A Practical Guide to Family Law

Donnie Perkins
146-04 228 Street
Rosedale, Queens
NY   11413.

A Practical Guide to Family Law

Matthew S. Cornick

WEST PUBLISHING COMPANY

Minneapolis/St. Paul
New York
Los Angeles
San Francisco

Copyeditor: Chris Thillen
Text and Cover Design: Jeanne Lee
Composition: Parkwood Composition Services, Inc.
Cover image: "Legal Aids," by Morris J. Shubin
Production, Prepress, Printing and Binding by West Publishing Company

West's Commitment to the Environment

In 1906, West Publishing Company began recycling materials left over from the production of books. This began a tradition of efficient and responsible use of resources. Today, up to 95 percent of our legal books and 70 percent of our college and school texts are printed on recycled, acid-free stock. West also recycles nearly 22 million pounds of scrap paper annually—the equivalent of 181,717 trees. Since the 1960s, West has devised ways to capture and recycle waste inks, solvents, oils, and vapors created in the printing process. We also recycle plastics of all kinds, wood, glass, corrugated cardboard, and batteries, and have eliminated the use of Styrofoam book packaging. We at West are proud of the longevity and the scope of our commitment to the environment.

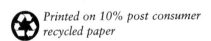 *Printed on 10% post consumer recycled paper*

COPYRIGHT © 1995   By WEST PUBLISHING COMPANY
                        610 Opperman Drive
                        P.O. Box 64526
                        St. Paul, MN 55164-0526

Library of Congress Cataloging-in-Publication Data

Cornick, Matthew S.
    A practical guide to family law / Matthew S. Cornick
        p.   cm.
    Includes index.
    ISBN 0-314-04451-5 (soft : acid-free paper)
    1. Domestic relations—United States.   I. Title.
KF505.C67   1995
346.7301'5—dc20   94-46248
[347.30615]   CIP

For my parents, Arthur and Dorothy Cornick
and
for Renda, my wife and best friend.

Contents in Brief

Table of Cases

The page numbers of principal cases are in bold type. Cases cited in principal cases and within other quoted materials are not included.

Contents

Preface

Introduction to Family Law

You have the opportunity to help people through what can be the most difficult period in a person's life. Paralegals play a critical role in this balance of head and heart, beginnings and endings. It is the intent of this text to provide you with a realistic and practical portrayal of family law and the paralegal's role within family law.

The study of law is an interactive exercise. It is not enough simply to study or memorize the bare facts of an area of law. To learn the law, you must put into practice the theories you have studied. Accordingly, the purpose of this book is twofold: to introduce you to the basic concepts of family law and to afford you the opportunity to put these principles into practice. A primary goal of this text is to promote hands-on application—a dialogue, rather than a monologue.

This text contains chapters detailing the most commonly occurring family law issues: annulment, divorce, enforcement of court-ordered support, and adoption. Typically, clients are aware when they have one of these problems and require legal advice. But most clients are unaware of all the options available to them, not to mention the advantages and disadvantages of each option. If paralegals are to perform to the full extent of their abilities, they must be able to analyze a situation, determine the nature of the problem, and formulate the possible solutions (if any) to the problem. The paralegal must be able to translate a client's problem from English into "legalese" and back again.

The most important skill of any legal professional, including paralegals, is the ability to ask the appropriate questions. When you learn what questions to ask of the client, of your supervising attorney, and of yourself, you will inevitably find the answer you are seeking. It is this skill, the ability to ask the right question at the right time, that makes you a valued member of a law office; and it is this skill that you will practice throughout your study of family law.

Legal questions can be divided into two general categories. Questions of law include interpretations of the law and determination of strategy (i.e., deciding when to file a particular motion and when to object to a question posed to a client). Questions of law are generally the responsibility of the attorneys. Questions of fact include determination of the facts in a particular case (i.e., what salary a person earns; whether a person physically abused their spouse, etc.). Questions of fact are primarily the responsibility of the paralegal. The importance of this role of the paralegal cannot be overstated; without the correct facts, the attorneys will be unable to properly address questions of law. Family law practitioners are afforded the opportunity to engage in every facet of modern litigation—motion practice, discovery, courtroom exposure (pretrial hearings are especially prevalent), collection of judgments, and appellate work. They are also given the opportunity to work in a relatively new facet of litigation: alternative dispute resolution, including mediation and arbitration. Paralegals working in this area experience a great deal of client contact, perhaps more so than in any other area of the law.

A qualified family law paralegal must also have a broad knowledge of other areas of the law that interact with the family. Accordingly, in this text we also discuss the impact of tax laws on the settlement of a marital dispute; the effect of the laws of estates and wills in determining how they affect the rights of married people to transfer property; how property laws affect a couple when they decide to get married (and when they decide to terminate the marriage); and the interplay of family law with criminal law and contract law, among others.

One of the most important abilities a legal professional can have is the ability to foresee problems, and therefore prevent problems, before they mature. This is only possible with a thorough knowledge of all of the areas of law that affect a family law practice. For example, there are times when it may be advantageous for a party to pay $500 per month in child support as opposed to paying $400 per month in alimony (also called spousal support). But this anomaly can be understood only upon recognizing the tax consequences of the above payments to the parties. (The rationale for this example can be found in Chapter 14.)

Family law is unique among the areas of practice open to you in that the paralegal is present for some of the most traumatic moments in a person's life. Family law is society's attempt to regulate and organize the most basic of human relationships. The pain of a contested child custody hearing and the joy of a successful adoption—family law touches people in ways that other areas of the law cannot.

Finally, few areas of law have undergone such radical change in recent years. The American family has experienced a significant metamorphosis, and family law has had to adjust accordingly. Even the very definition of *family* is no longer automatically assumed to be Mom, Dad, and a couple of kids. Same-sex marriages, artificial reproduction, children "divorcing" their parents—no other area of the law has allowed its practitioners to venture into such unchartered waters. Furthermore, it is likely that in the coming years, we will see even more significant changes in the laws relating to the family. This assures the family law practitioner that life at the office will never be boring.

STUDENT LEARNING FEATURES

In addition to the text, each chapter of this book contains some or all of the following features:

— *Chapter Objectives* list the specific skills and areas of knowledge to be discussed within each chapter.
— An *Introduction* sets out the highlights of each chapter.

— *Focus on Ethics* boxes highlight the application of appropriate ethical standards to family law.

— *Case Law* excerpts of legal opinions demonstrate how a rule of law is applied "in real life," followed by *Discussion Questions* designed to foster understanding of the cases and the legal principals they embody.

— *Practice Pointers* give practical advice about real-world problems.

— *Focus* boxes highlight topics of current interest in family law, such as domestic partnerships or cryopreservation.

— *Interview Checklists* provide insight into the factual issues confronting family law. A basic interview checklist is provided in Chapter 2; successive chapters include additional checklists that highlight the specific issues discussed in those chapters.

— *Sample Forms and Documents* put into practice the theoretical concepts set out in the chapter; *Margin Annotations* provide a clear understanding of specific parts of the forms.

— *Important Terminology* is emphasized and reinforced throughout the text in the following ways: Key terms are set in bold type, defined in context, and defined in the margin for quick access where they first appear. All key terms are also listed at the end of each chapter and defined in the end-of-text glossary.

— *Review Questions and Practice Exercises* require both knowledge of the basic concepts and understanding of their application to on-the-job tasks.

— *State Research Assignments* allow each student to discover what the law is in their own jurisdiction, and to better learn the process of legal reasoning.

— *Ethical Problems* present ethical dilemmas specific to family law and ask students how they would handle the situation.

By the time you reach the end of each chapter, you should be able to understand 1) the principles detailed therein and 2) how the information contained in that chapter relates to the information presented in all preceding chapters. You should also know *why* laws exist and the *purpose* sought to be achieved by those laws. If you understand why the law exists in a particular manner, you will find it easier to memorize a series of legal concepts. You will naturally remember the laws as part of a program for processing a family law problem. The difference between knowing the law (otherwise known as memorization) and understanding the law is the ability to understand *why* the law achieves its intended result. But when confronted with a legal question, you should always refer to the appropriate statute or case to ensure that the law you are relying on has not been modified, repealed, or reversed.

As the title *A Practical Guide to Family Law* indicates, this text aspires to be something of a "how-to" book. Paralegal training is, or at least should be, vocational training in the best sense of the phrase. Paralegal students are ultimately hired to perform tasks in the law office, so the reader is encouraged to pay special attention to the portions of the text relating to the various tasks of a family law paralegal.

REAL-WORLD ORIENTATION

In keeping with the title, *A Practical Guide to Family Law,* the text includes numerous practical ideas and tips. These are designed to allow the reader to use this text in the "real world," where tests occur daily and the failure of any such test affects the client as well as the paralegal.

STUDY GUIDE

Prepared by Dorothy Moore, Broward Community College. This study guide provides extensive review of chapter concepts through the use of approximately 40 true/false, fill-in, and short-answer questions. In addition, the study guide contains Practice Exercises designed to provide hands-on practice with the concepts and tasks discussed in the text.

INSTRUCTOR'S MANUAL WITH TEST BANK

Prepared by Matthew Cornick, this manual is designed to provide the instructor with useful information, including lecture outlines, answers to all the text problems, and approximately 40 test questions for each chapter.

TEACHING AND LEARNING PACKAGE

In addition, the following teaching and learning aids are available with the text:

— West's Paralegal Video Library Qualified adopters can select and exchange from a variety of tapes.
— WESTLAW™ allows qualified adopters to receive ten free hours during nonprohibited hours. WESTMORE® Tutorial is also available.
— *Strategies and Tips for Paralegal Educators* pamphlet by Anita Tebbe, Johnson Community College, provides teaching strategies specifically designed for paralegal educators.

A NOTE ON TERMINOLOGY

Just as the law of domestic relations has undergone pronounced changes in recent years, so too the terminology of family law has changed. What is called *divorce* in one state may be known as *dissolution* in another. Similarly, *alimony* may also be called *maintenance* or *spousal support.* For clarity, we use the traditional and more familiar terms of *divorce* and *alimony* throughout this text. You are advised to ascertain the appropriate terminology for a specific jurisdiction.

Note also that family law can be called either *domestic relations* or *matrimonial law,* depending on the jurisdiction.

One of the most noticeable trends in paralegal education is the increasing proportion of male students. Similarly, it is no longer true that the lawyer is male and the paralegal is female. Accordingly, throughout this text, both attorneys and paralegals are alternately referred to as male and female. Additionally, the clients referred to throughout the text are alternately either husband or wife. In any event, unless specifically noted, the use of *he, him,* and *his* also indicates *she, her,* and *hers* and no inference is to be made by the use or disuse of a specific gender reference.

STATE LAW DIFFERENCES

From state to state, there is no such thing as a standard in "family law." That is, the law in New York is different from the law in Texas, which is different from the law in Oregon. Accordingly, this text is a survey of family law in the United States. Keep in mind, however, that this text makes reference to a number of laws that are accepted generally, but may not be accepted in your state. The "State Research Problems" throughout the text, and your instructor, will help you discern the laws applicable in your state.

ACKNOWLEDGMENTS

I am grateful to all my friends and colleagues for their support and encouragement during the long process of bringing this project to fruition. Whatever skills I have acquired as a teacher are due in large part to the opportunities provided to me by the staff and students at The National Center for Paralegal Training in Atlanta. My thanks to my friend Mark Panfel, JD, CPA, for his invaluable assistance in the preparation of the chapter on the tax considerations of divorce. I want to thank everyone at West Publishing; they have all been so patient and cooperative. I will always be thankful for an acquiring editor like Elizabeth Hannan. No matter how badly I would miss a deadline, she would cheer every small step on the road to publication. Particular thanks go to Production Editor Matt Thurber, Developmental Editor Patty Bryant, and Copyeditor Chris Thillen.

My thanks to the following people for their comments and suggestions as reviewers of this text:

Joseph Annacarto
Star Technical Institute

Jeptha Clemens
Northwest Mississippi Community College

John D. DeLeo, Esq.
Central Pennsylvania Business College

Susan De George
Iona College—Seton School

Holly Enterline
State Technical Institute at Memphis

Sumner Freedman
Fisher Junior College

Susan W. Harrell
University of West Florida

Deborah A. Howard
University of Evansville

Barbara L. Jones
Minnesota Legal Assistant Institute

Mary Kubichek
Casper College

Mary Louis Kurr
University of Maine, University College

Jennifer Allen Labosky
Davidson County Community College

Mary Hatfield Lowe
Westark Community College

Donna Kay Mettz
Southwestern Paralegal Institute

Michelle Migdal, Esq.
Florida Atlantic University

Virginia C. Noonan
Northern Essex Community College

Barbara Quigley
Kensington College

Gina-Marie Reitano
St. John's University

Kathleen M. Smith
The Career Institute

George Urban
ETI Technical College

Leo R. Villalobos
El Paso Community College

Most of all, thank you to Renda and Peter. I love you both.

Marriage

CHAPTER OBJECTIVES

In this chapter you will learn:

- *The requirements for a valid marriage*

- *The necessary elements for both ceremonial and common-law marriages*

- *The legal consequences of marriage upon the parties married*

- *The legal consequences of marriage upon third parties*

- *The rights of a party upon the breach of a promise to marry*

- *How unmarried cohabitants may seek to enter into agreements to protect their respective rights*

- *The effect and design of domestic partnership laws*

When people get married, they make significant changes in both the rights and obligations they are entitled to receive from each other and those they are obligated to provide each other. Because marriage is a contract regulated by state government, a couple wishing to marry must meet certain minimum requirements. These requirements include minimum age limits, physical and mental health requirements, and prohibitions against marrying within certain degrees of family relationship. Additionally, while all states have a procedure for ceremonial marriages (obtaining a marriage license and having an official wedding ceremony), some states also recognize common-law marriages. In those states, common-law marriages are no less valid than ceremonial marriages. A common-law marriage is created when two people have the capacity to be married, intend to be married, hold themselves out to the public as husband and wife, and cohabitate. Regardless of the method of marriage, married people have different property rights than those afforded to unmarried individuals. These include the right to receive and the obligation to provide financial support, a claim to the property of their spouse, and the right

1

to inherit property from their spouse. Married people also have several non-property rights, such as the right to use a single family surname, the right of consortium, the right to prevent testimony by a spouse in certain cases, and a degree of immunity from some tort claims by a spouse. A relatively new trend, however, has expanded the rights of married people to sue their spouse for torts such as battery. Marriage also affects a spouse's relationships with third parties under both contract law and tort law. Finally, a limited number of jurisdictions have enacted laws that give unmarried cohabitants some of the privileges normally reserved for married couples.

HISTORY OF MARRIAGE

dowry
The property that a wife brings to her husband in marriage.

common-law
The ancient, traditional law that serves as the foundation for the United States legal system.

The history of marriage mirrors the history of the society in which it exists. In ancient Rome, marriage was not a function of the law; rather, it was entirely a component of the religious life of the society. Further, marriage was not a romantic notion, but a necessary part of the economic life of the community. The prospective bride's family was typically expected to make a payment to the groom (this payment was called a **dowry**). Such marriages were arranged by the spouse's families with little, if any, input from the spouses themselves. Such marriages continue today in portions of India, Africa, and the Middle East. Marriage in America owes its roots to the English common and canon (religious) laws. At **common law** (the original source for modern American law, based on the laws of England and the colonies at the time of American Revolution), a married woman did not exist as an independent person. Rather, the husband and wife were treated as one person under the law, and that "one person" was the husband. This effectively denied married women any property rights, and granted husbands complete control over the couple's property. By the end of the nineteenth century, the individual states had enacted laws (i.e., "Married Women's Property Acts") designed to permit married women to own and transfer property and to enter into contracts. Through the past one hundred years, married women have been accorded privileges and obligations identical to those of their husbands.

REQUIREMENTS FOR A VALID MARRIAGE

marriage
A legal union of two persons.

Marriage may be defined as the legal union of a man and woman as husband and wife. It has been referred to as a legal status, or condition, that two people attain by entering into a contract with each other. For example, federal tax laws treat two couples with identical income levels differently depending on their marital status. Marriage is also a contract between two people. As with all contracts, it requires these four elements:

1. An *offer*

2. An *acceptance* of the offer

3. Parties with the *capacity* (mental and legal ability) to make the contract

4. Adequate and mutual *consideration*

"Consideration" is what each party to a contract receives from the other party. It is the *quid pro quo* ("this for that"). Consideration can take the form of some tangible benefit (i.e., money or property), or it can be a promise to do (or not to do) some act. When each partner agrees to marry the other, the mutual promises form the consideration for the contract.

Furthermore, a valid contract cannot be created by *fraud* (a misrepresentation of a significant fact) or *duress* (induced by the threat of an unlawful act). If either of these defenses to contract exist, there never really was a voluntary and intelligent "meeting of the minds" between the parties and, accordingly, no contract. For example, a "shotgun" marriage, wherein the groom marries the bride because of threats of physical violence by the bride's father, would be a marriage entered into under duress. Any marriage thus created could be annulled by the "victim" of the fraud or duress. (See Chapter 5 for a discussion of annulment.)

The Marriage Contract

The marriage contract is different from most other contracts in many ways. First, the marriage contract cannot be terminated at will by either party. Termination of the marriage contract can be granted only by the state. Second, the obligations incurred through a marriage contract are personal and cannot be assigned or transferred to a third party. Third, a marriage contract requires the approval of the state government. Although the right to marry is considered a fundamental right, historically the state has restricted who may enter into a contract for marriage. To varying degrees, all states in the United States impose these requirements:

1. Each partner must be of a *different sex*. Homosexual marriages are currently illegal. But several cities, such as New York City and San Francisco, have legislation, either enacted or proposed, that would extend many of the benefits of marriage to "nontraditional" families. In addition, in 1993, the Hawaii Supreme Court may have opened the door for same-sex marriages. A discussion of "domestic partnerships" and same-sex marriages follows later in this chapter.

2. Each partner must have attained a *minimum age*. This is to help ensure that the parties fully understand the consequences of getting married, and that they will be capable of bearing the responsibility of raising children of their own. Typically, a state establishes one age at which a person may marry without the consent of his or her parents (i.e., 18 years) and a lower age at which a person may marry with either proof of parental consent or with court consent (i.e., 16 years). At one time, states had varying minimum-age

requirements for males and females, with a lower age requirement for females. Such laws have largely been struck down as an unconstitutional denial of equal protection. The age requirement may be waived by a court if the female is pregnant at the time the marriage license is sought or if either party has become **emancipated.**

emancipation
Acts by which a person under the age of majority can be granted the legal rights afforded adults.

legal capacity
As relates to family law, the ability to enter into marriage.

bigamy; polygamy
Bigamy occurs when one person is married to two persons at the same time. Polygamy occurs when one person is married to more than two persons at the same time.

mental capacity
The ability to understand the consequences of specific actions.

3. Both partners must have the **legal capacity** to be married. That means they must not already be married to anyone else at the time they enter into the contract for marriage. Being married to two persons at one time constitutes the crime of **bigamy;** being married to *more than two* persons at the same time is called **polygamy.** Bigamy and polygamy are punishable crimes even when committed under the guise of a religious practice. Until it is terminated, a prior marriage voids all later marriages. One noticeable exception to this rule is encompassed by what have come to be known as "Enoch Arden" laws. Named after a long-absent sailor in a poem by Alfred, Lord Tennyson, these laws absolve persons from possible charges of bigamy when the second marriage is entered into after the spouse of the first marriage has been missing for a statutorily prescribed time. These statutes affect only the criminal aspect of the multiple marriages; the second marriage may still be void unless the missing spouse from the first marriage has been legally declared dead.

4. Both partners must have the **mental capacity** to enter into the contract for marriage. The key question is whether at the time they enter into the marriage the parties have the ability to understand the consequences of being married. The traditional basis for this requirement was the fear that the offspring of the marriage of mentally deficient persons would suffer the same affliction, and thus be a burden on society. All states currently have laws regulating the ability of mentally retarded persons to marry. The concept of mental capacity also relates to instances in which one or both of the parties may have been under the influence of alcohol or drugs (prescription or illegal), and thus unable to understand the ramifications of their actions. Questions of mental illness, mental retardation, and the influence of alcohol or drugs at the time the marriage is entered into are usually raised when one party seeks an annulment to terminate the marriage. (See Chapter 5.)

physical capacity
As relates to family law, the ability to engage in a sexual relationship.

5. Each partner must have the **physical capacity** to enter into marriage. This requirement typically takes the form of a blood test that tests for various communicable diseases, especially venereal diseases. A finding that either partner has such a disease does not necessarily prevent a marriage; it does allow both parties to make a fully informed decision as to whether to enter into marriage. These tests do not carry the same weight they did years ago, before the introduction of penicillin and other medications that can effectively treat venereal diseases. However, as AIDS continues to make

inroads into the general population, states may consider imposing mandatory AIDS testing before issuing a marriage license. Additionally, because one traditional ground for terminating a marriage (by annulment or divorce) is the incapacity of one spouse to consummate the marriage by sexual intercourse, such ability may be viewed as a requirement for marriage. This requirement does not relate to the ability to have children, only to the ability to engage in intercourse. Furthermore, the inability to engage in intercourse would not impede marriage if both parties were aware of this condition at the time of the marriage. This subject is covered more fully in the discussion of annulment in Chapter 5.

6. Each partner *must not be related to the other* within certain degrees. All states have laws prohibiting incestuous marriages between parent and child and between siblings (brothers and sisters). These laws are designed to prevent marriage between people related by a close degree of **consanguinity** (a family relationship based on a common blood relationship) and result from the traditional religious and cultural prohibitions against incest as well as from fears of creating genetically defective offspring. Accordingly, most states also prohibit marriage between first cousins. To a lesser degree, many states also have laws designed to prevent marriage between people related only by **affinity** (a family relationship created through marriage), for example, marriage between a stepfather and stepdaughter. The rationale for this prohibition is not medical (since the partners are not related by blood); marriages like these are contrary to public policy because they foster ill feelings between family members. This is an area of the law in which individual state prohibitions vary significantly.

> **affinity; consanguinity**
> Two variations of incest. Affinity is a relationship between persons related by marriage. Consanguinity is a relationship between persons related by blood.

What if parties do "marry" without satisfying all of these requirements? The result may be a "void" or "voidable" marriage, but generally, at a minimum, the marriage may be annulled. (See Chapter 5.)

Ceremonial Marriage

A **ceremonial marriage** is a marriage celebrated by a ceremony (a wedding or marriage solemnization) in which a representative of the state formally officiates over the creation of the marriage between two people. In addition to the requirements outlined earlier, all states have legal formalities and technicalities that parties must satisfy before entering into marriage. Marriage is noticeably different from other forms of contracts in that the state places certain restrictions on the ability of its citizens to enter into marriage. The state has various reasons for instituting these restrictions, many of which are based on the state's traditional role as *parens patriae* (the state as the parent or guardian of its citizens). The reasons include preventing hasty marriages, maintaining a public and official record of all marriages, and collecting statistical data.

> **ceremonial marriage**
> As opposed to a common-law marriage; a marriage involving a ceremony officiated over by a person authorized by the state to perform weddings.

1. All states require prospective brides and grooms to obtain a *marriage license*. Typically, the marriage license must be obtained before the marriage ceremony. If all the state-imposed requirements discussed earlier have been satisfied, a clerk of the appropriate court in the county where at least one of the parties resides will issue the marriage license. The application for the marriage license typically requires the prospective couple to set out their name, address, date and place of birth, social security number, and information regarding any prior marriages. A sample application and marriage license are given in Exhibit 1–1.

2. Most states have instituted a *waiting period* between the time the license is issued and the time of the wedding. This restriction was originally intended to prevent couples from getting married without fully considering the consequences of their decision to be married. Waiting periods generally range from one to six days. But couples who fervently desire to be married *now* are usually not deterred by a lengthy waiting period. Those couples are the reason for the success of the many marriage chapels in Reno and Las Vegas, Nevada, where there is no such waiting period. (For the same reason, states also have waiting periods before a divorce can be obtained.)

3. The actual *marriage ceremony* is intended to force the prospective bride and groom to face the seriousness of their actions. The couple typically takes an oath to "love, honor, and cherish" one another. (The obligation of the wife to "obey" her husband has gone the way of white gloves and pill-box hats.) In many ways, this is the epitome of a contract. Both parties simultaneously offer to marry the other and accept their partner's offer, and their mutual promises act as consideration for the contract. The ceremony also provides witnesses for the couple's exchange of vows. State statutory laws list the persons authorized to officiate at wedding ceremonies. These persons may include duly ordained ministers, priests, and rabbis, as well as certain judges and justices of the peace. After conducting the wedding ceremony, the official signs and returns the marriage license to the appropriate state authority, where it is recorded and made a part of the state's public records.

Common-Law Marriage

common-law marriage
As opposed to a ceremonial marriage; a marriage that occurs when two persons capable of being married, intend to be married to each other, hold themselves out to the public as being married and cohabit.

Generally, a **common-law marriage** is one in which a man and a woman:

1. Hold themselves out to the public as husband and wife

2. Intend to be married to each other

3. Have the legal capacity to be married

4. Openly live together (cohabit)

EXHIBIT 1–1

SAMPLE APPLICATION FOR A MARRIAGE LICENSE

DEPARTMENT OF HUMAN RESOURCES
VITAL RECORDS SERVICE

COUNTY OF _____

STATE FILE NO. _____

COUNTY NO. _____

PERSONAL PARTICULARS	CONTRACTING PARTIES		CODE
	GROOM	BRIDE (MAIDEN NAME)	A
1. FULL NAME			B
2. RESIDENCE STREET ADDRESS			C
CITY	IN CITY LIMITS YES ☐ NO ☐	IN CITY LIMITS YES ☐ NO ☐	D
COUNTY AND STATE			E
3. AGE LAST BIRTHDAY DATE OF BIRTH AND RACE	AGE / DATE OF BIRTH / BLACK / WHITE / OTHER	AGE / DATE OF BIRTH / BLACK / WHITE / OTHER	F
4. BIRTHPLACE			G
5. RELATIONSHIP			H
6. USUAL OCCUPATION (OPTIONAL)			I
7. DESIGNATED SURNAME			J
8A. NUMBER OF PREVIOUS MARRIAGES	☐ NONE ☐ ONE ☐ TWO ☐ OTHER (SPECIFY)	☐ NONE ☐ ONE ☐ TWO ☐ OTHER (SPECIFY)	K
8B. IF PREVIOUSLY MARRIED HOW DISSOLVED			L
8C. UPON WHAT GROUNDS			M
8D. WHEN AND WHERE			N
9. ANY LEGAL IMPEDIMENT			O
10. FATHER'S NAME			P
11. FATHER'S BIRTHPLACE			Q
12. MOTHER'S MAIDEN NAME			R
13. MOTHER'S BIRTHPLACE			S
14. PARENT'S RESIDENCE			T
15. DATE AND PLACE Of CONTEMPLATED MARRIAGE			

I HEREBY CERTIFY THAT THE FOREGOING ANSWERS WERE MADE UNDER OATH AND SUBSCRIBED BEFORE ME BY BOTH OF THE CONTRACTING PARTIES.

I HEREBY CERTIFY THAT I HAVE RECEIVED THE DHR AIDS BROCHURE AND LIST OF TEST SITES.

THIS _____ DAY OF _____ 19 _____

APPLICANT ▶ _____

▶ _____
Signature of Probate Judge

APPLICANT ▶ _____

The effect of a common-law marriage is the same as a ceremonial marriage, although there is no marriage license or ceremony. At this writing, only twelve states recognize the validity of a common-law marriage: Alabama, Colorado, Georgia, Idaho, Iowa, Kansas, Montana, Oklahoma, Pennsylvania, Rhode Island, South Carolina, Texas, and the District of Columbia. Their number is likely to decrease in the future, since the trend among the states is now decidedly against common-law marriages. This was not always so; in the eighteenth and nineteenth centuries, most jurisdictions permitted common-law marriages. The historical reasons favoring common-law marriage included the difficulty of traveling to the county seat to obtain a marriage license, the inability of ministers or civil officials to travel throughout an ever-expanding frontier, and the desire to cloak the relationships and the resulting children in the respectability of marriage. Of course, these are no longer cogent reasons for continuing the practice of common-law marriage.

The reasons cited for discontinuing common-law marriage include the need to keep accurate marriage records to best protect the property rights of spouses; the inability to mandate medical tests to prevent the spread of disease; and the lack of a waiting period that prevents hasty marriages.

Here are the individual elements of a common-law marriage:

1. A couple must *hold themselves out to the public as husband and wife.* This is generally accomplished when a person refers to another person as "my wife" or "my husband." Another indication is the female partner's adoption of the male partner's surname (last name) or the parties' mutual adoption of a hyphenated surname, thus leading third parties to reasonably believe the couple is married. This can also occur when a couple designate themselves as husband and wife on a lease, joint checking account, insurance contract, or any other manner of contract.

2. The couple must *intend to be married* to one another. Obviously, it is not possible to truly know what another person actually intends to do. But a person's intent can be determined by his statements and actions. Accordingly, to know whether two people intend to be married to each other, we must examine what, if any, actions they took to demonstrate their intent. For example, if a couple were to discover after their ceremonial "wedding" that the person who had officiated at the ceremony was not legally authorized to do so, it would be fair to state that those individuals intended to marry each other. Thus, in a state that recognizes common-law marriage, the parties would be considered married. Note that this mutual intent need only exist for an instant. Generally, there is no minimum time during which a couple must intend to be married. The acts by which a couple hold themselves out as husband and wife may also indicate their intent to be married to each other. For example, if the parties referred to each other as their "husband" or "wife," they would be both holding themselves out as husband and wife and manifesting a present intent to be married.

3. The parties must have both *legal and mental capacity* to be married. See "The Marriage Contract" for a discussion of legal and mental capacity.

4. The couple must *cohabit* (live together) as husband and wife. This generally also presumes a physical consummation of the marriage, although the law may not require consummation.

This is not to say that two persons merely "living together" are in danger of awaking one morning to find themselves married. All four elements listed above must exist simultaneously in a state that recognizes the validity of common-law marriage before a common-law marriage exists. Therefore, as long as the couple does not intend to be married and does not hold themselves out to the public as being married, they will not "accidentally" marry one another.

A typical question is whether a couple with a common-law marriage is still considered married if they travel to a state that does not recognize the validity of common-law marriages. The answer is yes. Under Article IV, Section 1 of the U.S. Constitution, the laws of one state are given **full faith and credit** (requires that the legislative acts, public records, and judicial decisions of the individual states must be honored by all other states within the United States) by other states even if the other states do not have similar laws. The validity of such a marriage is judged in accordance with the laws of the marriage state. Conversely, what happens if a couple cohabits in State A, which does not recognize common-law marriage, and travels to State B, which does recognize common-law marriage? Will the couple find themselves married if they spend one night together in a hotel room in State B? The answer to this question is more problematic. The constitutional guarantee of full faith and credit dictates that the validity of a marriage is to be determined by the laws of the state of a couple's **domicile** (the geographic location where the parties intend to live on a permanent basis). But at least two states (Illinois and Minnesota) refuse to recognize the foreign common-law marriages of their own residents. Other states will recognize a foreign common-law marriage only upon a showing that the parties had significant minimum contacts with the marriage state. For example, if the parties jointly own vacation property in a common-law marriage state, that is more likely to be deemed a sufficient contact with the state. On the other hand, a single visit to that state would be less likely to constitute a sufficient contact with the common-law marriage state. These questions typically arise when a couple cohabits for many years in a state that does not recognize common-law marriage and one of the partners dies. The surviving partner may attempt to show that because of extended joint visits in a common-law marriage state, the parties were married and the surviving partner is entitled to share in the estate, or other benefits, of the deceased partner.

Putative Spouse Doctrine

Another theory similar to common-law marriage is the **putative spouse doctrine,** which holds that when one or both of the participants in a formal mar-

full faith and credit
U.S. Constitutional guarantee that the judgments and judicial decisions of one jurisdiction will be recognized by other jurisdictions.

domicile
A person's permanent place of residence.

putative spouse doctrine
Theory which provides a party who mistakenly, although reasonably, believes they are married, with the legal benefits of marriage.

CASE

COLLIER v.
CITY OF MILFORD

Supreme Court of Connecticut.
Decided Feb. 9, 1988.

. . . .

Before PETERS, C.J., and SHEA, CALLAHAN, COVELLO and HULL, JJ.

CALLAHAN, Associate Justice.

Charles Collier, an employee of the city of Milford suffered work related injuries when he fell from a truck on April 24, 1978. He died from those injuries on May 3, 1978. It is undisputed that Collier's injuries and death arose out of and in the course of his employment. Subsequent to Collier's death, Fontella Rudene Williams the daughter of the decedent and of Juanita Felder Williams, filed a claim for workers' compensation benefits as a presumptive dependent under General Statutes § 31–306(a)(3). (Footnote omitted.) At the time of Collier's death, Fontella was eleven years old, had been supported by Collier, and had been living with Collier and the plaintiff Juanita Williams. (Footnote omitted.)

The daughter's claim was uncontested and, after a hearing on January 7, 1980, the workers' compensation commissioner for the third district issued a finding and award ordering compensation to be paid to Fontella Rudene Williams at the rate of $139.83 per week commencing May 4, 1978. The commissioner also ordered burial expenses in the amount of $1500 to reimburse Juanita Williams who had paid the funeral bill.

On September 21, 1981, Juanita Williams moved to open the January 7, 1980 order of compensation on the ground that she had an interest superior to that of her daughter in the receipt of any workers' compensation benefits resulting from Collier's death. The commissioner denied the plaintiff's motion to open. The plaintiff thereafter appealed to the compensation review division, pursuant to General Statutes § 31–301(a). (Footnote omitted.)

The compensation review division dismissed the plaintiff's appeal and affirmed the commissioner's denial of the plaintiff's motion to open. Thereafter the plaintiff appealed the decision of the compensation review division to the Appellate Court under General Statutes § 31–301b. This court transferred the appeal to itself. (Citation omitted.)

The gravamen of the plaintiff's claim, as stated in her brief to this court, is that "she had lived with Charles Collier for sixteen years, that her union with Charles Collier was a valid common law marriage, that she was dependent on him for support, and that under the Workers' Compensation Act she is a presumptive dependent and entitled to compensation." (Footnote omitted.) The commissioner and the compensation review division both found that the union of Juanita Williams and Collier did not constitute a common law marriage cognizable under Connecticut law. Therefore, the commissioner held, and the compensation review division affirmed, that "[t]he claims of Juanita Williams do not comply with the provisions of the Workers' Compensation Act and must be denied."

The plaintiff contends that the commissioner and the review division erred when they determined that she was not married to Collier and was, therefore, not entitled to compensation as a presumptive dependent under General Statutes § 31–306(a)(1). Her argument is premised on the claim that her testimony before the commissioner compelled a finding that she and Collier had contracted a valid common law marriage. (Footnote omitted.)

The plaintiff's testimony revealed that she was born Juanita Felder in Alabama on April 20, 1934. On May 7, 1952, she married Luke Williams in Montgomery, Alabama. "[A]bout 1959" Luke Williams left her and their five children in Alabama and moved to Ohio. In the "early 1960s" the plaintiff moved from Alabama, first to Rye, New York, and later to Connecticut. Shortly after moving to Connecticut she met and formed a relationship with Charles Collier. In approximately 1962 she and Collier commenced living together in Bridgeport. Their child, Fontella, was born of their liaison on October 16, 1966. Luke Williams, Juanita Williams' husband, from whom she had never been divorced, died in Cleveland, Ohio, on December 31, 1968.

The plaintiff's testimony also disclosed that, after the death of Luke Williams, she and Collier continued to live together in Bridgeport until Collier's death in 1978. During their years together, both before and after the death of her husband in Ohio, she and Collier took annual vacation trips together of approximately two weeks duration. On these trips, in alternate years, they visited Collier's mother in Orangeburg, South Carolina, and the plaintiff's sister in Montgomery, Alabama. While in South Carolina and Alabama, she and Collier stayed with the family member whom they were visiting. There they slept together, had sexual relations, generally represented themselves as being married to each other, and were generally regarded as married by those with whom they came in contact. (Footnote omitted.)

It is the plaintiff's contention that, because of their living arrangements while on vacation, their representations and the perception of their relationship by the community, and the fact that South Carolina and Alabama both recognize common law marriages, she and Collier entered into a valid common law marriage on their trips to those states. She concedes that she never went through a marriage ceremony with Collier anywhere.

In order to qualify as a presumptive dependent . . . , and to have a claim for compensation superior to that of her daughter, the statute requires that the plaintiff be the legal "wife" of the deceased. (Footnote and citation omitted.)

Connecticut does not presently recognize, as valid marriages, living arrangements or informal commitments entered into in this state and loosely categorized as common law marriages. (Citations omitted.) Only recently this rule of law has been reaffirmed. "In this jurisdiction, common law marriages are not accorded validity. The rights and obligations that attend a valid marriage simply do not arise where the parties choose to cohabit outside the marital relationship." (Citations omitted.) *Boland v. Catalano*, 202 Conn. 333, 339, 521 A.2d 142 (1987).

In order to have any possible claim for benefits under the workers' compensation act, therefore, the plaintiff must demonstrate that the commissioner and the compensation review division erred when they determined that the periodic sojourns of the plaintiff and Collier in South Carolina and Alabama did not result in a valid common law marriage. Both South Carolina and Alabama recognize as valid common law marriages contracted within those states. (Citations omitted.)

This court has never had the occasion to rule directly on the question of the validity in this state of a common law marriage validly contracted in accordance with the law of another state. The Superior Court in *Delaney v. Delaney*, 35 Conn.Sup. 230, 405 A.2d 91 (1979), however, held that the validity of a marriage is governed by lex loci contractus and recognized the validity of a common law marriage contracted in Rhode Island. (Citation omitted.) Further, it is the generally accepted rule that a marriage that is valid in the state where contracted is valid everywhere (citations omitted); unless for some reason the marriage is

contrary to the strong public policy of the state required to rule on its validity. (Citations omitted.)

We are not, however, called upon to decide that question. The commissioner found that it would be "spurious to contemplate under the facts presented that said Juanita Williams and Charles Collier contracted a valid common law marriage in the States of South Carolina and Alabama." The compensation review division also determined that a valid marriage had not been contracted in South Carolina or Alabama. The review division, therefore, affirmed the commissioner's decision that the plaintiff was not entitled to benefits and that the commissioner did not err when she refused to open the compensation award to the plaintiff's daughter.

The existence of a common law marriage is a question of fact. (Citations omitted.) Where the evidence is in conflict, the determination of whether there exists a common law marriage is for the trier. (Citations omitted.) . . .

To constitute a valid common law marriage there must first be a present agreement, that is, a present mutual understanding or a present mutual consent to enter at that time into the marriage relationship. (Citations omitted.) That mutual understanding or consent must be conveyed with such a demonstration of intent and with such clarity on the part of the parties that marriage does not creep up on either of them and catch them unawares. One cannot be married unwittingly or accidentally. (Citation omitted.) The intention of the parties to enter into a marriage contract may be demonstrated by words of present assent (citation omitted); or may be inferred from facts and circumstances and need not rest exclusively on the declarations of the parties. (Citation omitted.) There must, however, be evidenced a present, mutual, intention to marry. (Citation omitted.) An "[i]llicit relationship, though accompanied by cohabitation, is not transformed into a legal state of marriage by the mere lapse of time." (Citation omitted.) Moreover, "due to the serious nature of the marriage relationship, the courts will closely scrutinize a claim of common-law marriage and require clear and convincing proof thereof." (Citations omitted.)

The plaintiff's testimony was the only evidence that was introduced before the commissioner and the compensation review division concerning the relationship that existed between Collier and her. (Footnote omitted.) Under the circumstances revealed by her testimony, we cannot say that there was error when the commissioner found, and the compensation review division affirmed, that the plaintiff and Collier had not entered into a valid common law marriage in either South Carolina or Alabama. It cannot be gleaned from the plaintiff's testimony that any contemporaneous agreement was ever entered into or even contemplated in either of those two states to change the status of the relationship of the parties that existed in Connecticut. Further, there is nothing in the plaintiff's testimony to signal a change in the status of her relationship with Collier in Connecticut after the death of her husband in 1968 had removed him as an impediment to her remarriage. (Citations omitted.) Therefore, even if, as the plaintiff testified, on their vacation trips to South Carolina and Alabama she and Collier had slept together, had sexual relations and generally held themselves out to be married, a finding that a valid common law marriage was contracted was not required.

The plaintiff's testimony, in fact, is wholly consistent with a finding that, while on vacation in South Carolina and Alabama, the parties simply continued cohabiting without benefit of marriage, as they had at home. As previously indicated, however, cohabitation is not enough to create a valid common law marriage nor is an intention to marry sometime in the future. (Footnote and citation omitted.) There must, at a minimum, have been some evidence of a present contemporaneous mutual intention to marry, in either South Carolina or Alabama, when the parties were present in those states, to give rise to a valid common law marriage. The plaintiff's testimony was devoid of any such evidence.

There is no error.

In this opinion the other Justices concurred.

DISCUSSION QUESTIONS

Consider the above case of *Collier v. City of Milford*, 537 A.2d 474 (Conn., 1988), and answer the following questions:

1. What evidence did the plaintiff offer to establish the existence of a common-law marriage?
2. What was the court's decision, and what was the rationale offered in support of that decision?
3. How would your state resolve this problem?

riage ceremony have a good-faith belief in the validity of their marriage, they will be entitled to some of the benefits of marriage, even if the marriage is not valid due to a technical deficiency.

For example, suppose Paula marries Paul, believing Paul to be unmarried. If Paula were later to discover that Paul was still married to another woman, Paula might be able to assert a claim for a share of all "marital" property and for support as Paul's putative spouse. The rationale behind this policy is that when a person, in good faith, enters into marriage, that person should have legal authority to claim the same rights as a validly married person, regardless of any unknown technical defects of the marriage. In some states (i.e., Minnesota, Illinois) the putative spouse doctrine has been codified, while in others it remains a function of a court's equity power. (See Chapter 4 for a discussion of equity.)

A primary difference between common-law marriage and the putative spouse doctrine is that the putative spouse must have actually participated in a marriage ceremony. Another difference is that the benefits of a common-law marriage continue to accrue until the marriage is terminated, while the benefits obtained under the putative spouse doctrine accrue only until the nullity of the ceremonial marriage is discovered by the party acting in good faith. The putative spouse doctrine originated under French and Spanish law, and as such is generally available in states with a French or Spanish legal influence.

EFFECT OF MARRIAGE ON THE SPOUSES

Marriage (whether ceremonial or common law) changes the status of the two persons married. Marriage gives the new husband and wife a set of new rights and obligations. Most of the issues mentioned below are discussed in greater detail in later chapters; cross-references are provided where applicable.

The Obligation to Provide Support and the Right to Receive Support

At common law, only the husband had the legal obligation to provide adequate support (food, clothing, shelter, etc.) for his family. Today, the Equal Protection clause of the U.S. Constitution demands that both spouses be held legally accountable to provide adequate support for each other and for all minor children. Note that the level of support owed to a spouse may vary from the level of support owed to minor children. Each state has specific statutes detailing the extent of the obligations recognized in that state.

Certain states require a spouse to pay for all family expenses, while others require only that the **necessities** be provided. This requirement allows one spouse to purchase necessities on credit and to hold the other spouse responsible for payment of the resulting bill. A common usage of necessities today is the practice of hospitals to collect for medical services rendered for a spouse or child.

necessities
Food, shelter, utilities, medical treatment, etc.

The doctrine of necessities dates to common law, which imposed this duty only on husbands. As this doctrine is applied today, it must address charges that it is violative of the Equal Protection clause of the U.S. Constitution. In response, the individual states are divided. Some have abolished the doctrine of necessities completely, while others have expanded it to impose an identical responsibility on wives as well. Of course, the definition of *necessities* varies from state to state and among families within a single state.

At a minimum, necessities will always include basic food, clothing, shelter, and medical services. The level of necessities often rises with the income level of the family in question. For example, cable television and lawn maintenance may be included under the umbrella of necessities. The obligation to provide support for a spouse may continue until the termination of the marriage. The obligation to provide support for minor children continues until they reach the age of majority (typically 18 years of age) or otherwise become emancipated (i.e., if a minor child should marry).

The Right to Claim an Interest in All Marital Property

Once married, a husband and wife may acquire an interest (a stake or claim) in all **marital property** (property acquired, other than by gift or inheritance, by either spouse during the marriage). The extent of this particular interest is

marital property
Property acquired by persons while married to each other.

controlled by the property laws of the state of the couple's domicile. (See Chapter 9 for a detailed discussion of property rights.) This interest may be extended or limited by the execution of a valid antenuptial agreement. (See Chapter 3 for a discussion of antenuptial agreements.)

The Right to Use a Single Family Surname

Traditionally, women have adopted the surname (last name or family name) of their husband. But no state currently requires a wife to adopt her husband's surname if she chooses not to do so. Therefore, a married woman may adopt her husband's surname, retain her maiden name, or join her surname with her husband's to form a hyphenated surname (i.e., Penny Thomas marries James Hampton and assumes the name Penny Thomas-Hampton). A married woman does not relinquish the right to use her husband's surname upon divorce. In some states, upon divorce a woman may have to specifically request that the court restore her maiden name if that is her desire. Note that some courts may limit a woman's ability to restore her maiden name if minor children bearing their father's surname are involved.

The Right to Inherit Property from a Spouse

When two people marry one another, they are then entitled to inherit at least a portion of their spouse's estate (property owned at the time of death) upon the death of that spouse. Naturally, these rights vary greatly from state to state.

curtesy; dower
Laws providing for the passage of property from a deceased spouse to a widower (curtesy) or widow (dower).

intestate; testate
A person who dies with a valid will dies testate. A person who dies without a valid will dies intestate.

descent and distribution; intestate distribution
The laws that determine the distribution of property when a person dies without a valid will.

These rights originated in the common-law rules of **dower** and **curtesy,** which generally provided for the support of a surviving wife (dower) or husband (curtesy) from the estate of the deceased spouse. It is well worth noting the difference between inheriting from someone who died **intestate** (without having executed a valid last will and testament) and someone who died **testate** (having executed a valid last will and testament). Inheriting property from a spouse who died intestate is controlled by the laws of **intestate distribution** or **descent and distribution** of the state where the deceased spouse was domiciled. (When a person dies, his property "descends" down the family tree and is "distributed" to his heirs.) These laws control the passing of property from one generation to the next. Typically, a surviving spouse inherits all of the deceased spouse's property either individually or jointly with any surviving children of the deceased spouse.

Inheriting property from a spouse who died testate is controlled by the terms of the last will and testament of the deceased spouse. But, it is important to note that some states have laws designed to prevent the total disinheritance of a surviving spouse. The rationale for these laws is that the obligation to support a spouse continues even after the death of the supporting spouse. It also furthers public policy against increasing the number of widows on the welfare rolls. Of course, spouses do not normally execute wills designed to disinherit their spouses; however, a couple that has separated and/or has commenced divorce proceedings at the time of death may not be inclined to bequeath property to one another.

These laws ensure that while a couple is married, the obligation to support a spouse is not completely interrupted by death. Generally, these laws guarantee the surviving spouse a certain minimum percentage (i.e., 25 percent; 50 percent) of the deceased spouse's estate. This statutorily guaranteed minimum share of the estate is called the "spousal share" or "widow's share."

This mandatory share for the surviving spouse is especially important when a spouse dies while divorce litigation is pending, or when a surviving spouse claims a share of the deceased spouse's estate as a result of a common-law marriage, because it provides a share of the estate to someone whom the deceased may not have intended. When a spouse dies while divorce litigation is still pending, the litigation is dismissed and the surviving spouse is entitled to be treated as a widow(er). Finally, as with the right to claim an interest in marital property, the execution of a valid antenuptial agreement may alter the parties' testamentary rights.

The Right of Consortium

A married person has the right to receive (and obligation to provide) services, support, companionship, and sexual relations from his or her spouse. This is known as the right of **consortium**. (Note how this relates to the physical requirements for marriage.) In later chapters, we will discuss how the withholding of these services can provide the basis for annulment (see Chapter 5) or a divorce action (see Chapter 6).

When a married person is seriously injured by a third party's **tort** (either negligence or an intentional tort) and as a result cannot provide the services described herein, both spouses will have a cause of action against the *tortfeasor* (party committing the tort). The physically injured spouse would have a cause of action for the injuries suffered. Additionally, the other spouse would also have a cause of action against the tortfeasor for the interference in the marital relationship—the "loss of consortium."

consortium
The right to receive society, affection, companionship and assistance from a spouse.

tort
A noncriminal wrong, such as negligence or libel.

Immunity from Tort Claims Made by a Spouse

At common law, spouses were immune from claims of tort liability from their spouses. In other words, a husband could not sue his wife for injuries she caused. The rationale for this intrafamily tort **immunity** was that the family harmony was considered to be more important to society than the right of an injured party to recover compensation for injuries caused by her spouse. Further, at common law, a married couple was considered to be a single person legally, and that "person" was embodied by the husband. A wife had little status as an individual. It was also thought that this immunity would prevent collusion between the spouses (i.e., fraudulent claims made by one spouse against the other, with both spouses ultimately enjoying any money damages thus awarded).

Today, this intrafamily tort immunity has been sharply limited or completely eliminated in most states. In recent times, the theory that family harmony can be disrupted or destroyed by intrafamily tort litigation has been

immunity
As relates to family law, the traditional prohibition against tort actions between spouses.

criticized largely on the ground that if the family harmony is disrupted by such litigation, there was probably precious little family harmony present in the first place. Today both spouses are treated as individuals, and most of these claims are covered by insurance, so the family has nothing at risk in such litigation. The law today recognizes the existence of "domestic torts," as explained in Chapter 7.

The Obligation to Pay Taxes

Married persons must file income tax returns as married persons (either filing jointly or separately), thus paying taxes at a different rate than similarly situated unmarried individuals. This often results in the payment of a "marriage tax," a euphemism for the extra amount of taxes paid by a married couple as compared to a single person under identical financial circumstances. Numerous other tax consequences of marriage are discussed in Chapter 14.

The Right to Prevent Testimony by a Spouse

privilege for marital communications
Prohibition against coerced disclosure of certain statements made within the marital relationship.

A married person has the right to prevent his or her spouse from revealing in court proceedings any confidential communications made to the spouse during the marriage. This is the rule of evidence known as the **privilege for marital communications.** The traditional foundation of this privilege has been that society places a great value on the sanctity and harmony of marriage and does not wish to see it threatened by forcing one spouse to testify against another. Additionally, our society wants a married couple to be able to confide in each other without the fear that a confidential communication will be made public. This privilege continues even after a couple is divorced, as long as the confidential communication was made while the couple was still married. This privilege applies only to testimony at court actions initiated by a third party against one of the spouses and not to a court action between the spouses. Accordingly, the privilege for marital communications does not apply to court actions such as the following:

— Divorce, annulment, or other civil actions relating to the termination of the marriage or actions for support

— Court proceedings involving allegations of child molestation or abuse brought by one spouse against the other spouse

Additionally, the immunity only applies to communications between the spouses, not to acts that one spouse saw the other commit, and the communication must be directed to the spouse, not to a third party.

The Right to Receive Government Benefits

Surviving spouses are entitled to receive various entitlements based on their relationships with a qualified individual. The benefits may include Social Security, worker's compensation, or military and unemployment compensation. The degree to which these benefits may be payable to a surviving spouse depends on the degree to which the benefits are "vested" (earned and not subject to revocation); the existence of any additional, former, surviving spouses; the length of the marriage; the age of the surviving spouse; and the income level of the surviving spouse. The effect of marriage (and the termination of marriage) on these property rights is discussed in Chapter 9.

EFFECT OF MARRIAGE ON THIRD PARTIES

Agency is the legal theory that imposes liability on one party (the *principal*) for the actions of a second party (the *agent*) when those actions are undertaken on behalf of the first party. Just as an employer may be liable for the actions of its employee, a spouse may be liable for the actions of her spouse and children. This affects third parties (parties other than the spouses) in both tort law and contract law.

agency
A legal relationship in which the agent acts on behalf of the principal, and the principal is responsible for the actions of the agent.

Tort Law

Typically, spouses are not liable for torts committed by one another. But many states have specific laws regarding liability for automobile collisions. These laws, often called *family purpose laws*, allow a person injured in an automobile collision to seek compensation from both (1) the insurance company that issues the automobile insurance for the driver of the car that caused the accident and (2) the insurance companies that issue automobile insurance policies for all other family members living in the same household. For example, if Mr. Jones causes an automobile collision, the injured third party could make a claim against Mr. Jones' automobile insurance policy and against Mrs. Jones' automobile insurance policy, even though she had no involvement with the accident.

Contract Law

As already discussed, spouses have the legal obligation to provide support for each other and for the minor children. Accordingly, when one spouse makes a purchase and fails to pay for it, the merchant may be able to sue the other spouse to recover the purchase price. Usually this requires the authority or permission of the spouse not making the purchase. Additionally, as already noted, certain states have statutory provisions that provide a remedy to a spouse who is not receiving necessary support. These laws allow such a spouse to purchase necessities using the other spouse's credit, even without that spouse's authority to do so. For example, a wife could purchase milk, bacon, and eggs for the children's breakfast and pay for them with her husband's credit card. The merchant could seek payment from the husband even if the husband did not permit the wife to use his credit card, if the merchant can show that the purchase was for necessities.

BREACH OF THE PROMISE TO MARRY

A broken engagement is also a breach of contract. While not as prevalent as in years past, a minority of jurisdictions still recognize the validity of this cause of action. According to a noted authority in domestic relations[1], the claim of breach of the promise to marry has existed for at least two hundred years. But today the engagement period before marriage is viewed as a trial period between the parties. Further, it is now far more acceptable to marry later in life, so the loss of an opportunity to marry is no longer fatal to a person's eventual chances to marry.

As with any cause of action, there are specific defenses and damages. Among the defenses to a claim of breach of the promise to marry are misrepresentation of a material fact by the recipient of the promise to marry. For example, a misrepresentation of one's ability to conceive children or the existence of a prior marriage may be valid defenses. Additionally, if the consideration for the promise to marry is the offer of sexual relations, the promise is not enforceable. This is because sexual services may not serve as valid consideration for a contract. The basis of damages include the plaintiff's hurt feelings, embarrassment, and damage to reputation. A related cause of action is one for actual monetary losses caused by the breach of a promise to marry. For example, if one party is left at the altar, she could have a cause of action for the nonrefundable expenses of the wedding. This second cause of action is recognized even where no cause of action is recognized for the breach of promise to marry.

The decline of the cause of action for breach of the promise to marry is one aspect of what are known as **heartbalm statutes**. These statues abolished a number of traditional torts that sought to remedy hurt feelings. The torts include the breach of the promise to marry, as well as the following:

heartbalm statutes
Laws abolishing the right of action for alienation of affections, seduction, and criminal conversion.

— *Seduction*—The cause of action of seduction gave the father of a young girl who had been seduced monetary damages from the seducer. This usually required that the girl was a virgin at the time of the seduction.

— *Alienation of affections*—A cause of action against a third party for interference with a marital relationship. Potential defendants could include meddling family members as well as adulterous partners of a spouse.

— *Criminal conversation*—A cause of action for adultery with one's spouse.

The marriage contract is unique in that its formation precipitates a series of gifts to, and between, the parties. Who gets the presents when the wedding is called off? Usually, the most expensive "gift" is the engagement ring. The general rule is that if the bride cancels the wedding, she forfeits the ring. If the groom cancels the wedding, the bride is entitled to keep the ring. What about

---

1. Clark, *The Law of Domestic Relations,* Second Edition, West Publishing Company, 1988.

gifts received from third parties? Generally, if the motivation for the gift was the impending wedding, the gift should be returned.

UNMARRIED COHABITATION

One of the most noticeable changes in recent years is the increased social acceptability of unmarried persons living together. As a contrast to common-law marriage, in unmarried cohabitation the partners are not married and have no present intent to marry. This custom affects the practice of family law in two ways: First, unmarried cohabitants may want to enter into a written contract contemplative of their relationship; and second, when such a relationship dissolves, the parties may have to deal with many of the same issues raised in divorce litigation.

Traditionally, unmarried cohabitants received little, if any, protection under the law. Agreements made between the cohabitants were unenforceable, since courts found them to be based on illegal consideration—the parties' sexual relationship. Note that under state law, any sexual activity outside of marriage may be illegal.

Cohabitation Agreements

The traditional view held that any contract between unmarried persons engaged in an illicit relationship was unenforceable due to the illegality of the parties' relationship. Today, such contracts are enforceable as long as sexual services do not serve as the sole consideration for the contract. To the extent that sexual services are made a part of the contract, depending on the law of the jurisdiction, the contract will be at least partially unenforceable. The contract will be completely unenforceable unless the jurisdiction recognizes the theory of contract law known as the doctrine of severability, which permits the enforcement of valid portions of an otherwise invalid contract.

The most famous and trendsetting case in the area is *Marvin v. Marvin*, 18 Cal.3d 660, 134 Cal. Rptr. 815, 557 P.2d 106 (1976). In that case, the actor Lee Marvin lived with his girlfriend for approximately six years. When the couple split up, Mrs. Marvin (she had adopted his surname) brought suit seeking enforcement of an alleged oral agreement by which they would share all property acquired by either of them during the relationship. Among other things, this case introduced the term **palimony**, which refers to a claim for property or support resulting from the termination of a nonmarital relationship. The California Supreme Court held that an express agreement between the parties would be enforceable unless it was based solely on immoral and illicit consideration. But the court also held that where the contract did contemplate such consideration, the "doctrine of severability" would permit the court to sever the illegal aspects of the contract, and still enforce the remainder of the agreement. The California Supreme Court also stated that in the absence of an express agreement, other remedies may be available to enforce the lawful expectations of the parties. Other states have adopted some or all of the remedies mentioned by the California court, including

palimony
A slang term for support payment that may be owed to a former partner other than a spouse.

— *Implied contract.* A contract inferred from the parties' unexpressed intentions as evidenced by the parties' actions. For example, where two unmarried persons jointly purchase a residence, it may be inferred that each of them will be responsible for the maintenance of the premises, and that each would share in the proceeds of the eventual sale of the property.

— *Constructive trust.* A judicially created trust. If it is established that one party holds property that properly belongs to another, a constructive trust will transfer title to the property to the rightful owner of the property.

— *Resulting trust.* A trust created when one party contributes services or funds toward the acquisition of property, and title to that property is taken by another party.

— *Quantum meruit.* Where it can be established that one party provided domestic services with the reasonable expectation of compensation, the court may award the reasonable value of the services rendered, less any support actually received.

Traditionally, courts have found a way of affording relief to unmarried cohabitants when *equity* (a system of justice that seeks fairness for all parties, regardless of the strict construction of relevant statutes) demanded such relief. Common-law marriage is one such remedy.

Cohabitation Agreement Provisions

To better avoid judicial intervention, unmarried cohabitants may execute a written contract, clearly delineating the parties' respective rights and obligations. Here are some issues to be considered in a cohabitation agreement:

— That the parties do not intend to be married to each other (prevents the possibility of any claims that a common-law marriage exists)

— The parties' obligations toward their children

— How property acquired by the couple is to be owned (individually, tenants in common, joint tenants, etc.)

— Modification, enforcement, and termination of the agreement

— Who is responsible for which bills, and whether the parties are entitled to use each other's credit

A sample of typical provisions found in a cohabitation agreement follows at Exhibit 1–2.

EXHIBIT 1–2

SAMPLE COHABITATION AGREEMENT PROVISIONS[2]

I.

No Promises. Nothing contained herein shall be deemed, or construed, to be a promise on the part of either party to marry the other, or to support the other, or to continue to cohabit with the other.

Clearly setting forth that the parties do not intend to be married to each other, preventing the possibility of a claim that a common-law marriage exists.

II.

Relationship. The parties agree that this Agreement will totally determine their legal rights with respect to each other arising out of their cohabitation. Both parties agree not to assert any claims against the other arising out of their cohabitation or out of any common-law marriage or any contract or agreement, whether oral or written, express or implied, other than this Agreement and any amendments hereto which may be executed in accordance with the other provisions of this Agreement.

III.

Real Property. The parties are the owners, as joint tenants, of a parcel of improved real estate, located at 123 Main Street, Blackstone, Florida. The parties agree that each shall be responsible for the payment, out of his or her own separate income and property, of 50% of the mortgage, taxes, insurance, and maintenance and improvement of the real property.

Sets out the parties' agreement as to the ownership, maintenance, and payment for their jointly owned property. This provision more closely resembles a business "buy-sell" agreement than an agreement between lovers. However, a cohabitation agreement is a business contract and should be treated as such.

   If either party pays more than the required 50% share of the aforementioned expenses (hereafter referred to as the "Overpayment"), the other party will reimburse the amount of the overpayment to the paying party within thirty days of the date of the Overpayment. If either party fails to reimburse the other for an Overpayment within the thirty-day period, the amount of the Overpayment will become a "Sales Debit" of the party failing to make reimbursement. After the expiration of the thirty-day period, an offer to reimburse will not affect the existence of the Sales Debit unless agreed to, in writing, by the party to whom the reimbursement, relating to the particular Sales Debit, was owed. Each party shall keep a record of the Sales Debits owed to him or her by the other party as well as the proof of the debt. Upon the sale of the real property, the total Sales Debits owed to each party shall be calculated. The parties shall each be entitled to receive 50% of the net proceeds of the sale of the real property; however, each shall also be entitled to receive from the other an amount equal to the sum of the Sales Debits owed.

   If either party wishes to sell the real property ("Selling Party"), but the other does not agree to do so ("Non-Selling Party"), the parties agree that the real property will be sold. The parties will endeavor, in good faith, to agree upon an appropriate sales price for the real property. If they do agree, that price will be denominated the "Putative Sales Price." If they do not agree, the Putative Sales Price of the real property shall be determined by an appraisal made by independent appraisers or real estate brokers selected by the parties to this contract. In such case, each party shall select one appraiser or real estate broker, and then the two persons selected shall select a third.

---

2. Copyright 1986. The Michie Company. Reprinted with permission from *Separation Agreements and Marital Contracts.* The Michie Company, Charlottesville, Virginia, (800) 446-3410. All Rights Reserved.

IV.

Personal Property. The parties will agree upon an appropriate amount for each to contribute to the normal living expenses in connection with the real property, such as food, cleaning supplies, linens, paper goods, etc. Each party shall be responsible for his or her own personal expenses, such as clothing, toiletries, etc.

The parties are the owners as tenants in common (each with a 50% interest) of the furniture presently located upon the real property. Each party is the sole and separate owner of any items of personalty now, or hereafter, located upon the real property of an obviously personal nature to such party, such as jewelry, clothing, etc. Each particular item of property not described above shall belong to the party who has legal title to that property, or to the party to whose income or property the particular item of property is traceable. If the ownership of any particular item of property cannot be determined, it shall be determined that each party shall own a 50% interest in the property.

Except as specifically provided in this Agreement, each party shall keep and retain sole ownership, control, and enjoyment of all income and all property, real or personal, tangible or intangible, and any and all interest therein or income therefrom, now or hereafter owned by, possessed by, or standing of record in his or her name or in the nominee or trustee for his or her benefit and that each shall be free to dispose of all or any part of such property and interests and income as he or she may at any time and from time to time determine. Further that no claim or interest in the property of the other will arise by virtue of their cohabitation or by virtue of any contract, written or oral, express or implied.

V.

> *Each party affirmatively waives any entitlement to continuing support from the other party.*

Support. Except as may be provided in any future amendment to this Agreement, both parties waive, release, renounce, and relinquish any right or claim to support from the other party, whether that claim arises, or is alleged to arise, by virtue of their cohabitation, or by virtue of any common-law marriage or any contract, written or oral, express or implied.

VI.

Estate Rights. Except as may be provided in any future amendment to this Agreement, both parties acknowledge that neither has promised or represented to the other that he or she will bequeath any portion of his or her estate to the other, and both parties release, waive, renounce, and relinquish any right or claim against the estate of the other whether that right or claim arises, or is alleged to arise, by virtue of their cohabitation, or by virtue of any contract, written or oral, express or implied. However, the foregoing is not to be deemed to constitute a waiver by either party of any devise or bequest to him or her actually contained in the Last Will and Testament of the other.

VII.

> *Each party has entered into this agreement, and relationship, with full knowledge of the other party's financial status.*

Full Disclosure of Financial Status. Each party acknowledges that they have been advised of the other party's current net worth and annual income. Further, that each party has had the opportunity to make a full inquiry and to request all documents desired, with respect to the other's financial status, and that all such inquiries and requests have been satisfactorily fulfilled.

FOCUS ON DOMESTIC PARTNERSHIPS AND SAME-SEX MARRIAGES

As already noted, the very definition of *family* has been assailed in recent years as being discriminatory against those living what has been called "alternative life-styles." Such life-styles include persons of the opposite sex living together without benefit of marriage as well as persons of the same sex living together in a marriage-like relationship. The discrimination is alleged to occur because these relationships are not legally recognized (in some jurisdictions, they may even be illegal) and therefore the parties involved do not receive the same benefits accorded persons who are legally married. Domestic partnerships may be the most likely avenue if the benefits of marriage are to be bestowed upon unmarried persons.

First, what is a family? A *family* has been defined by the U.S. Census Bureau as "two or more persons related by birth, marriage, or adoption who reside in the same household." A *domestic partnership* is a unit of two persons who have registered with a governmental authority, which in turn confers upon the partnership many of the benefits usually reserved for married persons. These benefits may include extending insurance coverage to the partners of insured partners, the right to take a leave of absence from work to care for the domestic partner, and the right to receive a distribution from a deceased intestate partner. The rationale put forth by proponents of such laws is that homosexual couples, as well as different-sex couples who prefer not to enter into marriage, are denied the privileges afforded married couples, such as the right to adopt children, intestate succession, and insurance benefits for their partners and other dependents.

In 1993, the Hawaii Supreme Court decided the case of *Baehr v. Lewin,* 852 P.2d 44. The court ruled that the Hawaii statutes permitting only opposite-sex couples to obtain a marriage license are presumed to be unconstitutional unless it can be shown that the statute's sex-based requirements are justified by compelling state interests and are narrowly drawn to avoid unnecessary abridgements of constitutional rights. The Hawaii Supreme Court held that marriage is a fundamental right, and that statutes impinging upon such rights are subject to "strict scrutiny." At this writing, the case has not been finally adjudicated, but this is clearly an issue that will create much spirited debate.

CASE

BAEHR v. LEWIN

Supreme Court of Hawaii.
May 5, 1993.

. . . .

LEVINSON, Judge, in which MOON, Chief Judge, joins.

The plaintiffs-appellants Ninia Baehr (Baehr), Genora Dancel (Dancel), Tammy Rodrigues (Rodrigues), Antoinette Pregil (Pregil), Pat Lagon (Lagon), and Joseph Melilio (Melilio) (collectively "the plaintiffs") appeal the circuit court's order (and judgment entered pursuant thereto) granting the motion of the defendant-appellee John C. Lewin (Lewin), in his official capacity as Director of the Department of Health (DOH), State of Hawaii, for judgment on the pleadings, resulting in the dismissal of the plaintiffs' action with prejudice for failure to state a claim against Lewin upon which relief can be granted. Because, for purposes of Lewin's motion, it is our duty to view the factual allegations of the plaintiffs' complaint in a light most favorable to them (*i.e.,* because we must deem such allegations as true) and because it does *not* appear beyond doubt that the plaintiffs cannot prove any set of facts in support of their claim that would entitle them to the relief they seek, we hold that the circuit court erroneously dismissed the plaintiffs' complaint.

Accordingly, we vacate the circuit court's order and judgment and remand this matter to the circuit court for further proceedings consistent with this opinion.

I. BACKGROUND

On May 1, 1991, the plaintiffs filed a complaint for injunctive and declaratory relief in the Circuit Court of the First Circuit, State of Hawaii, seeking, *inter alia*: (1) a declaration that Hawaii Revised Statutes (HRS) § 572–1 (1985) (footnote omitted)—the section of the Hawaii Marriage Law enumerating the [r]equisites of [a] valid marriage contract—is unconstitutional insofar as it is construed and applied by the DOH to justify refusing to issue a marriage license on the *sole* basis that the applicant couple is of the same sex; and (2) preliminary and permanent injunctions prohibiting the future withholding of marriage licenses on that sole basis.

In addition to the necessary jurisdictional and venue-related averments, the plaintiffs' complaint alleges the following facts: (1) on or about December 17, 1990, Baehr/Dancel, Rodrigues/Pregil, and Lagon/Melilio (collectively "the applicant couples") filed applications for marriage licenses with the DOH, pursuant to HRS § 572-6 (Supp.1992)(footnote omitted); (2) the DOH denied the applicant couples' marriage license applications solely on the ground that the applicant couples were of the same sex (footnote omitted); (3) the applicant couples have complied with all marriage contract requirements and provisions under HRS ch. 572, except that each applicant couple is of the same sex; (4) the applicant couples are otherwise eligible to secure marriage licenses from the DOH, absent the statutory prohibition or construction of HRS § 572-1 excluding couples of the same sex from securing marriage licenses; and (5) in denying the applicant couples' marriage license applications, the DOH was acting in its official capacity and under color of state law.

Based on the foregoing factual allegations, the plaintiffs' complaint avers that: (1) the DOH's interpretation and application of HRS § 572-1 to deny same-sex couples access to marriage licenses violates the plaintiffs' right to privacy, as guaranteed by article I, section 6 of the Hawaii Constitution (footnote omitted), as well as to the equal protection of the laws and due process of law, as guaranteed by article I, section 5 of the Hawaii Constitution (footnote omitted); (2) the plaintiffs have no plain, adequate, or complete remedy at law to redress their alleged injuries; and (3) the plaintiffs are presently suffering and will continue to suffer irreparable injury from the DOH's acts, policies, and practices in the absence of declaratory and injuctive relief.

. . . .

B. The Right to Privacy Does Not Include a Fundamental Right to Same-Sex Marriage.

It is now well established that "'a right to personal privacy, or a guarantee of certain areas or zones of privacy,' is implicit in the United States Constitution." (Citation omitted.) And article I, section 6 of the Hawaii Constitution expressly states that "[t]he right of the people to privacy is recognized and shall not be infringed without the showing of a compelling state interest." Haw. Const. art. I, § 6 (1978). The framers of the Hawaii Constitution declared that the "privacy concept" embodied in article I, section 6 is to be "treated as a fundamental right[.]" (Citations omitted.)

. . . .

Accordingly, there is no doubt that, at a minimum, article I, section 6 of the Hawaii Constitution encompasses all of the fundamental rights expressly recognized as being subsumed within the privacy protections of the United States Constitution. In this connection, the United States Supreme Court has declared that "the right to marry is part of the fundamental 'right of privacy' implicit in the Fourteenth Amendment's Due Process Clause." *Zablocki v. Redhail*, 434 U.S. 374, 384, 98 S.Ct. 673, 680, 54 L.Ed.2d 618 (1978). The issue in the present case is, therefore, whether the "right to marry" protected by article I, section 6 of the Hawaii Constitution extends to same-sex couples. Because article I, section 6 was expressly derived from the general right to privacy under the United States Constitution and because there are no Hawaii cases that have delineated the fundamental right to marry, this court, . . . looks to federal cases for guidance.

The United States Supreme Court first characterized the right of marriage as fundamental in *Skinner v. Oklahoma ex rel. Williamson*, 316 U.S. 535, 62 S.Ct. 1110, 86 L.Ed. 1655 (1942). In *Skinner*, the right to marry was inextricably linked to the right of procreation. The dispute before the Court rose out of an Oklahoma statute that allowed the state to sterilize "habitual criminals" without their consent. In striking down the statute, the *Skinner* court indicated that it was "dealing . . . with legislation which involve[d] *one of the basic civil rights of man. Marriage and procreation are fundamental to the very existence and survival of the race.*" *Id.* at 541, 62 S.Ct. at 1113 (emphasis added). Whether the Court viewed marriage and procreation as a single indivisible right, the least that can be said is that it was obviously contemplating unions between men and women when it ruled that the right to marry was fundamental. This is hardly surprising inasmuch as none of the United States sanctioned any other marriage configuration at the time.

The United States Supreme Court has set forth its most detailed discussion of the fundamental right to marry in *Zablocki, supra,* which involved a Wisconsin statute that prohibited any resident of the state with minor children "not in his custody and which he is under obligation to support" from obtaining a marriage license until the resident demonstrated to a court that he was in compliance with his child support obligations. (Citation omitted.) The *Zablocki* court held that the statute burdened the fundamental right to marry; applying the "strict scrutiny" standard to the statute, the Court invalidated it as violative of the fourteenth amendment to the United States Constitution. (Citations omitted.) . . .

. . . .

The foregoing case law demonstrates that the federal construct of the fundamental right to marry—subsumed within the right to privacy implicitly protected by the United States Constitution—presently contemplates unions between men and women. (Once again, this is hardly surprising inasmuch as such unions are the only state-sanctioned marriages currently acknowledged in this country.)

Therefore, the precise question facing this court is whether we will extend the *present* boundaries of the fundamental right of marriage to include same-sex couples, or, put another way, whether we will hold that same-sex couples possess a fundamental right to marry. In effect, as the applicant couples frankly admit, we are being asked to recognize a new fundamental right. . . .

. . . [W]e do not believe that a right to same-sex marriage is so rooted in the traditions and collective conscience of our people that failure to recognize it would violate the fundamental principles of liberty and justice that lie at the base of all our civil and political institutions. Neither do we believe that a right to same-sex marriage is implicit in the concept of ordered liberty, such that neither liberty nor justice would exist if it were sacrificed. Accordingly, we hold that the applicant couples do not have a fundamental constitutional right to same-sex marriage arising out of the right to privacy or otherwise.

Our holding, however, does not leave the applicant couples without a potential remedy in this case. As we will discuss below, the applicant couples are free to press their equal protection claim. If they are successful, the State of Hawaii will no longer be permitted to refuse marriage licenses to couples merely on the basis that they are of the same sex. But there is no fundamental right to marriage for same-sex couples under article I, section 6 of the Hawaii Constitution.

. . . .

In addition to the alleged violation of their constitutional rights to privacy and due process of law, the applicant couples contend that they have been denied the equal protection of the laws as guaranteed by article I, section 5 of the Hawaii Constitution. On appeal, the plaintiffs urge and, on the state of the bare record before us, we agree that the circuit court erred when it concluded, *as a matter of law,* that: (1) homosexuals do not constitute a "suspect class" for purposes of equal protection analysis under article I, section 5 of the Hawaii Constitution (footnote omitted); (2) the classification created by HRS § 572-1 is not subject to "strict scrutiny," but must satisfy only the "rational relationship" test; and (3) HRS § 572-1 satisfies the rational relationship test because the legislature "obviously designed [it] to promote the general welfare interests of the community be sanctioning traditional man-woman family units and procreation."

. . . [M]arriage is a state-conferred legal status, the existence of which gives rise to rights and benefits reserved exclusively to that particular relationship. This court construes marriage as "'a partnership to which both partners bring their financial resources as well as their individual energies and efforts.'" (Citations omitted.) So zealously has this court guarded the state's role as the exclusive progenitor of the marital partnership that it declared, over seventy years ago, that "common law" marriages—*i.e.,* "marital" unions existing in the absence of a state-issued license and not performed by a person or society possessing governmental authority to solemnize marriages—would no longer be recognized in the Territory of Hawaii. (Citation and footnote omitted.)

. . . .

The applicant couples correctly contend that the DOH's refusal to allow them to marry on the basis that they are members of the same sex deprives them of access to a multiplicity of rights and benefits that are contingent upon that status. Although it is unnecessary in this opinion to engage in an encyclopedic recitation of all of them, a number of the most salient marital rights and benefits are worthy of note. They include: (1) a variety of state income tax advantages, including deductions, credits, rates, exemptions, and estimates (citation omitted); (2) public assistance from and exemptions relating to the Department of Human Services (citation omitted); (3) control, division, acquisition, and disposition of community property (citation omitted); (4) rights relating to dower, curtesy, and inheritance (citation omitted); (5) rights to notice, protection, benefits, and inheritance under the Uniform

Probate Code (citation omitted); (6) award of child custody and support payments in divorce proceedings (citation omitted); (7) the right to spousal support (citation omitted); (8) the right to enter into premarital agreements (citation omitted); (9) the right to change of name (citation omitted); (10) the right to file a nonsupport action (citation omitted); (11) post-divorce rights relating to support and property division (citation omitted); (12) the benefit of the spousal privilege and confidential marital communications (citation omitted); (13) the benefit of the exemption of real property from attachment or execution (citation omitted); and (14) the right to bring a wrongful death action (citation omitted). For present purposes, it is not disputed that the applicant couples would be entitled to all of these marital rights and benefits, but for the fact that they are denied access to the state-conferred legal status of marriage.

. . . .

Notwithstanding the state's acknowledged stewardship over the institution of marriage, the extent of permissible state regulation of the right of access to the marital relationship is subject to constitutional limitations or constraints. (Citations omitted.) It has been held that a state may deny the right to marry only for compelling reasons. (Citation and footnote omitted.)

The equal protection clauses of the United States and Hawaii Constitutions are not mirror images of one another. The fourteenth amendment to the United States Constitution somewhat concisely provides, in relevant part, that a state may not "deny to any person within its jurisdiction the equal protection of the laws." Hawaii's counterpart is more elaborate. Article I, section 5 of the Hawaii Constitution provides in relevant part that "[n]o person shall . . . be denied the equal protection of the laws, *nor be denied the enjoyment of the person's civil rights or be discriminated against in the exercise thereof because of* race, religion, *sex*, or ancestry." (Emphasis added.) Thus, by its plain language, the Hawaii Constitution prohibits state-sanctioned discrimination against any person in the exercise of his or her civil rights on the basis of sex.

. . . .

Jones v. Hallahan, 501 S.W.2d 588 (Ky. Ct.App.1973), (citations omitted), warrant . . . analysis. In *Jones,* the appellants, both females, sought review of a judgment that held that they were not entitled to have a marriage license issued to them, contending that refusal to issue the license deprived them of the basic constitutional rights to marry, associate, and exercise religion freely. In an opinion acknowledged to be "a case of first impression in Kentucky,"

the Court of Appeals summarily affirmed, ruling as follows:

> Marriage was a custom long before the state commenced to issue licenses for that purpose. . . . [M]arriage has always been considered as a union of a man and a woman. . . .
>
> It appears to us that appellants are prevented from marrying, not by the statutes of Kentucky or the refusal of the County Clerk . . . to issue them a license, but rather by their own incapability of entering into a marriage as that term is defined.
>
> . . . [I]n substance, the relationship proposed by the appellants does not authorize the issuance of a marriage license because what they propose is not a marriage. 501 S.W.2d at 589–90.

Significantly, the appellants' equal protection rights—federal or state—were not asserted in *Jones,* and, accordingly, the appeals court was relieved of the necessity of addressing and attempting to distinguish the decision of the United States Supreme Court in *Loving v. Virginia. Loving* involved the appeal of a black woman and a caucasian man (the Lovings) who were married in the District of Columbia and thereafter returned to their home state of Virginia to establish their marital abode. (Citation omitted.) The Lovings were duly indicted for and convicted of violating Virginia's miscegenation laws (footnote omitted), which banned interracial marriages. (Footnote omitted.) . . .

. . . .

The Lovings appealed the constitutionality of the state's miscegenation laws to the Virginia Supreme Court of Appeals, which, *inter alia,* upheld their constitutionality and affirmed the Lovings' convictions. (Footnote and citation omitted.) The Lovings then pressed their appeal to the United States Supreme Court. . . .

In a landmark decision, the United States Supreme Court, through Chief Justice Warren, struck down the Virginia miscegenation laws on both equal protection and due process grounds. The Court's holding as to the former is pertinent for present purposes:

[T]he Equal Protection Clause requires the consideration of whether the classifications drawn by any statute constitute an arbitrary and invidious discrimination. . . .

There can be no question but that Virginia's miscegenation statutes rest solely upon distinctions drawn according to race. *The statutes proscribe generally accepted conduct* if engaged in by members of different races. . . . At the very least, the Equal Protection Clause demands that racial classifications . . . be subjected to the "most rigid scrutiny," . . . and, if they are ever to be upheld, *they must be shown to be necessary to the accomplishment of some permissible state objective, independent of the* racial *discrimination which it was the object of the Fourteenth Amendment to eliminate. . . .*

There is patently no legitimate overriding purpose independent of invidious discrimination which justifies this classification. . . . We have consistently denied the constitutionality of measures which restrict the rights of citizens on account of race. There can be no doubt that restricting the freedom to marry solely because of racial classifications violates the central meaning of the Equal Protection Clause. . . . (Emphasis added and citation and footnote omitted).

The facts in *Loving* and the respective reasoning of the Virginia courts, on the one hand, and the United States Supreme Court, on the other, both discredit the reasoning of *Jones* and unmask the tautological and circular nature of Lewin's argument that HRS § 572–1 does not implicate article I, section 5 of the Hawaii Constitution because same sex marriage is an innate impossibility. Analogously to Lewin's argument and the rationale of the *Jones* court, the Virginia courts declared that interracial marriage simply could not exist because the Deity had deemed such a union intrinsically unnatural, (1974) (citation omitted) and, in effect, because it had therefore never been the "custom" of the state to recognize mixed marriages, marriage "always" having been construed to presuppose a different configuration. With all due respect to the Virginia courts of a bygone era, we do not believe that trial judges are the ultimate authorities on the subject of Divine Will, and, as *Loving* amply demonstrates, constitutional law may mandate, like it or not, that customs change with an evolving social order.

Singer v. Hara, 11 Wash.App. 247, 522 P.2d 1187, (1974) (citation omitted) suffers the same fate as does *Jones.* In *Singer,* two males appealed from a trial court's order denying their motion to show cause by which they sought to compel the county auditor to issue them a marriage license. On appeal, the unsuccessful applicants argued that: (1) the trial court erred in concluding that the Washington state marriage laws prohibited same-sex marriages; (2) the trial court's order violated the equal rights amendment to the state constitution; and (3) the trial court's order violated various provisions of the United States Constitution, including the fourteenth amendment.

The Washington Court of Appeals affirmed the trial court's order, rejecting all three of the appellants'

contentions. Predictably, and for the same reasons that we have reached the identical conclusion regarding HRS § 572-1, the *Singer* court determined that it was "apparent from a plain reading of our marriage statutes that the legislature has not authorized same-sex marriages." (Citation omitted.) Regarding the appellants' federal and state claims, the court specifically "[did] not take exception to the proposition that *the Equal Protection Clause of the Fourteenth Amendment requires strict judicial scrutiny of legislative attempts at sexual discrimination.*" (Citation and footnote omitted and emphasis added.) Nevertheless, the *Singer* court found no defect in the state's marriage laws, under either the United States Constitution or the state constitution's equal rights amendment based upon the rationale of *Jones:* "[a]ppellants were not denied a marriage license because of their sex; rather, they were denied a marriage license because of the nature of marriage itself." As in *Jones,* we reject this exercise in tortured and conclusory sophistry.

3. Equal Protection Analysis under
Article I, Section 5 of the
Hawaii Constitution

"Whenever a denial of equal protection of the laws is alleged, as a rule our initial inquiry has been whether the legislation in question should be subjected to 'strict scrutiny' or to a 'rational basis' test." (Citations omitted.) This court has applied "strict scrutiny" analysis to "'laws classifying on the basis of suspect categories or impinging upon fundamental rights expressly or impliedly granted by the [c]onstitution,'" in which case the laws are "'presumed to be unconstitutional (footnote omitted) unless the state shows compelling state interests which justify such classifications,'" (citations omitted) and that the laws are "narrowly drawn to avoid unnecessary abridgments of constitutional rights." *Nagle,* 63 Haw. at 392, 629 P.2d at 111 (citations omitted).

By contrast, "[w]here 'suspect' classifications or fundamental rights are not at issue, this court has traditionally employed the rational basis test." (Citation omitted.) "Under the rational basis test, we inquire as to whether a statute rationally furthers a legitimate state interest." (Citation omitted.) "Our inquiry seeks only to determine whether any reasonable justification can be found for the legislative enactment." . . .

As we have indicated HRS § 572–1, on its face and as applied, regulates access to the marital status and its concomitant rights and benefits on the basis of the applicants' sex. . . . As such, HRS § 572-1 establishes a sex-based classification.

    . . . .

Accordingly, we hold that sex is a "suspect category" for purposes of equal protection analysis under article I, section 5 of the Hawaii Constitution (footnote omitted) and that HRS § 572–1 is subject to the "strict scrutiny" test. It therefore follows, and we so hold, that (1) HRS § 572–1 is presumed to be unconstitutional (2) unless Lewin, as an agent of the State of Hawaii, can show that (a) the statute's sex-based classification is justified by compelling state interests and (b) the statute is narrowly drawn to avoid unnecessary abridgments of the applicant couples' contitutional rights.

. . . .

III. CONCLUSION

Because, for the reasons stated in this opinion, the circuit court erroneously granted Lewin's motion for judgment on the pleadings and dismissed the plaintiffs' complaint, we vacate the circuit court's order and judgment and remand this matter for further proceedings consistent with this opinion. On remand, in accordance with the "strict scrutiny" standard, the burden will rest on Lewin to overcome the presumption that HRS § 572-1 is unconstitutional by demonstrating that it furthers compelling state interests and is narrowly drawn to avoid unnecessary abridgements of constitutional rights. (Citations omitted.)

Vacated and remanded.

DISCUSSION QUESTIONS

Consider the above case *Baehr v. Lewin*, 852 P.2d 44 (Haw. 1993), and answer these questions:

1. What is the basis of the plaintiff's claim against the state?

2. What is the difference between the "rational basis" test and the "strict scrutiny" test, and why did this court decide to use the strict scrutiny test?

3. What is to happen to this case after the Hawaii Supreme Court has ruled?

REVIEW QUESTIONS

For questions 1 through 8, determine whether the following statements are true or false. If false, determine what portions of the statement are false and make the necessary additions, deletions, or modifications to correct the statement.

1. While two people of the same sex cannot enter into a ceremonial marriage, there is no restriction against two people of the same sex entering into a common-law marriage.

2. If two people get married while under the influence of alcohol, the marriage may be voided because the parties did not have the capacity to marry.

3. In a state that recognizes the validity of common-law marriages, a couple will be married if they simultaneously hold themselves out to the public as husband and wife, intend to be married to one another, and cohabit as husband and wife.

4. In most states, only the husband has the legal obligation to provide adequate support for his family.

5. A person who died without a valid last will and testament died testate.

6. If a wife is injured in an accident caused by a third party, and as a result is unable to engage in sexual relations with her husband, the husband may have a cause of action for loss of consortium against the third party.

7. If a wife confesses to her husband that she had embezzled funds from her employer, the husband could be compelled to testify against his wife in later court proceedings.

8. Same facts as in question 7, except this time the husband and wife have obtained a divorce since the time the wife confessed to her husband. The ex-husband can be compelled to testify against the ex-wife in later court proceedings.

9. What are the differences between a same-sex marriage and a domestic partnership?

10. How does the putative spouse doctrine differ from a common-law marriage?

11. What claim does a surviving spouse have to the estate of her deceased spouse? What difference

does it make, if any, if the deceased spouse had a valid last will and testament?

12. What are the legal prerequisities for a person to be married?

13. What are the requirements for a common-law marriage in states in which it is recognized?

14. What are the requirements for a valid ceremonial marriage?

15. What is the right of consortium, and how does a loss of consortium occur?

KEY TERMS

affinity	family
agency	full faith and credit
bigamy	heartbalm statutes
ceremonial marriage	immunity
cohabitation	intestate
agreements	intestate distribution
common law	legal capacity
common-law	marital property
marriage	marriage
consanguinity	mental capacity
consortium	necessities
curtesy	palimony
descent and	physical capacity
distribution	polygamy
domestic	privilege for marital
partnership	communications
domicile	putative spouse
dower	doctrine
dowry	testate
emancipation	tort

STATE RESEARCH PROBLEMS

While the answers to many of these questions can be found in your state code, some of these questions may best be answered by an official at the local courthouse.

1. What relationships are prohibited from marriage in your state? List the relationships prohibited because of consanguinity separately from those prohibited because of affinity.

2. Review the relevant statutes of your state, and determine the definition of *necessities*.

3. What is the minimum age for a person to be married? Is the minimum age different for common-law as opposed to ceremonial marriages? Does parental consent have any effect on the age limit? If required, how must parental consent be proven (must the parent be present at the wedding; is an affidavit required)?

4. What court in your county or district issues marriage licenses?

5. How soon before the wedding can/must the license be obtained? How much does the license cost?

6. What types of medical tests must be performed on the applicants? How soon before the wedding can/must these tests be performed?

7. Who is empowered to perform the wedding ceremony? Does that party have the responsibility for filing the marriage license once it has been executed (signed)?

8. How many, if any, witnesses are required to attend the ceremony? What, if anything, must they sign?

Initial Client Interview

CHAPTER OBJECTIVES

In this chapter, you will learn:

- *The goals of a successful initial client interview and the procedure for accomplishing them*

- *The roles of the attorney and paralegal in an initial client interview*

- *The definition of conflicts of interest and how to avoid them*

- *The requirement to preserve the confidences and secrets of a client*

- *How to avoid participating in the unauthorized practice of law*

- *The different forms of attorney's fees*

- *How to document the attorney-client relationship*

The initial client interview (ICI) is the foundation of the relationship between a law firm and a client. The ICI gives the law firm an opportunity to appraise clients and their cases. The ICI also allows the client to determine whether to retain the law firm. An initial concern is the potential for any conflict of interests that might exist between the new client and either another client or the law firm itself. Paralegals are an integral part of the client interviewing process. They often meet with the client, without the attorney present, to obtain the facts necessary to properly represent the client. Paralegals usually refer to an interview checklist when interviewing a client to ensure that the appropriate information is obtained. But paralegals must take care not to give a client legal advice, or to reveal the client's secrets and confidences. Although paralegals cannot ultimately decide whether the law firm will represent a particular client, paralegals do have input into these decisions. After the ICI, paralegals prepare a report to their supervising attorney detailing the facts of the case and giving their opinion of the client and the case.

Although this text uses the abbreviation *ICI* for the term *initial client interview,* you will soon learn that every firm has its own name for the initial client interview (i.e., intake interview, initial consultation, etc.).

OVERVIEW OF THE INITIAL CLIENT INTERVIEW

For a paralegal, an attractive feature of working in family law is the opportunity for contact with clients. Naturally, one of the best opportunities to interact directly with clients is the ICI. The ICI is an integral part of an attorney-client relationship for many reasons. Perhaps none is more important than this: The ICI sets the tone for the working relationship between the client and the law firm. It is a relationship that can last months, if not years. A successful ICI allows both the client and the attorney to achieve their goals. Clients want to leave the law office after the ICI confident that they have made an intelligent choice to retain your law firm to represent them. Attorneys want to be certain that they have obtained enough information to be comfortable with the decision to take on this new client.

The ICI is, above all else, an interview. Clients are conducting what essentially amounts to a job interview; they are looking for someone to represent them in a lawsuit. The law firm is conducting what essentially amounts to an audition; they want to know how well this person might do as a witness in a courtroom. If the attorney or the paralegal conducting the ICI does not believe a client as she relates her "story," there is little chance that the law firm would accept her as a client. Additionally, as with any relationship, there is an intangible factor or a "chemistry" that must exist, or the client and the attorney may very well be at each other's throat throughout the litigation.

Goals of the Interview

A successful ICI accomplishes many goals and lays the foundation for a mutually beneficial relationship between the client and the law firm. In addition to establishing a good rapport and learning about the clients and their case, the ICI should accomplish the following:

— Educate clients concerning the laws affecting them and the legal procedures likely to be used in the case (to be accomplished by the attorney).

— Discuss office procedures, that is, how the firm uses attorneys and paralegals; what to do in an emergency; etc. (to be accomplished by either the attorney or the paralegal).

— Discuss the legal fees: how much, when it is to be paid, etc. The client's obligation to pay the costs of litigation (court reporter fees, subpoena fees, etc.) should also be fully explained (to be accomplished by the attorney).

— Alleviate the clients' anxiety and convince them that your law firm is the appropriate source of relief to their legal woes (to be accomplished by both the attorney and the paralegal).

The Paralegal's Role

The paralegal's role in the ICI can vary from almost no participation whatsoever (an increasingly rare phenomenon) to sitting in with an attorney throughout the entire ICI to conducting a portion of the ICI without the attorney. As a paralegal, remember that even when you conduct a part of an ICI without an attorney present, both law and professional **ethics** limit what you can say to the client and what agreements you can reach with the client. You cannot respond to a client's question about what they should do, or what your firm will do for them. You cannot make an agreement about the type of fee that will be paid, how it will be paid, when it will be paid, etc. You cannot make the ultimate decision whether your firm will accept the representation of a particular client. Failure to follow any of these rules may lead to a claim of the unauthorized practice of law.

Regardless of the extent of the paralegal's participation in an ICI, the paralegal usually performs certain tasks before the interview:

ethics

Legal ethics relate to the legal and professional duties that lawyers owe to each other, their clients, and the courts.

1. Check the firm's master list of all clients and adverse parties to ascertain whether representation of that party would constitute a conflict of interest. (See "Focus on Ethics: Conflicts of Interest")

2. Be certain that the reception area is prepared for the new client. Although this is usually the responsibility of the receptionist, everyone in the office should be in the habit of checking that the reception area is clean and neat.

3. Determine why the client is coming to the office. The receptionist, or whoever schedules the ICI, should already have asked the potential client why they desire an appointment. This step serves the dual purposes of a) ensuring that the service the client seeks is offered by your firm, and b) allowing you to be fully prepared for the ICI (having the right interview forms ready, etc.).

4. Most firms ask a client to fill out a brief form or questionnaire before meeting with the attorney and paralegal, in which the client provides the basic information. A sample new client questionnaire is provided in Exhibit 2–1.

5. Prepare the site for the ICI. Some firms use an attorney's or paralegal's office; others prefer to use a conference or interviewing room. The advantage of the latter is that it allows a potential client to be interviewed in a room free from the clutter that inevitably seems to take over an office. Instruct the support staff to hold all calls and interruptions. Position the furniture properly. Some firms prefer a traditional configuration, with the interviewer sitting behind a desk across from the client. Others now prefer a more

FOCUS ON ETHICS

Unauthorized Practice of Law

Paralegals can do many, if not most, of the tasks traditionally performed by attorneys *if* they do so under the supervision and control of an attorney. A paralegal engaging in any of these tasks for another person without the supervision of a licensed attorney would be engaging in the *unauthorized practice of law,* in other words, practicing law without a license. This conduct is prohibited by the attorney's rules of ethics in every state in the nation. Furthermore, it is a criminal act subject to prosecution and punishment. (Of course anyone, including a paralegal, can represent themselves in a legal matter.)

What acts constitute the unauthorized practice of law?

— A paralegal cannot represent another person in a court of law. Generally, a paralegal can sit with the attorney and client in a courtroom and assist during trial. Note that this prohibition is limited to courts of law. Many governmental agencies, such as the Social Security Administration and Veterans Administration, as well as many other state and federal agencies, have their own administrative law courts that permit someone who is not an attorney to represent a third party before them.

— A paralegal cannot sign any document requiring the signature of a licensed attorney (i.e., a complaint for divorce). Paralegals can help the attorney draft the complaint; they can even draft the complaint by themselves. But, the attorney *must* read and sign the complaint before it can be filed in court.

— A paralegal cannot make the ultimate decision whether to accept a person as a client. But paralegals can, and do, participate in initial client interviews.

— A paralegal cannot give legal advice. In practice, this is the element of the rule that proves most troubling for paralegals. What can you say when a client asks you, "What should I do?" For example, suppose that a prospective client calls your office and tells you that he has just been served with a complaint for divorce. He is very upset and he wants to know what he should do, what he can do, what you will do, etc. How do you respond if this is your first day on the job? How do you respond if this is your tenth year on the job? The answer to both questions is the same: You must respond by saying that you are not an attorney, and that the client needs to speak with the attorney for advice about the proper course of action. As a paralegal, you are permitted to provide information to clients (i.e., "What is an interrogatory?" or "What is a counterclaim?"). But you are not permitted to advise clients what they should do with the interrogatory or counterclaim. That would constitute the practice of law.

As a paralegal, you have the affirmative duty to be certain that everyone you deal with is aware that you are not an attorney. This eliminates the possibility that anyone contacting a law firm will assume that you are an attorney. This duty requires you to include the title *Paralegal* or *Legal Assistant* after your signature on law firm correspondence. The same rationale prohibits a paralegal's name from appearing on the firm letterhead unless it specifically identifies the individual as a paralegal. Some states prohibit law firm employees who are not attorneys from having a law firm business card, even if it clearly identifies the person as a paralegal.

Before you decide that these rules are designed solely to aggravate, demean, or otherwise irritate paralegals, please remember the rationale supporting these rules. First, society has decided that the general public needs to be protected from unqualified persons attempting to practice law. Licensed attorneys have the necessary training that enables them to use their professional judgment on their client's behalf. Further, attorneys have the exclusive privilege to practice law on the behalf of other people, because the process for obtaining a license to practice law examines them for two significant attributes: one is competence, which is measured by the bar admissions exam that each lawyer must pass; the other is integrity, which is measured by the bar admissions committee inquiry into the character of the bar applicant. Attorneys are also under the continuing jurisdiction and scrutiny of the state bar association or state supreme court, which can sanction an attorney for failure to abide by any of the ethical rules of that state.

Avoiding the unauthorized practice of law is an increasingly difficult problem in many law offices. Because so many paralegals have become so adept at the tasks assigned to them, they receive increasingly complex assignments. Attorneys want to use paralegals to the full extent of their capabilities, because the attorney is then free to concentrate on tasks specifically requiring the attention of an attorney. The client prefers to have a paralegal perform as many tasks as possible, to help reduce legal fees. And of course, paralegals enjoy the additional responsibilities assigned to them. Throughout the text, we will emphasize those areas in which the paralegal is most likely to encounter the unauthorized practice of law.

intimate setting, with the interviewer and client at a conference table or in two chairs without a desk. Of course, always keep a box or two of tissues available.

You must also be certain that the prospective client does not see any other clients' files, which would result in a breach of confidentiality. Failure to keep files secure tells prospective clients that your law firm is a slipshod organization, and that they cannot rely on any promises of confidentiality.

Later in this chapter, we discuss a paralegal's role in two different situations: participating in an ICI with an attorney present and conducting part of an ICI without an attorney present. But first we will look at a sample checklist of questions that can be asked at an ICI. And finally, we will discuss preparing your report to the supervising attorney.

EXHIBIT 2–1

NEW CLIENT QUESTIONNAIRE

Name _____   Date _____

Current Address _____

Current Mailing Address (if different) _____

Home Tel. No. _____   Office Tel. No. _____

Brief Description of Case (divorce, adoption, etc.) _____

_____

_____

Who referred you to our firm? _____

FOCUS ON ETHICS

Conflicts of Interest

Attorneys owe their clients the duty of complete, undivided loyalty. The goal is to allow attorneys to provide independent judgment on behalf of each of their clients. *Conflicts of interest* generally occur when the interests of the attorney are not identical to the interests of the client. Such conflicts may occur in a variety of settings: between the attorney and the client, between two or more clients of the same attorneys, or between a current client and a former client.

Conflicts between Attorney and Client

A conflict of interest can occur if an attorney enters into a business transaction with a client or loans money to a client. The basis for the conflict is the possibility that the attorney will not be able to provide appropriate and competent legal advice because the client's interests may be contrary to the attorney's interests. For example, if an attorney loans money to a client who is suing for divorce, she might be tempted to persuade her client to accept a less than satisfactory offer to settle the divorce litigation just to help the client repay the loan. Or, an attorney being paid under a contingent fee agreement may urge his client to accept a less than favorable settlement solely to provide the attorney with immediate compensation. (As noted below, contingent fee agreements are not permitted within divorce litigation.)

Conflicts between Two Current Clients

The most obvious conflict that can occur between two clients of the same attorney occurs during common representation—when one attorney represents both parties in the same adversarial action. For example, Attorney Smith cannot represent both husband and wife in the same divorce. Obviously, these two parties have interests that are antithetical to each other (i.e., the husband would like to pay less money in alimony and the wife would like to receive more).

Having said this, it is possible for one attorney to represent both the husband and wife in a divorce action if:

— The divorce is an **uncontested divorce**, meaning that the parties have voluntarily decided all issues, such as property settlement, child custody and visitation, etc.

— The parties agree to the common representation.

— The attorney reasonably believes that the common representation will not adversely affect his ability to represent either client.

— The ethical rules of that particular state permit common representation (most states permit common representation if the first three conditions above are satisfied).

For example, consider David and Julie, who are both in their late twenties, live in an apartment, and have no children. They have recently realized that they no longer wish to stay together as husband and wife; however, they harbor no malice against each other. They are an ideal couple to use common representation for their divorce. David and Julie need an attorney more to shepherd them through the legal process than to act as an advocate.

On the other hand, conflicts between two current clients can be avoided entirely by making it clear at the outset of the legal representation that the attorney will represent only one of the spouses, and that the other spouse has the right to seek alternative legal advice. In this scenario, when David and Julie first go to the attorney, the attorney informs them that he is willing to formally represent either one of them (suppose it is David). Julie is then told that the attorney will draft the necessary papers as requested by the parties, but that if a dispute should develop between her and David, the attorney will represent David. Further, Julie is told that the attorney will not be responsible for her welfare. This understanding would be included in the parties' separation agreement (see Chapter 6).

Conflicts between a Current Client and a Former Client

A common problem that an attorney faces is the conflict between a current client and a former client. The basis for this conflict of interest is that the loyalty an attorney owes a client does not terminate when a particular piece of litigation ends.

Accordingly, an attorney cannot represent an adverse party in litigation against a former client. The exception to this prohibition would allow an attorney to litigate against a former client if the new litigation is completely unrelated to the subject matter of the prior representation.

Here are some examples of a conflict of interest:

— An attorney representing a married couple jointly when they file for bankruptcy cannot represent one of the spouses in a subsequent divorce action. The rationale is that both parties had to reveal confidential information to the attorney during the course of the bankruptcy action, and it would be unfair to give the same attorney the potential to use that information against a spouse in a later divorce action.

— Conversely, consider that a lawyer representing a married couple jointly when they purchase a parcel of real estate *may* represent the husband in a later divorce action *if* the attorney did not obtain any confidential information from the wife that could be used to the husband's advantage in the divorce action. This conflict differs from the first example based on the degree to which a client must confide in an attorney (less to purchase real estate; more to file for bankruptcy).

Another conflict unique to family law occurs when one spouse confers with many or all of the family law practitioners in town, with the intent of disqualifying them from representing the other spouse. This can be accomplished with relative ease in small towns with few attorneys. Should it be established that the first spouse met with the attorneys for the purpose of disqualifying them from further participation in the litigation, a court could exercise its equity jurisdiction to grant the other spouse permission to retain one of those law firms.

Imputed Disqualification of Law Firm

It is important to remember that generally, when an attorney has a conflict of interest in a particular case, that attorney's law firm shares the conflict of interest. This means that an entire law firm can be disqualified from participating in a lawsuit because one of its attorneys has a conflict of interest.

Furthermore, a law firm can be disqualified from participating in a lawsuit if one of its paralegals has a conflict of interest that would bar participation. This is usually not a problem for paralegals until they move from one law firm to another. For example, before Law Firm A hires a paralegal who has previously worked for Law Firm B, they ask whether the new paralegal would cause a conflict of interest for Law Firm A.

A possible solution to the problem of law firm disqualification would be to install a **Chinese Wall** around the conflicting files and information. (The name derives from an analogy with the Great Wall of China, which protected China against invaders.) The Chinese Wall effectively cuts off the disqualified attorney or paralegal from the conflicting files. The erection of a Chinese Wall may include prohibiting the disqualified legal professional from having any connection with the conflicting case, informing all other employees not to discuss that case with the disqualified personnel, placing those case files in a restricted area and prohibiting the disqualified legal professional from entering the area (in large firms, it may be necessary to post photographs of the prohibited legal professionals, so they cannot gain entry by walking past an unwary guard), and placing the work space of the disqualified legal professionals on a separate floor or in another office.

Preventing Conflicts of Interest

As should be evident by now, it is all too easy for the unwary attorney to enter into a lawsuit that can result in a conflict of interest. To prevent conflicts of interest from occurring, law firms usually have master lists of all parties any of their attorneys or paralegals have represented previously. Then, when a new client comes to the law office for the initial client interview, you can review the master list of clients to determine whether the party adverse to your new client was a former client.

USING INTERVIEW CHECKLISTS

This book is designed to teach you, among other things, what facts are relevant in various types of family law actions. One way of accomplishing this goal is by using sample interview checklists. What follows is that portion of the interview checklist that would be appropriate for practically all circumstances except adoption. Throughout the book, you will find additional sections entitled "Interview Checklist." These sections serve as addenda to the basic interview checklist that follows. For example, the interview checklist for an action to obtain past-due child support payments consists of the basic interview checklist and the additional interview checklist to be found in Chapter 12.

BASIC INTERVIEW CHECKLIST

Client name

S.S.N.

Other names (including maiden)

Address

Previous address (within last 12 months)

Occupation

Employer

Home telephone no.

Work telephone no.

Date of birth   Age

Place of birth

Spouse's name

S.S.N.

Other names (including maiden)

Highest level of education completed:
H. S.   College   Other

Previous employer

Position

Period of employment

Highest salary

Previous employer

Position

Period of employment

Highest salary

Are you presently under any obligation to any military service? _____ If so, state which branch of the military, where you are stationed, and when your obligations will terminate.

Address (if different from your own)

continued on page 38

continued from page 37

Other addresses (within last 12 months)

_____

_____

Occupation

_____

Employer

_____

Home telephone no.

_____

Work telephone no.

_____

Date of birth   Age

_____

Place of birth

_____

Highest level of education completed:
H. S.   College   Other

_____

Previous employer

_____

Position

_____

Period of employment

_____

Highest salary

_____

Previous employer

_____

Position

_____

Period of employment

_____

Highest salary

_____

Is spouse currently under an obligation to any military service? _____ If so, state which branch of the military, where spouse is stationed, and when the obligation will terminate.

_____

_____

Name of child from this marriage

_____

Date of birth   Age

_____

Sex

_____

Name of child from this marriage

_____

Date of birth   Age

_____

Sex

_____

(List additional children on reverse side.)

Is the wife currently pregnant?

If so, when is baby due?

Have you legally adopted any children from a spouse's prior marriage?

Name of child(ren)

_____

Court granting adoption

_____

Date

_____

Has spouse legally adopted any children from your prior marriage?

Name of child(ren)

_____

Court granting adoption

_____

Date

_____

Are there any minor children with severe disabilities and/or illnesses that will require special care now and/or beyond the age of 18?

If so, state name of child and nature of disability and/or illness.

_____

_____

Are any children under the jurisdiction of a court at this time, for example, Juvenile Court, Family Court, etc.?

If so, state name of child, name of court, and why child came before that court.

_____

continued on page 39

continued from page 38

Do you anticipate that child custody will be a contested issue? _____

If so, why? _____

_____

Date of marriage _____

Do you have a copy of the marriage license? _____

Place of marriage _____

Where? _____

Have you ever been married before? _____

Where was marriage terminated? _____

If so, state spouses' names. _____

Names of any children of prior marriage _____

Date of marriage _____

Ages of children _____

Place of marriage _____

Custodial parent _____

How was marriage terminated? _____

Parent with support obligation _____

When was marriage terminated? _____

(Use other side if necessary.)

Has spouse ever been married before? _____

Where was marriage terminated? _____

If so, state spouses' names. _____

Names of children of prior marriage _____

Date of marriage _____

Ages of children _____

Place of marriage _____

Custodial parent _____

How was marriage terminated? _____

Parent with support obligation _____

When was marriage terminated? _____

(Use other side if necessary.)

Date of last sexual relations with current spouse _____

It may be necessary to serve legal papers on your spouse. To facilitate this process, please state where you believe your spouse can be located most often, and when he or she is likely to be there (for example, when he is at home, when he is at work, etc.).

What are the most important objectives to you in this litigation? Please state them in order of importance.

Please provide a brief physical description of your spouse.

PARTICIPATING IN AN ICI WITH AN ATTORNEY PRESENT

Many law offices have both an attorney and a paralegal attend the ICI. This allows the client to meet the team that will represent him or her during the course of the litigation and instills in the client the notion that the paralegal is an essential part of the team. Ideally, this practice also encourages the client to direct calls to the paralegal rather than the attorney. This saves the client money and allows the attorney to spend more time on other matters requiring the attention of an attorney. Having both an attorney and a paralegal at the ICI also permits a division of labor not otherwise available. Generally, the attorney concentrates on interviewing the client and can interact on a more personal basis without the burden of taking notes. The paralegal concentrates on recording the information revealed by the client and can help evaluate the client without having to conduct the interview.

Typically, when a new client comes to the law office for the first time, the attorney greets the client and then introduces the client to you, the paralegal. The attorney normally assures the client that the rules of confidentiality still apply, and tells the client how much he depends on you. During the ICI, while the attorney questions the client, the paralegal does the following:

1. *Watch the client.* After participating in a number of ICIs, you will develop an ability to gauge how a client would conduct themselves as a witness in a courtroom. For example, does the client appear excessively nervous, angry, confused, etc.? Does the client sound sincere? Do you believe the client? Remember, not only is the client interviewing your firm, but your firm is interviewing the client. Watch the client's eyes—this is what a jury will do. Watch the client's body language—is the client fidgeting?

2. *Take complete notes.* The attorney generally asks questions from an interview checklist, so you should be able to anticipate the next question. Since you are preparing these notes for yourself, use any abbreviations you wish. After the ICI, you will have the time to prepare a written summary of the client statement. (You may also want to make a tape recording of the ICI, although some clients are inhibited by microphones and other recording equipment.)

3. *Watch the attorney.* This is how you will learn how to conduct part of an ICI without an attorney present. When does the attorney interrupt the client, and when does the attorney let the client tell her story in her own fashion? How does the attorney ask questions concerning sensitive issues (i.e., allegations of physical abuse, lack of sexual fidelity)?

4. *Remind the attorney* of any questions or topics he or she might have forgotten to inquire into.

PARTICIPATING IN AN ICI WITHOUT AN ATTORNEY PRESENT

An experienced paralegal often conducts the fact-finding portion of the ICI without the presence of an attorney. Certain portions of the ICI require an attorney, including the discussion of legal fees and litigation costs; an assessment of the client's case and the prospects for the future; and what the law firm specifically will and will not do for the client. When the attorney turns the ICI over to you, the paralegal, you should consider following these recommendations:

1. Refer to the clients as "Mr.," "Mrs.," "Dr.," etc. Always be respectful and courteous. Avoid using slang terms or "legalese."

2. Make certain clients are fully aware that you are not authorized to offer legal advice, and that the purpose of this portion of the ICI is to elicit facts from the client. After the attorney has received all the information necessary to form an opinion or provide legal advice, the client will meet with the attorney. All the client's questions will be answered then.

3. Make certain clients are aware that everything they tell you is protected by the attorney-client privilege, just as if they were speaking to the attorney. It may be necessary to remind clients of this several times if the ICI delves into embarrassing or sensitive issues. (See "Focus on Ethics: Confidentiality.")

4. Use the appropriate interview checklist as a guide. But let clients move from one topic to another if they want to. Clients often feel the need to tell you "their story." Allow them to do so without interrupting. This encourages them to speak freely. You can always return to a particular topic later for additional details.

   The interview checklists included in this book (as well as those used in most law offices) are long and quite detailed. Accordingly, many firms prefer to send the client a copy of the appropriate interview checklist before the ICI to allow the client to obtain the information requested. Alternatively, some firms give a copy of the appropriate interview checklist to the client after the ICI to allow the client to obtain the information requested. In any event, do not worry when a client cannot answer every question at the ICI. There will always be time to obtain the necessary information.

5. Show clients that you are paying attention to them. Look them in the eyes. Do not spend all of your time writing down the clients' every word. You can always ask the clients to repeat some of the details again later in the ICI.

6. Family law deals with emotional issues—allow clients to show their emotions. Do not be afraid of getting emotional yourself when appropriate—this shows the clients that you genuinely empathize with them. It may well be the emotional aspect of divorce litigation that distinguishes it from other varieties of civil litigation. Paralegals, as well as attorneys, must be capable of working with individuals enduring great psychological trauma.

7. Do not be afraid to ask the "embarrassing" questions. Divorce litigation involves the most intimate of issues. Ask the necessary questions in a straightforward, matter-of-fact manner. This approach helps a timid client who otherwise might not reveal private details of the marriage. (For example, "When was the last time you had sex with your husband?")

8. Never argue with a client. If the client says something you disagree with or find distasteful, remember you are not required to like every client. If a client is very argumentative and seems determined to get into a fight with you, contact the attorney.

9. Determine the client's expectations. If they are unreasonable, alert the attorney to this so that he or she can discuss this issue with the client. Clients with unreasonably high expectations are bound to be disappointed with the law firm that represented them. This is an invitation to malpractice.

10. Know when to end your portion of the ICI. Clients do not usually appreciate unnecessary conversation when they are paying for it by the hour.

Inform clients if they need to obtain any necessary information and documentation, and give them a deadline to provide this information. This gives clients a greater feeling of participation and control over their litigation and makes your job easier.

REPORTING TO YOUR SUPERVISING ATTORNEY

After you conduct part of an ICI without an attorney present, you must then prepare a report for your supervising attorney. Remember that ethically only an attorney can ultimately decide whether to undertake the representation of a particular client. Typically, your report will be in writing and will contain a condensed version of the completed interview checklist used in the ICI. (The attorney will also review the completed interview checklist.)

However, most attorneys will also be interested in *your* assessment of the client and the client's case. Your input is critical to the attorney—you spent that time with the client; the attorney did not. If your supervising attorney so desires, tell him or her *why* you believe that the person you interviewed would, or would not, be a suitable client for your firm. (Of course, other

FOCUS ON ETHICS

Confidentiality

Attorneys should preserve the confidences and secrets of their clients. This obligation exists so that clients will be more inclined to reveal all relevant information to the attorney. You should distinguish between an attorney's (and paralegal's) professional duty not to reveal a client's confidences and a client's right, or privilege, to prevent such disclosures. The professional duty is imposed on attorneys by state bar associations. The client's privilege is a rule of law, usually found in a state's laws of evidence.

This prohibition against revealing a client's confidences and secrets applies equally to paralegals, legal secretaries, and all other law office personnel who come into contact with a client's confidential information. The attorney has the affirmative obligation to ensure that all employees comply with this requirement to maintain a client's confidences and secrets. Failure to honor this obligation can result in disciplinary measures being meted out against the attorney. Furthermore, in many states a violation of this obligation is a criminal act that can result in criminal sanctions. Many firms require their employees, including their paralegals, to sign an agreement in which the employee agrees not to reveal any confidences of the firm's clients. There is no more certain path to the unemployment line than to violate the attorney-client privilege. This can be especially difficult in family law, because you will be privy to a great deal of intimate information. Remember, this privilege is absolute. You cannot reveal any confidential information to your spouse, your friends—to anyone!

There are several prerequisites for the prohibition of **confidentiality** to become effective: A *client* must communicate some information *to another party acting as a legal professional at that time,* the communication *must have been made in confidence,* and it must have been made *for the purpose of obtaining legal advice.*

First, what is a **client**? A client is any person who seeks legal advice from an attorney or paralegal, regardless of whether that person actually becomes a paying client of that law firm. Therefore, a person can come into your office for an initial consultation but later retain a different law firm, and all information the person revealed to your firm is still protected by the privilege. This privilege extends even to the question of whether a person is a client. For example, it would be a violation of the privilege to reveal that David Smith was a client even if you did not reveal the purpose of his visit.

The communication must be made to someone acting as a legal professional at that time. What happens when a friend tells you a secret about a mutual friend? Are you permitted to reveal this information to a third party? Putting aside all issues of morality, the answer is yes. The information was not revealed to you while you were acting as a legal professional. The essence of this part of the prohibition is that clients must be aware that they are talking to the attorney—*or someone acting in the place of an attorney, such as a paralegal,*—to obtain legal assistance. Therefore, if a man walks up to an attorney at a party and proceeds to discuss his crumbling marriage, it is possible that the information revealed to the attorney may be protected under this ethical rule. But before this hypothetical problem can be resolved, we must ask whether this information was revealed in confidence. Did the man talk to the attorney in hushed tones in the corner of the room, or did he talk to the attorney while standing with a group of other people who were listening? Only information that is revealed in confidence is protected under this rule of ethics. Finally, the information must be revealed in the hope of *receiving legal advice.* If the despondent partygoer described in the preceding paragraph revealed the information merely to unburden his breaking heart, it would not be considered confidential information.

There are exceptions to the rule protecting a client's confidences and secrets. The first allows an attorney to reveal confidential information to prevent a criminal act that would cause injury or death to a third party. One example of this exception would be where a client reveals to an attorney that he is going to kill his wife so he will not have to pay alimony. Additionally, in family law, the whereabouts of a client may be important (i.e., if the client has absconded with one or more of the spouses' children). Normally, a client's location cannot be revealed by the attorney. But if a client is in violation of a court order (i.e., to allow visitation), an attorney may be obligated to reveal the client's whereabouts. Another exception allows an attorney to reveal confidential information about the client if the attorney and the client litigate with each other (i.e., if the client is suing the attorney for malpractice or the attorney is suing the client for nonpayment of legal fees). Lest this appear to be a sleazy attempt to extort payment from clients, remember that in order to sue a client for nonpayment, the law firm must prove that services were rendered. This proof may necessitate at least a partial breach of the client's confidences.

attorneys may want "just the facts.") This is not a skill you can acquire overnight. It requires significant client contact, so take advantage of all opportunities to work directly with clients. A sample report to a supervising attorney is given in Exhibit 2–2.

HANDLING ADMINISTRATIVE MATTERS

Once the decision is made whether to represent the new client, the terms of this relationship must be reduced to writing. Even if the law firm decides not to represent the client, or if the attorney-client relationship is to be severed, that fact must be clearly stated in writing. These matters may technically be called "administrative" matters, but they are essential. All litigation has setbacks; at such times, a written agreement between the law firm and the client can be the difference between a continuing relationship and malpractice. One of the most important administrative matters is the establishment of the fees and costs of litigation: the form they are to take, when they are to be paid, etc.

Fees and Costs

Attorneys may charge for their services in a variety of methods, including **flat fees,** a set fee to be paid to the attorney without regard as to the amount of work actually performed or the result achieved (i.e., $400 for a simple, uncontested divorce); **hourly rates,** when the client is charged a set fee for each hour of work performed, without regard to the result achieved (i.e., $100 per hour for an attorney and $60 per hour for a paralegal—when attorneys charge for their services by the hour, a **retainer,** a lump sum paid in advance, is collected and used to offset the hourly charges); and **contingent fees,** when the attorney receives a fee based on the result achieved (i.e., under an agreement to be paid 25 percent of the amount recovered, attorney receives $2,500 when client receives $10,000 in compensation for injuries).

While all family law attorneys use flat fees or hourly rates, or some combination of the two, it is unethical for an attorney to charge a contingent fee in almost all family law matters. (The one exception is when an attorney seeks to collect unpaid alimony and/or child support payments.) The basis for this rule is the fear that under a contingent fee arrangement, attorneys would not encourage the spouses to reconcile because they would not collect a fee if there is no divorce.

---

flat fee
A preset fee for a specified legal task, such as $500, plus costs of litigation, for an uncontested divorce.

hourly rate
Legal fees based on a specified fee for each hour of labor performed.

retainer
A lump sum of money paid to a law firm from which hourly fees are deducted.

contingent fees
Legal fees based on the ultimate result obtained by law firm. Not available in divorce cases.

EXHIBIT 2-2

REPORT TO SUPERVISING ATTORNEY

To: Attorney Smith

From: Paralegal Jones

Re: Initial Client Interview of Wendy Taylor

Client is a 38-year-old female with two children (boy, Chris, 14; girl, Jessica, 9). Married 16 years to Tony Taylor. Client works outside of house as a CPA, annual salary of $65,000. Children are **latchkey.** Husband owns a construction company. Client does not know value of company; husband does not take a salary, but uses profits from company. Client wants custody of both children, child support, marital residence (owned as joint tenants w/husband) which was purchased 8 yrs. ago for $145,000. No spousal alimony is sought, nor does she want to pay any to husband. Parties do not have substantial debt. Reasons for divorce are 1) Client's suspicion that husband is having an affair with co-worker, and 2) general dissatisfaction with marriage and desire for "something better." Client believes that husband will consent to divorce, but will contest her property demands. There are no allegations of physical abuse of Client or children. Client does not demonstrate anger or resentment toward husband. If anything, she appears genuinely weary of the emotional toll the marriage has been causing recently.

[NOTE TO READER—*This report is written in an abbreviated fashion. Some firms will require that the report be written in a more formal fashion.*]

latchkey children
Children who stay at home after school without adult supervision.

When one spouse has significantly greater financial resources than the other, the financially disadvantaged spouse (usually the wife) may seek the recovery of attorney's fees and costs of litigation from the financially superior spouse (usually the husband). The determination of an award of attorney's fees is based on the receiving party's need, not on any fault on the part of the paying spouse. Attorney's fees can be sought as early as the initial court appearance. The court may also award attorney's fees based on a determination that a party has been stubbornly litigious or has acted in bad faith. This means that a party has unnecessarily prolonged the litigation or has used the litigation as a means of harassment. For example, if it can be established that a husband seeks custody of the children solely to discourage the wife from seeking permanent alimony, that could justify an award of attorney's fees.

As opposed to fees, which is payment for legal services rendered, **costs of litigation** are monies paid to the law firm as reimbursement for expenses incurred by the firm on behalf of the client. Examples of costs include filing, witness and subpoena fees, court reporter fees, long distance telephone charges, copying and facsimile (fax) charges, travel expenses, postage, etc. While law firms often advance the funds for such expenses, clients are ultimately responsible for them. Accordingly, the client must be made aware of the costs of litigation. It is a common practice to have clients pay an additional sum as an advance for costs.

costs of litigation
Usually includes all costs other than attorney's fees, such as filing fees, deposition costs, etc.

Letters of Engagement

engagement letter; disengagement letter; nonengagement letter
An engagement letter memorializes the creation of a contract between a client and a law firm. A disengagement letter memorializes the termination of a contract between a client and a law firm. A nonengagement letter memorializes the lack of a contract between a client and a law firm.

When the client and attorney reach a consensus as to the legal fees to be paid, it is necessary to document this agreement. A **letter of engagement** (also called a fee agreement) must be prepared for the client's signature. A letter of engagement should reflect the entire agreement between the attorney and the client: the purpose and goals of the representation; the nature of the legal fees (flat fee, hourly rates, etc.); the amount of any retainer to be paid at the commencement of the representation; the amount of any monies to be paid at later stages of the representation; how and when the costs of the litigation are to be paid; a disclaimer as to what acts are not included in the representation (i.e., attorney agrees to seek divorce for client, but does not agree to pursue a contempt action to collect support payments); and the client's obligations and duties. A sample letter of engagement is given in Exhibit 2–3.

Letters of Nonengagement

By the same token, if the attorney makes the determination *not* to accept a client's case, that fact should also be memorialized in a **nonengagement letter** (also called a declination letter). The purpose of the nonengagement letter is to ensure that the client is aware that the law firm will not be able to represent him or her, and that alternative representation should be obtained. (It is not unheard of for a "client" to appear in court and complain to the judge that "his" lawyer has failed to appear, when in fact no agreement for representation was ever reached. A letter of nonengagement would save the lawyer considerable trouble.) It is not necessary to detail the reasons for the nonengagement. It is necessary to clearly inform the client of any pending deadlines

---

EXHIBIT 2–3

LETTER OF ENGAGEMENT

_____, 19___

Name of client
Client address
City, State, ZIP
Re: Legal representation

Dear Client:

This letter confirms our recent agreement regarding your engagement of our firm to represent you and render legal advice in connection with your divorce. We appreciate the opportunity to work with you in this matter and set forth below our practice for billing our legal services.

1.

Hourly Charges. We will bill you on a periodic basis for the time expended by our firm's professional personnel in performing legal services with respect to this matter at our hourly rates. The hourly rate for Attorney Smith is currently $_____ per hour. The rate for Paralegal Anderson is currently $_____ per hour. We shall offset these hourly charges against the retainer of $_____ you paid at the initial client interview. We reserve the right to increase these hourly rates thirty (30) days after the delivery of written notice of the increase. We reserve the right to request that you replenish the retainer as circumstances dictate.

2.

Fees Charged by Others. In all litigation there are necessary costs that must be incurred. These costs include filing and recording costs, court reporting services, witness and subpoena fees, air freight, courier and messenger services, long distance telephone charges, facsimile charges, photocopying costs, travel expenses, and word processing. Therefore, we shall require that you pay a costs deposit of $_____. These funds shall remain in the law firm trust account until needed to pay for such costs. We shall be reimbursed on a current basis for any other charges or expenses which we advance or incur on your behalf.

3.

Scope of Representation. We shall represent you in your divorce action against _____. This shall include an investigation of all of your claims and all of your spouse's defenses to such claims; preparation and filing of all necessary pleadings, motions, briefs, and discovery requests; representation for any counterclaims made by your spouse; and preparation for and appearance at all court hearings and trials of this action. Considerations included are the issues of termination of the marriage, child support, child custody, alimony, and division of marital property and debts. Specifically excluded from this representation are any attempts to enforce a court order for support, appeals of any court ruling or order, or any other litigation.

4.

Duties of Client. You are expected to respond to all of our requests for information promptly and completely. Please understand that we cannot do our job properly without this information. Do not speak to your spouse about this litigation, and inform us immediately if your spouse attempts to contact you. If these terms meet with your approval, please sign below and forward one copy of this agreement to us.

Thank you for the opportunity to be of service to you.

Sincerely,

_____
Attorney

I understand the terms of this agreement and agree to abide by them.

_____
Client

or other items requiring immediate attention. A sample letter of nonengagement is given in Exhibit 2–4.

Letters of Disengagement

Finally, there are times when the relationship between law firm and client cannot (or should not) continue. The reasons for this are many, and may include

— The development of a conflict of interests

— The discovery that the client has participated, is participating, or will participate in a fraud upon the court (i.e., telling a lie under oath)

— The failure (willful or intentional) to pay attorney's fees

— Personal differences between the client and lawyer and/or paralegal

---

EXHIBIT 2–4

LETTER OF NONENGAGEMENT

_____ , 19___

Name
Address
City, State, ZIP
Re: Legal representation

Dear _____:

This letter is to inform you that after careful consideration, this firm will not represent you in the _____ matter. It is also our understanding that we do not currently represent you in any other matter.

Because we are not representing you on any matter currently, we cannot monitor any changes in the law or your circumstances as they might affect the validity of your claims. We must therefore disclaim any duty to do so.

If you wish to pursue your claim with another law firm, you will need to act promptly. Several deadlines are involved in your claim, and the first one is _____. If you fail to file a _____ or take other appropriate action by that date, you may permanently lose some, if not all, of your rights.

Please sign the enclosed copy of this letter and return it to this office. Thank you.

Sincerely,

_____
Attorney

I have read this letter and understand its contents.

_____
Name

When the relationship must be terminated, court permission must be received if the law firm is listed as counsel of record in ongoing litigation. In all such cases, however, the client must receive a **disengagement letter,** detailing the terms of the separation. A sample disengagement letter is given in Exhibit 2–5. Note that the following letter contains provisions covering a wide range of fact patterns, not all of which will exist in any one case.

EXHIBIT 2–5

LETTER OF DISENGAGEMENT

_____, 19___

Former Client
Client Address
City, State, ZIP
Re: Legal representation

Dear Client:

This is to notify you that effective ten (10) days from the date of this letter, this office shall withdraw as your legal representative in your divorce litigation. A Motion to Withdraw has been filed with the court this day. A copy of that motion has been enclosed with this letter. You have the right to object to our withdrawal from this litigation, and you are hereby advised that you have ten (10) days to file any such objections with the court. You are also advised to retain new counsel as soon as possible. We shall make available to your representatives all information and documentation.

You are also advised that there is a balance still owing on your account of $_____ for services rendered to date, and payment in full is expected immediately.

You are further advised of the upcoming deadlines relevant to your litigation. You must provide the documents listed in the defendant's Request for Production of Documents no later than _____. All discovery must be completed no later than _____. A Consolidated Pretrial Order must be filed with the court no later than _____.

If you have any questions concerning any of the above, please contact me.

Thank you for your attention to this matter.

Sincerely,

_____
Attorney

I have read and understand this letter, and I consent to the withdrawal of this firm as my legal representation in the above referenced litigation.

_____
Former client

REVIEW QUESTIONS

1. A successful initial client interview (ICI) should accomplish, at a minimum, the following three goals:

   _____

   _____

   _____

2. During an ICI conducted without an attorney present, the client becomes exasperated with all the questions she is being asked. She asks the paralegal whether the law firm plans to ask all of the same questions of her husband. The paralegal replies that they probably will and proceeds to explain how discovery works. Check one of the following:

   _____ The paralegal properly responded to the client's question.

   _____ The paralegal did not properly respond to the client's question because _____

   _____

3. What are three different types of fee agreements? What are the distinguishing characteristics of each?

4. Which fee agreement(s) is (are) inappropriate for divorce cases, and why?

5. What is a Chinese Wall? How, when, and why is one used?

6. Under what circumstances may the confidences and secrets of a client be disclosed? What is the rationale for these exceptions?

7. What are the purposes of a nonengagement letter? How does it differ from a disengagement letter?

8. What is a "client" for the purposes of invoking the ethical obligation to maintain a client's secrets and confidences? Under what circumstances may a client's secrets and confidences be revealed?

9. What is "common representation," and under what circumstances is it generally permissible?

10. What types of acts would constitute the unauthorized practice of law if performed by a paralegal?

KEY TERMS

Chinese Wall
client
common representation
confidentiality
conflict of interest
contingent fees
costs of litigation
disengagement letter
engagement letter
ethics
fiduciary relationship
flat fee
hourly rate
latchkey children
nonengagement letter
retainer
unauthorized practice
    of law
uncontested divorce

STATE RESEARCH PROBLEMS

Review the law of your state to answer the following questions:

1. What state agency has the authority to license attorneys?

2. Review the ethical regulations of your state and list the conditions, if any, under which a law firm can undertake common representation.

ETHICAL PROBLEMS

1. It is your first day on the job. Your "supervising" attorney asks you to draft and file a complaint for divorce for a new client. The attorney offers no assistance, and tells you to file the complaint "as soon as you have finished it." What ethical problems are raised by this scenario, and how can they be resolved?

2. Tom Murphy is a paralegal who previously worked for Bass & Associates. Two years ago, he left for a new job with another firm. Today, Mrs. Murphy calls Bass & Associates and says Tom has had her served with a complaint for divorce. She wants Bass & Associates to represent her in the divorce. What, if any, ethical problems would this pose? What additional information would you need to be certain you have answered this question completely?

3. A new client arrives for his initial client interview with his brother. When invited to come to the conference room, the client says that he wants his brother to accompany him for "moral support." What are the ethical ramifications if the brother is present during the initial client interview?

PRACTICE EXERCISE

Read the sample deposition in Appendix B. Using the facts contained therein, fill out the basic interview checklist for your client, Thomas James Morrison. What additional questions would you ask the client in that case?

Antenuptial Agreements

Antenuptial agreements are contracts that a couple contemplating marriage can enter into, thereby altering the property rights of the parties upon the termination of the marriage. Some requirements for a valid antenuptial agreement are that the agreement be in writing, that each party fully disclose all assets to the other party, and that the terms of the ultimate distribution of the parties' property be fair and reasonable. While such agreements contemplating the death of a spouse have long been enforceable, today an increasing number of states are enforcing antenuptial agreements that contemplate the divorce of the parties. An antenuptial agreement can govern both distribution of property and the payment of alimony (not child custody or support) upon termination of the marriage. If an antenuptial agreement is breached, the party seeking to enforce the agreement can sue for breach of contract, but the remedies available to the plaintiff are more limited than in a typical breach of contract action.

REQUIREMENTS OF AN ANTENUPTIAL AGREEMENT

antenuptial agreement; prenuptial agreement
A written agreement made by two persons contemplating marriage, setting forth the disposition of their property upon the dissolution of the marriage.

Antenuptial agreements (also called **premarital agreements** or **prenuptial agreements**) are contracts made by two people before marrying each other in which the parties agree to the ultimate disposition of their property upon the termination of the marriage. (Note the spelling of the word *antenuptial*—it means before marriage, as opposed to *antinuptial,* which means against marriage.) Antenuptial agreements are becoming more commonplace with every passing year. The reasons for this include the comparative ease of obtaining a divorce today because of the advent of no-fault divorces and the lessening stigma attached to divorce, an increasing number of marriages between individuals with children from previous marriages, and the emergence of the two-income family resulting in two prospective spouses wanting to protect their property.

At this point, let's define the phrase "termination of the marriage." Before you assume that "termination" is always a euphemism for divorce, remember the three different ways a marriage can end: 1) death of a spouse, 2) divorce, and 3) annulment. For reasons we examine in detail later in this chapter, courts are more likely to enforce antenuptial agreements made in contemplation of death than those made in contemplation of either divorce or annulment.

Until recently, antenuptial agreements have been executed by people who are older, well-to-do, and desire to protect the interests of third parties who might otherwise be adversely affected financially by the marriage (i.e., children from a prior marriage.) A common example would involve someone meeting the above description who wants to ensure that her children from a prior marriage would receive their fair share of her assets upon her death. Antenuptial agreements will no doubt continue to grow in popularity as successive marriages become more common, and as life expectancies continue to rise providing even greater opportunities for remarriages.

As noted in Chapter 1, marriage comes with a litany of rights and obligations affecting the spouses' property rights. Antenuptial agreements are executed to alter the effect of marriage on the distribution of property upon the termination of the parties' marriage. As with any attempt to change the effect of the law, various requirements must be satisfied for the antenuptial agreement to be valid:

— The contractual elements of offer, acceptance, *consideration,* and meeting of the minds must be included.

— The agreement must be in *writing.*

— There must be *full disclosure* by each party of his or her assets and liabilities.

— The agreement must be *fair and reasonable* to all parties.

— Both parties should have the opportunity to obtain *independent legal advice* before executing the agreement.

— The *subject matter* of the agreement should be confined to those areas permitted by law.

In the following sections, we examine the elements of a valid antenuptial agreement.

Consideration

The only consideration required in connection with antenuptial agreements is the marriage between the parties. In cases where marriage is the sole consideration, the parties must actually marry each other for the antenuptial agreement to be effective. Additional consideration includes the parties' promise to divide their property in a certain manner upon termination of the marriage.

As in any transfer of property between two or more persons, it is always necessary to consider and allow for any taxes that might be incurred as a result of the transaction. Accordingly, the provisions of the agreement relating to the consideration given and received by each party must be drafted carefully. Should one party give some property and/or benefit to the other without receiving adequate consideration in return, that transaction may be deemed a gift by the Internal Revenue Service and could trigger a gift tax liability for the party receiving the property and/or benefit.

Also as with any form of contract, the agreement must reflect the true, voluntary intentions of the parties. For example, an agreement procured by fraud or duress would be unenforceable. Fraud may be found where one party asks the other to sign a document (the antenuptial agreement) without telling the other party what she or he is signing. Fraud also occurs when a party fails to fully disclose all assets and liabilities. Duress is most often cited when the demand to sign an antenuptial agreement is made on the eve of the wedding, or later.

Written Agreement

Most contracts are valid regardless of whether they are oral or written. However, each state has a **Statute of Frauds:** a set of laws that delineates which types of contracts *must* be in writing, and signed by the party against whom enforcement is sought, in order to be enforced by a court of law. The types of contracts regulated by the Statute of Frauds typically have such significance that you would naturally assume they would be in writing.

The Statute of Frauds of most states requires antenuptial agreements to be in writing. Some states require further formalities to be complied with, such as requiring the antenuptial agreement to be informally witnessed and/or formally witnessed by a notary public. Some states also require that antenuptial agreements be recorded with the appropriate court. Certain states require that the antenuptial agreement be recorded with all of the other public records at the local courthouse, especially if the agreement affects any interests in real property. Without the requirement for a written agreement, there would be ample opportunity and motivation for a spouse facing the prospect of divorce to make a claim for relief under a fictitious oral antenuptial agreement.

Statute of Frauds
Laws requiring that particular contracts be in writing and signed by the party against whom enforcement of the contract is sought.

Exceptions to the requirement for a written agreement may be allowed where it can be shown that there was an oral antenuptial agreement and that the parties have partially performed the agreement, or that it would be patently unfair to one of the parties not to enforce the oral antenuptial agreement. This exception is known as the **partial performance doctrine.**

Regardless of whether your state requires antenuptial agreements to be in writing, it is always advisable to put these agreements in writing. As a matter of fact, for a law firm to create an antenuptial agreement without reducing it to writing is an invitation to legal malpractice.

partial performance doctrine
The ability to prove the existence of a contract by the performance of at least some of the terms of the contract.

Full Disclosure

Each party must fully disclose all material facts relating to the quantity, character, and value of his or her property. Without this full disclosure, it would be practically impossible for the parties to have fair and evenhanded agreement. (Imagine buying a car without knowing its age, condition, options, etc.) Historically, this requirement protected women whose husbands had an economic advantage over them. Before a court would enforce an antenuptial agreement, it would have to be proven that the husband had fully informed his prospective wife of the true nature and extent of his property. Today this requirement is applied to both husbands and wives. Only with full disclosure can a fair exchange of promises and a fair antenuptial agreement be obtained. Of course, every rule has at least one exception: Some states permit the enforcement of an antenuptial agreement made without a full disclosure of each party's assets if the ultimate distribution of the property in accordance with the antenuptial agreement is determined to be fair and reasonable.

Fair and Reasonable Agreement

The antenuptial agreement must provide a fair and reasonable distribution of the parties' property. While such a determination is always subjective, courts typically consider factors such as: a) the respective property of each spouse; b) the respective ages, health, and experience of each spouse; c) the financial needs of each spouse after the termination of the marriage; and d) whether both spouses fully understood the ramifications of the antenuptial agreement before executing it. It is important to note that the issue is whether the antenuptial agreement is fair and reasonable at the time the distribution is to be made, not at the time the agreement is originally executed.

Independent Legal Advice

Independent legal counsel for both parties is recommended for two reasons. First, as noted in Chapter 2, common representation would pose a serious conflict of interests for any attorney attempting to represent both sides in the negotiation of an antenuptial agreement. It is generally assumed that to properly prepare an antenuptial agreement, the attorney must have confidential communications with the client. Obviously, an attorney cannot have confidential communications with both the prospective bride and groom when their interests are antithetical to each other. Second, common representation creates the appearance of, and the opportunity for, one party to take an unfair advantage of the other. Therefore, even if both parties come to the law office together, it should be clearly understood which party is to be represented by that law office, and that the other party should seek the advice of independent counsel. In any event, each party must have at least the *opportunity* to obtain independent legal counsel.

Appropriate Subject Matter

Today antenuptial agreements can be formulated to protect the parties in a variety of circumstances. Traditionally, these agreements were enforceable only when they were created to protect the parties upon the death of one of the spouses. Antenuptial agreements created to provide for the parties in the event of divorce were not enforceable. The rationale for this approach was that public policy favored marriage and disfavored divorce, and that antenuptial agreements promoted divorce (by allowing the parties to know in advance what their financial rights and obligations would be) and therefore were contrary to public policy. This rationale holds less sway today, for a number of reasons:

— The advent of the "no-fault" divorce

— A greater emphasis on settlements and agreements contained in the no-fault statutes, including a greater willingness to recognize antenuptial agreements

— A general improvement in the economic condition of most women compared to their status just a few decades ago

— The lack of any empirical evidence to bolster the argument that such agreements really did foster marital disharmony

Currently there are only a handful of states in which antenuptial agreements made in contemplation of divorce are not enforceable in a court of law.

UNIFORM PREMARITAL AGREEMENT ACT

Approximately one-third of the states have adopted the Uniform Premarital Agreement Act (UPAA).[1] First promulgated in 1983, the UPAA incorporates many of the requirements detailed above. States having adopted the UPAA will enforce antenuptial agreements unless the court deems the provisions of the agreement unconscionable, and the party seeking to avoid enforcement

---

1. The following states have adopted the UPAA: Arizona, Arkansas, California, Colorado, Hawaii, Illinois, Iowa, Kansas, Maine, Montana, Nevada, New Jersey, North Carolina, North Dakota, Oregon, Rhode Island, South Dakota, Texas, and Virginia.

was not given the opportunity to review the agreement before its execution. The UPAA also contemplates agreements covering nonfinancial areas of married life, including child rearing and household chores. *Each state has its own particular requirements regarding the formation of a valid antenuptial agreement. The paralegal should review all relevant statutory and case law to ensure full compliance.*

◄ **PRACTICE** ►
POINTER

As the *Edwardson* case demonstrates, the law in this area is still in a state of flux, but the trend is unmistakably in favor of upholding antenuptial agreements that are made in contemplation of the possibility of divorce. Such antenuptial agreements can be further divided between those attempting to fix potential alimony payments and those attempting to determine the property division between the parties. Of course, some antenuptial agreements attempt to perform both functions. Courts have historically been more inclined to enforce antenuptial agreements dealing with property settlements than those attempting to pre-set alimony payments.

When you are meeting with a client to discuss the preparation of an antenuptial agreement, the most important information to obtain in the initial client interview is the objective the client wishes to achieve with the antenuptial agreement. Remember, unless you are aware of the client's reason for wanting the antenuptial agreement, it is highly unlikely that the client will be satisfied with the final product. For example, an antenuptial agreement can define the property rights of the prospective spouses, namely, to prevent either prospective spouse from acquiring an interest in the other's property; or to provide for joint contribution to household expenses. The antenuptial agreement *cannot* affect most issues regarding the minor children, such as provisions for child support, child custody, and visitation; only the court is empowered to do so. The antenuptial agreement can provide specific property for the prospective spouse at the termination of the marriage in consideration for the release of statutory rights in the other spouse's property—for example, a lump-sum payment, the transfer of specific property, and the agreement to provide life insurance for the prospective spouse, among many other options. Naturally, it must be clear that both parties fully understand the implications and significance of the antenuptial agreement and the impact it will have on their rights and interests.

Remember that while an antenuptial agreement can, and often does, provide additional rights and benefits to third parties, it cannot relieve a third party of any right they might possess unless they specifically agree to it in writing. For example, a minor child of either party cannot lose any rights of inheritance by virtue of an antenuptial agreement entered into by a parent or stepparent.

INTERVIEW CHECKLIST

The following questions should be considered when a client comes into the law office seeking an antenuptial agreement. Use these questions in tandem with the questions provided in the basic interview checklist in Chapter 2.

INTERVIEW CHECKLIST

(Each party should complete this form carefully, listing all property of any kind. Failure to fully disclose all assets may invalidate the resulting antenuptial agreement.)

List the street address for each piece of real property you currently own or have an interest in.

For each piece of real property, state the nature of your interest in the property (i.e., fee simple, life estate, time share, etc.).

In whose name(s) is the real property titled?

Are there any encumbrances on the real property?

If so, state the name of the lienholder, the nature of the encumbrance, the total amount still owed, how often payments are due, the date of the final payment, the amount of each payment, and whether a lump sum (or balloon) payment is to be paid (and if so, the amount of the payment and when the payment is due to be paid).

Was the property acquired by purchase or inheritance?

If by inheritance, state from whom it was inherited, the date of inheritance, and, if known, the value of the property at the time of the inheritance.

If by purchase, state the date of purchase, the purchase price, the name of the seller, and the source of the funds used to purchase the property.

State whether any or all of the real property listed above is to be retained by owner free from any interest or claim the other may acquire by virtue of the impending marriage between the parties.

List each piece of personal property (i.e., cars, boats, jewelry, furniture, clothing, business property) with a value of $250.00 or greater, and state the nature of the property.

State the nature of your interest in the property (i.e., owned, leased, etc.).

Was the property acquired by inheritance or by purchase?

If by inheritance, state the date of inheritance, from whom it was inherited, and, if known, the value of the property at the time it was inherited.

If by purchase, state the date of purchase, the purchase price, and the source of the funds used to purchase the property.

Are there any encumbrances on any piece of personal property?

If so, state the name of the lienholder, the nature of the encumbrance, the amount still owed, how often payments are due, the date of the final payment, the amount of each payment, and whether a lump sum payment (balloon) is to be paid (and, if so, the amount of the payment and when the payment is due to be paid).

State whether any or all of the personal property listed above is to be retained by the owner free from any interest or claim that the other party may acquire by virtue of the impending marriage between the parties.

continued on page 58

continued from page 57

List all savings and checking accounts in your name or control.

Name of bank or financial institution

_____

Name(s) on account

_____

Type of account

_____

Account number

_____

Amount currently in account

_____

Average monthly balance for last six months

_____

State whether any or all of the savings or checking accounts listed above is to be retained by the owner free from any interest or claim of the other acquired by virtue of the impending marriage between the parties.

_____

_____

List all certificates of deposit (CD) in your name or control.

Name of bank or financial institution

_____

Name(s) on account

_____

Account number

_____

Amount

_____

Date purchased   Interest rate

_____

Source of funds used to purchase CD

_____

State whether any or all of the CDs listed above is to be retained by the owner free from any interest or claim of the other acquired by virtue of the impending marriage between the parties.

_____

_____

List all shares of stock or mutual funds owned in your name or control. _____

Name of corporation or mutual fund

_____

Public or closed corporation

_____

Name(s) of owner of stock on certificate

_____

Number of shares owned

_____

Date(s) acquired

_____

Purchase price of stock (If stock was purchased at different times, list the number of shares bought at each price.)

_____

Source of funds used to purchase stock

_____

State whether any or all of the stock listed above is to be retained by the owner free from any interest or claim by the other acquired by virtue of the impending marriage between the parties.

_____

List all bonds owned in your name or control.

_____

Name of obligor

_____

Name(s) of owner shown on bond

_____

Face amount due at maturity

_____

Maturity date

_____

Date acquired

_____

Purchase price of bond (If bonds were purchased at different times, list the specific bonds bought at each price.)

_____

Rate of interest

_____

Date interest paid

_____

State whether any or all of the bonds listed above is to be retained by the owner free from any inter-

continued on page 59

continued from page 58

est or claim by the other acquired by virtue of the impending marriage between the parties.

_____

_____

List all income received in your name or control.

Employer

_____

Present annual salary

_____

Position

_____

Date hired

_____

Original salary

_____

Bonus received last three years

_____

Amount and nature of pension plan

_____

Source of other income (royalties, real estate, etc.)

_____

CASE

EDWARDSON v. EDWARDSON

Supreme Court of Kentucky.
Nov. 8, 1990.

. . . .

LAMBERT, Justice

Almost seventy-five years ago this Court declared "the law will not permit parties contemplating marriage to enter into a contract providing for, and looking to, future separation after marriage." *Stratton v. Wilson,* 170 Ky. 61, 185 S.W. 522, 523 (1916). In subsequent decisions we have adhered to the foregoing rule, although a fine distinction was drawn in *Jackson v. Jackson,* Ky., 626 S.W.2d 630 (1981), wherein the Court enforced an antenuptial agreement in a divorce action which required the husband to furnish the wife "a decent support during his natural life." (Citation omitted). This Court granted appellant's motion for discretionary review to reconsider the position taken in *Stratton* and its progeny to determine whether the underlying policy is still valid; if not, whether other policy considerations have emerged making it desirable to retain the *Stratton* rule; or whether societal changes render its modification appropriate.

Prior to their marriage to each other, both parties had been married previously. In the divorce decree dissolving her prior marriage, appellant was awarded the sum of seventy-five dollars ($75.00) per week as maintenance, the payment of which was to be terminated upon her remarriage. Appellant and appellee executed an agreement prior to the time their marriage was solemnized which contained, *inter alia,* the following provision:

"In the event that the marriage of the parties shall be dissolved or the parties become legally separated, to the extent permitted under Kentucky law or the state of residence where said action is filed, the Party of the First Part shall receive SEVENTY-FIVE DOLLARS ($75.00) per week as maintenance (alimony) from the Party of the Second Part for her life, or until her remarriage. Furthermore, Party of the Second Part shall maintain medical/hospitalization insurance for the Party of the First Part for her life or her remarriage, which insurance program shall have benefits substantially similar to those presently held by the Party of the First Part through the ROTHROCK INSURANCE SERVICE. Other than as provided in this paragraph, neither party shall have any obligation to the other for alimony or support, and neither party shall have any claim against the property of the other nor any claim thereto by reason of the marriage or the manner or cause thereto by reason of the marriage or the manner or cause of dissolution thereof, it being the intent hereof that the parties, each having adequate separate estates on the date of marriage, shall each retain their separate estates, any increase in the value thereof and accretions thereto, free of any and all claims or interest in property or other rights which may come into existence or arise by reason of the marriage of the parties hereto, except as stated herein."

After about two and a half years of marital turbulence, the parties finally separated. In the divorce action which followed, appellant sought enforcement of the agreement. Enforcement was denied in the trial court and on appeal the judgment of the trial court was affirmed. The courts below relied upon the principles set forth in *Stratton v. Wilson, supra,* for their decisions.

From the facts just stated, the precise issue which emerges is whether parties may enter into an enforceable agreement in advance of their marriage for the amount of maintenance to be paid by one to the other in the event the marriage is dissolved. The larger issue before the Court is whether any antenuptial agreement which contemplates divorce and provides for the payment of maintenance and the disposition of property upon subsequent dissolution of the marriage is enforceable.

. . . .

In unmistakable terms, the Court in *Stratton* held the portion of the agreement which provided for payment of alimony in the event of separation or divorce to be void. The decision was based on the view that such an agreement was destabilizing to the marital relationship and might promote or encourage marital breakup.

It is an indisputable fact that since rendition of our decision in *Stratton,* the incidence of divorce in Kentucky has followed the national experience and risen steadily. Further, the Kentucky General Assembly has abandoned the fault-based system of allowing dissolution of marriage which prevailed prior to 1972 and adopted portions of the Uniform Marriage and Divorce Act which is substantially a "no-fault" marriage dissolution system. A legislative determination has been made that abandoning the necessity of proving fault would, *inter alia* "[s]trengthen and preserve the integrity of marriage and safeguard family relationships." (Citation omitted.) While the rising incidence of divorces and the existence of profound legislative changes do not *per se* render the *Stratton* rule invalid,

neither do they support its continuation. Unless the continued validity of this rule of law which restricts the rights of parties and is subject to change without disrupting settled expectations (footnote omitted) can be demonstrated or reasonably assumed, it should not be blindly followed. In view of the foregoing, it is appropriate to re-examine *Stratton* to determine whether such a broad restriction is necessary to promote the substantial state interest in marital stability (citation omitted).

A number of other jurisdictions have confronted the question before this Court and abandoned or modified the prohibition against enforcement of antenuptial agreements which contemplate divorce. In a leading decision, *Posner v. Posner,* 233 So.2d 381 (Fla.1970), the Supreme Court of Florida reviewed a number of authorities and noted a "clearly discernible" trend in favor of enforcing antenuptial agreements. The Court observed that in some circumstances, the exisistence of an antenuptial agreement might actually promote the continuation of marriage rather than its dissolution and further noted the widespread enforcement of antenuptial agreements to settle property rights upon the death of a spouse. Abandoning its prior rule, the Court held that such agreements should no longer be void *ab initio,* but should be measured by the stringent standards prescribed in *Del Vecchio v. Del Vecchio,* 143 So.2d 17 (Fla.1962), for agreements which settle property rights on the death of a spouse, and the additional requirement that it not appear the agreement promoted procurement of the divorce. In another leading case, *Scherer v. Scherer,* 249 Ga. 635, 292 S.E.2d 662 (1982), the Supreme Court of Georgia overruled its prior decisions holding antenuptial agreements in contemplation of divorce invalid. As grounds for its decision, the Court recognized that divorce is a commonplace fact of life, that state law and public policy permit married persons to obtain divorces, and the absence of empirical evidence to show that antenuptial agreements in contemplation of divorce actually encourage or incite divorce. . . .

While the foregoing cases present differing factual circumstances and subtle differences in the legal issues addressed and answered, a common theme may be found throughout. The notion that divorce is promoted by an antenuptial agreement which contemplates such a possibility has been rejected and the right of parties to enter into appropriate agreements has been upheld. We concur with this view.

Finally, we observe that the legal status of marriage partners is vastly different today than it was when *Stratton v. Wilson* was decided. At that time the Nineteenth Amendment to the Constitution of the

United States had not yet been ratified, married women's property acts were not yet in existence or were in their infancy, and in general the status of women in this society was decidedly second class. In 1916 it may have been entirely logical to restrict the nature of agreements available to persons contemplating marriage in an effort to avoid marital instability. Subsequent changes in society and seventy-five years of experience have rendered such restrictions inappropriate. . . .

From the foregoing, we are unable to conclude that the *ratio decidendi* for *Stratton* remains valid.

. . . .

The first limitation upon parties to an antenuptial agreement is the requirement of full disclosure. Before parties should be bound by agreements which affect their substantial rights upon dissolution of marriage, it should appear that the agreement was free of any material omission or misrepresentation (citation omitted). The second limitation to be observed is that the agreement must not be unconscionable at the time enforcement is sought. Regardless of the terms of the agreement and regardless of the subsequent acquisition or loss of assets, at the time enforcement is sought, the court should be satisfied that the agreement is not unconscionable (footnote omitted). Upon a finding of unconscionability, the trial court entertaining such an action may modify the parties' agreement to satisfy the necessary standard, but should otherwise give effect to the agreement as nearly as possible providing the agreement was not procured by fraud or duress.

While it may go without saying, we observe that antenuptial agreements may apply only to disposition of property and maintenance. Questions of child support, child custody and visitation are not subject to such agreements; and unless the parties otherwise agree, non-marital property retains its character as such.

. . . Parties and their counsel should be admonished to refrain from entering into agreements lacking mutuality and without a rational basis. Courts reviewing antenuptial agreements and faced with a claim of unconscionability should not overlook the wisdom, which is fully applicable to both spouses, expressed in this Court's decision rendered in *Clark v. Clark,* 301 Ky. 682, 192 S.W.2d 968, 970 (1946):

"A separation agreement will be closely scrutinized by a court of equity, ... It must appear that the husband exercised the utmost good faith; that there was a full disclosure of all material facts, including the husband's circumstances and any other fact which might affect the terms of the contract; and that the provisions made in the agreement . . . were fair, reasonable, just, equitable, and adequate in view of the conditions and circumstances of the parties. . . ."

For the reasons stated, we reverse and remand this cause to the Jefferson Circuit Court for further proceedings consistent herewith.

DISCUSSION QUESTIONS

Consider the above case of *Edwardson v. Edwardson,* 798 S.W.2d 941 (Ky. 1990), and answer the following questions:

1. How did this case change the law in Kentucky as to the enforceability of antenuptial agreements?

2. What is the name of the case that formed the basis of the existing precedent? What was the court's rationale for its reversal of that case?

Exhibit 3–1 is a sample antenuptial agreement made in contemplation of both death and divorce.

BREACH OF THE ANTENUPTIAL AGREEMENT

Elements

A breach of the antenuptial agreement occurs when a party fails to honor any provision contained in the agreement. Should such a breach occur, the

EXHIBIT 3–1

SAMPLE ANTENUPTIAL AGREEMENT[2]

STATE OF _____

COUNTY OF _____

*(Introductory paragraphs are **boilerplate** provisions (provisions that are used in all such agreements) providing, among other things, the date of the agreement, the identity of the parties to the agreement, and the parties' individual schedules of assets. Boilerplate should always be used carefully so that inappropriate paragraphs are not inadvertently included.)*

This Agreement, made this ____ day of ____ , 199__, by and between ROBERT BROWNING, hereinafter referred to as "BROWNING," and ELIZABETH BARRETT, hereinafter referred to as "BARRETT."

WHEREAS, a marriage is contemplated between the parties hereto in the immediate future;

WHEREAS, said parties are severally (individually) possessed of property in their own rights, respectively;

WHEREAS, by Schedule A, a copy of which is attached hereto and incorporated herein as part hereof, BROWNING has fully and completely disclosed to BARRETT and her independent counsel the nature and extent of his various property and interest and sources of income; and

WHEREAS, by Schedule B, a copy of which is attached hereto and incorporated herein as a part hereof, BARRETT has fully and completely disclosed to BROWNING and his independent counsel the nature and extent of her various property and interest and sources of income; and

WHEREAS, the parties have agreed that each is economically independent of the other;

WHEREAS, the parties hereto enter this Agreement with the desire to define the interest which each of them shall have in the property of the other during and after marriage, and in the estate of the other after the death of one of them; and

WHEREAS, both parties have been afforded the opportunity to retain, advise, and consult with independent counsel of their own choice;

NOW, THEREFORE, in consideration of the contemplated marriage about to be solemnized, and the mutual covenants and promises herein contained, the parties do hereby agree as follows:

1.

Husband relinquishes all legal claim, present and future, to the property of the Wife. (Boilerplate.)

BROWNING hereby waives and relinquishes all right, title, estate and interest, statutory and otherwise, including but not limited to dower, year's support, statutory allowance, distribution in intestacy and right to take against the will of BARRETT, as well as the right to act as personal representative of her Estate, which he might acquire under the present or future law of any jurisdiction as the Husband, Widower, Heir at Law, Next of Kin, or Distributee of BARRETT in her property, owned by her at the time of the marriage or acquired by her any time thereafter and in her Estate upon her death.

2.

Wife relinquishes all legal claim, present and future, to the property of the Husband. (Boilerplate.)

BARRETT hereby waives and relinquishes all right, title, estate and interest, statutory and otherwise, including but not limited to curtesy, year's support, statutory allowance, distribution in intestacy and right to take against the will of BROWNING, as well as the right to act as personal representative of his Estate, which she might acquire under the present or future law of any jurisdiction as the Wife, Widow, Heir at Law, Next of Kin, or Distributee of BROWNING in his property, owned by him at the time of the marriage or acquired by him any time thereafter and in his Estate upon his death.

3.

After the marriage, each party shall keep and retain sole ownership and control of all property, real or personal, now owned or hereafter acquired by such property. Each party shall, upon the request of the other, execute, acknowledge, and deliver any and all instruments necessary or appropriate to carry into effect the intention of the parties here expressed.

Both Husband and Wife agree to sign any documents necessary to implement their desire not to commingle their property. (Boilerplate.)

4.

Within thirty days after solemnization of the marriage between the parties, BROWNING shall effect insurance on his life in a minimum sum of $100,000.00 with ELIZABETH BARRETT as the beneficiary thereof. So long as BARRETT remains his wife, BROWNING shall not change the designation of beneficiary on such insurance, and he shall keep the same in full force and effect during his lifetime, at his expense. To the extent that BROWNING shall fail to comply with the provisions of this paragraph, his Estate shall be charged with the obligation herein assumed.

In exchange for relinquishing all legal claim to Husband's property, Wife is made the sole beneficiary of life insurance policy on Husband's life, providing the assurance of some income should Husband predecease Wife.

5.

Within thirty days after solemnization of the marriage between the parties, BARRETT shall pay to BROWNING the sum of $25,000.00. It is understood and agreed that the aforesaid payment constitutes a part of the consideration upon which this Agreement is based, and the failure of BARRETT timely to make such payment shall render this Agreement null, void, and of no effect.

In exchange for relinquishing all legal claim to Wife's property, Husband is to receive an immediate payment of money. If Wife fails to make this payment within the time permitted, the whole agreement is void.

6.

BROWNING agrees to provide in his Last Will and Testament that in the event of his death, BARRETT shall receive the sum of no less than $100,000.00 from his Estate, if she survives BROWNING as his widow. To the extent that BROWNING shall fail to comply with the provisions of this Paragraph, his Estate shall be charged with the obligation herein assumed.

Husband agrees to provide for Wife no less than $100,000.00 in his Will. If the Will fails to provide for this amount, Wife would be able to receive the deficiency from Husband's estate.

7.

If the parties separate from one another at any time following their marriage, for any reason, it is their mutual desire that each shall maintain and support himself or herself separately and independently from the other. Accordingly, each party releases and discharges the other, absolutely and forever, for the rest of his or her life, from any and all claims and demands for alimony or support, either temporarily or permanently.

Each party forever waives the right to claim any alimony. Note that this does not mention or include the right to claim child support payments.

8.

Each of the parties hereby expressly waives any legal right either may have under any federal or state law as a spouse to participate as a payee or beneficiary under any interest the other may have in any pension plan, profit-sharing plan, or any other form of retirement or deferred income plan, including, but not limited to, the right either spouse may have to receive any benefits, in the form of lump-sum death benefit, joint or survivor annuity, or

Federal law guarantees surviving spouses the right to receive a deceased spouse's pension, retirement, or deferred income plan (i.e., 401(k) plans). Each spouse here forever relin

preretirement survivor annuity, and each of the parties hereby expressly consents to any election made by the other, now or at any time hereafter, with respect to the recipient and the form of payment of any benefit upon retirement or death under any such pension plan, profit-sharing plan, or other retirement or deferred income plan.

9.

quishes any claim to any such property.

Notwithstanding the provisions of this Agreement, either party shall have the right to transfer or convey to the other any property or interest therein which may be lawfully conveyed or transferred during his or her lifetime or by will, and neither party intends by this Agreement to limit or restrict in any way the rights and power to receive any such transfer or conveyance to the other. However, the parties acknowledge that no representations or promises of any kind whatsoever have been made by either of them to the other with respect to any transfer or conveyance.

Each party still has the right to give and receive property to and from each other; however, they have no legal obligation to do so.

10.

Each party covenants and represents to the other that he or she has disclosed to the other the nature and extent of his or her various property, interest, and sources of income, and that Schedules A and B, which are attached hereto and incorporated as a part hereof, fully and fairly reflect the said property, interest, and sources of income of each party, respectively.

Both parties promise that they have completely revealed the amount and type of all of their property to the other spouse in the schedule of assets.

11.

BROWNING declares that he fully understands the terms and provisions of this Agreement; that he as been fully informed of his legal rights and liabilities; that he believes that the provisions of this Agreement are fair, just, and reasonable; and that he signs this Agreement freely and voluntarily, acting under the advice of independent legal counsel, (name of Browning's attorney).

Husband states that he has his own attorney, and Husband believes the agreement is fair.

12.

BARRETT declares that she fully understands the terms and provisions of this Agreement; that she has been fully informed of her legal rights and liabilities; that she believes that the provisions of this Agreement are fair, just, and reasonable; and that she signs this Agreement freely and voluntarily, acting under the advice of independent legal counsel, (name of Barrett's attorney).

Wife states that she has her own attorney, and Wife believes the agreement is fair.

13.

This Agreement is made in the State of _____ and shall be construed in accordance with the laws of that State.

The laws of each state are different, so it is essential to agree in advance which laws apply.

14.

Should any provision of this Agreement be found, held, or deemed unenforceable, voidable, or void, as contrary to the laws or public policy of the State of _____ or any other state of the United States, the parties intend that the remaining provisions of this Agreement shall nevertheless continue in full force and be binding upon the parties, their heirs, personal representatives, executors, and assigns.

A severability clause; this provision ensures that even if one clause is found to be void or otherwise unenforceable, the rest of the agreement shall survive.

15.

This Agreement contains the entire understanding of the parties. There are no representations, warranties, promises, convenants, or undertakings, oral or otherwise, other than those expressly set forth herein.

A merger clause ensures that the parties' agreement shall be limited to that specifically stated within the agreement.

16.

This Agreement shall become effective only upon the marriage of the parties, shall inure to the benefit of, and shall be binding upon the parties hereto, their heirs, executors, administrators, and assigns.

The agreement becomes effective only when the parties marry one another.

IN WITNESS WHEREOF, the parties hereto have hereunto set their hands and affixed their seals, on the day and year first above-written.

_____ (SEAL)
ROBERT BROWNING

Witnesses:

_____

_____

Notary Public: _____

My commission expires _____

The two witnesses should be independent (i.e., not the best friend of one of the parties). This agreement calls for two informal witnesses and one formal witness (a notary public).

_____ (SEAL)
ELIZABETH BARRETT

Witnesses:

_____

_____

Notary Public: _____

My commission expires _____

---

burden of proof
The burden to prove all elements of a cause of action. Also, the duty of a plaintiff to present a prima facie case and of a defendant to rebut or contradict the plaintiff's prima facie case.

aggrieved party will have a cause of action for breach of contract against the defaulting party if they can carry their **burden of proof;** that is, they have to prove with a **preponderance of the evidence** the basic elements of a cause of action for breach of antenuptial agreement: 1) the existence of the agreement, 2) the terms of the agreement, and 3) the specific breach of the agreement.

If that burden of proof *can* be carried, then:

— If the terms of the agreement are fair and reasonable on its face (if they are clearly fair and reasonable), the party claiming the invalidity of the agreement has the burden of proving the impropriety of the agreement or clause.

— If, however, the terms of the agreement appear to be unfair on its face (they are clearly not fair and reasonable), then the proponent

preponderance of evidence
A majority of the evidence.

of the agreement has the burden of establishing the validity of the agreement or clause, especially that the opponent to the agreement had full and complete knowledge of the circumstances surrounding the execution of the agreement. (Note that in certain states, the opponent of the agreement will still have the burden of establishing the impropriety of the agreement or clause.)

Remedies

The remedies available to a plaintiff in an action for breach of an antenuptial agreement are somewhat more restricted, however, than in a typical breach of contract action. The court can award the plaintiff **specific performance;** that is, the court can order the defaulting party to do, or refrain from doing, the act referred to in the complaint. For example, a court could award a party the property accorded her in the antenuptial agreement. But the court cannot **rescind** (cancel or undo) the agreement, because the court cannot completely restore the parties to their prior condition (i.e., the consideration cannot be restored because the marriage cannot be undone). Nor can the court award a plaintiff money damages for an economic loss or for emotional distress incurred due to the breach of the antenuptial agreement.

Defenses

The defendant in an action for breach of an antenuptial agreement can raise certain **defenses** in addition to the assertion that the agreement itself is vague, unconscionable, or otherwise unenforceable.

The first of these defenses deals with the time within which the lawsuit is filed. Every state has a **statute of limitations,** or statutory period of time within which a cause of action must be filed with a court. For example, the statute of limitations for filing a negligence cause of action may be two years, while the statute of limitations for a breach of contract may be four years. These statutes vary from state to state. The failure to file the lawsuit within the statutory period of time acts to permanently bar the cause of action. Note that usually the statute of limitations for breach of an antenuptial agreement begins to run with the termination of the marriage; in other words, the statute of limitations is "tolled" during the parties' marriage.

A similar defense is the equitable defense of **laches,** which allows a court to dismiss a lawsuit if the plaintiff delayed filing it for so long (although within the statute of limitations) that the defendant's ability to defend himself would be prejudiced or disadvantaged. The other defense is **estoppel,** also an equitable defense, under which a party who knowingly accepts the benefits of a breach of an antenuptial agreement is later prevented, or estopped, from attacking the agreement because of that breach. The defending party always has the burden of proving the existence of any defense to a cause of action. A complete discussion of these equitable defenses can be found in Chapter 4.

---

specific performance
A remedy in a breach of contract action in which the plaintiff seeks a court order compelling the defendant to comply by the terms of the parties' contract.

rescission
A remedy in a breach of contract action in which the plaintiff seeks that the contract be nullified, or rescinded.

defense
A legal justification for some act. As opposed to a denial of the act.

statute of limitations
The period of time permitted by law for a claimant to file a law suit.

laches
Equitable rule that requires persons having a claim file it before the defending party loses the ability to defend themselves.

estoppel
An equitable theory which prevents a party from claiming one fact to be true after asserting the truthfulness of a contrary fact.

FOCUS ON BEING A WITNESS

Paralegals are often called upon to act as a witness for the execution of a legal document, such as the antenuptial agreement in Exhibit 3–1. To protect yourself from a charge of assisting with a fraud, always be certain that the person signing the document is who they say they are—you should ask to see a picture identification if you are unsure of their indentity. Always be certain that the person signing the document knows what they are signing and what consequences follow from signing the document. Always be certain that you actually witness the signature—do not take anyone's word for it. Never allow anyone to pressure you into acting as a witness when you feel uncomfortable about so doing. This is even more important when you are acting as a formal or official witness—a notary public. It is not unheard of for a notary public to be sued for malpractice for failure to properly execute his or her duties.

To summarize what occurs in an action for breach of an antenuptial agreement, assume an antenuptial agreement between Husband and Wife, stating that upon dissolution of the marriage, Husband and Wife are each entitled to one-half of the parties' marital property. Assume further that upon the dissolution of the parties' marriage, Wife withdraws all of the funds from the parties accounts. If Husband wishes to initiate a lawsuit for breach of the antenuptial agreement, he bears the initial burden of proving the existence and terms of their agreement. If Husband can prove these elements, then because the terms of the agreement are fair and reasonable on its face, Wife then has the burden of proving that the antenuptial agreement is unfair. As a plaintiff, Husband can seek relief, including an order for specific performance—an order directed to the defendant Wife ordering her to comply with the terms of the antenuptial agreement and to return any funds obtained in contravention of the agreement.

REVIEW QUESTIONS

1. What are the six requirements for a valid antenuptial agreement and the reasons for each requirement?

2. What is the purpose of the Statute of Frauds, and why do many states provide for antenuptial agreements in their respective Statutes of Frauds?

3. What is specific performance, and how is it applicable in an action for breach of an antenuptial agreement?

4. How are antenuptial agreements made in contemplation of death treated differently from those made in contemplation of divorce?

5. Name at least three rights normally granted through marriage that can be altered via an antenuptial agreement, and describe how they can be altered.

6. What are the effects of a merger clause in a written contract (i.e., an antenuptial agreement)?

7. What defenses are available to a claim of breach of an antenuptial agreement?

8. What remedies are available for such a breach?

9. Which legal claims cannot be affected by an antenuptial agreement? What is the rationale for excluding these claims?

10. What is the difference between a witness and an formal witness?

KEY TERMS

antenuptial agreement
boilerplate
burden of proof
defense
estoppel
laches
partial performance doctrine

premarital agreement
prenuptial agreement
preponderance of evidence
rescind (rescission)
specific performance
Statue of Frauds
statute of limitations

STATE RESEARCH PROBLEMS

Review the laws of your state and answer the following questions.

1. Locate the Statute of Frauds. List the various types of contracts regulated by that Statute of Frauds. Does it include contracts made in consideration of marriage? If so, what are the requirements of that statute?

2. Locate the statutes and most recent case law regulating antenuptial agreements. Are antenuptial agreements made in contemplation of divorce (as opposed to death) enforceable? If so, is it permissible for an antenuptial agreement to regulate the property settlement and alimony?

3. Find several recent cases involving a breach of an antenuptial agreement. For each case, detail a) the provision of the agreement that was allegedly breached; b) the defense put forth by the defendant; c) the remedy, if any, granted by the court; and d) the court's rationale for its decision.

ETHICAL PROBLEM

A young, unmarried couple makes an appointment to discuss the details of an antenuptial agreement they want your office to prepare. They both come to your office and meet with you and your supervising attorney. Later, you review their original financial documents and discover that the husband had a bank account that he had not listed on his schedule of assets. What ethical issues are raised by this scenario, and what are the appropriate responses to each?

PRACTICE EXERCISES

1. Consider the example of two people who execute an antenuptial agreement in which they agree to divide all of their marital property equally. They are both artists who support themselves by selling their work at local fairs. Ten years later, the wife files for divorce and seeks to enforce the antenuptial agreement. During the course of the marriage, the wife has inherited a substantial amount of property, which she has kept in her name only. She has also earned a Masters in Business Administration and now earns a salary in excess of $100,000.00. The husband is still a "starving artist."

What questions do you need answered before a determination can be made regarding whether the agreement should be enforced? List at least ten questions for each party to answer, and state why that information is requested.

2. Working with a classmate, draft an antenuptial agreement contemplating the possibility of either death or divorce for your client, Eugene Michaels, assuming the following facts: Mr. Michaels, who is divorced and has two minor children, is engaged to marry Janet Banker, a widow with one minor child of her own. Both parties own their own homes, although they have decided to sell Ms. Banker's house and use the profit to renovate Mr. Michaels' house. Both parties are gainfully employed, and they do not plan to have more children. You may assume any other facts you deem necessary, but you must state all such assumptions.

Termination of Marriage—
An Overview

CHAPTER OBJECTIVES

In this chapter, you will learn:

- *How the legal concepts of "law" and "equity" differ from each other*

- *The general nature of divorce*

- *The specific issues to be considered in the different stages of litigation*

- *The religious aspects of divorce*

- *How alternative dispute resolution methods, such as arbitration and mediation, can be used in divorce litigation*

Marriage and the termination of a marriage are governed by a general area of the law called equity, in which the courts do not so much implement rules as they use discretion and judgment to decide each case on its own merits. Equitable theories include estoppel, clean hands, and laches. Divorce and (in some cases) annulment necessitate a resolution of issues including paying alimony and child support, agreeing on child custody and visitation, and dividing of all marital property. The end of a marriage, whether by annulment or divorce, is a revocation of many of the rights discussed in Chapter 1. All of these issues must be investigated and considered by the client and the legal professionals.

EQUITY

As noted in Chapter 1, family law is an area of the law in which society, through the courts, maintains a significant amount of control. In many ways, the law still contains remnants of the days when the king was the law. It acts

in loco parentis
Latin for "in the place of a parent."

equity
The ability of a court to use its discretion and judgment to fashion a remedy appropriate to a particular case.

laws
Specific rules of conduct promulgated by government.

in loco parentis, or as legal parent; and as the "parent," it wants what it believes to be best for all of its "children." Accordingly, the law often does whatever is necessary to achieve the desired result. Thus family law is considered an area of law controlled by **equity**. Equity can be thought of as the ability of a court to use its discretion and judgment to fashion a remedy appropriate to a particular case, as opposed to the strict application of rigid laws.

Many years ago, there were two kinds of courts: law courts which interpreted and enforced the statutes and precedent case law; chancery courts exercised equity power, resolving the problems for which no law existed. Today in most states, the trial court has the authority to act as both a law court and a chancery court; that is, to interpret the laws and to use discretion and judgment to fashion an appropriate remedy. But be aware that in many states, trial courts *do not* have equity jurisdiction. All matters relevant to the termination of a marriage are equitable issues requiring a court with the authority to use equity in deciding a case.

The concepts of law and equity are not identical. **Laws** are rules that are enforced in the same way in different cases. Equity involves the application of conscience and justice as opposed to the application of rigid legal rules. For an example of a nonequity case, consider this: Jeanne lends Tom $100, which he does not repay as agreed; Jeanne seeks a judicial remedy. The court is limited as to the relief it can award—the original $100, and perhaps accrued interest and attorney's fees. But, if Jeanne seeks to terminate her marriage to Tom, the court has very broad discretion in determining what relief, and in what amount, it will award to each party.

In other words, the court in an equity action has the ability to shape the remedy to meet the needs of the parties in a particular case. The court can and does attempt to do whatever it believes is fair and equitable for the parties. This is why the court decisions in a divorce action sometimes seem incongruous (i.e., declaring that a child born as issue of an annulled marriage is legitimate, even though the parents were never legally married to each other). Any set of rules or laws can be twisted or perverted to obtain an unfair or improper advantage if applied strictly and without discretion; equity gives a court the authority to bend the rules when appropriate.

Several equitable theories must be understood, since they appear time and again in the study of family law.

Estoppel

Estoppel is a defense used when the adverse party seeks to take advantage of a wrongful act that is at least partially of his or her own making. For example, if Marsha marries John based on John's misrepresentation that he was physically capable of consummating the marriage, John would be estopped from seeking an annulment (although Marsha could). Estoppel has three elements, as illustrated by the example:

1. One party (John) has knowledge of the true facts and misrepresents—by word, deed, or silence—those facts to the second party (Marsha).

2. The second party relies on the misrepresentation of the first party.

3. The first party (John) seeks to take advantage of a legal right that accrued to him as a result of the second party's reliance on his misrepresentation.

In short, John knew the true facts and misrepresented them to Marsha; Marsha relied upon the misrepresentation; and now John seeks an annulment of the marriage that resulted from Marsha's reliance on his false statements. As we shall see in Chapter 5, physical inability to consummate a marriage is usually a ground for annulment. But in this case, it would not be "equitable" to permit John to annul this marriage; therefore, Marsha could claim that John is estopped from seeking an annulment of the marriage.

Clean Hands

Equity is reserved for "innocent" parties only, as provided by the defense known as **clean hands.** If a party (Marsha, for example) seeks equity (i.e., claims that an opposing party is estopped from claiming certain relief), that party must show that she is entitled to equity—that she has not participated in any related intentional wrongdoing herself. If, for example, it could be shown that Marsha was still married to a third party at the time of her marriage to John, a court would rule that since she does not have clean hands, she cannot claim that John is estopped from seeking an annulment.

clean hands
An equitable doctrine requiring that a person seeking an equitable remedy must be innocent of any wrongdoing.

Laches

Laches can be thought of as an equitable version of the statute of limitations—laws that establish the time period within which a person has to file a civil action upon a particular cause of action. For example, in a certain state the statute of limitations for a breach of a written contract may be four years after the breach allegedly occurs. So if a contract is breached on April 25, 1993, the statute of limitations for that cause of action can be calculated precisely. But suppose a plaintiff purposefully waited until the last day of the statutory period to file the law suit. If the defendant can establish that she was prejudiced, or injured, by the plaintiff's delay in filing the law suit, then the defendant could use the defense of laches.

The elements of a claim for laches are (1) that the party to whom the cause of action has accrued intentionally delays the initiation of litigation, and (2) that the party defending against the cause of action is prejudiced by the intentional delay. A good example of an application of this theory in the arena of family law exists where a husband files for annulment on the grounds that his wife was under the minimum age for marriage at the time of the commencement of the marriage.

If the husband discovers the defect concerning his wife's nonage, but fails to seek an annulment for a significant period of time (i.e., five years), the wife can use the defense of laches if she can show that she was prejudiced by the delay (i.e., in the interim, a child was born of issue of the marriage; or she gave up a career to stay home and raise a family, etc.).

laches
An equitable theory that prevents the prosecution of a legal claim if the claimant delays prosecution until the defending party's ability to defend the claim is impaired.

NATURE OF DIVORCE AND ANNULMENT

annulment; divorce
Annulment is a judicial determination that a "marriage" never existed. As opposed to divorce, which is a judicial determination that a marriage is legally terminated.

Divorce (also called dissolution) is the legal procedure by which a marriage is terminated. Even with a common-law marriage, court intervention is required to terminate it; in the United States, there is no such thing as a common-law *divorce*. The marriage thus terminated, the parties are no longer entitled to receive nor obligated to provide the litany of rights discussed in Chapter 1.

That said, it is of paramount importance to note that the parties are *not* relieved of certain obligations incurred during the marriage. Hence, there is alimony (also called maintenance or spousal support), a postdivorce payment from one spouse for the maintenance of the other spouse; child custody, a judicial determination as to which of the spouses shall have the exclusive, permanent right to the physical custody of the minor children of the parties, that parent being declared the custodial parent and the other spouse the noncustodial parent; property division, the apportionment of all assets and debts acquired by the parties during their marriage; child support, a postdivorce payment made by the noncustodial parent to the custodial parent for the support of the minor children of the marriage; and child visitation, the right of the noncustodial parent to have periodic physical custody of the minor children of the marriage. In the following sections, we examine each of these elements more closely.

Alimony

Alimony payments can generally be made either as a lump sum, in periodic payments (i.e., monthly or weekly payments), or some combination of the two. The method of payment is generally a function of the payor's ability to pay and the recipient's desire to be paid at the onset of the divorce. Additionally, if alimony is paid as periodic payments, the amount paid can be structured to remain constant; or it can fluctuate with the payor's ability to pay, or the rate of inflation. For income tax purposes, alimony is considered income to the recipient and a deduction from the income of the payor. Other payments or transfers from one party to another are not treated in the same fashion. Accordingly, when negotiating a settlement or compromise of divorce litigation, the amount of alimony may increase or decrease to maximize the tax benefits for all concerned. Chapter 9 contains a complete discussion of alimony.

Property Division

When the parties to a divorce (or annulment, for that matter) separate, they must divide their property. But only the marital property (the property acquired by the spouses during the term of the marriage) is subject to division. Property acquired by a party before the marriage remains the property of that spouse. The states have two theories of property ownership to choose from in determining the appropriate distribution of the marital property.

The most frequently used theory is called equitable distribution under which the court apportions the marital property between the spouses in a manner that, under the circumstances and facts of each case, is fair and equitable to each party. (Although each party need not receive an equal share.)

The other theory, currently in use in eight states (Arizona, California, Idaho, Louisiana, New Mexico, Nevada, Texas, and Washington), is called community property. In community property states, marital property is divided equally between the spouses. Chapter 9 contains a more complete discussion of the property division considerations of divorce.

Child Support

The obligations of a parent to a minor child do not terminate with the termination of the marriage. While financial support was once the sole obligation of the father, today each parent shares this duty. For income tax purposes, child support payments are not income to the recipient nor deductible for the payor. The court oversees the assessment and collection of child support, always keeping "the best interests of the children" in the forefront. In Chapter 10, we discuss all the implications and considerations of child support.

Child Custody

The adjudication of the custody of any minor children of the parties lies with the discretion of the trial court. Once again the controlling factor is always what will be "in the best interests of the children." Custody can be awarded exclusively to one parent or to both parents jointly. This issue is often the most divisive issue raised in divorce litigation. Child custody is discussed more fully in Chapter 10.

Child Visitation

Barring extraordinary circumstances that make the visitation with minor children by the noncustodial parent injurious to the mental or physical health of the minor child, the noncustodial parent is awarded specific visitation rights with the minor children. As already noted, the "best interests of the minor child" determine the schedule of visitation. Visitation with minor children is discussed more fully in Chapter 10.

Annulment

Unlike divorce, which ends an existing marriage, **annulment** is the legal recognition that a particular "marriage" never existed in the first place. The right to grant an annulment stems from the fact that the marriage may be either void or voidable because of the existence of a technical defect in the inception of the marriage. Annulment is covered in Chapter 5.

ISSUES TO BE CONSIDERED

One effect of divorce or annulment is to change the status of the parties, just as their status had changed when they were first married. The practice of a family law office deals primarily with the termination of a marriage, usually by divorce, and the consequences of divorce. The bulk of this text and your studies will therefore be devoted to the myriad problems and solutions related to those issues.

Divorce and annulment not only end a legal relationship, they also profoundly change economic and emotional relationships. In fully litigated divorce (and in certain annulment) litigation, the following issues will inevitably require your attention. They can be generally categorized as problems that must be considered before initiating the litigation; those that must be considered during the pendency of the litigation; and those that must be considered after the divorce or annulment is granted.

Before Filing the Litigation

The following issues must be addressed before filing the litigation:

— Where (in which court) should the action for divorce or annulment be filed?

— Do the parties have to comply with court-mandated arbitration or mediation?

— Are the parties willing to undergo voluntary arbitration or mediation?

— What are the grounds (reasons), if any, for the divorce or annulment?

— Does one of the spouses require court protection against physical abuse from the other spouse?

— Do any minor children require court protection against physical abuse from one or more of their parents?

— What, if any, religious considerations of divorce or annulment will be encountered?

— What, if any, are the immigration considerations of either or both parties as a result of this divorce?

While the Litigation Is Pending

While the litigation is pending, your law office must consider these issues:

— Is the party seeking relief entitled to an annulment as opposed to a divorce? If so, which remedy provides the most protection for the parties and any minor children born as issue of the marriage?

— Will the court grant the parties' divorce separate from all the other issues that must be resolved, or must the final divorce await determination of all other issues?

— Who shall remain in possession of the marital residence, and who shall be responsible for its upkeep and payments?

— Who shall have custody of any minor children?

— When shall visitation by the noncustodial parent be permitted, and what (if any) limitations shall be placed upon it?

— Are grandparents to be allowed visitation rights with the minor children? To what extent?

— What amount shall be paid by the noncustodial parent to the custodial parent as support for the minor children?

— Which party shall be responsible for providing health and medical insurance for any minor children?

— Are either or both parties entitled to receive any retirement benefits?

— Are either or both spouses entitled to receive benefits from a branch of the U.S. military services?

— Which party shall retain possession of particular pieces of personal property, such as automobiles and furniture, etc.?

— How shall the value of particular pieces of real and personal property be determined?

— How shall the value of an interest in a business or the assets of a business be determined?

— How shall the value of a professional degree (i.e., M.D., Ph.D., etc.) held by a spouse be determined?

— What are the tax consequences of the court order or settlement between the parties?

— How can a court order relating to any of the above-mentioned concerns be enforced against a reluctant spouse?

— What happens if one party cannot afford the services of an attorney?

— Shall the marital residence be sold, and if so, how will the proceeds of the sale be divided?

After the Divorce or Annulment Is Granted

These issues must be addressed after the court grants the divorce or annulment:

— When and how can a court order or voluntary settlement for support, custody, or visitation be appealed?

— When and how can a court order or voluntary settlement for support, custody, or visitation be modified?

— When does the obligation to support an ex-spouse terminate?

— When does the obligation to support minor children terminate?

— What methods of collecting alimony and support payments are to be used, for both past due and current obligations?

RELIGIOUS CONSIDERATIONS OF DIVORCE

While the emphasis today is on the civil laws governing marriage and divorce, it is worth remembering that the origins of marriage are rooted in the religions of the world. Those origins continue in the rituals of the marriage ceremony, and in the religious considerations of divorce. For the followers of a given religion, it may be one thing for a civil court to grant a divorce. It may be quite another to obtain religious recognition of the termination of the marriage. The importance of this recognition cannot be understated; without it, remarriage within the religion is not possible. It should also be noted that while certain religions may grant their adherents a divorce, others may grant an annulment. A common thread running through the specific examples that follow is the relative, and historic preeminence of the husband over the wife. *When first meeting a new client, it is important to inquire whether either spouse considers the religious elements of divorce important.*

PRACTICE POINTER

Jewish

get
A Jewish divorce.

The Jewish version of divorce is called a **get**—a written bill of divorce that the husband can deliver to the wife. Under Jewish law, only the husband may obtain a *get,* although the wife may refuse to accept it. Obviously, this provides the husband with potential leverage that may be used against the wife. A Jewish wife thus remains married under Jewish law until the husband delivers and the wife accepts the *get.* Should a woman who fails to obtain a *get* remarry in a secular ceremony, she is considered an adulteress under Jewish law. Further, any children born as a result of the secular marriage are considered illegitimate under Jewish law. Conversely, should a husband remarry without first obtaining a *get,* while not treated as an adulterer, he is guilty of polygamy (which, strangely enough, does not carry the same stigma as adultery). The children of the remarriage of a husband who does not first obtain a *get* are not considered illegitimate.

In other countries, the courts issuing the secular divorce may order a reluctant husband to give his wife a *get.* In the United States, however, the Establishment Clause of the First Amendment of the Constitution, as well as other constitutional provisions, makes such judicial intervention problematic. One such attempt at secular intervention is the New York "*get* statute" (section 253 of the New York Domestic Relations Law). The practical effect of section 253 is to prevent a Jewish husband from obtaining a civil divorce until he swears that he has given his wife a *get.* While the constitutional problems with section 253 appear obvious, the statute has yet to be declared unconstitutional.

Islamic

An Islamic divorce is called *talaq* (also spelled *talak*.) It is an *ex parte* ceremony in which the Islamic husband simply says "talaq" (which roughly trans-
lates to "I divorce you") three times. In some Islamic countries, the *talaq* must
occur before a religious or governmental official, while this is not required in
other countries.

talaq
An Islamic divorce.

Roman Catholic

Unlike the two previous examples, the Roman Catholic Church does not
grant divorces. It will grant an annulment if it can be established that the marriage was not valid upon its inception, for example, immaturity or psychological factors which may have seriously impeded the freedom of one or both
of the parties to marry. The church maintains a tribunal that acts as a court
and determines whether the necessary grounds for annulment are present.

Recognition of Foreign Religious Divorces

A related problem is whether a religious divorce (such as a *talaq*) rendered in
a country in which religious divorces also serve as secular divorces will be recognized as valid in the United States. This problem is encompassed in an area
of the law known as conflicts of law. Generally, if a court in a foreign country grants a divorce and all rights required by its laws are satisfied, the divorce
will be recognized as valid in the United States.

THE CHANGING LANDSCAPE OF DIVORCE

The laws related to divorce, alimony, and the support and custody of children
bear little resemblance to the laws that were in effect just 25 years ago. In
1971, California passed the first no-fault divorce laws. Since that time, laws
permitting some version of no-fault divorce have been passed in all fifty states.
Prior to the promulgation of the no-fault divorce laws, a divorce could be had
only upon a showing of fault (i.e., adultery, desertion, cruelty) by one of the
parties, even if both parties desired a divorce.

    The requirement of fault had several ramifications. First, the spouse
found to be "guilty" for the failure of the marriage would often be treated
more harshly when the marital assets were divided. The rationale for this was
that a spouse should not benefit from his own inappropriate behavior.
Second, if a husband wanted "out" of a marriage to pursue other romantic
interests, the wife had an opportunity to negotiate a favorable economic settlement that would allow her to continue to live in the style to which she had
become accustomed. This situation arose because in such a case, unless the
wife had committed some act constituting marital fault, only the wife had the
right to seek a divorce. It also meant that many women continued to live in a
loveless marriage, rather than agree to a divorce and the possibility of spending subsequent years in poverty.

The onset of no-fault divorce changed everything. Thereafter, fault was no longer a primary issue, and even the "guilty" spouse could seek a divorce. Further, a no-fault divorce requires only that the parties have irreconcilable differences and that the marriage be irretrievably broken. Accordingly, the decision to divorce can now be made unilaterally, because it requires only one spouse to claim that reconciliation is impossible.

The economic consequences of divorce have also changed. It is widely believed that the economic status of women suffers a dramatic decline after divorce, while their former husbands enjoy enhanced economic prospects. A well-publicized study[1] indicated that after divorce a woman's standard of living decreased by 73 percent in the first year after divorce, while in the same time period, a man's standard of living increased by 42 percent.

Several theories have been put forth to explain this phenomenon. One theory focuses on the division of the parties' marital property. Under no-fault divorce theory, marital property is usually divided equally—or roughly equally—between the parties, regardless of either party's marital fault. Thus, a philandering husband no longer need fear the loss of all of his stake in the marital property. Another theory holds that because the advent of no-fault divorce occurred at the same time as the beginning of the "women's rights" movement of the 1970s, awards of permanent alimony were viewed as antithetical to a woman's ability to care for her own needs.

Thus, when alimony was awarded, it was often in the form of rehabilitative alimony, the purpose of which is to provide the recipient with the training and education necessary to obtain gainful employment. But even with such training, there is a statistical difference between the average pay earned by women as compared to that earned by men. On average, women earn approximately $.71 for every $1.00 earned by men, and in combination with the modern trend against awarding permanent alimony, this tends to provide men with a more substantial economic base.

A ROAD MAP THROUGH DIVORCE

Rome was not built in a day. Nor can a party obtain a divorce in a day. If divorce were easy, clients would not need lawyers and paralegals—and we would all be out of a job! Divorce, like any litigation, involves many complex and interwoven tasks. Paralegal students (and legal professionals) sometimes "fail to see the forest for the trees." In other words, it may be easy to lose sight of the main objectives in litigation because so much time is spent on tasks that, while essential, seem unrelated to the ultimate resolution of the litigation. Accordingly, the chart in Exhibit 4–1 is designed to act as a reference guide through divorce, a "road map," if you will. You may want to refer to this section if you later find yourself wondering, "What does this have to do with divorce?"

---

1. Lenore J. Weitzman, *The Divorce Revolution: The Unexpected Social and Economic Consequences for Women and Children in America*, The Free Press, 1985.

EXHIBIT 4–1

A ROAD MAP THROUGH DIVORCE

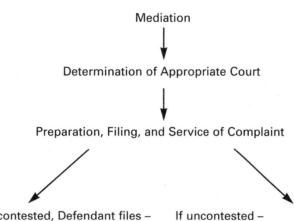

Mediation

↓

Determination of Appropriate Court

↓

Preparation, Filing, and Service of Complaint

If contested, Defendant files –
- Motion to dismiss
- Answer
- Counterclaim

If uncontested –
- Preparation of settlement agreement
- Hearing for final decree

↓

Interlocutory Relief

↓

Discovery

↓

Preparation for Trial

↓

Trial of Case

↓

Posttrial Motions

↓

Appeals

↓

Collection of Judgment

↓

Enforcement of Judgment

↓

Modification of Judgment

ALTERNATIVE DISPUTE RESOLUTION

alternative dispute resolution
Nonjudicial methods of dispute resolution.

arbitration
A process by which a dispute is taken outside the judicial system and is determined by a neutral third party. May be either binding or nonbinding.

mediation
A process by which parties to a dispute are aided in negotiations by a neutral third party.

Alternative dispute resolution (ADR) refers to various nonjudicial means of resolving disputes. The primary forms of alternative dispute resolution are **arbitration** and **mediation**.

Arbitration

Arbitration is a process in which the parties take their dispute to one or more neutral third parties, who will make an award to the prevailing party. It is similar to a court of law in that after hearing evidence from both parties, the arbitrator ultimately hands down an award to one of the parties. Arbitration can be either binding or nonbinding. Binding arbitration is usually entered into by the parties voluntarily. The award made in binding arbitration cannot be appealed to a court of law. (The television program "People's Court" was actually binding arbitration.) On the other hand, nonbinding arbitration is usually judicially imposed. The parties have the right to reject the arbitrator's award.

Mediation

Mediation has been defined in the American Bar Association (ABA) *Divorce and Family Mediation Standards of Practice* as:

> A process in which the lawyer helps family members resolve their disputes in an informative and consensual manner. This process requires that the mediator be qualified by training, experience, and temperament; that the mediator be impartial; that the participants reach decisions voluntarily; that their decisions be based on sufficient factual data; and, that each participant understands the information upon which decisions are reached.

In litigation generally, ADR has become a growth industry, as the public tires of the long delays and hefty legal bills that are so much a part of traditional litigation. This is even more so in the arena of family law, where the parties' relationship does not terminate with the close of the litigation. ADR is blossoming in family law because it is seen as a method of resolving deeply emotional issues without causing further damage to an already damaged relationship.

Of special interest in family law is mediation. Mediation can be entered into voluntarily, or it may be judicially mandated. For example, many courts now require divorce litigants with minor children to participate in mediation to attempt to forge a mutually satisfactory agreement relating to child custody and visitation. Proponents of mediation point to the following factors:

— Traditional litigation, especially protracted divorce litigation, can be very expensive for both parties and may take several years to come to a conclusion.

— The adversarial nature of litigation, in which there is a "winner" and a "loser," is often contrary to the best interests of the parties;

a mediator can act as a counselor and seek to lessen the hostility between the parties, which lessens the possibility of postdivorce conflicts between the parties.

— Mediation allows, even requires, the parties to negotiate personally with each other, as opposed to litigation, in which the attorneys do all of the talking.

— In litigation, attorneys are ethically obligated to zealously represent their clients and to obtain the best deal possible for them, even if the resulting agreement creates an inequity for the other party.

Divorce mediation is sometimes conducted with therapists or other mental health professionals, as opposed to legal professionals, acting as the neutral third party. Regardless, the mediator cannot advise either party as to what he or she should do. Instead, each party should have independent counsel to review and advise on all issues. And remember that even with mediation, a complaint for divorce will have to be filed. The resulting agreement will still be subject to approval of the court in which the divorce is filed.

A Step-by-Step Comparison

The following steps trace the significant points in divorce and describe the similarities and differences between the adversarial and mediation processes.

Adversarial Process	**Mediation Process**
Decision to Divorce	
— Couples have usually made the decision to divorce before visiting a lawyer, although many individual spouses obtain information about their rights prior to actually making a decision to proceed with the divorce process. In the event one spouse wishes the other to refrain from some type of behavior, a divorce or separate maintenance action must be filed to activate the court's power to force the other spouse to act.	— The decision to divorce need not be a firm decision, and the couple may take advantage of the mediation process without filing papers. Voluntary decisions about management of money, separation, and freezing of assets can be obtained without commencing legal action. However, such mediated decisions do not have binding legal effect.
Commencement of Legal Action	
— Filing of a petition for divorce by service of process upon the opposing spouse is usually completed prior to beginning	— Filing of a petition for divorce is usually done after the couple have completed mediation and they and their attorneys are

negotiations about a possible settlement.

provided with a memorandum of understanding that serves as the basis for the stipulated settlement agreement and divorce decree.

Temporary Hearing

— A temporary hearing is seldom scheduled unless court restraint is deemed necessary because one spouse is in physical danger or it appears possible that one spouse will abscond with or significantly deplete marital funds or property. Where uncertainty about support exists, the hearing establishes temporary levels of child and spousal support and determines occupancy and use of homestead and other property during pendency of the proceeding.

— Signing an agreement to mediate, where the couple contractually agree to rules and conditions prohibiting depletion of assets, cancellation of insurance policies, and so forth, serves as a substitute for the orders issued at a temporary hearing. The first mediation sessions will cover other temporary or immediate decisions that must be made before the couple begin to work on settlement of long-term issues. The mediator asks the couple if they wish to have their temporary agreements filed with the court by their attorneys, and where trust level is low, some couples will ask their attorneys to prepare a temporary agreement based upon the mediation decisions reached at the initial sessions. Converting temporary mediated agreements into temporary legal orders may be desirable, to take advantage of the spousal support tax deduction.

Discovery

— Discovery is accomplished informally or formally through motions to produce, depositions, and interrogatories. Because comprehensive formal discovery is expensive, it is only used in those cases with sufficient assets to justify the expense, although discovery of

— The mediator supervises and manages discovery. Should one party become uncooperative, the sessions are usually terminated and the couple is returned to their lawyers, who will then proceed with formal, court-supervised discovery. Documentation of assets and expert witnesses' opinions and possible testimony is used in contested custody matters. Since fair divorces are based on complete disclosure, the integrity of the discovery process is supervised and managed by the individual attorneys, with resort to the court system for assistance if the other attorney or spouse becomes uncooperative. Under existing rules of ethics, attorneys are generally not required to volunteer information unless and until it is requested by the other side.

identification of property and income are quite similar to the adversarial method. Couples beginning mediation are asked to sign an agreement to mediate that requires them to produce copies of tax returns, pay stubs, business records, and all other documents and records requested either by the mediator or the other spouse. Because the mediator supervises and manages disclosure, he or she must be familiar with the documents needed by the attorneys who are asked to review and approve mediated decisions.

Settlement Documents

— The attorneys prepare the settlement document after reaching agreement on all issues in the divorce. The jurisdiction may call it a stipulation for settlement, marital settlement agreement, or marital termination agreement. The language most often has special legal significance and contains legal descriptions and boilerplate language as dictated by local custom.

— The mediator prepares a memorandum of the decisions or a mediated plan. The mediation document is not signed by the couple and has no binding legal effect until reviewed and converted to a legal document. Some mediators ask the couple to sign the mediation memorandum after it is reviewed and approved by the attorneys, so that it can be attached as an exhibit to the court papers. The memorandum of understanding is drafted in plain English and usually contains background information about how the decisions were negotiated and reached, providing a basis for evaluating the entire settlement.

Contested Hearings

— Contested hearings are the last resort if negotiations fail, and may be used by attorneys to coerce a better settlement. This stage of the adversarial process

— Most couples attempting settlement through the mediation process wish to avoid the cost, stress, and delay of acrimonious, contested proceedings.

often presents some internal conflict for the divorce attorney, who understands that settlement may be desirable but is wary of being viewed as soft or unwilling to do what is necessary to represent fully the interests of his or her client.

Resort to contested proceedings represents a failure of the mediation process to the extent that the couple have placed themselves in the position of allowing the court to make decisions for them. Mediation may be partially successful in narrowing issues to be litigated.

Law or Legal Precedent

— The law is the foundation of most settlement choices, and the divorce outcome is judged according to what might have happened in court or how the court will rule on a particular factual situation. Where the law does not mandate certain agreements, attorneys will approve such agreements with caution.

— The law is seldom discussed because divorce mediation is not viewed as the practice of law. Thus, all legal predictions about the outcome or result in a particular case or issue are referred back to the couple's attorneys. Couples are asked to determine their own law of fairness rather than to speculate on what the litigation outcome might be.*

Time to Complete

— In a contested case, the divorce process is long, often in excess of one year. In a negotiated settlement, the time to complete depends on how fast the attorneys complete discovery and conclude the negotiations.

— In most cases the mediation process is quicker than the adversarial, as mediators generally meet with the couple either weekly or every other week. The total time spent in mediation ranges from six to twenty hours and varies with the complexity of the case, the skill of the mediator, and the attitudes of the couple.

Compliance with Decree

— In theory, the adversarial system should have a good record of compliance because the court's power of contempt stands behind each order that

— Research has shown high rates of compliance with mediated agreements, compared to compliance with adversarial decrees. Couples are more

*(NOTE: *Not all attorney-mediators adhere to this model.—Ed.)*

it issues. However, statistics show high levels of nonpayment of child and spousal support and many contempt proceedings on issues of custody and visitation.

likely to abide by an order that they helped create, and most couples choose to include an agreement to mediate future disagreements or changes of circumstances.

Qualifications of Professional

— Attorneys must have met the requirements for admission to the bar. All attorneys are licensed by the state, and many states require mandatory continuing education for attorneys. There is no requirement that an attorney have any specialized training in counseling, human behavior, or conflict resolution.

— At present, no state has enacted licensure of mediators. Most professional divorce mediators are either mental health professionals or attorneys. The Academy of Family Mediators has recommended training requirements for divorce mediators, and special training is required of lawyers who mediate in some Canadian provinces.

Ethics

— The attorney has a duty of vigorous advocacy on behalf of a client. An attorney is required to advance the position or cause of the client, regardless of the impact upon the rest of the family. Attorneys must guard against conflicts of interest and are generally prevented from representing divorcing couples.

— The mediator has a duty to remain neutral and impartial while managing the discussions. The mediator does not represent either party and has a duty to prevent overreaching. Some critics of mediation claim that the mediation will not work where there are disparities in power and negotiating abilities. Defenders of mediation claim that couples, regardless of their strengths and weaknesses, can be taught effective bargaining skills in mediation.

Cost

— The adversarial system is presently under attack from many quarters because of the increasingly high costs of legal services. It is not uncommon to pay fees in excess of $10,000 for representation in a long, contested divorce.

— A mediated settlement is probably less costly than settlement through the adversarial process, although there is no accurate way to compare the costs in a particular case because only one method is used. It is certainly less costly when com-

Newer attorneys apply pressure by offering low-cost packages for divorce cases where there are no children, no real estate, and no contest.

pared to contested litigation.

Outcome

— Since the outcome is the product of a competitive conflict-resolution process, it is viewed as a victory or defeat.

— The outcome is a win–win solution that attempts to balance the needs of each spouse, through compromise.[2]

---

2. Erickson, Stephen K., "The Legal Dimension of Divorce Mediation." In *Divorce Mediation Theory and Practice,* edited by Jay Folberg and Ann Milne, The Guilford Press, 1988.

INTERVIEW CHECKLIST

The following questions for the interview checklist for divorce would be used in tandem with the questions of the Basic Interview Checklist in Chapter 2. The Interview Checklist for annulment appears in Chapter 5.

INTERVIEW CHECKLIST

What is your religion?

Your spouse's?

Your children's?

Do your religious beliefs mandate the execution of a "religious divorce"? _____ If so, provide details.

Assets

List the street address for each piece of real property that you or your spouse currently own or have an interest in.

For each piece of real property, state the nature of the interest in the property you and your spouse have (i.e., fee simple, life estate, time share, etc.).

In whose name(s) is the real property titled?

Are there any encumbrances on the real property?

If so, state the name of the lienholder, the nature of the encumbrance, the total amount still owed, how often payments are due, the date of the final payment, the amount of each payment, and whether a lump-sum (or balloon) payment is to be

continued on page 87

continued from page 86

paid (and if so, the amount and due date of the payment).

_____

_____

Was the property acquired by purchase or inheritance?

_____

If by inheritance, state from whom it was inherited, the date of inheritance, and, if known, the value of the property at the time of the inheritance.

_____

_____

If by purchase, state the date of purchase, the purchase price, the name of the seller, and the source of the funds used to purchase the property.

_____

_____

List each piece of personal property you or your spouse own (i.e., cars, boats, jewelry, furniture, clothing, business property) with a value of $250.00 or greater.

_____

_____

State the nature of the interest in the property (i.e., owned, leased, etc.).

_____

Was the property acquired by inheritance or by purchase?

_____

If by inheritance, state the date of inheritance, from whom it was inherited, and, if known, the value of the property at the time it was inherited.

_____

_____

If by purchase, state the date of purchase, the purchase price, and the source of the funds used to purchase the property.

_____

_____

Are there any encumbrances on any piece of personal property?

_____

If so, state the name of the lienholder, the nature of the encumbrance, the amount still owed, how

often payments are due, the date of the final payment, the amount of each payment, whether a lump-sum payment (balloon) is to be paid (and, if so, the amount and due date of the payment).

_____

_____

List all savings and checking accounts in either your name or control or your spouse's name and control, jointly or individually.

Name of bank or financial institution

_____

Name(s) on account

_____

Type of account

_____

Account number

_____

Amount currently in account

_____

Average monthly balance for past six months

_____

List all certificates of deposit (CD) in your name or control or your spouse's name or control, jointly or individually.

Name of bank or financial institution

_____

Name(s) on account

_____

Account number

_____

Amount

_____

Date purchased

_____

Interest rate

_____

Source of funds used to purchase CD.

_____

List all shares of stock or mutual funds owned in your name or control or your spouse's name or control, jointly or individually.

continued on page 88

continued from page 87

Name of corporation or mutual fund

Public or closed corporation

Name(s) of owner of stock on certificate

Number of shares owned

Date(s) acquired

Purchase price of stock (If stock was purchased at different times, list the number of shares bought at each price.)

Source of funds used to purchase stock

List all bonds owned in your name or control or your spouse's name or control, jointly or individually.

Name of obligor

Name(s) of owner shown on bond

Face amount due at maturity

Maturity date

Date acquired

Purchase price of bond (If bonds were purchased at different times, list the specific bonds bought at each price.)

Rate of interest

Date interest paid

List all income received in your name.

Employer

Address of employer

Present annual salary

Position

Date hired

Original salary

Bonus received in past three years

Amount and nature of pension plan

Source of other income (royalties, real estate, etc.)

List all income received by your spouse.

Employer

Address of employer

Present annual salary

Position

Date hired

Original salary

Bonus received in past three years

Amount and nature of pension plan

Source of other income (royalties, real estate, etc.)

Monthly Expenses

List all monthly expenses for both yourself and for any minor children in your custody.

Housing

Rent or mortgage

Electricity

continued on page 89

continued from page 88

Gas or oil

Telephone (w/long distance)

Water

Sewer

Maintenance

Lawn care

Home or apartment insurance

Automobile payments (incl. lease payments)

Gasoline

Automobile maintenance

Automobile insurance

Other

Food, Health, and Clothing

Groceries

Food eaten away from home

Clothing for you

Clothing for children

Shoes for you

Shoes for children

Laundry and dry cleaning

Life insurance premiums for you

Personal hygiene for you

For children

Medical insurance for you

For children

Doctor bills for you

For children

Drug expenses for you

For children

Dentist bills for you

For children

Orthodontist expenses for children

Other

Personal and Leisure Expenses

Haircuts/hairstyle for you

For children

Books, records, movies, videos, other entertainment

Music/dance lessons for children

Pet food, veterinarian expenses

Charity

Misc. cash

Vacation expenses

Savings

REVIEW QUESTIONS

1. What does it mean to say that divorce and annulment are actions in equity as opposed to actions at law?

2. Consider the following scenario: When Julie and David are married, Julie tells David that she is 18, even though she is actually only 15 years old, and thus is under the minimum age requirement for the state in which they are married.

   For each of the following scenarios, state which equitable defense would be applicable and then explain how it could be applied.

   a) If two weeks after the wedding Julie wants to annul the marriage, which equitable defense exists?

   b) If David finds out about Julie's nonage within one month of the wedding, but does not seek to annul the marriage until three years later when he learns that Julie is pregnant, which defense is applicable?

   c) Same facts as (b) above, but now consider which equitable defense David might seek to use to counter the defense raised by Julie.

3. What is a *get,* and what is the procedure for obtaining one? How are husbands and wives treated differently under Jewish law?

4. What are arbitration and mediation, and how do they differ from each other?

5. What is a *talaq,* and what is the procedure for getting it? How are husbands and wives treated differently under Islamic law?

6. What are the advantages of mediation in a divorce case?

7. How are the concepts of "statute of limitations" and "laches" similar? How are they different?

8. In your own words, what are the elements of estoppel?

9. What is the relevance of the concept of "clean hands" to a divorce or annulment case?

10. List three ways in which divorce has changed since 1970.

KEY TERMS

alternative dispute resolution

annulment

arbitration

clean hands

divorce

equity

get

in loco parentis

laches

laws

mediation

talaq

STATE RESEARCH PROBLEMS

Review the laws of your state and answer the following questions:

1. What court(s) in your state have the authority to exercise equity power? What court(s) in your state do not have the authority to exercise equity power?

2. What, if any, requirements does your jurisdiction have concerning arbitration and/or mediation for divorce litigation? Are those requirements imposed by state law or by the rules of the local court?

ETHICAL PROBLEM

The parties in a divorce case are Jewish. Your firm represents the husband. The wife wants a *get* so that she can remarry properly under Jewish law. Your client refuses to grant the *get* unless the wife agrees to forgo her claim to any equity in the parties' marital residence. This claim is worth well over $25,000 and under the law of your jurisdiction, the wife would be entitled to it. What, if any, ethical concerns does the husband's demand raise for the law firm?

PRACTICE EXERCISE

Compare the questions contained in the interview checklist for antenuptial agreements (Chapter 3) and the questions that appear on pages 86–89. Which questions appear in both interview checklists? Why are they appropriate for both client problems? Which questions appear in only one of the interview checklists?

Why are they not appropriate for both client problems?

Annulment

In this chapter, you will learn:

- *How annulment differs from divorce*

- *How annulment is similar to divorce*

- *The difference between a void marriage and a voidable marriage*

- *The procedure for annulment*

- *The grounds for and defenses to annulment*

- *The procedure for separate maintenance*

Annulment is a judicial procedure in which the relief sought is an official court ruling that a marriage between two persons is a nullity and that as a matter of law, the marriage never existed at all. The specific remedies available to a party in an annulment action vary from those available in a divorce action. That is, alimony may not be available in annulment, but child support and property settlements are available. The retroactive nature of annulment requires a careful analysis of the effect of the annulment on the rights conferred upon the parties by virtue of their "marriage." A distinction is made between void marriages, which are void from their inception as an operation of law, and voidable marriages, which remain valid until a court grants an annulment. A complaint for annulment must allege that a defect existed at the inception of the marriage; a successful defense would establish that the defect did not exist at that time.

Separate maintenance is a judicial proceeding in which the court does not terminate the marriage, but rather sanctions the legal separation of a married couple and issues an order providing for the support of the economically dependent spouse. This can be compared with a judicial separation, which is identical to a complete divorce except that the parties do not have the right to marry anyone else.

COMPARISON BETWEEN ANNULMENT AND DIVORCE

The essential difference between an action for annulment and an action for divorce is that an action for annulment seeks a court order declaring that the marriage between the parties never existed, while an action for divorce recognizes the existence of the marriage and seeks a court order terminating it. And because the result of a successful action for annulment is a court order ruling that the parties were never legally married, there is no continuing obligation for support. Therefore, alimony is generally not available to either of the spouses. Property settlements are available through annulment, however. In those rare cases where children were born to the parties, the issues of child support and visitation fall within the court's jurisdiction.

Following is a brief summary of the differences between annulment and divorce.

Divorce	Annulment
—Court order terminates an existing marriage.	—Court order declares that marriage never legally existed.
—Relief available includes alimony, child custody/support, and property division.	—Relief available includes child custody/support and property division.
—Grounds for divorce may occur after time of marriage.	—Grounds for annulment must exist at time of marriage.

Grounds for Annulment

The grounds for annulment all relate to the validity of the marriage *at the inception of the marriage.* Should any of these defects occur after the parties marry each other, the defect may provide grounds for divorce, but not annulment. In cases when a couple marries without satisfying the requirements for marriage described in Chapter 1, that failure can provide a sufficient ground for annulment. These grounds include

— Bigamy

— Nonage of a spouse at the time of the marriage

— Lack of mental capacity of a spouse at the time of the marriage

— A spouse with a venereal disease or physical disability at the time of the marriage

— Incest either by affinity or consanguinity

— The use of fraud in inducing the marriage

— The use of duress to induce the marriage

— The parties did not really intend to get married (i.e., marriage entered into on a dare or as a joke)

If these factors look familiar, that is because they are all discussed in Chapter 1 as factors in a valid marriage. Thus, the failure to satisfy any of these requirements can serve as legal grounds for annulment. Contrast these grounds with the grounds for a fault-based divorce in Chapter 6.

Since annulment acts to nullify an already existing marriage, it is necessary to distinguish between those marriages that are "void" and those that are merely "voidable." A **void marriage** is one that is clearly illegal on its face and therefore is null and void from the inception of the marriage; the annulment simply makes the voiding of the marriage official. Examples of a void marriage include marriages involving incest and bigamy. A **voidable marriage** is one in which a defect exists at the time the marriage is entered into, but it is not actually null and void until a court of law issues an order annulling the marriage. The difference is that the defect in a voidable marriage is one requiring proof, while the defect in a void marriage speaks for itself. Examples of voidable marriage include marriage based on fraud, duress, and lack of mental capacity.

void marriage; voidable marriage
A void marriage is one that was never considered a valid marriage; a voidable marriage is one that is valid until a court declares it to be void.

Relief Available

Regardless of how a marriage is terminated, the parties still have to deal with the ramifications of its dissolution. Following is a discussion of how these issues are treated in actions for annulment.

Alimony
As noted, alimony is not usually available to a party in annulment action. Those states that do permit some manner of alimony do so when the equities of the case dictate that some form of maintenance be provided (i.e., the degree of neediness of the dependent spouse, and whether that spouse is deserving of such equity—does she have "clean hands"?).

Issues Involving Minor Children
A typical question about annulment is: What is the status of any children born of an annulled marriage? Such children were legitimate at the time they were born, but do they remain legitimate after a court decrees that their parents were never legally married? Until recent years, the common law would have declared such children illegitimate retroactively. However, most states have abrogated the common law to provide that such children would remain legitimate after their parents' annulment. (See Chapter 15 for a full discussion of legitimation.)

Additionally, a court still must decide those issues incumbent with the termination of the marriage related to any minor children of the couple, such as child custody, visitation, support payments, etc., which are decided in the same manner as in a divorce action. (See Chapter 10 for a full discussion of issues involving minor children.)

Division of Property

Property is apportioned between the parties in an annulment action in the same manner as in a divorce action. (See Chapter 9 for a full discussion of issues involving division of property.)

EFFECTS OF ANNULMENT

The status of marriage carries with it a series of rights: the right of inheritance, interspousal tort immunity, the privilege to prevent the publication of any marital communications, etc. When the marriage is annulled, what is the effect of the annulment upon those rights? Often the effect is that the parties are treated as if they had never married. This is known as the **relation back doctrine** of annulment—the annulment relates back to the time of the initiation of the marriage. But because equity often seeks to do what is right, a court may grant limited benefits to parties to an annulled marriage.

relation back doctrine
An annulment relates back in time to the date the "marriage" occurred, thus creating the legal theory that an annulled marriage never existed at all.

Effect on the Right to Prevent Testimony of a Former Spouse

As noted in Chapter 1, a party has the right to prevent a spouse from testifying against him or her in a civil action (other than one for divorce, annulment, or child abuse). For example, consider an example in which the husband is called to testify about his wife's confession of her alleged drug habit, and the marriage between them has been annulled since the time of the marital communication. While there is disagreement on this point among the states, the prevailing view is that because the purpose of this privilege is to allow spouses to confide in each other without fearing that any such communications will be made public, the privilege against the disclosure of marital communications remains intact even if the marriage is later annulled (or terminated by divorce).

Effect on Immigration Status

Ingrid, a foreign national, marries a citizen of the United States, and as a result obtains permanent residence status to remain in the United States. If the marriage is annulled, what happens to Ingrid's immigration status? All things being equal, if the marriage was not a sham executed for the sole purpose of obtaining improved immigration status, Ingrid will be able to remain in the United States as though the annulment had not occurred. But the burden will

FERNANDEZ v. FERNANDEZ
Court of Appeals of Texas, El Paso.
Oct. 8, 1986.

. . . .

OPINION
FULLER, Justice.

Appellant filed a motion for contempt and for other relief against Appellee, her former husband, for failure to pay child support as ordered for their daughter, Jo-Ann Fernandez. Appellee's sole defense as pled and argued was that the minor child had married, thereby was emancipated, and that his duty of support therefore ended. The trial court agreed, even though the child's marriage had been annulled. We affirm in part, and reverse and render in part.

The sparse amount of largely uncontested evidence showed that the minor daughter, at fourteen years of age, married under a belief that she was pregnant. Sixty days thereafter, the parties separated after discovery that she was not expecting a child. Annulment of the marriage followed some months later. The natural mother then filed the motion for contempt against the natural father for his failure to pay the court-ordered child support. The father's defense was that the minor child became emancipated when she married, and even though an annulment of that marriage took place, it in no way affected her emancipation; therefore, he owed no duty of support.

Appellant's Points of Error Nos. One and Two assert that the trial court erred in finding that the annulment of the marriage did not affect the minor daughter's emancipation, and also erred in finding no duty of support by the father after the minor daughter's marriage was annulled.

There is no question in our state that by virtue of the Tex.Fam.Code Ann. art. 4.03 (Vernon 1975), a married person becomes emancipated and has the power and capacity of an adult; otherwise, majority is not attained until age eighteen years (citation omitted). The duty of support terminates by marriage of the child (citation omitted). However, generally annulment voids ab initio the marriage (citation omitted).

Appellant relies primarily on *Home of Holy Infancy v. Kaska*, 397 S.W.2d 208 (Tex.1965). In that case, Kaska's child was conceived before marriage, and Kaska then married the mother; but, before the child

was born, the marriage was annulled. The mother placed the child for adoption, and Kaska filed a custody suit. If the relation-back doctrine applied, Kaska had no standing because the child would be illegitimate. In that case, the court refused to apply the relation-back doctrine as it would bastardize the child. (Citation omitted.) Therefore, it is apparent that although a voidable marriage is void ab initio, it is really not void for all purposes, such as division of property and legitimacy of children (citations omitted).

In the instant case, Appellee's fourteen-year-old daughter, the product of a broken home, believed she was pregnant and then married. The marriage was annulled, and the minor daughter moved back with her mother who was unemployed, and sought work at a local pizza parlor. The minor daughter had a limited education, having left school in the ninth grade. She testified that her mother "buys me . . . personal things. She buys my clothes. She buys my food, my shampoo, my toothbrush, my toothpaste." The Court notes that the motion to hold the natural father in contempt was filed under pauper's oath, whereby the natural mother stated she was unemployed and too poor to pay the court costs.

Should that marriage, which consisted of living with a husband for sixty days resulting in annulment of the marriage, forever free the natural father of any support obligation? In 1900, our Supreme Court in *State v. Deaton*, 93 Tex. 243, 54 S.W. 901, at 903, so aptly said, and it is worth repeating in this day and age:

> God, in his wisdom has placed upon the father and mother the obligation to nuture, educate, protect and guide their offspring, and has qualified them to discharge those important duties by writing in their hearts sentiments of affection, and establishing between them and their children ties which cannot exist between the children and any other persons.

Apparently, Appellee feels no legal or moral obligation to further support this child of a broken marriage.

On the record before this Court, we find that the annulment of the Appellee's minor daughter reinstated her minority and, also, reinstated Appellee's duty of support as provided in the previous court orders. We sustain Points of Error Nos. One and Two.

We affirm the trial court's decision on failure to find the Appellee in contempt; but, that part of the judgment finding the minor child emancipated and terminating Appellee's duty of child support is reversed and judgment is rendered that Appellee's duty of support is hereby reinstated effective from the date of the granting of the annulment of the marriage of the minor daughter, Jo-Ann Fernandez.

DISCUSSION QUESTIONS

Based on the preceding case of *Fernandez v. Fernandez*, 717 S.W.2d 781 (Tex., 1986), answer the following questions:

1. Was the theory of the relation back doctrine used in this case? What rationale was used in determining whether the relation back doctrine should be applied?

2. What is the effective date of the reinstatement of the father's child support obligation? What argument can be made that the reinstatement date should be the date of the minor daughter's marriage?

be on Ingrid to establish that she entered into her "marriage" in good faith rather than to slip through a loophole in the immigration laws. On the other hand, consider the following effect on the right of inheritance.

Effect on the Right of Inheritance

Once the marriage is annulled (or ends in divorce, for that matter), the right of inheritance from a deceased spouse ends. But what happens if a spouse had previously executed a last will and testament, leaving all his worldly belongings "to my beloved wife?" Generally, most states have statutes that nullify, as an operation of law, a will of a person who has been divorced or annulled since the execution of the will.

PROCEDURE FOR ANNULMENT

As with any litigation, a request to a court for an annulment begins with a complaint filed by the party seeking the relief. See Chapter 6 for a discussion of the general procedural rules of family law litigation.

Following is Exhibit 5–1, a complaint for annulment. As with any complaint, the plaintiff must establish a **prima facie** case for annulment. That is, she must allege the existence of all the necessary **elements** of an action for annulment, including

— That the court in which the action is filed has the necessary personal jurisdiction and venue to hear the case

— That the parties married each other

— Whether any children were born as issue of the marriage (born to the parties as a result of the marriage)

— That (most importantly) some defect existed at the inception of the marriage, thus causing the marriage to be either void or voidable

The complaint must also ask for the relief desired (i.e., annulment of the marriage, division of property, etc.). The facts set forth in the complaint must be

prima facie; elements
A prima facie case is one in which the plaintiff can present some evidence on each element of his cause of action, thus shifting the burden of persuasion to the defendant. Elements are the individual factors that must be established to prevail in a particular cause of action.

EXHIBIT 5–1

<table>
<tr>
<td>Caption, including the name of the court where action is filed, name of the parties, the civil action file number, and designation as a complaint for annulment.</td>
<td>

IN THE _____ COURT OF _____ COUNTY
STATE OF _____

ANGELA P. MARTIN,
Plaintiff,

v.   CIVIL ACTION NO. _____

GERALD D. LEWIS,
Defendant.

</td>
</tr>
</table>

Complaint for Annulment

<table>
<tr>
<td>Introductory paragraph.</td>
<td>COMES NOW, Angela P. Martin, Plaintiff in the above-styled action, and for her Complaint against the Defendant, shows the Court as follows:</td>
</tr>
</table>

1.

<table>
<tr>
<td>Allegation regarding residency requirement of state where filed.</td>
<td>Plaintiff is now and has been a resident of the State of _____ for at least ___ months prior to the filing of this Complaint.</td>
</tr>
</table>

2.

<table>
<tr>
<td>Allegation regarding court's personal jurisdiction over the defendant and where he can be served with process.</td>
<td>Defendant is a resident of _____, County, State of _____, and is subject to the personal jurisdiction of this Court. Defendant may be personally served with a copy of this Complaint and Summons at his principal place of residence, 433 Main Street, City of _____.</td>
</tr>
</table>

3.

<table>
<tr>
<td>Allegation regarding existence of parties' marriage—a necessary element for cause of action of annulment.</td>
<td>Plaintiff and Defendant entered into a purported marriage on the 14th day of February, 1988, in Charlotte, North Carolina.</td>
</tr>
</table>

4.

No children have been born of issue as a result of this purported marriage, and Plaintiff is not pregnant at this time.

5.

<table>
<tr>
<td>Allegation regarding grounds for annulment; note the required allegation that the marriage was void from the onset (void ab initio).</td>
<td>Plaintiff has now learned for the first time that Defendant was never legally divorced from his first wife, Carrie Ann Lewis, and that therefore Defendant remains legally married to Carrie Ann Lewis.</td>
</tr>
</table>

OR

Plaintiff has now learned for the first time that Plaintiff did not have the mental capacity to enter into marriage at the time the purported marriage was entered into, and that Plaintiff's marriage to Defendant is void ab initio.

<table>
<tr>
<td>Demand for relief (Wherefore clause). Demand that summons be issued by the court, that</td>
<td>

WHEREFORE, Plaintiff prays that the Court grant the following relief:

a)   that Summons issue as required by law;
b)   that her marriage to Defendant be annulled; and,

</td>
</tr>
</table>

c) that she be awarded all such other and further relief deemed appropriate by the Court.

Respectfully submitted,

_____
ATTORNEY FOR PLAINTIFF
State Bar No. 123456

Address
City, State, Zip
Telephone Number

marriage be annulled, and for all other relief— usually included in all claims for relief as a savings clause in case party fails to specifically request certain relief in the pleading.

EXHIBIT 5–2

IN THE _____ COURT OF _____ COUNTY
STATE OF _____

ANGELA P. MARTIN,
Plaintiff,

v.

CIVIL ACTION NO. _____

GERALD D. LEWIS,
Defendant.

Verification

Personally appeared Angela P. Martin, Plaintiff above, who states, upon oath, that the facts contained in the foregoing Complaint for Annulment are true and correct.

_____
ANGELA P. MARTIN

Sworn to and subscribed before me
this _____ day of _____ , 199__.

_____
Notary Public

_____
My commission expires _____

verified (sworn to by the party seeking relief), so a notarized verification (given in Exhibit 5–2) signed by the plaintiff must be filed with the complaint.

DEFENSES TO ANNULMENT

Defenses to an action for annulment usually depend on a number of factors including whether the plaintiff is the "innocent" or "guilty" spouse, and whether the marriage sought to be annulled is void or voidable.

Requirements of Clean Hands

Because annulment is an action in equity, courts will not grant relief to a plaintiff who has done wrong or does not have "clean hands." For example, if the plaintiff is the party who committed the fraud or knowingly married a person of nonage, that plaintiff would not be granted an annulment. To do so would in essence reward the party responsible for the defective marriage. In such cases, the "innocent" party must be the plaintiff for an annulment to be granted.

Traditional Defenses

When the marriage is void, barring extraordinary circumstances, there are no valid defenses to an action for annulment. Traditional defenses are possible with voidable marriages, including

— Where the plaintiff was aware of the defect existing at the time the marriage was entered into and still married the defendant with full knowledge of the existing defect

— Where the plaintiff continues to live with the defendant after learning of the preexisting defect and fails to immediately initiate annulment or divorce proceedings (In such cases, the plaintiff is said to have "ratified" the marriage.)

— Where the defendant denies that the alleged marital defect existed at the time the marriage was commenced

In cases where the annulment is contested by the defendant, the issue may not be the continued existence of the marriage, but rather the method of dissolution to be used. In such cases, the defendant may respond to the complaint for annulment with an answer denying the existence of the marital defect at the time of the commencement of the marriage and with a counterclaim for divorce. See Chapter 6 for the format and procedure used with answers and counterclaims.

INTERVIEW CHECKLIST

The following questions should be submitted to any client seeking an annulment in addition to the basic interview checklist questions provided in Chapter 2.

INTERVIEW CHECKLIST

Who officiated at your wedding? _____

Who witnessed your wedding (including any guests)?

_____

_____

_____

Date of separation from spouse.

How long did you actually cohabitate with your spouse? _____

Were you or your spouse under the influence of alcohol or any intoxicating drugs at the time of your marriage? _____ If so, explain.

_____

Were you or your spouse under any threat or duress at the time of your marriage? _____ If so, explain

Were you or your spouse legally married to another party at the time of your marriage? _____ If so, please explain, and include the name of any other such spouses and the date and location of such prior marriages.

_____

_____

If you answered yes to the above question, state whether the prior existing marriage has been legally terminated (by divorce, death of spouse, etc.) since the time of your marriage.

What was your age at the time of your marriage?

_____

What was your spouse's age at the time of your marriage?

Are you and your spouse related to each other by blood? _____ If so, provide specific details.

_____

Are you and your spouse related to each other by marriage? _____ If so, provide specific details.

_____

Did either you or your spouse have a venereal disease at the time of your marriage? _____ If so, explain.

_____

Have you and your spouse had marital relations at any time since the time of your marriage? _____ If so, has a child been born of issue of the marriage, or is the wife pregnant at this time? _____ If, so, provide specific details.

_____

Was the wife pregnant with the child of a man other than her husband at the time of this marriage? _____ If so, provide specific details.

_____

Are you or your spouse unwilling to engage in sexual relations or to have and raise children? _____ If so, explain.

_____

_____

Did you rely on any representations of your spouse that you now know were false when you entered into marriage with your spouse? _____ If so, provide specific details.

_____

_____

Were you or your spouse suffering from any mental illness at the time of your marriage? _____ If so, provide specific details.

_____

_____

OTHER FORMS OF RELIEF

Divorce and annulment are not the only forms of relief available to spouses seeking to end, or at least suspend, their marriage. Two other remedies are separate maintenance and judicial separation.

Separate Maintenance

separate maintenance
In an action for separate maintenance, the parties separate but remain married.

Separate maintenance is a legal procedure whereby a couple legally separates from each other and the court issues an order setting forth the parties' rights and obligations. The key to separate maintenance is that the spouses do not terminate their marriage; rather, it may be considered as a suspension of the marriage. A court order for separate maintenance determines the nature and amount of any alimony, child custody, support and visitation, insurance, etc. But separate maintenance orders do not contemplate the division of the spouses' property, because the parties remain married to each other. Generally, separate maintenance is appropriate only when the spouse seeking support is genuinely dependent on the spouse from whom support is sought. Further, it must be shown that the supporting spouse has the ability to provide the support requested.

The grounds required for an action for separate maintenance vary among the states. Some states require only that the parties separate, without any consideration of fault. Other states require a showing of fault by the defendant. Among these states, there are several grounds for an action for separate maintenance. Chief among them is the willful abandonment of the dependent spouse. Other grounds include the supporting spouse's cruelty, violence, abuse, and excessive use of alcohol and/or narcotics.

abandonment; constructive abandonment
Abandonment occurs when one spouse permanently leaves the marital home. Constructive abandonment occurs when one spouse permanently leaves the marital home in response to the inappropriate behavior of the other spouse.

Abandonment occurs when one spouse terminates cohabitation without justification, without the consent of the other spouse, and without the intent to resume cohabitation. What happens if the dependent spouse is the one who leaves the marital home? Can an action for separate maintenance still be successful? The answer is—maybe. The determining factor is whether the dependent spouse was "constructively abandoned." **Constructive abandonment** occurs when the dependent spouse leaves the marital home because of the acts of the supporting spouse. Such acts include those that would constitute adequate grounds for divorce or separate maintenance. This allows a spouse to seek separate maintenance when the circumstances at home are deleterious, but the supporting spouse will not leave. Many states require that an applicant for separate maintenance be a "needy" and "innocent" spouse; for example, where a husband has abandoned his wife and is not providing for her support, the wife would be an appropriate candidate for separate maintenance.

Separate maintenance is similar to divorce in that pending a final adjudication, the court may award the dependent spouse temporary support. Separate maintenance ceases upon the termination of the marriage. No action for separate maintenance may be brought after the dissolution of the marriage.

Judicial Separation

Contrast separate maintenance with a **judicial separation**, also called a limited divorce, a divorce from bed and board, or a *divorce a mensa et thoro*. (A complete divorce is called a *divorce a vinculo matrimonii*.) A judicial separation is similar to a "normal" divorce in that the court adjudicates alimony, child custody, visitation and support, and division of the parties' property. The significant difference is that a judicial separation does not completely terminate the parties' marital status, because it does not grant the parties the right to marry other parties. Additionally, the parties may still be entitled to receive certain benefits reserved for spouses, such as Social Security benefits, pension and retirement benefits, and inheritance rights.

judicial separation
A judicial separation grants all the relief available in a complete divorce except for the right to remarry.

REVIEW QUESTIONS

1. In the following circumstances, is the marriage void or voidable?

    a) At the time of the marriage, one of the spouses is still legally married to a third party.

    b) At the time of the marriage, one of the parties was under the influence of alcohol or drugs.

    c) At the time of the marriage, one of the parties was physically unable to consummate the marriage.

2. What is the difference between a void marriage and a voidable marriage?

3. What are the differences between separate maintenance and a judicial separation?

4. What are the various legal grounds for the granting of an annulment?

5. What are the elements of a valid complaint for annulment?

6. What are the defenses available to a defendant in annulment litigation? What difference, if any, does it make if the marriage is voidable as opposed to void?

7. What forms of relief are available in an annulment action?

8. What are three differences between divorce and annulment?

9. Provide three examples of how equity or equitable theories are applied in annulment cases.

10. What is the difference between separate maintenance and annulment? Divorce?

KEY TERMS

abandonment	prima facie
constructive	relation back doctrine
abandonment	separate maintenance
elements	voidable marriage
judicial separation	void marriage

STATE RESEARCH PROBLEMS

Research the laws of your state and answer the following questions:

1. What are the accepted grounds for annulment?

2. What relief is available through annulment? Specifically, may alimony be awarded pursuant to an annulment?

3. What distinction does your state make between "void" and "voidable" marriages?

4. Find a sample form for an annulment for your state. How does it differ from the example provided on pages 98–99?

5. Does your state recognize a right to separate maintenance? If so, what are the requirements for a successful action for separate maintenance?

ETHICAL PROBLEM

Assume for hypothetical purposes that your state does not permit the awarding of alimony pursuant to annulment. Your client states in the ICI that he wants to obtain an annulment rather than a divorce from his wife. When pressed for an explanation, he says that he does not want to pay alimony, and that an annulment would eliminate that concern. He further states that he has just learned that when he and his wife were married, his wife lied on the marriage license; at that time, she was actually younger than the minimum age for marriage. After reviewing all the facts of the case, it appears that a valid case can be made for annulment. It also appears that in a divorce action, the wife would qualify for an award of alimony, and that without some form of support, she would be severely disadvantaged economically. What, if any, ethical concerns are raised by this scenario?

PRACTICE EXERCISE

Using the following facts, draft a complaint for annulment, being certain to satisfy all procedural requirements for your state.

Your client, Sally Baker, tells you that her new husband, Glen, has a physical disability that prevents him from participating in sexual relations. She says that she was unaware of this disability before marrying Glen, and that Glen never informed her of it. She now wants to terminate the marriage. They do not have any children, and neither party requires any support from the other. Prepare a complaint for annulment for Sally.

Divorce—Pleadings

CHAPTER OBJECTIVES

In this chapter, you will learn:

- *How subject matter jurisdiction, personal jurisdiction, and venue determine the appropriate court in which to file an action for divorce*

- *The grounds and defenses available in an action for divorce*

- *How to draft a complaint for divorce*

- *How to draft an answer to a complaint for divorce*

- *The nature of an uncontested divorce*

- *The requirements for a valid separation agreement*

Litigation is conducted through a series of pleadings, in which the parties detail their various claims and defenses. The first consideration in litigation is where the action should be filed. This involves questions of subject matter jurisdiction (the type of court where the action can be filed), personal jurisdiction (the individual states that have authority over the defendant), and venue (the specific county or district where the action is to be filed). The complaint for divorce must allege that the necessary jurisdictional requirements have been met, state the grounds for the divorce (or that the divorce is being sought as a "no-fault" divorce), and include a demand for the specific relief desired. The complaint and summons must then be served upon the defendant, who can then file an answer (containing any defenses to the complaint) and a counterclaim (for any affirmative relief desired by the defendant). Motions can be filed seeking to immediately dismiss pleadings that contain technical defects. A separation agreement can be prepared and filed as soon as the parties can agree to the resolution of all issues raised by the divorce.

JURISDICTION AND VENUE

"Everyone" knows that if a person wants to terminate a marriage, he or she can file papers with a court and ask for a divorce. Everyone does not know, however, *where* to file for the divorce. How many courthouses are there in your city, county, or district? Chances are, there are more than one, and that means a decision has to be made. This decision concerns the topics of subject matter jurisdiction, personal jurisdiction, and venue.

Subject Matter Jurisdiction

subject matter jurisdiction
A court's authority to hear a particular case or type of claim.

Subject matter jurisdiction is the authority of a court to hear and decide a particular subject matter or type of case. For example, many localities have a court specifically designated as a family or divorce court; usually, such a court has the authority to grant a divorce. In other jurisdictions, divorces are granted by a **court of general jurisdiction**—a court having the authority to hear and determine a wide range of cases (i.e., Superior Court, District Court, Court of Common Pleas, etc.). By the same token, a United States Bankruptcy Court obviously does not have subject matter jurisdiction to preside over a divorce case. Nor do federal trial courts have the subject matter jurisdiction to hear and decide divorce cases. Divorce is one of the few areas of the law (ownership of real estate is another) in which state trial courts have exclusive subject matter jurisdiction. This actually makes the question of "where do I file this case?" much easier because the answer must be a state court.

court of general jurisdiction
A court having jurisdiction over a wide range of claims.

A vital question in determining whether a court within a particular state has subject matter jurisdiction to hear a divorce is the **residency** requirement of that state. Every state requires a person filing for a divorce be a resident of that state for at least some minimum period of time prior to the filing of the divorce action. For example, in a divorce action filed in California, the plaintiff must have been a resident of California for at least 6 months. In Nevada, it is necessary to be a resident for only 6 weeks before filing a petition for divorce. (Now you know one of the reasons why some people talk about going to Nevada for a "quickie" divorce.)

residency
As it relates to family law, the requirement that a plaintiff seeking a divorce live in the state in which the divorce is filed for a defined minimum period of time.

Personal Jurisdiction

personal jurisdiction
A court's authority to enforce its rulings on a particular person.

Personal jurisdiction is the authority of a court to enforce its rulings and decisions against a particular person. The general rule is that each state has the authority to enforce the rulings and decisions of its courts on those persons then present in that state. For example, if you are currently in North Carolina, either because that is the place of your permanent residence or because you happen to be driving through North Carolina on your way to Virginia, you are subject to the authority of the courts of the state of North Carolina. (If you don't believe this, next time you are in North Carolina, try driving 80 miles per hour.)

What is the flaw with such a rule? Suppose Clark is sued by Lois in Texas for divorce or breach of contract (or for any cause of action) and Clark then moves to Arizona to avoid the jurisdiction of the Texas courts. What can Lois do? As noted, the general rule requires the plaintiff to go to the state of the defendant's residence to file suit, as opposed to forcing the defendant to appear in the state of the plaintiff's residence.

The exception to this rule permits a plaintiff to obtain personal jurisdiction over a nonresident defendant if that defendant has had "sufficient minimum contacts" with the nonresident state so that the exercise of personal jurisdiction by that state is fair and equitable. (The concept of sufficient minimum contacts was introduced in a series of U.S. Supreme Court cases.) This legal theory has been codified by the states in the laws commonly referred to as long-arm statutes.

Long-Arm Statutes

Long-arm statutes are laws that grant a state personal jurisdiction over those persons not currently present in that state based on that person's prior sufficient minimum contacts with the state. Each state has its own long-arm statute, and the specific grounds for obtaining personal jurisdiction over a nonresident can differ among the states.

Generally, a long-arm statute grants a court personal jurisdiction over a nonresident when the claim being litigated relates to some act or transaction by the nonresident within the state. Specifically, many long-arm statutes provide a court with personal jurisdiction over a nonresident when, with respect to actions of termination of a marriage and legal separation, a nonresident had previously maintained a residence in the state. Some states require that the nonresident has maintained a *marital residence* (a residence wherein spouses cohabitate as husband and wife) within the state, while others merely require that the nonresident lived within the state at one time. This has obvious implications for a family law practice.

Remember the general rule—a plaintiff must file suit against a defendant in the state in which the defendant resides. But what about a party whose spouse has fled the state? Is it fair to force that party to follow the fleeing spouse to another state so relief can be sought? This inequity is the rationale for the application of the long-arm statute to divorce cases.

Thus, to continue the example of Clark and Lois, if Clark and Lois lived together in Texas before Clark's departure for Arizona, Lois could still sue Clark for divorce in Texas. His prior residency in Texas would be a sufficient minimum contact with Texas, thus permitting Texas to retain personal jurisdiction over him. Of course, Lois could also go to Arizona and (after residing there for the required period of time) file for divorce against Clark. But could Clark file for divorce against Lois in Arizona? The answer is no, a complete divorce may not be had unless Lois had some sufficient minimum contact with Arizona.

(NOTE—*This discussion of personal jurisdiction, and of venue below, relates only to the issue of divorce. There are other considerations when the issue is personal jurisdiction or venue for child custody (Chapter 10) or adoption of a minor child (Chapter 16).)*

long-arm statute
A state law which gives that state personal jurisdiction over a nonresident of that state.

Divisible Divorce

divisible divorce

A court proceeding that terminates the parties' marriage, but does not adjudicate all of the other issues related to a divorce, i.e., child custody, alimony, etc.

Now consider the **divisible divorce,** in which the marriage is terminated but without an adjudication of the other issues typically decided in a divorce, such as alimony, child custody and visitation, etc. For example, assume a woman in California wants to obtain a divorce from her husband, who now lives in the Philippines. If the husband never lived in California, how can the woman get the relief she seeks? At this point, you may ask, "How can the court gain personal jurisdiction over the defendant/husband if he never resided in California?" The answer is that while the courts of California may not have personal jurisdiction over the defendant, it can have *in rem* jurisdiction over the divorce itself.

In Rem Jurisdiction

in rem jurisdiction

A court's jurisdiction over a thing.

res

Latin for a "thing."

In rem **jurisdiction** is the authority a court has over a thing, as opposed to jurisdiction over a person. For example, a court in New York will always have the authority to determine who owns land in New York, even if the parties do not reside in New York. Similarly, the law recognizes a marriage as a "thing"; a *res* (pronounced "race") to use the legal term. Since a marriage is a *res* possessed by each of the spouses, a marriage exists in whatever state(s) either of the spouses reside in. Therefore, in our example, the state of California has *in rem* jurisdiction over the plaintiff's marriage.

in personam jurisdiction

A court's jurisdiction over a person.

In rem jurisdiction grants the court authority to determine only whether the marriage should be terminated. All other issues—child custody and support, alimony, division of marital property, etc.—require personal jurisdiction over the defendant (*in personam* **jurisdiction**) and therefore are left unresolved for now. The woman in our example can terminate the marriage, but she cannot obtain any other relief without going to a state that has personal jurisdiction over the defendant. Some states, however, do not permit divisible divorce because it permits a couple to obtain a divorce without confronting the issues of alimony, child support, and custody.

Venue

venue

The particular county or district in which litigation is to be filed.

Once it has been determined that the courts of a particular state (or states) have both proper subject matter jurisdiction and personal jurisdiction, it still remains to be determined where within that state (or states) the lawsuit can be filed. **Venue** is the particular geographic location in which a lawsuit can be filed.

(NOTE—*For the purposes of this text, we use the term county to denote such a geographic unit; however, in many jurisdictions the terms district, parish, borough, etc. are the equivalent of county.*)

The general rule requires a plaintiff to file suit against the defendant in the county in which the defendant resides. For example, suppose both parties live in the same state, but the husband currently resides in Smith County and the wife currently resides in Jones County. If the husband wishes to initiate divorce proceedings against his wife, he must do so in Jones County. If the defendant is a nonresident of the state (and if both subject matter and personal jurisdictional requirements are satisfied), the general rule is to file the lawsuit in the county where the plaintiff resides.

GROUNDS FOR DIVORCE

At common law, a marriage could be dissolved only if sufficient grounds (reasons) could be established. Today, all fifty states have adopted some version of "no-fault" divorces. The historical requirement for a fault-based divorce lies with the state's traditional interest in preserving marriages whenever possible.

Common Grounds

Each state has its own specific grounds for divorce. Following are the most common grounds for divorce (note how some of them might also provide grounds for annulment):

— Adultery

— Habitual drunkenness and/or drug addiction

— Insanity of a spouse

— Criminal conviction of a spouse

— Duress

— Underage spouse

— Fraud

— Spouse has a sexually transmitted disease

— Nonsupport

— Impotence

— Desertion or abandonment—This ground requires more than the mere absence of a spouse. It requires the voluntary, intentional, and permanent absence of a spouse for a specified period of time (i.e., one year). Constructive desertion or abandonment requires that the conduct of one spouse actually force the other spouse to leave the marital home. Thus the spouse who leaves has a defense to the claim that they deserted the marital home and a claim of constructive desertion that they can use as their own ground for divorce. For example, when the husband physically or emotionally abuses the wife, causing the wife to flee the marital residence, she could claim that the husband has committed constructive desertion.

— Cruelty—This ground can take the form of mental cruelty, physical cruelty, or some combination of the two. In recent years, society (and accordingly, the courts) has taken claims of cruelty and violence between spouses more seriously. (See Chapter 7 for a discussion of family violence.) To support a claim of cruelty, it is generally necessary to show (a) the specific acts of the other spouse, (b) that these acts were intentionally performed, and (c) that these acts had a deleterious effect on the party seeking the divorce.

No-Fault Divorce

Various states use different standards for a no-fault divorce. Some states require the plaintiff to allege that the marriage between the parties is "irretrievably broken" and that there is no hope of reconciliation. Other states require that the parties have "irreconcilable differences." Both standards essentially require a showing that the marriage between the parties is beyond repair, and that at least one spouse wants to terminate the marriage. Some states require the parties to live separate and apart from each other for a specified period of time. Note that "separate and apart" does not necessarily mean in different locations. In economically disadvantaged families, divorcing spouses occasionally remain under the same roof because neither spouse can afford to live separately. As long as the parties do not engage in normal marital relations during the period of "separation," such an arrangement may satisfy the requirement for living separate and apart. Other jurisdictions, on the other hand, require the parties to actually live in two different locations.

DRAFTING THE COMPLAINT FOR DIVORCE

complaint
A claim for relief filed by a plaintiff to state a claim against the defendant.

Litigation begins with the filing of a **complaint** with a court having proper subject matter jurisdiction, personal jurisdiction over the defendant, and venue. (Some states call this pleading a petition; regardless of the name attached to it, the theory remains the same.) The complaint is a "pleading." A pleading is a document filed with the court that sets out a party's claims or defenses. It generally does not detail the reasons or justifications for the claims or defenses.

A property pled complaint contains the following elements:

1. A caption, setting forth the name of the parties, the name of the court in which the complaint was filed, the file number assigned to the case by the court, and a designation as to the type of pleading (i.e., Complaint for Divorce)

2. A brief statement setting forth the court's authority to hear that particular case (This means that subject matter jurisdiction, personal jurisdiction, and venue must be properly pled.)

3. A brief statement of the elements of the cause of action of divorce, including the vital statistics of the plaintiff's marriage, allegations

supporting the prayers for relief sought by the plaintiff, and the plaintiff's grounds for divorce (or that a no-fault divorce is sought)

4. A prayer for relief (also called a wherefore clause) in which the plaintiff asks for the specific relief desired

When a complaint for divorce is properly pled and alleges each element or requirement of the cause of action of divorce, it sets forth a *prima facie* case for divorce. A *prima facie* case is a case that would permit a plaintiff to recover the relief sought in the complaint unless the defendant later presents evidence that contradicts or overcomes the plaintiff's evidence.

Every cause of action, or claim for relief, has particular requirements that must be satisfied if relief is to be granted. These requirements are often referred to as the elements of the cause of action. Here are the elements of divorce:

— The parties are currently married to each other.

— The plaintiff has resided in that state for at least the statutory minimum period of time.

— The parties are living separately and apart from each other and have done so for at least the minimum period of time prescribed by state law.

— The marriage between the parties should be terminated because of some action by the defendant (if divorce is fault-based), or the marriage is irretrievably broken and there is no hope of reconciliation (if divorce is no-fault).

— Whether plaintiff is entitled to receive alimony, custody of any minor children, child support, child visitation, marital property or other relief.

Note how these requirements are presented in the sample complaint for divorce at Exhibit 6–1.

(NOTE—The Student is advised that all forms appearing in this text are samples. They are not intended to represent the specific requirements of any particular state.)

Certain jurisdictions may have standardized form complaints for divorce that are to be used for divorce actions. In those jurisdictions, the paralegal drafts the complaint by selecting the appropriate relevant paragraphs from the standard forms and revises them to reflect the specific facts of that case.

In addition to the complaint for divorce, the plaintiff's law firm must typically prepare and file several other documents, including a Verification, as was used with the complaint for annulment, and an Affidavit Under the Uniform Child Custody Jurisdiction Act, in which the plaintiff (and defendant if an uncontested divorce) states under oath the whereabouts of the minor children for at least the past 5 years prior to the filing of the complaint for divorce and whether any party other than the spouses has any claim to cus-

EXHIBIT 6–1   COMPLAINT FOR DIVORCE

Caption indicating names of parties, name of court where action was filed, the civil action file number, and the nature of the pleading.

IN THE _____ COURT OF _____ COUNTY
STATE OF _____

JEANNE CLAIRE MORRISON,

Plaintiff,

v.   CIVIL ACTION NO. _____

THOMAS JAMES MORRISON,

Defendant.

Introductory paragraph.

Complaint For Divorce

COMES NOW Plaintiff and for her Complaint shows the Court as follows:

Allegation as to residency requirement.

1.

Plaintiff is now and has been for more than _____ months prior to the filing of this Complaint a resident of the State of _____ .

Allegation as to personal jurisdiction.

2.

Defendant has acknowledged service of this Complaint and jurisdiction of this Court, as evidenced by Exhibit A, attached hereto and made a part thereof.

OR

Defendant resides at 10 Beverly Lane, Hicksville, County of _____, State of_____ , and may be served with Summons and this Complaint. Defendant is subject to the jurisdiction of this Court.

Allegation as to venue.

3.

Venue properly lies with this Court.

Allegation as to the existence of the parties' marriage.

4.

Plaintiff and Defendant were married on June 6, 1978, in Chattanooga, Tennessee.

Allegation as to separation of the parties.

5.

The parties separated on or about November 15, 19___, and since that date have continuously lived in a bona fide state of separation.

Allegation as to the grounds for divorce, a necessary element of the cause of action for divorce.

6.

Plaintiff is entitled to and desires a total divorce from Defendant on the grounds that the marriage between the parties is irretrievably broken and there is no hope of reconciliation.

OR

Plaintiff is entitled to and desires a total divorce from Defendant on the grounds of mental cruelty (or abandonment, adultery, etc.).

Allegation as to the existence of any minor children, and if any,

7.

No children were born as issue of the parties' marriage.

OR

One child was born an issue of this marriage and Plaintiff seeks permanent custody of Tiffany Crystal Morrison, born on July 4, 1982. Plaintiff is not pregnant at this time.

allegation as to plaintiff's right to custody.

8.

Plaintiff desires and is entitled to have temporary and permanent custody of the parties' minor child.

9.

Plaintiff desires and is entitled to receive from Defendant an amount no less than the sum of $ _____ per month (or week) as temporary and permanent child support.

Allegation as to plaintiff's right to receive temporary (interlocutory) and permanent child support.

10.

Plaintiff desires and is entitled to receive from Defendant an amount no less than the sum of $ _____ per month (or week) as temporary and permanent alimony.

Allegation as to plaintiff's right to receive temporary (interlocutory) and permanent alimony.

11.

Plaintiff desires and is entitled to receive an equitable distribution of the marital property of the parties.

Allegation as to plaintiff's right to receive a share of the parties' marital property (depending on state's rules of property distribution).

OR

Plaintiff desires and is entitled to receive one half of all marital property of the parties.

WHEREFORE, Plaintiff respectly prays that:

Demand for relief (wherefore clause)—Demand for complete divorce, issuance of summons, and all relief to which plaintiff alleged entitlement.

(a) She be granted a total divorce, that is a divorce a vinculo matrimonii, from Defendant;

(b) Summons and process issue as required by law;

(c) She receive temporary and permanent custody of the parties' minor child;

(d) She receive temporary and permanent child support in an amount no less than $ _____ per month (or week);

(e) She receive temporary and permanent alimony in an amount no less than $ _____ per month (or week);

(f) She receive an equitable distribution of the marital property of the parties; OR, She receive one half of all marital property of the parties;

(g) She receives a trial by jury; and,

(h) She have such other and further relief as the Court may deem just and proper.

Respectfully Submittted,

Signature of plaintiff's attorney(s)

_____

MATTHEW S. CORNICK
Attorney for Plaintiff
State Bar No. 123456
Address, City, State
Telephone number

tody of the minor children of the marriage. The Uniform Child Custody Jurisdiction Act is discussed in Chapter 10. An example of the affidavit follows as Exhibit 6–2.

EXHIBIT 6–2   AFFIDAVIT UNDER UNIFORM CHILD CUSTODY JURISDICTION ACT

IN THE ———— COURT OF———— COUNTY
STATE OF ————

JEANNE CLAIRE MORRISON,

Plaintiff,

v.   CIVIL ACTION NO.   ————————

THOMAS JAMES MORRISON,

Defendant.

<u>Affidavit Under Uniform Child
Custody Jurisdiction Act</u>

STATE OF ————————

COUNTY OF ————————

JEANNE CLAIRE MORRISON, Plaintiff herein, being duly sworn, respectfully represents to the Court:

1. Plaintiff's minor child, TIFFANY CRYSTAL MORRISON:

A. Lives at 433 Jerold Street, Plainview, ———————— .

B. Lives with Plaintiff

C. During the last five (5) years has lived at the following places with the custodian indicated:

Residence	**Custodian**
433 Jerold Street, Plainview,————————	Both Parents July 1982–November 19——
433 Jerold Street, Plainview,————————	Mother November 19——–present

2. Plaintiff has not participated in any capacity in other litigation concerning the custody of said minor child in this or any other state.

3. Plaintiff has no information of a custody proceeding concerning said minor child in this or any other state.

4. Plaintiff does not know of any person, not a party to these proceedings, who has physical custody of said minor child or who claims custody or visitation rights with the child.

————————————————————
JEANNE CLAIRE MORRISON

Notary Seal

FOCUS ON ETHICS
The Duty to Investigate

While the rules of ethics impose the obligation upon an attorney to represent a client zealously within the bounds of the law, that zeal must be tempered by other considerations. Obviously, the attorney cannot engage in any fraudulent or dishonest conduct on behalf of a client. But the obligation extends far beyond this minimum standard of conduct.

Attorneys are prohibited from filing any civil action or asserting any defense to a civil action that cannot be supported by existing law or by a good-faith argument for the extension, modification, or reversal of existing law. Accordingly, claims and defenses that are frivolous or designed merely to delay or harass the adverse party are prohibited. This ethical duty has been codified by Rule 11 of the Federal Rules of Civil Procedure (FRCP) and by similar, if not identical, rules for the individual state courts. By virtue of these rules, an attorney's signature on a pleading, motion, discovery request, etc., certifies that the attorney has determined that the relief sought by the document is justified under the law. Thus, an attorney should not accept a client's version of the facts without conducting an independent investigation to ascertain whether a claim (or defense) can properly be filed on behalf of that client. The failure to abide by these rules may result in the adverse party making a claim for the tort of abusive litigation, and in the judge issuing sanctions against *both* the client making the frivolous claim *and* his attorney.

This rule has important ramifications for paralegals, because in many offices paralegals have primary responsibility for conducting the factual investigation of the client's claim or defense. And while paralegals cannot be sanctioned for their actions, they may be sued for legal malpractice—and they almost certainly would be terminated from their employment. Therefore, a cautious paralegal seeks independent verification of all relevant "facts" presented by their clients before relying on those facts in a pleading or motion. For example, all claims of expenses and income by a client should be corroborated by appropriate documentation. This documentation is going to be necessary should the client ever appear before a court. If the documentation does not exist, it is better to learn that earlier, rather than later.

Most divorce complaints are very similar to other divorce complaints. You do not have to reinvent the wheel. Find a reliable form book for your jurisdiction, and take a divorce complaint from an old (and hopefully successful) file. Use those samples as guides for the complaints you are asked to draft. On the other hand, do not blindly copy allegations from a sample complaint. Make sure that they are applicable in your case.

PRACTICE
POINTER

SERVICE OF PROCESS

To obtain personal jurisdiction over the defendant and compel him to respond to the plaintiff's complaint for divorce, the complaint must first be properly delivered, or "served," upon the defendant. The bundle of papers containing the complaint and **summons** (the formal notification of pending litigation issued by the court) is called the process; accordingly, this procedure is called **service of process.** Questions to be considered here are a) how does the court issue a summons, b) how can the service of process be effected, and c) who may serve process upon the defendant.

summons
Official notification from a court to a defendant that a complaint has been filed against him/her.

service of process
Delivery of the summons and complaint upon a defendant.

The Summons

A summons officially informs the defendant that litigation has been commenced against him. It details the name of the plaintiff, the name of the court in which the litigation is pending, the civil action number of the litigation (the file number used by the court to keep track of litigation), the name of the plaintiff's attorney, and the period of time the defendant has to file an answer to the complaint. A summons is issued by a court after it has been completed by the attorney or paralegal for the plaintiff. Failure to properly prepare a summons can lead to the dismissal of the action. See "Motion Practice" later in this chapter. A sample summons is presented at Exhibit 6–3.

EXHIBIT 6-3   SAMPLE SUMMONS

IN THE SUPERIOR COURT OF ——————— COUNTY
STATE OF ———————

_____

_____

_____
                    Plaintiff

VS   CIVIL ACTION NO. ———————————

_____

_____

_____
                    Defendant

                    Summons

TO THE ABOVE NAMED DEFENDANT:

You are hereby summoned and required to file with the Clerk of said court and serve upon the Plaintiff's attorney, whose name and address is:

an answer to the complaint which is herewith served upon you, within 30 days after service of this summons upon you, exclusive of the day of service. If you fail to do so, judgment by default will be taken against you for the relief demanded in the complaint.

This _____ day of _____, 19_____.

Clerk of Superior Court

By _____
            DEPUTY CLERK
Notary Seal

The Service

Generally, unless special circumstances dictate otherwise, statutes require that a complaint for divorce (or any other cause of action, for that matter) be served personally upon the defendant. A defendant can be served personally at home, at work, in the supermarket—anywhere. Effective service of process is proven by the filing of a *return of service,* a sworn statement by the party delivering the process to the defendant, that she served the defendant at a particular time and at a particular place.

If service of process is not effected, the return of service will so state. A defendant cannot attempt to escape proper service of process by refusing to accept the papers. As long as the process server properly notifies the defendant of the nature of the papers, the service is properly effected, even if the defendant lets the papers fall to the ground and runs away.

The Process Server

The process is typically served by either a *process server* or by a sheriff, marshal, or other constable of the county. A process server is a person, hired by the plaintiff, to deliver the complaint and summons upon the defendant. Some states require court permission to use either a process server or a sheriff; some permit either without any court permission required. The plaintiff himself cannot serve process in his own case. Similarly, it is not recommended that anyone from the plaintiff's law firm participate in the service of process for their own cases. The reasoning here is that if the defendant later questions the validity of the service, the representative of the plaintiff's law firm would be placed in the uncomfortable, and ethically tenuous, position of being both an advocate and a witness for the plaintiff.

Under certain circumstances, it is possible to serve a defendant by *publishing* the summons in a publication authorized to publish legal notices. Such circumstances may include when the defendant spouse resides outside the United States; when the defendant resides in a different state from the plaintiff; and when the plaintiff does not know where the defendant can be located for service of process. Since the defendant in such cases cannot be personally served, the law permits the defendant to be "served" by publishing the summons in a newspaper authorized to print such notices. You have probably seen these notices in a newspaper in your locality. Service by publication generally gives the court only *in rem* jurisdiction.

The Paralegal's Role

One of the most important tasks for a paralegal is to calendar litigation—that is, to determine and keep track of the deadlines for performance of all required action. Once the complaint is properly served, the defendant has a specific period of time within which to respond, for example 30 days. The time to respond does not include the day in which the document requiring a response was served. If the last day of the period falls on a Saturday, Sunday, a legal holiday, or is a day when the courthouse is closed for other reasons

NOBLE

v.

NOBLE

Supreme Court of Mississippi.
Feb. 4, 1987.

. . . .

PRATHER, Justice, for the Court:

. . . .

I.

Dorothy J. Noble and Eli W. Noble were married June 5, 1956, in Ellisville, Mississippi and from that union two children were born. The husband/appellee was permanent military personnel in the United States Armed Forces and claimed Mississippi as his residence at all times pertinent here until his retirement from the military on May 15, 1984. The parties separated in Frankfurt, Germany on January 10, 1982, when the appellant returned to Jones County, Mississippi. After retirement, appellee resided in Columbia, South Carolina, where he still resides.

Dorothy Noble filed for a divorce, attorneys' fees, alimony, and other relief on October 22, 1985, and summons upon the defendant was issued by non-resident publication in the newspaper. Copy of the publication notice was mailed, first class, to defendant at his post office address in Columbia, South Carolina. The defendant did not answer the complaint or make any other response. On January 31, 1986, the chancery court granted Dorothy Noble a divorce, but retained jurisdiction to award permanent alimony, attorney's fees and other relief. . . .

Thereafter, on February 7, 1986 appellant filed a motion to alter the final decree regarding the monetary items on the ground that the court erred in ruling that it had no jurisdiction to render a personal judgment. From a denial of the motion this appeal was pursued.

II.

The issue presented here is whether summons issued under Mississippi Rule of Civil Procedure 4(c)(4)(C) is sufficient to confer personnel jurisdiction over a non-resident defendant for purposes of rendering a monetary judgment against such defendant.

. . . .

For purposes of this opinion, Rule 4(c)(4)(A) and Rule 4(c)(4)(C) were the sections followed for summons upon Eli Noble as a non-resident defendant as follows:

(4) By Publication

(A) If the defendant in any proceeding in a chancery court, or in any proceeding in any other court where process by publication is authorized, by statute, be shown by sworn complaint or sworn petition, or by a filed affidavit, to be a non-resident of this state or not to be found therein on diligent inquiry and the post office address of such defendant be stated in the complaint, petition, or affidavit, or if it be stated in such sworn complaint or petition that the post office address of the defendant is not known to the plaintiff or petitioner after diligent inquiry, or if the affidavit be made by another for the plaintiff or petitioner, that such post office address is unknown to the affiant after diligent inquiry and he believes it is unknown to the plaintiff or petitioner after diligent inquiry by the plaintiff or petitioner, the clerk, upon filing the complaint or petition, account, or other commencement of a proceeding, shall promptly prepare and publish a summons to the defendant to appear and

. . . .

(C) It shall be the duty of the clerk to hand the summons to the plaintiff or petitioner to be published, or, at his request, and at his expense, to hand it to the publisher of the proper newspaper for publication. Where the post office address of the absent defendant is stated, it shall be the duty of the clerk to send by mail (first class mail, postage prepaid) to the address of the defendant, at his post office, a copy of the summons and complaint and to note the fact of issuing the same and mailing the copy, on the general docket, and this shall be the evidence of the summons having been mailed to the defendant.

. . . .

There is an additional section in Rule 4(c)(5) providing for an alternate method of service on non-residents as follows:

(5) Alternate Service on Person Outside State. In addition to service by any other method provided by this rule, a summons may be served on a person outside this state by sending a copy of the summons and of the complaint to the person to be served by certified mail, return receipt requested. Where the defendant is a natural person, the envelope containing the summons and complaint shall be marked "restricted delivery." Service by this method shall be deemed complete as of the date of delivery as evidenced by the return receipt or by the returned envelope marked "Refused."

. . . .

In this case, the plaintiff followed Rule 4(c)(4)(A) by publication and a mailing of the publication, first class mail service, postage prepaid, to the defendant at his post office address. The question is whether the forum court in Mississippi has personal jurisdiction over the non-resident defendant in South Carolina under federal and state laws. The United States Supreme Court has set forth the federal constitutional requirements in *Kulko v. California Superior Court,* 436 U.S. 84, 91, 98 S.Ct. 1690, 1696, 56 L.Ed.2d 132, 140 (1978), in this language:

> The Due Process Clause of the Fourteenth Amendment operates as a limitation on the jurisdiction of state courts to enter judgments affecting rights or interests of nonresident defendants. (Citation omitted.) It has long been the rule that a valid judgment imposing a personal obligation or duty in favor of the plaintiff may be entered only by a court having jurisdiction over the person of the defendant. (Citations omitted.) The existence of personal jurisdiction, in turn, depends upon the presence of reasonable notice to the defendant that an action has been brought. (Citation omitted.) and a sufficient connection between the defendant and the forum State as to make it fair to require defense of the action in the forum. (Citation omitted.) In this case appellant does not dispute the adequacy of the notice that he received, but contends that his connection with the State of California is too attenuated, under the standards implicit in the Due Process Clause of the Constitution, to justify imposing upon him the burden and inconvenience of defense in California.

Applying these federal standards, as well as our state standards for summons, this Court concludes that the defendant/appellee had more than sufficient nexus with the forum state of Mississippi to satisfy the latter requirement. As to the requirement of adequate notice to the defendant, this Court concludes that, absent some proof of defendant's receipt of summons, the reasonableness of notice is questionable. It is acknowledged that the mail was not returned to the clerk, but this Court holds that at the trial court level, the adequacy of notice test is not met for rendition of a monetary judgment. There can be no "valid judgment imposing a personal obligation or duty in favor of the plaintiff" against this defendant under this process.

This summons does not confer personal jurisdiction over the defendant without answer or general appearance by the defendant. This publication method under M.R.C.P. 4(c)(4)(C) does not authorize rendition of a personal judgment against the defendant without his appearance. *Campbell v. Campbell,* 357 So.2d 129 (Miss.1978).

Had the plaintiff followed the procedure of Rule 4(c)(5) and secured service of process by certified mail, return receipt requested, restricted delivery, personal jurisdiction over the defendant to render a personal judgment would have been accomplished under the facts of this case.

It is noteworthy to add, however, that notwithstanding this Court's holding that the Chancery Court of Jones County properly held that it could not render a personal monetary judgment against the non-resident defendant on this summons, it was not totally without jurisdiction. The Chancery Court did have jurisdiction over the subject matter of the divorce action and personal jurisdiction over one of the parties to the marriage who did meet residency requirements for a divorce action. Miss. Code Ann. §93-5-5 (Supp.1986). This statutory authority and the publication notice gives the chancery court its authority to grant a divorce on constructive notice by publication.

This appeal is affirmed, but without prejudice to allow plaintiff to file new pleadings and secure proper process for a trial on issues retained by the chancery court. AFFIRMED.

DISCUSSION QUESTIONS

Consider the preceding case of *Noble v. Noble,* 502 So.2d 317 (Miss. 1987) and answer the following questions:

1. What form of jurisdiction was obtained over the defendant?

2. What form of jurisdiction was required to render a judgment as to permanent alimony, attorney's fees, and division of the husband's military retirement pay?

3. What action by the plaintiff was required to effect the proper personal jurisdiction?

4. What is the relevance of the Due Process Clause of the Fourteenth Amendment?

(i.e., inclement weather), the time period to respond is extended to the next business day the courthouse is open. For example, suppose a defendant is served with a complaint for divorce on Thursday, March 21, in a state requiring a response to a complaint within 30 days. It may help to think of March 21 as day zero, and March 22 as day one. Day thirty is Saturday, April 20, and therefore the response to the complaint must be filed with the court (actually received by the court, not just postmarked) no later than the next business day, Monday, April 22.

DRAFTING THE ANSWER TO A COMPLAINT FOR DIVORCE

answer

Filed by a defendant in response to the plaintiff's complaint.

Unless the divorce is uncontested, when a defendant is served with the summons and complaint for divorce, an answer must be prepared and filed with the court. The **answer** is a pleading setting out the defenses alleged by the defendant. As can be seen by the sample answer at Exhibit 6–4, the caption of an answer is identical to that of the complaint (see Exhibit 6–1). The body of the answer is made up of two different types of responses: (1) general defenses to the complaint as a whole, and (2) admissions or denials of the specific allegations of the plaintiff's complaint. General defenses attack the validity of the complaint and the plaintiff's entitlement to relief. General defenses can include "technical" defenses such as improper jurisdiction (subject matter or personal), improper venue, insufficient process or service of process, and/or that the complaint fails to state a claim upon which relief can be granted (failure to state a *prima facie* case).

There are also traditional defenses, which are used in fault-based divorces. The most frequently used of these traditional defenses include

— *Condonation.* If the defendant can prove that the plaintiff has forgiven the defendant for the acts complained of in the complaint, the defendant can use the defense of condonation. This forgiveness can best be demonstrated by showing that the plaintiff resumed normal marital relations with the defendant at some point after learning of the defendant's alleged misconduct, for example, where the wife resumes marital relations with her husband after learning of his infidelity.

EXHIBIT 6–4   ANSWER TO A COMPLAINT FOR DIVORCE

IN THE _____ COURT OF_____ COUNTY
STATE OF _____

JEANNE CLAIRE MORRISON,

Plaintiff,

v.   CIVIL ACTION NO._____

THOMAS JAMES MORRISON,

Defendant.

The caption of the answer is same as that of the complaint, with the obvious exception of the designation ("Answer" vs. "Complaint"). There is an introductory paragraph, as in the complaint.

<u>Answer</u>

COME NOW, THOMAS JAMES MORRISON, Defendant in the above-styled action, and files his Answer to the Plaintiff's Complaint for Divorce as follows:

<u>First Defense</u>

Plaintiff's Complaint fails to state a claim upon which relief can be granted.

First Defense—Used when the defendant claims that the plaintiff has failed to allege a prima facie case. Can also be used in a motion to dismiss.

<u>Second Defense</u>

Plaintiff's Complaint should be barred because the Court lacks personal jurisdiction over the Defendant.

<u>Third Defense</u>

Defendant now responds to the individual allegations of Plaintiff's Complaint as follows:

1.

Defendant admits the allegations of Paragraph 1 of the Plaintiff's Complaint.

2.

Defendant admits the allegations of Paragraph 2 of the Plaintiff's Complaint.

3.

Defendant admits the allegations of Paragraph 3 of the Plaintiff's Complaint.

4.

Defendant admits the allegations of Paragraph 4 of the Plaintiff's Complaint.

5.

Defendant admits that the parties currently live in a bona fide state of separation, but denies that the date of separation is as alleged by Plaintiff. Defendant denies all other allegations contained in Paragraph 5 of the Plaintiff's Complaint.

Third Defense— Defendant now admits, denies, or states that he is without sufficient information to admit or deny. The answer should track the complaint so that, for example, Paragraph 1 of the answer refers to Paragraph 1 of the complaint. Failure to do so increases the risk that an allegation of the complaint will be omitted and therefore inadvertently admitted.

6.

Defendant denies the allegations of Paragraph 6 of the Plaintiff's Complaint.

7.

Defendant admits the allegations of Paragraph 7 of the Plaintiff's Complaint.

8.

Defendant denies the allegations of Paragraph 8 of the Plaintiff's Complaint.

9.

Defendant denies the allegations of Paragraph 9 of the Plaintiff's Complaint.

10.

Defendant denies the allegations of Paragraph 10 of the Plaintiff's Complaint.

11.

Defendant admits the allegations of paragraph 11 of the Plaintiff's Complaint; however, Defendant reserves the right to deny that certain property is to be considered "marital property."

Demand for relief. (wherefore clause)— Usually much shorter than a complaint's wherefore clause, although if the defendant had filed a counterclaim (see below), the specific demands for relief would be listed here.

WHEREFORE, Defendant respecfully requests that:

a) Plaintiff's claims for relief be denied in their entirety; and,

b) Defendant receive all other such relief deemed proper and appropriate by this Court.

NOTE—*Insert any counterclaim here, if affirmative relief is desired by defendant.*

Respectfully Submitted,

PETER A. BAIR
Attorney for Defendant
No. 789789
Address, City, State
Telephone number

Certificate of service— Attached to the answer (and to all subsequent pleadings, motions, briefs, discovery requests and responses, etc.) is a certificate of service. This is signed by the attorney charged with the responsibility of serving the document upon the other parties. The date that appears on the certificate is the date of service of that document. This is important in instances where the adverse party has to respond to a document served upon him or her.

Certificate of Service

This is to certify that I have this day served a copy of the foregoing Answer upon counsel for the Plaintiff, by U.S. Mail, first class, with sufficient postage affixed thereto, to:

MATTHEW S. CORNICK, Esq.
100 Peach Street
Suite 750
City, State 12345

This _____ day of _____ , 199____.

PETER A. BAIR, Esq.

— *Provocation.* If the defendant can prove that the plaintiff provoked the wrongs alleged in the complaint, the defendant can use the defense of provocation. For example, where the wife's abusive behavior forces the husband to leave the marital residence, the husband can claim that his "abandoment" of his wife was really the result of the wife's provocation (constructive abandonment).

— *Connivance.* If the defendant can prove that the plaintiff consented to, and possibly created the opportunity to commit the wrongful act complained of, the plaintiff may be denied the relief sought. For example, where one spouse files for divorce claiming infidelity even though the parties had agreed to have an "open marriage," and allow each other to engage in sexual relationships with third parties.

— *Collusion.* Collusion is not so much a defense to divorce as it is a legal bar to a complaint for divorce. Collusion is an express agreement between the parties in which the defendant does not deny the plaintiff's allegations of marital misconduct so they might obtain a mutually desired divorce. No-fault divorce laws have largely vitiated the need for collusion. But, where a fault-based divorce is sought, the court can refuse to grant the divorce if there is a finding of collusion between the parties. For example, where the wife claims that she was the victim of the husband's cruel treatment, and the husband does not deny these allegations even though no such cruelty ever occurred.

In addition to alleging the appropriate general defenses, the defendant must also respond to each and every individual allegation contained in the plaintiff's complaint. In responding to the allegations of the complaint, the defendant must either admit them, deny them, or state that he lacks the information to admit or deny the particular allegation—in other words, he can say, "I don't know." (For example, this can be stated as "The Defendant lacks the personal knowledge and information necessary to form a belief as to the truth of the matters asserted in Paragraph 4 of Plaintiff's Complaint.") If the defendant fails to respond (admit, deny, or "I don't know") to an allegation of the complaint, that allegation is automatically deemed to have been admitted. Therefore, it is essential that the paralegal drafting the answer be exceedingly careful not to overlook any allegation of the complaint.

Note how the defendant specifically admits the portion of Paragraph 5 of the Complaint that is true and denies all the remaining allegations of Paragraph 5. By responding in this fashion, a defendant admits only those facts that he specifically enumerates and denies all other allegations in a single stroke.

PRACTICE
POINTER

COUNTERCLAIMS

When a marriage disintegrates, both husband and wife may desire custody of minor children or possession of the marital residence. But only one party can

plaintiff

The party who initiates the litigation by filing a complaint against the defendant.

defendant

The party defending against the plaintiff's claim.

counterclaim

A claim for relief filed by a defendant to state a claim against the plaintiff.

be the **plaintiff.** That privilege belongs to the party who files for relief first. Once the complaint for divorce has been filed, the named **defendant** cannot then file an independent action for divorce. If the defendant wishes to make a claim for affirmative relief (rather than merely denying the plaintiff's claims for relief), he or she must file a counterclaim. A **counterclaim** (also called a cross bill, a cross complaint, or a cross petition) is a claim for relief made by the defendant against the plaintiff.

A counterclaim made by a defendant in a divorce action is a *compulsory* counterclaim, in that the counterclaim arises from the same cause of action (termination of the marriage) as the original complaint. The effect of the compulsory nature of the counterclaim is that if the counterclaim is not properly pled before the end of the litigation, it may not be filed in any subsequent litigation. This derives from the legal theory of *res judicata,* which literally means "the thing has been decided." *Res judicata* prevents the litigation of any claim that has already been litigated—or any related claim that should have been litigated. A complaint has no natural superiority over a counterclaim; the only difference between the two is that the plaintiff got to the courthouse first with his or her complaint.

A counterclaim, like the complaint and answer, is a pleading. Drafting a counterclaim is virtually identical to drafting a complaint—which should make sense, because they serve virtually identical purposes. A counterclaim can be filed and served either contemporaneously with the defendant's answer or separately. Pay attention to any time restrictions your state has concerning how soon a counterclaim must be filed. A counterclaim is filed with the court and served upon the plaintiff by delivering a copy, either by hand delivery or regular mail, to the attorney for the plaintiff. Formal service of process is not necessary because the plaintiff is already aware of the pending litigation.

The plaintiff then must respond to the defendant's counterclaim, just as the defendant had to respond to the plaintiff's complaint (note that the responsive pleading to a counterclaim is often referred to as a reply instead of an answer). The plaintiff will have the same amount of time to respond to the counterclaim as the defendant had to respond to the complaint. However, the defendant is served with the complaint only when it is actually delivered in accordance with the rules for service of process, while the plaintiff is served with the counterclaim when it is either hand-delivered or placed in the mail. (The date of service is the date appearing on the certificate of service.)

Thus the time for responding to the counterclaim may begin before the plaintiff is even aware of its existence. To be fair, the plaintiff receives an additional 3 days to respond to the counterclaim, if served by mail. For example, a counterclaim served by mail must be responded to within 33 days instead of 30. This requirement is not restricted to counterclaims, but rather applies to any deadline imposed by a document served by mail. And if the thirty-third day falls on a Saturday, Sunday, holiday, or any other day when the courthouse is closed, the deadline is extended to the next business day when the courthouse is open. (In some jurisdictions, the plaintiff is not required to respond to a counterclaim. The law presumes that the plaintiff denies the defendant's allegations.)

JURY TRIALS

Litigation usually triggers certain definite images, including a jury of the litigant's peers acting as the final arbiters of facts. But because divorce is essentially an action in equity, unless there are statutes providing to the contrary, it is typically a function of the court, acting without a jury, to determine divorce cases. (A trial in which the judge acts as both the trier of fact and trier of law is called a "bench" trial.)

A minority of the states do permit jury trials, including—but not limited to—Colorado, Georgia, Illinois, Louisiana, New York, and Texas. Even then a jury trial may not be permissible upon every issue requiring determination (i.e., child custody). If a jury trial is available and desired, a demand for jury trial should be made in the initial pleading filed on your client's behalf (complaint for plaintiff, answer, or counterclaim for defendant), since usually the time in which such a demand can be made is limited. The demand for jury trial is usually found in the "wherefore" clause of the complaint or answer. It can also be listed in the caption of the pleading.

MOTION PRACTICE

Whereas a complaint is a request to the court for a judgment, a **motion** is a request to a court for an order. Either party can file a motion; the party filing is called the movant and the party responding to the motion is called the respondent. In the course of any litigation, each party will file and respond to a series of different motions. Now we shall examine those motions typically filed immediately after the litigation begins, including the motion to dismiss, motion to strike, and the motion for a more definite statement.

motion
A request to a court for an order.

The Brief

In many jurisdictions, motions must be filed with an accompanying brief in support of the motion. A **brief** is a written, persuasive argument in which a party attempts to demonstrate to the court that their interpretation of the law is correct, and that they should be granted the relief sought. A brief cites (makes reference to) prior cases involving the same questions and similar fact patterns in which the relief desired by the party was granted. The movant will draw analogies between the prior cases and the present case (case at bar) to convince the court that he is entitled to the relief sought.

Within a specified period of time (i.e., 30 days), the respondent must file a brief in opposition to the motion. The respondent's brief (1) attempts to distinguish between the case at bar and the cases cited by the movant, so to persuade the court that those cases are either inapplicable or that they have been misconstrued by the movant, and (2) cite cases that the respondent believes are more on point and that support his contentions. After both parties have had an opportunity to submit their briefs, the court often, though not always, conducts a hearing on the motion. At that time each attorney orally argues in favor of their client, and the judge has an opportunity to ask questions of the counsel.

brief
A written, persuasive argument.   •

Since motions usually involve only questions of law, clients usually do not even attend, much less testify at these hearings. The court may rule on the motion at this hearing, or it may "take the matter under advisement" and rule upon it at a later date. In such cases, the court notifies counsel by mailing them an order granting or denying the relief sought.

Motion to Dismiss

motion to dismiss
A motion seeking that a claim for relief be dismissed due to a technical deficiency.

A **motion to dismiss** (also called a demurrer) is filed by the defending party (the defendant in the original claim; the plaintiff in the counterclaim) when she believes that the claim for relief contains a "technical" defect so that the court would be constrained to find for the defending party. Rule 12(b) (or the equivalent) of most civil practice acts details the different grounds for a motion to dismiss. The purpose of the motion to dismiss is to alert the court to a fatal defect in the claim for relief so that the lawsuit can be terminated, thus avoiding unnecessary litigation.

These technical defenses usually must be raised by the defending party at a very early stage of the litigation (i.e., no later than the time the answer is filed). Also note that these technical defenses can be raised either in a motion to dismiss or in the defending party's answer. The difference is that a court will rule on the defense immediately if raised in a motion and at trial if raised in the answer.

Motion to Strike

motion to strike
A motion seeking to eliminate a portion of a claim for relief.

A **motion to strike** works in much the same way as the motion to dismiss, except the goal of the motion to strike is not to have the entire claim for relief dismissed. Rather, it aims to strike, or delete, a portion of the claim for relief because it is either irrelevant, redundant, scandalous, or otherwise improper. For example, when a complaint refers to the husband as a "festering couch potato," or to the wife as a "decrepit old hag," a motion to strike would be appropriate to delete the slurs.

Motion for a More Definite Statement

motion for a more definite statement
A motion seeking that additional details be added to a claim for relief.

A **motion for a more definite statement** is a motion that a defendant can make when a plaintiff has presented their claim for relief in such a vague manner that the defendant cannot reasonably fashion a response. For example, if a complaint alleges that the defendant has "committed grievous and evil misfeasance and malfeasance towards both the plaintiff and the minor children" without providing any additional details, the defendant can seek an order from the court ordering the plaintiff to prepare a more specific complaint so that the allegations can be admitted, denied, or controverted.

UNCONTESTED DIVORCE

An **uncontested divorce** is a divorce in which the parties have voluntarily agreed to all terms of the divorce, including the need for the divorce; the grounds for the divorce (usually a no-fault divorce); whether alimony is to be paid by either spouse, and if so, the amount to be paid and the time period for the payments; child custody, support and visitation; life and health insurance for the spouses and minor children; and division of all marital property and debts. An uncontested divorce is one that does not require the intervention of the court to resolve any issues raised by the parties' divorce.

The uncontested divorce is prepared in much the same way as a contested divorce, with the following notable exceptions: (1) the parties execute a separation agreement and file it with the summons, complaint, and verification; (2) the complaint requests incorporation of the separation agreement in the final judgment and decree of divorce rather than requesting specific relief, as in a contested divorce; (3) the defendant can waive formal service of process and sign an acknowledgment of service, thus satisfying the legal requirement of service of the summons and complaint upon the defendant while saving the expense, time, and potential embarrassment incumbent with formal service of process (see Exhibit 6–5); and (4) the defendant may give permission to the court to grant the divorce in his absence (see Exhibit 6–6).

Certain jurisdictions may permit both parties to waive a final hearing before issuing the final decree and judgment of divorce.

EXHIBIT 6–5 ACKNOWLEDGMENT OF SERVICE

IN THE _____ COURT OF_____ COUNTY
STATE OF _____

JEANNE CLAIRE MORRISON,

Plaintiff,

v.   CIVIL ACTION NO. _____

THOMAS JAMES MORRISON,

Defendant.

Acknowledgment of Service

Defendant, Thomas James Morrison, hereby acknowledges service of process of the Complaint and all other accompanying papers in the above-styled action and consents to same. Defendant waives all further service of process.

This ____ day of _____ , 199 _ .

_____
Thomas James Morrison

Notary Seal

EXHIBIT 6–6   CONSENT TO FINAL HEARING

IN THE _____ COURT OF_____ COUNTY
STATE OF _____

JEANNE CLAIRE MORRISON,

Plaintiff,

v.   CIVIL ACTION NO. _____

THOMAS JAMES MORRISON,

Defendant.

Consent to Final Hearing

NOW COMES JEANNE CLAIRE MORRISON, Plaintiff herein, and THOMAS JAMES MORRISON, Defendant herein, who consent to the hearing of the instant case at the earliest time allowed by law.

Notary Seal

_____
Jeanne Claire Morrison

_____
Thomas James Morrison

SEPARATION   AGREEMENTS

The essence of an uncontested divorce is the **separation agreement,** a contract between the parties wherein they set out their understanding and agreement as to all of their respective rights and obligations to each other and the minor children of the marriage. The consideration for the contract is the parties' mutual promise to perform the acts recited in the agreement. Separation agreements are not used solely in uncontested divorces. Rather, unless there is a trial on the issues (which is relatively rare), sooner or later the parties will enter into a separation agreement.

Care must be taken in accounting for all issues raised by the divorce, and in drafting the separation agreement to prevent ambiguities. Ambiguities arise when the agreement does not carefully define all the terms used in the agreement. For example, what is wrong with a provision that states, "The noncustodial parent will have visitation privileges with the minor child every other weekend." Examples of typical errors include (1) What is a "weekend": When does it start, when does it end, and what about extended holiday weekends? (2) Which parent is responsible for picking up or dropping off the child? (3) How is it determined when "every other weekend" begins?

There would be other problems if the agreement did not have other provisions for visitation during summer vacation, holidays, etc. Clearly, the potential for problems is abundant. Most of these problems can be resolved by using form separation agreements—by adapting a separation agreement from a form book or from another case file in the office involving similar facts. Remember, there is no advantage in reinventing the wheel.

Following at Exhibit 6–7 is a sample separation agreement, with many of the most frequently used clauses. As with all forms in this text, it is intended only to demonstrate how the principles of family law may be put into practice. This particular form applies to a couple who own their own home and have one minor child.

EXHIBIT 6–7 SEPARATION AGREEMENT

IN THE _____ COURT OF _____ COUNTY
STATE OF _____

JEANNE CLAIRE MORRISON,

Plaintiff,

v.   CIVIL ACTION NO. _____

THOMAS JAMES MORRISON,

Defendant.

Separation Agreement

Pursuant to the laws of this state, this agreement ("Agreement") is made and entered into by and between Jeanne Claire Morrison ("Wife") and Thomas James Morrison ("Husband") on the date indicated below.

Recitals

WHEREAS, the parties hereto have been legally married at Chattanooga, Tennessee on June 6, 1978, and one child having been born as issue of said marriage, Tiffany Crystal Morrison, born July 4, 1982,

WHEREAS, unfortunate differences have arisen between the parties making the continuation of their marital relationship impossible; and

WHEREAS, the parties desire to settle all matters between them arising out of their marriage.

NOW THEREFORE, in consideration of these facts and circumstances and of the mutual promises made in this Agreement, Husband and Wife each agree:

1. *Separation.* The parties shall live separate and apart, and each shall go his or her own way without direction, control, or molestation from the other, as if unmarried, and each shall not annoy or interfere with the other in any manner whatsoever.

2. *Alimony.* Husband shall pay no alimony to Wife, and Wife shall pay no alimony to Husband.

Agreement as to the payment of permanent

alimony; if alimony is to be paid, consideration should be given to the effect of inflation over the years the alimony is paid.

OR

Husband shall pay alimony to Wife in the amount of Five Hundred Dollars ($500.00) per month, with all payments due no later than the fifth day of the month. The amount of alimony shall be adjusted annually on the anniversary date of this Agreement based on the Consumer Inflation Index as published in the *Wall Street Journal* or based on the rate of increase or decrease in the gross income of the Husband for the previous twelve months.

Agreement as to whether the parties waive the right to later modify the amount of alimony to be paid.

3. *Waiver of Future Modification.* The parties hereby waive their statutory right to future modifications, up or down, of the alimony provided for herein, based upon a change in the income or financial status of either party.

OR

The parties reserve their statutory right to future modifications, up or down, of the alimony provided for herein, either based on the provisions of this Agreement or upon a change in the income or financial status of either party.

Agreement as to permanent custody of minor children.

4. *Custody of Minor Child.* Subject to the further order of the Court, care, custody, and control of the minor child of the parties is hereby granted to Wife, referred to herein as "Custodial Parent." Husband is referred to herein as "Noncustodial Parent."

Agreement as to visitation by noncustodial parent. Considers the particular geographic situations of the parties. Visitation that is reasonable for a noncustodial parent living close to the minor child may be unworkable for one living a thousand miles away.

5. *Reasonable Visitation.* Noncustodial Parent shall have reasonable visitation rights with the child at all times as shall be agreed upon by the parties regardless of the child's location at any given time. Noncustodial Parent shall give Custodial Parent at least forty-eight (48) hours notice of any proposed visitation. Unless otherwise agreed, the Noncustodial Parent shall have the obligation for any transportation of the minor child necessary to implement the visitation provisions of this Agreement.

6. *Specific Visitation.* The Noncustodial Parent is hereby granted specific visitation rights, in addition to any times of visitation as the parties may agree, with the minor child as follows: Every other weekend from 6:00 P.M. Friday to 6:00 P.M. Sunday; three weeks in the period from June 15 through August 15, with at least two weeks notice to the Custodial Parent; Father's Day weekend in each year; the minor child's birthday, July 4, in even years; and the following holidays in even years: Easter Weekend and Christmas; the following holidays in odd years: New Year's Day, Memorial Day Weekend, Labor Day Weekend, and Thanksgiving Weekend.

Agreement as to payment of permanent child support. Includes provisions that payment is payable to custodial parent, not child; and when payment is due.

7. *Child Support.* Subject to the further order of the Court, Noncustodial Parent shall be obligated to pay to the Custodial Parent Two Hundred Dollars ($200.00) per month as and for support of the minor child of the parties. Said payment shall be sent each month so that it is received by Custodial Parent no later than the fifth day of each month.

Agreement for life insurance to guarantee an income source for child.

8. *Life Insurance.* Noncustodial Parent shall maintain a life insurance policy on his life in an amount of no less than Fifty Thousand Dollars ($50,000.00), with the minor child named as beneficiary.

Agreement as to payment of necessary medical expenses for minor child.

9. *Medical Expenses.* The parties will be equally responsible for all necessary medical, dental, and hospitalization expenses required for said minor child. The Noncustodial Parent shall maintain medical insurance coverage for the benefit

of the minor child. Should the Noncustodial Parent fail to maintain sufficient medical insurance for the benefit of the minor child, he shall be solely responsible for any expenses incurred as a result of such lapse.

10. *Post-Secondary Education.* Should the minor child be accepted into and attend an accredited post-secondary educational institution, Noncustodial Parent agrees to pay for the necessary tuition and fees, books and supplies, and room and board in an amount not to exceed the then-existing cost of such expenses at the State University, such obligation not to extend beyond four (4) academic years.

Agreement for the non-custodial parent to pay for no more than four years of college or vocational training.

11. *Debts.* Each party agrees to assume and pay all outstanding debts individually incurred by him or her whether such debt was incurred before the marriage, during the marriage, or during any period of separation, and each agrees to indemnify, defend, and hold the other absolutely harmless from any expense, loss, claim, or liability whatsoever arising from, or in any way connected with, such outstanding debts, except as herein otherwise agreed. Notwithstanding these provisions, Husband agrees to be solely responsible for, and to hold Wife harmless from, the parties' VISA credit card, account number 6365275, issued by the First National Bank in the principal amount of Seven Hundred Fifty Dollars ($750.00), and Wife agrees that she will relinquish all right to use said credit card as of the date of the execution of this Agreement.

Agreement as to the payment of all debts incurred by the parties. Contains indemnity or "hold harmless" clauses, in which the parties agree to reimburse each other for any losses caused by a failure to honor the covenants made herein.

12. *Household Goods.* Except as otherwise expressly agreed in writing, Husband and Wife have divided, to their mutual satisfaction, all household goods, furniture, furnishings, fixtures, and appliances. All such personal property, whether acquired before the marriage, during the marriage or during any period of separation, shall be, and remain, the sole property of the party in whose possession it presently is, free and clear of any claim on the part of the other.

Agreement as to the division of all household property.

13. *Automobiles.* Husband shall obtain or retain title and exclusive use of the 1989 Ford F-10 truck and become solely obligated for all payments due or which may become due for the use, operation, maintenance, and financing thereof, and Husband shall hold Wife harmless thereon. The parties shall execute title transfer documents, if necessary, accordingly.

Agreement as to the allocaton of the parties' automobiles. Consideration is given to both possession and the obligation to pay for the automobiles.

14. *Real Property.* The parties are owners as tenants in common (or joint tenants) of certain real property located at 433 Jerold Street, Plainview, State of _____ . It is agreed that the Wife shall have the exclusive use, control, and possession of said real property effective with the execution of this Agreement. It is further agreed that the Husband shall quit claim all his right, claim, and interest in said real property to Wife contemporaneously with the execution of this Agreement. Upon the ultimate sale of said property, Husband shall be entitled to receive the sum of Ten Thousand Dollars ($10,000.00) OR one-half of the equity presently existing in said property as determined by an independent and qualified real estate appraiser representing Husband's interest in the equity in said property, whichever is greater.

Agreement as to the rights and obligations regarding real property. Issues include possession of the land; obligation to pay any encumbrances; allocation of equity, either immediately or upon the ultimate sale of the land and; maintenance of the property.

15. *Effective Date.* This Agreement shall be effective upon the execution of the Agreement by the parties.

16. *Insurance Policies.* Unless and except as otherwise provided herein, each of the parties agrees that the other, after execution of this Agreement, shall

have the right to make any changes in his or her respective insurance policies, including, but not limited to, changing his or her beneficiary, increasing or decreasing the coverage amount, or canceling such policies.

Agreement not to use each other's credit, with an indemnity clause.

17. *Non-Use of Other's Credit.* Neither Husband nor Wife may hereafter incur any debts or obligations upon the credit of the other, and each shall indemnify, defend, and hold the other absolutely harmless from any debt or obligation so charged or otherwise incurred.

18. *Attorney Fees.* Each party agrees to pay their own attorney's fees incurred in preparation of this Agreement, after execution of this Agreement and in connection with this proceeding.

19. *Division of Other Property.* Except as set forth herein, the parties have effected to their mutual satisfaction a division of all other property, real or personal, in which they had an interest, either singly or jointly; all such property which Husband or Wife now has in his or her control and possession shall be and remain his or her property respectively, free from any claim whatsoever on the part of the other.

Agreement that any modification to the agreement must be executed in writing.

20. *Modification of This Agreement.* This Agreement may not be altered, changed, or modified except in a writing signed by each of the parties. After approval of this Agreement and entry of the Final Judgment and Decree of Divorce, this Agreement may not be altered, changed, or modified except pursuant to the Court's approval and order of modification.

Agreement that each party had the opportunity to seek and use the advice of independent counsel.

21. *Advice of Counsel.* Both parties acknowledge that they had an opportunity to seek the advice of legal counsel and that they are entering into this Agreement voluntarily of their own free will. Wife further acknowledges that this Separation Agreement and all pleadings filed contemporaneously with same were prepared by Husband's attorney, and that Wife has been advised to seek independent legal counsel and not to rely on any representations of Husband's attorney.

Agreement as to which state's law shall apply if a dispute arises after execution.

22. *Law Applicable.* The provisions of this Agreement shall be construed and enforced in accordance with the applicable laws of the State of_____.

23. *Enforcement Expenses.* If either Husband or Wife defaults in the performance of any of the terms, provisions, or obligations herein set forth, and it becomes necessary to institute legal proceedings to effectuate the performance of any provisions of this Agreement, then the party found to be in default shall pay all expenses, including reasonable attorney fees, incurred in connection with such enforcement proceedings.

Merger clause—neither can rely on any oral representations or promises unless included in this written agreement.

24. *Full Understanding.* Each party fully understands all of the terms of this Agreement, and the terms represent and constitute the entire understanding between them. Each party has read this Agreement and finds it to be in accordance with his or her understanding, and each voluntarily executes this Agreement and affixes his or her signature in the presence of the witnesses indicated below.

Agreement that each party will execute all documents necessary to implement the provisions

25. *Performance of Necessary Acts.* Each party shall execute any and all deeds, bills of sale, endorsements, forms, conveyances or other documents, and perform any act which may be required or necessary to carry out and effectuate any and all of the purposes and provisions herein set forth. Upon the failure of

either party to execute and deliver any such deed, bill of sale, endorsement, form, conveyance, or other document to the other party, this Agreement shall constitute and operate as such properly executed document. The County Auditor, County Recorder, and any and all other public and private officials are authorized and directed to accept this Agreement or a properly certified copy hereof in lieu of the document regularly required for the conveyance or transfer.

of this agreement, and that if either party fails to do so, this agreement shall act as a satisfactory substitute for the required document.

26. *Representations of Financial Status.* Each party has made a true and direct representation of his or her financial status, including possible expectancies and inheritances.

27. *Release.* Each party does hereby release and discharge the other from all other claims, rights, and duties arising out of said marital relationship, and said parties mutually agree that each party hereto may freely sell and encumber or otherwise dispose of his or her own property by gift, bill of sale, or Last Will and Testament. Each party is by these presents hereby barred from any and all rights or claims by way of dower, inheritance, descent and distribution, allowance of year's support, right to remain in the mansion house, all rights and claims as widow, widower, heir, distributee, survivor, or next of kin and all other rights or claims whatsoever in or to the estate of the other, whether real or personal, or whether now owned or hereafter acquired which may in any manner arise or occur by virtue of said marriage.

Agreement that each party releases any and all claims upon the property of the other obtained by virtue of the marriage. The general release in the second paragraph ensures that there will not be any post-decree litigation seeking redress for the tortious behavior of the other spouse.

Further, the parties do hereby generally release each other from any and all claims, whether in contract or tort, that may have arisen between the parties as of this date.

28. *Binding of Heirs.* All the covenants, promises, stipulations, agreements, and provisions herein contained shall bind the heirs, executors, administrators, personal representatives, and assigns of the parties hereto.

29. *Severability and Enforceability.* If any provision of this Agreement is held to be invalid or unenforceable, all other provisions shall nevertheless continue in full force and effect.

IN WITNESS WHEREOF, the parties have affixed their signatures hereto on the dates indicated.

WITNESSES to Husband's signature:

_____

_____

Notary Seal

          _____
          Thomas James Morrison

          _____
          Date

Signatures. With both informal witnesses and formal witnesses.

WITNESSES to Wife's signature:

_____

_____

Notary Seal

          _____
          Jeanne Claire Morrison

          _____
          Date

EXHIBIT 6–8   FINAL JUDGMENT AND DECREE

IN THE _____ COURT OF _____ COUNTY
STATE OF _____

_____

v.   CIVIL ACTION FILE NO. _____

_____

Final Judgment and Decree

Upon consideration of this case upon evidence submitted as provided by law, it is the judgment of the court that a total divorce be granted, that is to say a divorce a vinculo matrimonii, between the parties to the above stated case upon legal principles. And it is considered, ordered, and decreed by the court that the marriage contract heretofore entered into between the parties to this case, from and after this date, be and is set aside and dissolved as fully and effectually as if no such contract had ever been made or entered into and

Plaintiff and Defendant, in the future shall be held and considered as separate and distinct persons altogether unconnected by any nuptial union or civil contract, whatsoever, and both shall have the right to remarry. It is further ordered that the Separation Agreement executed by the parties be incorporated and made a part of the Final Judgment and Decree of Divorce.

The cost of the proceedings are taxed against the _____

_____

Decree entered this _____ day of _____ 19___ .

_____
Judge Superior Court

Of course, separation agreements are also used in contested divorces if and when the parties can reach a voluntary, mutually satisfactory accord. A separation agreement is a contract, and the failure of a party to satisfy any condition of the agreement can result in a claim of breach of contract. The separation agreement is effective upon the parties as soon as it is executed. But once the judge approves the separation agreement and either specifically incorporates its terms and conditions or incorporates the agreement by reference into the court's final judgment and decree of divorce (see Exhibit 6–8), it becomes a direct court order, and it is enforceable through the contempt power of the court. (See Chapter 12 for a discussion of the authority of a court to impose contempt on a party failing to obey an order of the court.) If the court merely approves the separation agreement, but fails to incorporate it into the final judgment and decree of divorce, that agreement does not become part of the divorce judgment and is not enforceable by contempt.

An uncontested divorce may not require a trial, but a court hearing is usually necessary for the judge to grant the divorce. Many times this can be performed in the **judge's chambers**, or the court may schedule an Uncontested Divorce calendar, during which a court may dispose of literally dozens of such cases in a single morning. The only evidence presented is a recitation under oath by the plaintiff of the facts contained in the complaint. A few judges will act only as a rubber stamp, approving almost any separation agreement; the majority of judges will already have scrutinized the separation agreement and will intervene only if they believe that the agreement is patently unfair to one of the parties. At the conclusion of the hearing, the judge signs a final judgment and decree of divorce, which was prepared by the attorney or paralegal representing the plaintiff. A sample of a final judgment and decree of divorce is presented at Exhibit 6–8.

REVIEW QUESTIONS

1. The type of jurisdiction that determines whether a court has the authority to hear a particular type of case is _____ ; while _____ jurisdiction determines which court(s) have the authority to impose their rulings on a party; and, the particular county or district in which a law suit is filed is determined by _____ .

2. When a court has only *in rem* jurisdiction in divorce litigation, what does the court have authority to do? How is this different from when a court has *in personam* jurisdiction in divorce litigation?

3. What is a pleading? What different types of pleadings were discussed in this chapter, and how are they alike or different from each other?

4. What must be alleged by a plaintiff if she is to plead a *prima facie* case for divorce?

5. In an answer to a complaint for divorce, what is the difference between a defense and a denial?

6. What is the difference in how a complaint is served on a defendant and how a counterclaim is served upon a plaintiff? What is the rationale for those differences?

7. What are the different purposes served by a counterclaim and an answer?

8. What is the purpose of a brief, and how does it achieve its goal?

9. Under what circumstances could, or should, a divorcing couple seek an uncontested divorce?

10. At what point in divorce litigation may the parties enter into a separation agreement? Once executed, at what point does the separation agreement become effective?

11. What issues may a separation agreement encompass?

12. If a counterclaim is served by U.S. Mail on July 25, and the period of time permitted for responding is 30 days, on what date is the response due? What if the court is closed on that date?

13. What is constructive abandonment? Give an example.

14. What is the purpose of the Affidavit Under the Uniform Child Custody Jurisdiction Act?

15. What is a long-arm statute, and what purpose does it play in divorce litigation?

KEY TERMS

answer	motion for more
brief	definite statement
complaint	motion to dismiss
counterclaim	motion to strike
court of general	personal jurisdiction
jurisdiction	plaintiff
defendant	*res*
divisible divorce	residency
domicile	separation agreement
in personam jurisdic-	service of process
tion	subject matter
in rem jurisdiction	jurisdiction
judge's chambers	summons
long-arm statute	uncontested divorce
motion	venue

STATE RESEARCH PROBLEMS

Review the law in your state and answer the following questions. Cite the authority for your answers.

1. Which court or courts have subject matter jurisdiction to hear divorce cases? Do those same courts have subject matter jurisdiction to determine alimony, child custody and support, contempt for willful violation of a court order relating to the divorce, etc.?

2. Find the long-arm statute in your state. Does it include a reference to nonresident defendants in divorce cases? If so, what are the requirements for personal jurisdiction over nonresidents?

3. What are the venue requirements in your state?

4. What is the minimum residency requirement for filing a complaint for divorce?

5. What are the grounds for divorce in your state? Provide your authority and list the grounds, giving an example of a spouse's behavior that might justify the assertion of each ground.

6. Find a form book for your state containing a complaint for divorce. Compare it to the one presented in this chapter and state what, if any, differences you note. (Where you notice differences, be certain to follow the procedures required by your state and not the general outline provided herein.) What other forms are required by your state?

7. Find the section in your state's Civil Practice Act relating to service of process. What is the proper citation for that statute or rule? Who is authorized to serve process? What, if any, authorization is required to do so? How may service of process be effected?

8. Is service by publication permitted? If so, what is the procedure for properly serving process by publication? What is the official newspaper, or outlet, for these notices? What is the cost to serve process by publication?

9. What, if any, defenses to divorce are available in your state? What is your authority for your answer? Use proper *Bluebook* citation form.

ETHICAL PROBLEM

You are instructed by your supervising attorney to prepare a list of a client's monthly expenses and income. The client tells you that his income is approximately $2,000.00 per month, and that his expenses are approximately $1,950.00 monthly. After reviewing the documentation assembled by the client, you discover that the client's income is actually closer to $2,300.00 per month, and that his expenses total less than $1,500.00 monthly. What are the possible ethical conflicts presented by this scenario? What steps should you take next?

PRACTICE EXERCISES

1. List the grounds for relief, defenses available, and relief available for both divorce and annulment.

2. Using the following facts, draft a complaint for divorce, being certain to satisfy all procedural requirements for your state.

   John and Marsha Thompson have been married for 11 years. They have two children: Anna, age 9, and Scott, age 5. Mrs. Thompson is not pregnant at this time. Although she has proof of her husband's infidelity, Mrs. Thompson wants to file for divorce in accordance with the no-fault divorce provisions of your state. She wants possession of the marital residence and custody of the children, as well as a sufficient level of child support. You should make up any other necessary information, such as specific dates and addresses.

3. Draft an answer and counterclaim for Mr. Thompson. He denies the allegations of his infidelity. Further, he believes that because of Mrs. Thompson's drinking problems, she cannot adequately care for the children. Accordingly, he desires permanent custody of the children, exclusive possession of the marital residence, and an adequate level of child support.

Divorce— Interlocutory Relief

CHAPTER OBJECTIVES

In this chapter, you will learn:

- Why interlocutory relief is often necessary in divorce litigation

- How courts provide for the immediate needs of divorce litigants while the divorce is pending

- The various types of relief available

- How a court seeks to remedy domestic violence

The nature of divorce litigation is such that at the time of the filing of the complaint for divorce, the parties have usually already begun living separate and apart from each other. This means that (1) the living expenses of the parties increase, and (2) a financially dependent spouse does not have the same access to the financial resources that were previously available. Further, the pace of modern litigation is such that there is often a significant time differential between the filing of the complaint for divorce and the conclusion of the litigation. As a result, once the divorce litigation begins, the court has the authority to determine some of the issues incident to a divorce (alimony, child custody, support and visitation, and possession of the marital residence) on a provisional basis until the court can provide final and permanent relief. The court may also issue any orders required to prevent or punish any incidents of domestic violence.

THE NEED FOR INTERLOCUTORY RELIEF

interlocutory relief
Temporary or nonfinal relief.

Interlocutory relief is provisional relief afforded to the litigants pending the ultimate outcome of the litigation. In various jurisdictions, this relief may also be called temporary relief, provisional relief, relief *pendente lite,* or *nisi* relief. The need for such relief exists because a significant time lag often occurs between the filing of a complaint for divorce and the conclusion of the litigation. In many jurisdictions, especially in densely populated urban areas, the wait for "a day in court" can be months, and as long as several years. During this period the parties to a contested divorce may need guidance as to the amount (if any) of alimony and child support to be paid, which party will assume the role of the custodial parent for any minor children, the amount and regulation of visitation with minor children, which party will retain possession of the marital residence, and so on.

The court may also need to intervene before trial to issue any orders necessary:

— To protect one spouse and/or minor children from a violent spouse/parent

— To prevent spouses from divesting themselves of certain property (the "If I can't have it, no one can!" syndrome)

— To prevent a spouse from removing a minor child from the jurisdiction

It is essential that this element of the divorce process receive the time and preparation it deserves because, aside from the obvious immediate impact it has on the parties, it also sets the stage for the remainder of the litigation. Very often, the final judgment of the court or settlement between the parties closely resembles the court's order for interlocutory relief. This is so because the period between the order for the interlocutory relief and the court's final order gives the parties, attorneys, and court an opportunity to see how well the provisions of the interlocutory relief work in actual practice. For example, suppose one party receives temporary custody of the children and, say, $500 a month in support payments. If neither party can demonstrate any difficulties caused by the temporary arrangement, the court may be inclined to make this arrangement permanent. This is the judicial version of "If it ain't broke, don't fix it."

PROCEDURAL REQUIREMENTS

Interlocutory relief must be specifically requested by one or both of the parties in a pleading or motion. The pleading should be carefully phrased so that "temporary and permanent" relief is sought for all relevant specific claims for relief. This requires both an allegation that the pleader is entitled to the temporary relief sought and an inclusion of temporary relief in the demand for relief. (See paragraphs seven through nine of Exhibit 6-1 for examples of this.)

Failure to do so could conceivably cause a party to forgo an otherwise valid claim for relief. A number of jurisdictions require parties seeking interlocutory relief to enter into mediation. This forces the parties to actually try to work together to reach a satisfactory accord. In such jurisdictions, the court does not intervene (barring allegations of physical abuse) until the parties can demonstrate that they have made a good-faith effort to mediate their differences.

Unless the parties reach a mutually satisfactory settlement, a court hearing must be scheduled at which the court addresses the issues detailed above. This temporary hearing is usually scheduled when the attorney for the party seeking the temporary relief files the original pleading. (Since interlocutory relief is most often sought by the plaintiff, for the purposes of this discussion, assume that the plaintiff has requested interlocutory relief in her complaint.) This hearing requires the preparation and filing of a "**show cause** order," which when signed requires the defendant to appear at the temporary hearing and show cause, or explain why, the temporary relief sought by the plaintiff should not be granted. This order may be taken to either the judge assigned to that particular case or to the judge assigned by the court to dispose of such cases. *The answer to this question usually cannot be found in the state code or case law. Instead it can be found in the local rules, the rules propounded by and for the judges of the trial courts, in which the judges describe in detail the procedures they want attorneys to employ.* In either event, the court then schedules the interlocutory hearing for the next available date. The date for the hearing is noted on the show cause order prepared by the plaintiff's attorney or paralegal. This order must then be served on the defendant along with the summons and complaint. Typically, the interlocutory hearing is conducted within a few weeks of the date of the filing of the request for relief.
(NOTE: *If there are allegations involving family violence, there are usually provisions for conducting the hearing even sooner. See "Relief from Domestic Violence" later in this chapter.*)

show cause
A court order to a person that he "show cause" why the court should or should not take specific action.

ISSUES FOR CONSIDERATION

The interlocutory relief sought by a party is intended to provide the necessary financial and custodial relief so the parties can continue to live day to day until the end of the litigation. The court determines, on an interim basis, how best to divide the financial rights and obligations of the parties and how the best interests of the minor children can be served through temporary custody and visitation. The court also determines which spouse shall have the exclusive right to use and possess the marital residence.

Temporary Alimony

Temporary alimony (also called alimony *pendente lite*) is not a matter of right; rather, it falls within the discretion of the trial court to determine whether there exists a need for temporary alimony, and if so, the amount to

pendente lite
Latin for "pending the suit."

be paid. The applicant's prospects for success in the ultimate trial of the case are not relevant to the decision whether to award temporary alimony. Until recently, temporary alimony was reserved solely for wives; constitutional challenges to that rule claiming violation of the "Equal Protection" provisions of the United States Constitution resulted in the expansion of this relief to include husbands. The award may include payment of the recipient's mortgage or other bills, attorney's fees and expenses of litigation, health, life and/or automobile insurance, and any other financial requirements.

The award of temporary alimony is an incident of litigation for divorce of an existing valid marriage, and therefore can occur only after the filing of a complaint for divorce, in which the applicant makes out a *prima facie* case for the relief sought. Temporary alimony can also be awarded pending the appeal of a final judgment of divorce for either party. Notice that either plaintiff or defendant, or both, may request temporary alimony.

The court considers each case on its individual merits and weighs each party's necessary expenses and their ability to provide for themselves. An interlocutory hearing is not a trial on the merits of the case; accordingly, any alleged wrongdoing or fault by either party is generally not germane to the issue under consideration. Temporary alimony is usually not awarded in instances where the "dependent" spouse has sufficient income to maintain her accustomed style of living during the pendency of the litigation. This is to be distinguished, however, from the situation where the dependent spouse has only property that would have to be liquidated to produce the necessary income. In the latter case, an award of temporary alimony would be appropriate. The court also considers the earning capacity of each party, rather than merely examining the amount of money each had earned within a given period of time. For example, if the wife is a licensed physician, but has not worked for a number of years, the court would hear evidence as to how much income she *could* earn. In cases where the parties entered into a valid antenuptial agreement that made provision for the payment, or nonpayment, of temporary alimony, the court does not grant temporary alimony, but rather enforces the applicable provisions of the antenuptial agreement (see Chapter 3). The award of temporary alimony can be modified if circumstances change significantly during the pendency of the litigation.

It is also important to note that there are different tax considerations for temporary alimony as opposed to permanent alimony, particularly that the payments to the dependent spouse are not deductible from the paying spouse's gross income and are not taxable income to the receiving spouse. The reason for this difference is that the parties are still married to each other at this point in the litigation, and there are no tax consequences for a transfer of funds between spouses.

Minor Children

As always when minor children are involved, the determination of all issues revolves around what is in the best interests of the children. Child support payments are awarded in accordance with the equities of the case and with consideration of any statutorily imposed guidelines as to the appropriate amount of child support to be paid, depending on the payor's income and the number of children for whom support is required. As a practical matter, the amount of child support ordered at an interlocutory hearing will be very close to, if not identical to, the amount ordered at a final trial for divorce. See Chapter 10 for a full discussion of the child support payments.

As to custody of the minor children, the court follows a methodology similar to that used at the final trial for divorce. Chapter 10 describes custody of and visitation with minor children.

Possession of the Marital Residence

When both spouses want to remain in the marital residence, the court must determine which party shall have the right to its exclusive use and possession. The court looks to the specific reasons each party presents for remaining in the marital residence. Often, the court awards possession to the custodial parent, with a view to mitigating the disruptive effect of divorce on the minor children. If that is not practical or if there are no minor children, the court considers factors such as the relative difficulty for either spouse to acquire new lodging (i.e., cost, location, space requirements). In addition, an adjudication must be made to determine which party shall have the obligation for the rent or mortgage payments, the necessary maintenance (i.e., painting, landscaping, pool upkeep, etc.), condominium association fees, pool or club dues, and so on. These payments may be included in the determination of temporary alimony, or they may be determined separately. It is not unusual for one spouse to be awarded the marital residence and the other spouse to be "awarded" the obligations incumbent with that residence.

CASE

WILKENS v. WILKENS

Appellate Court of Connecticut
Decided April 28, 1987.

. . . .

SPALLONE, Judge.

The defendant in this dissolution action is appealing from the order of the trial court denying his motion for modification of a pendente lite order for unallocated alimony and support.

The following facts are not in dispute. Pursuant to a pendente lite order entered by the trial court on June 11, 1984, the defendant was obligated to pay to the plaintiff as unallocated alimony and support the sum of $860 per month. At the time the order was entered, the defendant was a minister of a church. In addition to his salary of $370 per week, he received free use of a car and a parsonage.

On October 14, 1985, the defendant filed a motion for modification of the pendente lite order on the ground that he was no longer employed. When he filed the motion, the defendant was receiving severance pay which was to continue into December. Although he was still living in the parsonage at this time, he stated in the motion that he would be moving out in November. At the hearing on the motion on November

4, 1985, the defendant testified that he had voluntarily resigned from his position as a minister because his life situation interfered with his work. The court, ruling from the bench, denied the motion. The defendant has appealed from that denial.

Subsequently, on January 7, 1986, the defendant filed another motion to modify the pendente lite order on the grounds that he was still unemployed, had no income, and no longer had free housing or the free use of a car. After a hearing duly held on January 27, 1986, the trial court also denied this motion. The defendant filed an amended appeal to include the denial of this second motion.

The defendant claims that the trial court erred (1) in failing to modify the pendente lite order when the defendant's circumstances were clearly within the purview of General Statutes §46b–86(a),[1] (2) in abusing its discretion in failing to modify the defendant's pendente lite obligations, and (3) in denying his motions when such denials were clearly erroneous.

The purpose of an award of alimony and support pendente lite is to provide for the wife and dependent children while they are living apart from the husband pending determination of the issues in the case. (Citations omitted.) Under General Statutes §46b–86(a), an order for the periodic payment of alimony and support pendente lite may be modified upon a showing of a substantial change in the circumstances of either party. (Citation omitted.)

In reviewing the defendant's claims of error, we recognize that trial courts have a distinct advantage over appellate courts in addressing domestic relations issues because all of the surrounding circumstances as well as the appearance and attitude of the parties are observable by the court. The action of the trial court, therefore, will not be disturbed unless the court has abused its legal discretion. (Citations omitted.) We also recognize that support orders are not based solely on the needs of the children, but take into account what the parent can afford to pay. (Citations omitted.) Because great weight is due to the action of the trial court, every presumption should be given in favor of its correctness. (Citations omitted.)

. . . .

Turning to the court's action on the second motion, we find that the court did not err in denying this second motion to modify. The court carefully considered a variety of relevant factors when making its ruling. Initially, the court noted that the defendant's unemployment "may have significance in one fashion on a motion for contempt and significance in another fashion on the motion to modify." The court then observed that the defendant had not yet fallen behind on his payments. The court also considered the fact that the defendant had voluntarily terminated his position as a minister, although it recognized that the position was unique and there could be many valid reasons for the defendant's termination. The court particularly emphasized the defendant's earning capacity in light of his background, education, and experience. (Citation omitted) (courts may rely on earning capacity where party voluntarily terminates employment, even if termination not done wilfully to deny alimony to wife). Finally, the court considered the needs of the children in light of each party's ability to pay, and found that the plaintiff-wife's ability to support was virtually nil. After considering these factors, the court denied the motion to modify. In arriving at its conclusion, the court considered none of the extraneous factors referred to at the first hearing. In addition, the defendant does not claim, nor do we find, that the alleged improprieties at the first hearing in any way contaminated this second hearing. We thus find no abuse of discretion in the court's denial of the second motion to modify.

There is no error.

DISCUSSION QUESTIONS

Considering the preceding case of *Wilkens v. Wilkens,* 523 A.2d 1371 (1987, Connecticut), and answer the following questions:

1. What was the issue at the trial level in this case?

2. What is the purpose of alimony and child support *pendente lite,* according to the court in this case?

3. What factors were considered by the trial court in determining whether to modify the amount of alimony and child support *pendente lite?* What was the trial court's evaluation of those factors?

---

1.   Section 46b–86(a) provides: "Unless and to the extent that the decree precludes modification, any final order for the periodic payment of permanent alimony or support or alimony or support pendente lite may at any time thereafter be continued, set aside, altered or modified by said court upon a showing of a substantial change in the circumstances of either party. This section shall not apply to assignments under section 46b–81 or to any assignment of the estate or a portion thereof of one party to the other party under prior law."

PREPARATION FOR THE INTERLOCUTORY HEARING

At the court hearing for the interlocutory order, the court determines the most profound and personal issues of the parties and their minor children. The court, and that is essentially a euphemism for the judge, is looking to the legal professionals representing the parties to present the facts required to make a fair and equitable decision. Accordingly, a successful interlocutory hearing is a well-prepared interlocutory hearing.

Many courts require the parties to present the essential financial information in a detailed format by use of a **financial affidavit**. The forms vary from state to state, but the basic information required for a financial affidavit is essentially the same in all jurisdictions. An example of a financial affidavit is at Exhibit 7–1.

financial affidavit
A court-supplied form that, when completed under oath, details the current financial condition of a party in divorce litigation.

The client does most of the work in compiling the facts, and necessary proof or corroboration for same, needed to convince the judge to award the desired relief. The paralegal's primary responsibilities are to assist the client, organize the information as it is obtained, act as a liaison between the attorney and the client, and explain to the client why the requested information is necessary and relevant.

RELIEF FROM DOMESTIC VIOLENCE

Domestic or **family violence** has been defined as the use or threat of physical force (or psychological abuse) in a family or intimate relationship. The increase in domestic violence (and the increased reporting of it) is evidenced by research indicating that 25 to 40 percent of all women initiating divorce do so because of domestic violence. (Note that domestic violence can and does also include men as "victims" and woman as "abusers.") Domestic abuse can take many forms, such as hitting, pushing, punching, threatening with a weapon, psychological abuse, and nonconsensual sexual activity. Victims can include a spouse or partner, children residing in the household, or both.

domestic violence
Abusive behavior between family members or between partners in a romantic relationship.

Domestic violence is something of an anomaly. While it is certainly not a new phenomenon, it is only in the last few decades that domestic violence has been taken seriously by society, the police, and the courts, and therefore it has been reported more often than in years past. As a matter of fact, at one time a husband could legally beat his wife and children with a stick, as long as the stick was no thicker than his thumb (the origin of the phrase "rule of thumb").

All but a very few states have enacted legislation to protect victims of family violence. These laws typically include provisions relating to the following:

— Definition of persons entitled to protection

— The nature of relief available

— Provisions holding police authorities harmless from civil liability for arrests made without a warrant

EXHIBIT 7-1   SAMPLE FINANCIAL AFFIDAVIT

Attorney(s):
Office Address & Tel. No.
Attorney(s) for

SUPERIOR COURT OF NEW JERSEY
_____DIVISION, FAMILY PART
_____COUNTY

Plaintiff,

DOCKET NO. _____

vs.

CASE INFORMATION STATEMENT

Defendant.

OF _____

PART A—CASE INFORMATION:

Date of Statement _____

Date(s) of Prior Statement(s)_____

_____

Your Birthdate _____

Birthdate of Spouse _____

Date of Marriage _____

Date of Separation _____

Date of Complaint _____

ISSUES IN DISPUTE:

Cause of Action _____

Custody _____

Alimony _____

Child Support _____

Equitable Distribution _____

Counsel Fees _____

Other _____

_____

Does an agreement exist between parties relative to any issue?   ☐ Yes ☐ No. If Yes, attach a copy (if written) or a summary (if oral).

1. Name and Address of Parties:

Your Name _____

Street Address _____ City _____ State/Zip _____

Other Party's Name _____

Street Address (if different) _____ City _____ State/Zip _____

2. Name, Address, & Birthdate of all Child(ren); Person with whom Child(ren) Resides:

Child's Full Name	Address	Birthdate	Person's Name
_____	_____	_____	_____
_____	_____	_____	_____
_____	_____	_____	_____
_____	_____	_____	_____

PART B—MISCELLANEOUS INFORMATION:

1. Name and Address of Your Employer (Provide Name and Address of Co. if Self-Employed)

Name of Employer _____ Address _____

Name of Employer _____ Address _____

2. Name and Address of Your Health Insurance Company(ies); Policy Information:

Name of Company _____ Address _____

I.D. Number _____ Group Number _____

Coverage Type: Single ☐   Parent-Child ☐   Family ☐   Optical ☐

                Hospital ☐   Major-Medical ☐   Dental ☐   Drug ☐   Diagnostic ☐

Check if made available through employment ☐   or personally obtained ☐

Name of Company _____ Address _____

I.D. Number _____ Group Number _____

Coverage Type: Single ☐   Parent-Child ☐   Family ☐   Optical ☐

                Hospital ☐   Major-Medical ☐   Dental ☐   Drug ☐   Diagnostic ☐

Check if made available through employment ☐   or personally obtained ☐

3. Name and Address of Life Insurance Company(ies); Policy Information:

Name of Company _____ Address _____

Policy Number _____ Beneficiary _____

Face Amount $ _____ Name of Insured _____

Policy Owner _____

Name of Company _____ Address _____

Policy Number _____ Beneficiary _____

Face Amount $ _____ Name of Insured _____

Policy Owner _____

4. Additional Identification: Social Security Number

State Driver's License Number _____ Eye Color _____

5. Attach sheet listing all prior pending family actions involving support, custody, or domestic violence listing Docket Number, County, State, and the Disposition reached.

PART C—INCOME INFORMATION: Complete this section for self and (if known) for spouse. Attach to this form a corporate benefits statement as well as a statement of all fringe benefits of employment.

1. LAST YEAR'S INCOME

	Yours	Joint	Spouse or Former Spouse
1. Gross earned income last calendar year (19_)	$ _____	$_____	$ _____
2. Unearned income (same year)	_____	_____	_____
3. Total Income Taxes paid on above income (incl. Fed., State, F.I.C.A. and S.U.I.). If Joint Return, use middle line	_____	_____	_____
4. Net Income (1 + 2 − 3)	$ _____	$_____	$ _____

Attach a full and complete copy of last year's Federal and State Income Tax Returns. If none has been filed, attach W-2 statements, 1099's, Schedule C's, etc. to show total income plus a copy of the most recently filed Tax Returns. Check if attached: Fed. Tax Return ☐   State Tax Return ☐   W-2 ☐   Other ☐

2. PRESENT EARNED INCOME AND EXPENSES

	Yours	Spouse (if known)
1. Average Gross monthly income (based on last 3 pay periods—attach pay stubs) Commissions and bonuses, etc., are ( ) included* ( ) not included* ( ) not paid to you	$ _____	$ _____

*Attach details of basis thereof, including, but not limited to, percentage overrides, timing of payments, etc. Attach copies of last three statements of such bonuses, commissions, etc.

	Yours	Spouse (if known)
2. Deductions per month: check all types of withholdings ( ) Federal ( ) State ( ) F.I.C.A. ( ) S.U.I. ( ) Other	$ _____	$ _____
3. Net Income (1–2)	$ _____	$ _____

3. YOUR YEAR–TO–DATE INCOME

1. GROSS EARNED INCOME $ _____   Provide Dates: From _____   To _____

    Number of Weeks _____

2. TAX DEDUCTIONS: (Number of dependents _____)
    a. Federal Income Taxes   a. $ _____
    b. N.J. Income Taxes   b.   _____
    c. F.I.C.A.   c.   _____
    d. S.U.I.   d.   _____
    e. Estimated tax payments in excess of withholding actually made   e.   _____
    f. Other (specify)   f.   _____

    TOTAL $ _____

3. GROSS INCOME NET OF TAXES $_____

4. OTHER DEDUCTIONS   if mandatory, check box
    a. Hospitalization/Medical Insurance   a. $ _____   ☐
    b. Life Insurance   b. _____   ☐
    c. Pension/Profit Sharing Plan   c. _____   ☐
    d. Savings/Bond Plan   d. _____   ☐
    e. Wage Execution   e. _____   ☐
    f. Retirement Fund Payments   f. _____   ☐
    g. Other (specify)   g. _____   ☐
                      TOTAL $ _____

5. NET YEAR-TO-DATE EARNED INCOME $ _____

    NET AVERAGE EARNED INCOME PER MONTH $ _____

6. GROSS UNEARNED INCOME

Source	How Often Paid	Year to Date Amount
_____	_____	_____
_____	_____	_____
_____	_____	_____
_____	_____	_____

4. INCOME ANALYSIS UNDER THE CHILD SUPPORT GUIDELINES

To be completed if either parent contends that the child support guidelines apply or should be considered.

	Mother	**Father**
1. Weekly Earned and Unearned Gross Income From All Sources (excluding AFDC grants)	1. $ _____	1. $ _____
2. Weekly Mandatory Deductions		
a. Federal, State and Local Income Taxes	2a. _____	2a. _____
b. F.I.C.A. (Social Security)	b. _____	b. _____
c. Mandatory Union Dues	c. _____	c. _____
d. Mandatory Retirement	d. _____	d. _____
e. TOTAL MANDATORY DEDUCTIONS	e. _____	e. _____
3. Weekly Net Income (Line 1 minus Line 2e)	3. _____	3. _____
4. Weekly Allowable Exemptions		
a. Medical/Dental Insurance for Family (unreimbursed premium)	4a. _____	4a. _____
b. Prior Child Support and/or Alimony Orders	b. _____	b. _____
c. TOTAL ALLOWABLE EXEMPTIONS	c. _____	c. _____
5. Weekly Available Income (Line 3 Minus Line 4c)	5. _____	5. _____
6. COMBINED TOTAL WEEKLY AVAILABLE INCOME	6. _____	
7. Percent Contribution of each parent (line 5, each parent, divided by line 6)	7. _____	7. _____
8. WEEKLY CHILD SUPPORT AMOUNT (From Chart)	8. _____	
9. TOTAL WEEKLY CHILD SUPPORT AMOUNT EACH PARENT (percent line 7 each parent, times line 8)	9. _____	9. _____
10. Percent Contribution of Each Parent Toward Extraordinary Medical/Dental Expenses for Child(ren) and Work Related Child Care Expenses (from line 7)	10. _____	10. _____

PART D—MONTHLY EXPENSES (computed at 4.3 wks./mo.)
Should reflect standard of living established during marriage but
not repeat those income deductions listed on Part C.

	Yours and children (#___) residing with you	Expenses paid for spouse and/or children (#___) not residing with you
SCHEDULE A: SHELTER		
If Tenant:		
Rent	$ _____	$ _____
Heat (if not furnished)	_____	_____
Electric & Gas (if not furnished)	_____	_____
Renter's Insurance	_____	_____
Parking	_____	_____
Other Charges (Itemize)	_____	_____
If Homeowner:		
• Mortgage	$ _____	$ _____
Real Estate Taxes (prices included w/mortgage payment)	_____	_____
Homeowners Insurance (unless included w/mortgage payment)	_____	_____
Repairs and Maintenance		
Heat (unless electric or gas)	_____	_____
Electric & Gas	_____	_____
Water and Sewer	_____	_____
Garbage Removal	_____	_____
Other Mortgages (Specify)	_____	_____
	_____	_____
Snow Removal and Lawn Care	_____	_____
Maintenance Charges (condo/co-op)	_____	_____
Other Charges (Itemize)	_____	_____
	_____	_____
	_____	_____
	_____	_____
Tenant or Homeowner:	_____	_____
Telephone	_____	_____
Service Contracts on Equipment	_____	_____
Cable TV	_____	_____
Plumber/Electrician		
Equipment and furnishings	_____	_____
Other (Itemize)	_____	_____
	_____	_____
	_____	_____
TOTAL	$ _____	$ _____
SHELTER COMBINED TOTAL	$ _____	

SCHEDULE B: TRANSPORTATION

Auto Payment	$ _____	$ _____
Auto Insurance (number of vehicles ___)	_____	_____
Registration, License, Maintenance	_____	_____
Fuel and Oil	_____	_____
Commuting Expenses (state frequency and points of travel)	_____	_____
Other Charges (Itemize)	_____	_____
TOTAL	$ _____	_____
TRANSPORTATION COMBINED TOTAL	$ _____	

SCHEDULE C: PERSONAL

	Yours and children (#___) residing with you	Expenses paid for spouse and/or children (#___) not residing with you
Food at Home and Household Supplies	$ _____	$ _____
Prescription Drugs	_____	_____
Non-prescription Drugs, Cosmetics, Toiletries and Sundries	_____	_____
School Lunch	_____	_____
Restaurants	_____	_____
Clothing	_____	_____
Dry Cleaning, Commercial Laundry	_____	_____
Hair Care	_____	_____
Domestic Help	_____	_____
Medical (exclusive of psychiatric) [unreimbursed only]	_____	_____
Psychiatric/psychological/counseling	_____	_____
Dental (exclusive of orthodontic)	_____	_____
Orthodontic	_____	_____
Medical Insurance (hospitalization, etc.)	_____	_____
Club Dues and Memberships	_____	_____
Sports and Hobbies	_____	_____
Camps	_____	_____
Vacations	_____	_____
Children's Private School Costs	_____	_____
Parent's Educational Cost	_____	_____
Children's Lessons (dancing, music, sports, etc.)	_____	_____
Babysitting	_____	_____
Day Care Expenses	_____	_____
Entertainment	_____	_____
Alcohol and Tobacco	_____	_____
Newspapers and Periodicals	_____	_____
Gifts and Contributions	_____	_____
Payments to Non-Child Dependents	_____	_____
Prior Existing Support Obligations (this family)	_____	_____
(other families—specify)	_____	_____
Tax Reserve (not listed elsewhere)	_____	_____
Life Insurance	_____	_____
Savings/investment	_____	_____

Debt Service (from page 7)   _____   _____
Visitation Expenses   _____   _____
Professional Expenses (other than this proceeding)   _____   _____
Other (specify) _____   _____   _____

TOTAL $ _____ $ _____
PERSONAL COMBINED TOTAL $ _____

Summary of Monthly Expenses (Computed at 4.3 wks/mo):

	Yours & Children (#___) Residing With You		Expenses paid for spouse and/or Children (#___) Not Residing With You		Combined Total Expenses
Schedule A: Shelter	$ _____	+	$ _____	=	$ _____
Schedule B: Transportation	_____	+	_____	=	_____
Schedule C: Personal	_____	+	_____	=	_____
Grand Totals	$ _____	=	$ _____	=	$ _____

PART E—BALANCE SHEET OF ALL FAMILY ASSETS AND LIABILITIES

STATEMENT OF ASSETS Description	Title to Property (H,W,J)	If you contend asset is fully or partially exempt from equitable distribution, state reason:	Value ($)	Date of Evaluation Mo/Day/Yr
1. Real Property				
_____	_____	_____	_____	_____
_____	_____	_____	_____	_____
_____	_____	_____	_____	_____
2. Bank Accounts, Certificates of Deposit				
_____	_____	_____	_____	_____
_____	_____	_____	_____	_____
_____	_____	_____	_____	_____
3. Vehicles				
_____	_____	_____	_____	_____
_____	_____	_____	_____	_____
_____	_____	_____	_____	_____
4. Tangible Personal Property				
_____	_____	_____	_____	_____
_____	_____	_____	_____	_____
_____	_____	_____	_____	_____
_____	_____	_____	_____	_____
5. Stocks and Bonds				
_____	_____	_____	_____	_____
_____	_____	_____	_____	_____
_____	_____	_____	_____	_____
6. Pension, Profit-Sharing Retirement Plan(s), I.R.A.'s, 401(k)'s, etc.				
_____	_____	_____	_____	_____
_____	_____	_____	_____	_____
_____	_____	_____	_____	_____
_____	_____	_____	_____	_____

7. Businesses, Partnerships, Professional Practices

——————————— ——————— ———————————————— ———————— ————————

——————————— ——————— ———————————————— ———————— ————————

8. Life Insurance (cash surrender value)

——————————— ——————— ———————————————— ———————— ————————

——————————— ——————— ———————————————— ———————— ————————

9. Other (specify)

——————————— ——————— ———————————————— ———————— ————————

——————————— ——————— ———————————————— ———————— ————————

——————————— ——————— ———————————————— ———————— ————————

TOTAL GROSS ASSETS $ _____

STATEMENT OF LIABILITIES

Description	Name of Responsible Party (H,W,J)	If you contend liability should not be considered in equitable distribution, state reason	Monthly Payment	Total Owed	Date of Evaluation
1. Mortgages on Real Estate					
2. Other Long Term Debts					
3. Revolving Charges					
4. Other Short Term Debts					

5. Contingent Liabilities

_____   _____   _____   _____   _____

                    TOTAL GROSS LIABILITIES: $ _____
                    (Other than Contingent Liabilities)

                    NET WORTH: $ _____
                    (Other than Contingent Liabilities)

PART F—STATEMENT OF SPECIAL PROBLEMS (Provide a Brief Narrative Statement of Any Special Problems Involving This Case): As example, state if the matter involves complex valuation problems (such as for a closely held business) or special medical problems of any family member, etc.

I certify that the foregoing statements made by me are true. I am aware that if any of the foregoing statements made by me are wilfully false, I am subject to punishment.

DATED: _____   SIGNED: _____

CHECK IF YOU HAVE ATTACHED THE FOLLOWING REQUIRED DOCUMENTS:

1. A full and complete copy of your last federal and state income tax returns with all schedules and attachments.   _____

2. Your last calendar year's W-2 statements and 1099's.   _____

3. Your three most recent pay stubs.   _____

4. Bonus information including, but not limited to, percentage overrides, timing of payments, etc.; the last three statements of such bonuses, commissions, etc.   _____

5. Your most recent corporate benefit statement or a summary thereof, showing the nature, amount and status of retirement plans, savings plans, income deferral plans, insurance benefits, etc.   _____

6. Any agreements between the parties.   _____

7. A statement of prior/pending cases (Part B-5).   _____

The remedies available usually consist of immediate temporary (and ultimately permanent) injunctive relief: The court issues a direct order to the abusing party to cease and desist the behavior complained of and/or to vacate the marital household, to go through counseling, and/or to pay for any expenses incurred as a result of the violence. This order can be issued at an interlocutory hearing in which all of the issues discussed earlier in this chapter are resolved, or in a separate hearing.

A claim for relief from domestic violence can result in a court hearing in much less time than would otherwise be necessary; 10 days or less is not unusual. The hearing can be either *ex parte* or contested. A sample petition for immediate relief from domestic violence and the resulting order follow in Exhibit 7–2 and Exhibit 7–3. In addition, many courts issue a generic mutual restraining order when the complaint for divorce is filed. A criminal complaint can also be taken out for the purpose of having the abusing party arrested and tried for a criminal charge (i.e., assault, battery, etc.).

ex parte
Latin for "on one side only." At an *ex parte* hearing, only one side is present.

A violation of a protective order against domestic violence is usually punished by the imposition of civil contempt, resulting in financial penalty, incarceration, or both until the court is assured that the prohibited conduct will not be repeated. As a practical matter, no court order can deter someone who is determined to commit a violent act. Sometimes the best advice a victim of domestic violence can receive is to immediately vacate the marital residence and go to a shelter for battered women or some other form of "safe house." There, she can receive necessary emotional support as well as some time to evaluate the situation and decide what to do next. Remember that an act of domestic violence is a criminal act, and the proper authorities (police, district attorney) in the criminal justice system should be contacted.

Marital Rape

In recent years domestic violence has become newsworthy, especially as it relates to two specific cases. The first is the issue of **marital rape**. One of the rights of consortium created by marriage is the right to receive and obligation to provide sexual services. As discussed thus far, the failure of a spouse to meet this "obligation" could result in nothing more than a ground for divorce. But until very recently, that obligation of the wife was construed literally by the courts, thus relieving a husband of any criminal responsibility for any non-consensual sexual activity inflicted upon his wife.

marital rape
Forced sexual activity within the confines of a marital relationship.

Remember that the notion of equality of the sexes reflects a relatively recent change in long-held societal views. Originally, rape was viewed not as a crime against the person, but as a crime against property—the man's property. At a time when marriages were arranged for economic reasons, the rape of a daughter was seen as an infringement of the father's property rights.

Husbands had a similar property right in the fidelity of their wives, which was rendered valueless in the wake of rape. Once a couple was married, under the concept of "marital unity," the wife's rights were merged with those of the husband. Accordingly, there existed an exemption in the rape

EXHIBIT 7–2   PETITION FOR RELIEF FROM DOMESTIC VIOLENCE

IN THE SUPERIOR COURT OF _____ COUNTY_____
STATE OF _____

NANCY D. MARTIN,

Plaintiff,

v.   CIVIL ACTION NO. _____

WILLIAM Y. MARTIN,

Defendant.

<u>Petition for Relief from Family Violence</u>

COMES NOW the Plaintiff in the above-styled action, and files this Petition for relief from family violence requiring the imposition of a Temporary Restraining Order, and shows the Court as follows:

Allegations of personal jurisdiction and venue.

1.

Plaintiff is a resident of _____ County, State of _____, residing at
_____ .

2.

Defendant is a resident of _____ County, State of _____, residing at
_____ . Defendant is subject to the jurisdiction of this Court.

3.

Venue is proper in this Court.

4.

Plaintiff has filed a Complaint for Divorce in this Court, Civil Action Number 96–2134A.

Allegations establishing the family unit, location of marital residence, and the Plaintiff's forced flight from the marital residence.

5.

Plaintiff and Defendant are husband and wife with a minor child, age 5 years. The parties and their minor child have been residing in the marital residence, _____. Plaintiff and the parties' minor child fled the marital residence on September 3, 1996, after Defendant physically threatened and assaulted Plaintiff.

Specific allegations of abuse and violence.

6.

Defendant committed acts of physical violence against Plaintiff on September 3, 1996. These acts include being literally pushed around various rooms of the marital residence, as well as being slapped in the face more than once. Defendant was also verbally abusive and profane. The parties' minor child was awake and in the residence at the time these acts of violence occurred.

7.

As a result of these acts of family violence committed by Defendant, Plaintiff is in fear for her safety as well as the safety of her minor child, and is in immediate danger of additional acts of violence. She reasonably believes that there is a substantial likelihood of further family violence unless Defendant is restrained as requested.

Allegations regarding fear for personal safety and of future attacks.

8.

Due to the substantial likelihood of immediate danger of further family violence, a protective order should be issued before service of this action upon Defendant, restraining him from any such further acts of family violence.

Allegation of entitlement to protective order.

9.

Immediate and exclusive possession of the marital residence should be granted to the Plaintiff. Defendant should be enjoined from approaching the marital residence, or having any contact with Plaintiff or the parties' minor child at any other location.

Allegation of entitlement to the exclusion use and possession of the marital residence.

10.

It has been necessary for Plaintiff to employ an attorney to represent her in these proceedings, and she is entitled to recover her reasonable attorney's fees and costs of litigation from Defendant.

Allegation of entitlement to attorney's fees.

WHEREFORE, Plaintiff prays for relief as follows:

a) That this Court immediately issue a Temporary Restraining Order enjoining Defendant from committing further acts of family violence against Plaintiff and/or her minor child, and awarding to Plaintiff temporary exclusive possession of the marital residence;

b) That Defendant be ordered to pay Plaintiff's reasonable attorney's fees and costs of litigation;

c) That a hearing be held within ten (10) days of this date requiring Defendant to appear personally before this Court and show cause why the relief requested herein should be continued; and,

d) For all such other relief deemed proper by this Court.

Respectfully submitted,

_____
Attorney

(A Verification should be attached to the petition.)

EXHIBIT 7–3   SAMPLE EX PARTE ORDER

IN THE SUPERIOR COURT OF _____ COUNTY
STATE OF _____

NANCY D. MARTIN,

Plaintiff,

v.   CIVIL ACTION NO. _____

WILLIAM Y. MARTIN,

Defendant.

Order for Relief from Family Violence

The Verified Petition for Relief from Family Violence having been read and considered, and Plaintiff having prayed that a Temporary Restraining Order be issued *ex parte* having alleged that she is in immediate danger for her and her child's physical safety, and it appearing to this Court that there is a substantial likelihood of immediate danger of further family violence,

IT IS HEREBY ORDERED:

Allegation of entitlement to attorney's fees. Restraining order against further threat of harm by Defendant.

1.

Defendant is hereby restrained and enjoined from doing, or attempting to do, or threatening to do, any act of violence, molesting, harassing, or abusing Plaintiff or the parties' minor child.

Temporary grant of marital residence to Plaintiff.

2.

Temporary exclusive possession of the marital residence, located at _____, is hereby granted to Plaintiff, and Defendant is ordered removed from said residence immediately. Defendant shall not approach the marital residence or have any contact with Plaintiff or the parties' minor child at any other location.

Scheduled time for further hearing on these issues.

3.

The parties shall each appear before this Court on the ___ day of _____, 1996, to show cause why the demands of the Plaintiff should or should not be continued.

Assurance that local police or sheriff will ensure Defendant's removal from marital residence and compliance with the restraining order.

4.

The county sheriff's office shall oversee Defendant's compliance with this Order.

This ___ day of _____, 1996.

_____
Judge

CASE

BRYANT v. BURNETT

Superior Court of New Jersey, Appellate Division.
Decided April 22, 1993.

. . . .

The opinion of the court was delivered by
KING, P. J. A. D.

On this appeal, defendant claims that the evidence did not support the permanent restraining order entered against him on this domestic violence complaint. Plaintiff filed a sworn complaint under the Prevention of Domestic Violence Act of 1991 (Act), *N.J.S.A.* 2C:25–17 to –33, which sought temporary and permanent restraints against defendant. She alleged that on January 7, 1992 defendant hit her, pulled her hair, knocked her to the floor and threatened her with additional violence. She required emergency room treatment.

The Millville Municipal Court issued a temporary restraining order on January 7, 1992 and set a final hearing date for January 15. Defendant was required to pay for the emergency room services and was ordered not to return to the residence where he and plaintiff had lived. Defendant did not appear at the January 15 final hearing in the Superior Court before Judge Forester. He was in jail, apparently on another charge. After taking testimony from the plaintiff, the judge continued the temporary restraint and issued a bench warrant for defendant. The final hearing was rescheduled and held on March 18, 1992. By that time, plaintiff was incarcerated on an unrelated charge but she, along with defendant, did appear at the March 18 hearing.

The record reveals that the time of the January 7 altercation, plaintiff had been living with defendant for three months. Plaintiff testified that, "[h]e asked me to . . . come stay with him." She kept her possessions at defendant's address, and had lived there continuously for three months until the January 7 incident.

Defendant said that plaintiff had no place to stay and he offered her the opportunity to stay at his place as a favor. He did not intend any agreement to live together on any ongoing or permanent basis. He said, "She was supposed to get her own place," apparently after she found a job.

By the time of the March 18 final hearing, plaintiff though then in jail, had obtained her own residence. She no longer had any possessions at defendant's residence. The judge's final, permanent order excepts defendant's residence from the scope of the restraint. Defendant was otherwise restrained from any contact with plaintiff after she was released from jail. Defendant claims that even though he and plaintiff had lived together for three months, their intent at that time that the arrangement was "temporary" deprived plaintiff of standing to bring a complaint under the Act, since she was not a member of his "household."

The Act states that "it is the responsibility of the courts to protect victims of violence that occurs in a family or family-like setting." *N.J.S.A.* 2C:25–18. The Act defines "Victim of Domestic Violence" this way:

> [A] person protected under this act . . . shall include any person who is 18 years of age or older . . . who has been subjected to domestic violence by a spouse, former spouse, or any other person who is a present or former household member, or a person with whom the victim has a child in common. [*N.J.S.A.* 2C:25–19(d).]

The former domestic violence statute, *N.J.S.A.* 2C:25–3 to –16, L. 1981, *c.* 426 required that the victim have "cohabited" with defendant within the definition of that act.[1] The new Act deleted this definition of victim and adopted the more general term "present or former household member" in place of "cohabitants." (Citations omitted.) The new Act contains no requirement that a household member be of the opposite sex or related to the victim, as the former act did. (Citations omitted.) The new Act further provides:

> [T]he Legislature . . . encourages the broad application of the remedies available under

---

1. *N.J.S.A.* 2C:25–3, repealed by L. 1991, *c.* 261, §20, effective date November 12, 1991, stated:

As used in this act:

a. "Cohabitants" means emancipated minors or persons 18 years of age or older of the opposite sex who have resided together or who currently are residing in the same living quarters, persons who together are the parents of one or more children, regardless of their marital status or whether they have lived together at any time, or persons 18 years of age or older who are related by blood and who currently are residing in the same living quarters.

[this act in the civil and criminal courts of this State. It is further intended that the official response to domestic violence shall communicate the attitude that violent behavior will not be excused or tolerated, and shall make clear the fact that the existing criminal laws and civil remedies created under this act will be enforced without regard to the fact that the violence grows out of a domestic situation. [*N.J.S.A.* 2C:25–18.]

Our courts have applied the Act to nonmarital situations where the parties had no children. *Torres v. Lancellotti,* 257 N.J.Super. 126, 607 A.2d 1375 (Ch.Div.1992) (defendant was plaintiff's live-in male friend of eight years). Most recently, the Act was applied to a situation in which a young man and woman were "de facto" household members but maintained separate legal residences. The parties were constant companions, stayed overnight together frequently, and shared certain property.

We find that Judge Forester correctly applied the Domestic Violence Act of 1991 in this case. The parties

were members of the same household at the time of the domestic violence charged. Intent as to the permanency of the relationship and the circumstances of the invitation or agreement to live together were irrelevant in this case where plaintiff had lived in defendant's household for three months. No precise period of residence is specified by the statute to make one a household member. This case certainly involved more than assaultive conduct between casual friends or relative strangers and qualifies as "domestic violence."

DISCUSSION QUESTIONS

Based on the preceding case of *Bryant v. Burnett,* 624 A.2d 584 (New Jersey, 1993), answer the following questions:

1. What classes of persons are included as victims under the New Jersey Prevention of Domestic Violence Act?

2. What was the basis of the Defendant's appeal? How did the court rule on that issue?

laws for acts of sexual activity forced on a wife by her husband. Starting in 1978 in the Oregon case of *State v. Rideout,* 82 Or.App. 747, 728 P.2d 584, public awareness of the marital rape exemption began a trend that continues to this day. Today, the majority of states permit criminal prosecution of a husband who rapes his wife, especially if the spouses are not living together as "husband and wife" (thus reducing the possibility of a fraudulent claim of rape by the wife).

Battered Woman Syndrome

battered woman syndrome

Psychological theory that a woman who is repeatedly subjected to physical abuse by her mate may believe that she must kill her mate in self-defense to avoid future abuse.

Another domestic violence issue receiving public attention is the **battered woman syndrome,** perhaps best remembered from the book and movie, "The Burning Bed." The battered woman syndrome is a legal/psychological theory used in the defense of criminal prosecutions of a wife for the murder of her husband, wherein she claims that as a result of her husband's continuous abuse she was in imminent danger and therefore had to act in her own self-defense. The murder of the husband does not typically occur as an immediate response to an act of violence. More often, it occurs when the man is asleep or has his back to the battered woman. Thus, the traditional claim of self-defense is of no avail.

This is not a claim of insanity, although the wife's state of mind at the time she killed her husband is certainly central to the defense. A "battered woman" has been defined as a woman who is repeatedly subjected to any forceful physical or psychological behavior by a man in order to coerce her to do something he wants her to do without concern for her rights.[1] It has been theorized that such women suffer from "learned helplessness"—that the continuous beatings cause her to become increasingly passive. She no longer believes that any response she could make, including leaving the battering relationship, would have any effect on her situation.

Domestic Torts

There are domestic torts, other than those described above relating to physical abuse, for which relief may be sought, although not necessarily at this preliminary stage of litigation. Two of the other notable domestic torts include the intentional infliction of emotional distress and the intentional infliction of venereal diseases, including AIDS.

INTERVIEW CHECKLIST

The following questions could be asked of a client seeking relief from family violence. This checklist is to be used in conjunction with the basic interview checklist in Chapter 2.

INTERVIEW CHECKLIST

Relationship with abusing party

Name of abusing party

Address, if different than your own

Date of most recent violent act

Detailed description of that act

Dates and descriptions of all prior acts of violence (use additional paper if necessary)

Names and addresses of all witnesses to the acts described above

Did you seek medical treatment for any injuries received as a result of the acts described above?___ If yes, provide details, including names and addresses of all medical providers.

---

1. Lenore Walker, *The Battered Woman*. New York: Harper Collins (1979).

ENFORCEMENT OF INTERLOCUTORY ORDERS

If a party should fail to comply with the order of a court (interlocutory or otherwise) relating to the payment of alimony and/or child support or visitation with minor children, the court has the authority to enforce its orders using its power of contempt. Accordingly, the court in which the divorce litigation is pending has the authority to incarcerate (or otherwise coerce) a party that has been delinquent in meeting his or her obligations. Note that since the parties to an interlocutory order have not yet received their final relief from the court, they are typically less likely to default on their obligations for fear of facing the wrath of the trial judge later in the divorce proceedings. A full discussion of contempt and the other means available to enforce a court order is in Chapter 12.

APPEALS FROM INTERLOCUTORY ORDERS

As a general rule, interlocutory orders are not immediately appealable. If an appeal is to be taken from an interlocutory order, it is normally necessary to postpone any such appeal until a final order or judgment has been rendered terminating the litigation. Exceptions to this rule include interlocutory orders that immediately and directly affect the parties, such as an interlocutory order setting alimony, child custody/support, visitation, and so forth. The procedure and requirements of the appellate process are discussed in Chapter 13. But certain procedural requirements are peculiar to the appeal of interlocutory orders, including obtaining an order from the trial court authorizing an immediate appeal of the interlocutory order. Further, as a practical matter, since the time required to successfully prosecute an appeal can be longer than the effective period of the interlocutory relief, such appeals are relatively rare.

REVIEW QUESTIONS

1. What are three different terms used by different states to indicate "temporary" relief? What is the term used in your state?

2. What interlocutory remedies are available to a divorce litigant? What is the purpose of each remedy?

3. What are the procedural steps necessary to procure interlocutory relief?

4. How does the threat of domestic violence affect a claim for interlocutory relief?

5. What is the "battered woman syndrome," and in what context is it applied?

6. What is the "marital rape exemption," and what is the historical basis for it?

7. What is a financial affidavit, and what purpose does it play in interlocutory divorce proceedings?

8. Why is the relief awarded on an interlocutory basis so important in divorce litigation?

9. Is it possible to appeal either the granting or denial of interlocutory relief?

10. What specific remedies are available to a victim of domestic violence?

KEY TERMS

battered woman syndrome
domestic violence
ex parte
financial affidavit

interlocutory relief
local rules
marital rape
pendente lite
show cause

STATE RESEARCH PROBLEMS

Research the laws of your state and answer the following questions:

1. What is the procedure for obtaining interlocutory relief in your state, and more specifically, for the court in your community? (Remember that different courts within the same state can have differing rules.) What must be filed, and with whom is it filed? What is the average time required to have an interlocutory hearing?

2. Find out what, if any, affidavit or other documentary evidence is required to obtain interlocutory relief. In what resource did you find this information? Obtain a copy of the form required by the court in your locality.

3. What is the procedure for obtaining relief from domestic violence in your state and in your locality? What is the authority for your answer?

4. What proof is required to obtain relief from domestic violence, and what kinds of relief are available?

5. Are there any shelters for victims of domestic violence in your community? What are the requirements for obtaining shelter there? How long can someone stay? What is the cost?

PRACTICE EXERCISES

1. Review the financial affidavit in this chapter (Exhibit 7-1). What specific documentation would you tell a client to bring to your office that would allow you to complete this form?

2. Using either the form provided in this chapter (Exhibit 7-2) or a form used in your jurisdiction, prepare a petition for relief from domestic violence based on the facts contained in the case of *Bryant v. Burnett* (also in this chapter).

Divorce—Discovery and Investigation

CHAPTER OBJECTIVES

In this chapter, you will learn:

- *The goals of discovery and investigation in divorce litigation*

- *The scope of discovery in divorce litigation*

- *The procedure for using each of the discovery tools*

- *The advantages and disadvantages of each of the discovery tools*

- *The particular issues that are most often the target of discovery requests in divorce litigation*

After the pleadings have been filed, the process of discovery and investigation begins. Unlike television and the movies, real-life courtroom battles should not provide any surprises. Using formal discovery techniques such as depositions, written interrogatories, requests for the production of documents, requests for admission, and requests for physical and mental examinations, as well as informal discovery techniques (witness interviews, searches of official records, etc.), each party has a full opportunity to discover in advance of trial the facts known to their adversary. Discovery may also be had from nonparty witnesses through depositions and requests for production of documents. Typically, the information available through discovery is limited to what is relevant to the subject matter of the litigation and is not subject to any privilege (i.e., attorney-client). If the party to whom a discovery request is directed believes that the requested information falls beyond the proper scope of discovery or is propounded to harass or intimidate, an objection to the request may be offered in lieu of an answer. In preparing discovery requests, consideration must be given to the claims, defenses, and demands put forth by the other party. The factors that are most often the subject of divorce discovery requests are the parties' respective financial needs and abilities and their ability to act as the custodial parent of any minor children.

OVERVIEW OF DISCOVERY

Ignorance may be bliss, but in litigation ignorance is an invitation to malpractice. The essence of sound litigation is thorough and complete preparation. Paralegals have primary responsibility for the factual portion of the case. Accordingly, for many paralegals, discovery and investigation are among their most important activities. The term **discovery** is generally used to describe the formal process in litigation by which one party can obtain relevant facts and information from the other party, as well as nonparty witnesses, to assist in preparation for trial. The information thus obtained is provided under oath and as such is a form of **testimony.** Occasionally, the term *discovery* is used interchangeably with *investigation,* or *informal discovery,* which more accurately describes the informal process by which information can be obtained from either adverse parties or third parties to the litigation.

discovery
The formal process by which parties in litigation are entitled to receive factual information known to other parties.

testimony
Sworn statements of a witness.

Here are the various types of formal discovery:

— Depositions upon oral or written examination

— Written interrogatories

— Requests for production of documents and things

— Requests for admissions

— Requests for physical and mental examinations

(Be aware that while the exact names of these discovery tools may vary from state to state, the theory remains constant throughout.)

Examples of informal discovery or investigation include the use of private investigators, searches of public records, visits to sites of the incidents under investigation, and informal questioning of witnesses. Unlike formal discovery, informal discovery can, and should, commence before initiating the litigation, so it can be used to assist in formulating the theory of the plaintiff's case.

The scope of discovery, or the range of information that can be inquired into, is not without limit. Generally speaking, the scope of discovery is limited to that information which is

— Relevant to the subject matter of the litigation

— Not subject to a claim of privilege

Further, the information sought need not be admissible in court so long as it is likely to lead to the discovery of admissible information. As a practical matter, the issues that are most frequently the target of discovery requests in divorce litigation are

— *Financial status*—including a party's current income and expenses, as well as any assets owned or liabilities owed

— *Fitness as a parent*—including all aspects of the party's relationship with his or her minor children

— *Marital fault*—including allegations of adultery, cruelty, use of narcotics, etc.

Relevancy

relevance
The degree to which a piece of evidence tends to prove or disprove a fact in controversy.

Relevant information is that which tends to prove or disprove the existence of a fact that is of significance to a claim or defense at issue in litigation. For example, information concerning a party's income is relevant to the issue of how much alimony and/or child support should be paid; information concerning a spouse's drug addiction is relevant to the issue of which parent should be granted custody of the minor children of the marriage. In divorce actions, relevancy may become an issue when one party seeks to discover information relating to premarital conduct (i.e., whether a spouse's sexual history prior to marriage is relevant in a case involving a claim of adultery).

But merely because information is relevant, it is not necessarily discoverable, if it is duplicative or if its probative value (its value as proof of a fact) is outweighed by the prejudice the evidence might cause. For example, a court might not admit into evidence a videotape of a party engaging in sexual intercourse with a person other than his spouse, because while it may be relevant, it could unduly inflame the jury against the unfaithful spouse. Further, a party would not be permitted to prove his credibility by introducing the testimony of dozens of witnesses to that effect.

Privilege

privileged information
Information obtained through a privileged relationship.

Privileged information includes communications made within the scope of certain protected relationships (such as between physician and patient or between an attorney and client). They are immune from forced disclosure (see Chapter 2 for a discussion of the attorney-client privilege). Information that is privileged is not subject to discovery. For example, generally it would not be permissible for one party to seek discovery from another party's physician about her patient's physical condition. (But if a party were to make an issue of their own physical or mental status, they would waive that privilege and the relevant information and documentation would most likely be discoverable.) Also, while most states recognize the spousal privilege (in which a party can prevent testimony by a spouse), there is no spousal privilege in divorce litigation. (See Chapter 1 for a discussion of the spousal privilege.)

admissible evidence
Evidence deemed sufficiently reliable to be considered by a court.

Admissible Evidence

Admissible evidence is evidence that is of such a character and quality (relevant, nonprivileged, credible, etc.) that a court will allow it to be introduced at trial. In discovery, it is not necessary that the information sought be of such high character and quality, so long as it is designed to lead to admissible evidence. For example, in discovery it is permissible to ask a question that calls for an answer based on **hearsay** if the answer is designed to lead to admissible evidence.

For example:

Q. When did you learn of your husband's infidelity?
A. I was told of his affair by my neighbor, Dianne.
Q. What did Dianne tell you?
A. Dianne told me that Mary saw my husband entering the Good Times Motel and Grill with his secretary and a bottle of champagne.

This last question calls for a response based on hearsay, and while such a line of questioning would be inadmissible at trial, it is permissible in discovery. Armed with the information that Dianne knew of the defendant's affair and that she told the deponent, the attorney can now prepare to take depositions of Dianne and Mary to discover precisely what they know, when they learned it, and how they learned it.

hearsay
A statement made by an out-of-court declarant for the purpose of proving the truth of the statement.

Objections to Discovery Requests

The party receiving the discovery request has an affirmative obligation to comply with the request, but that obligation does not extend to all discovery requests. The recipient of the discovery requests may, in lieu of providing the information sought, object to all or part of a discovery request. Examples of some more common objections include

— That the information sought is not relevant to the subject matter of the litigation, and/or that it is being sought solely for the purpose of harassment

— That the information sought is privileged

— That the information sought is likely to subject the recipient of the request to unnecessary and/or undue hardship or expense

— That the information sought is cumulative

— That the form of the question is inappropriate (i.e., using a leading question to elicit information from a friendly witness)

If an objection is appropriate, it is stated in lieu of an answer, and the reason(s) for the objection must be specifically stated. Answers to any other discovery requests for which there are no legal objections must be provided. (NOTE: *Most states conduct discovery in a similar fashion. It is inevitable, however, that the rules of any particular state are likely to vary from the general outline presented here. You are cautioned to research the particular rules of your own state.)*

Duty to Supplement Responses

It may be possible to require the party responding to the discovery requests to supplement the responses should any new information become available prior to the end of the litigation. This is especially important when requesting information that is subject to change. For example, questions concerning income, expenses, and medical conditions should require supplementation of responses. Otherwise, the information obtained through discovery may become obsolete.

DEPOSITIONS

deposition upon oral examination

Questions posed to a live witness, answered orally, under oath.

A **deposition** is a discovery device in which one party asks questions addressed to a live witness or adverse party sworn to respond truthfully, and the answers are recorded verbatim for later review or use at trial. The person who is deposed is called the *deponent*. Depositions do not occur in open court; rather, they generally take place in a law office (although they can occur anywhere). Depositions may be taken via oral examination or written examination. The vast majority of depositions are taken through oral examination of the deponent. Accordingly, when this text refers to depositions, it is referring to depositions upon oral examination.

There are many advantages to a deposition over the other varieties of discovery:

— The attorney and paralegal have an opportunity to actually look deponents in the eye and evaluate their credibility and how they will perform as a witness in the courtroom.

— The attorney has the opportunity to ask follow-up questions if an answer is evasive or if additional information is sought.

— Depositions can provide necessary information in a relatively short period of time compared with other forms of discovery (hours versus weeks).

— Depositions are especially useful for obtaining information from nonparty expert witnesses (such as psychologists) for establishing or rebutting the fitness of a spouse to be the custodial parent or of a claim of cruelty or insanity. Depositions may also be taken from nonparty lay witnesses (such as neighbors and friends of the parties) to reveal the details of the spouses' daily life while living as husband and wife. (Generally, nonparty witnesses are not obligated to respond to written interrogatories.)

The primary disadvantage of a deposition is the cost. In addition to the hourly rate of the attorneys and paralegals for the preparation for, attendance at, and review of the deposition, the court reporter must also be paid for her time for taking down (or recording) the deposition, transcribing the notes, and copying the transcript. This can cost a client from $200–$300, and even up to $1,000 or more, depending on the length of the deposition. Other disadvantages of depositions are that they give witnesses an opportunity to practice their testimony before trial. The witness is better prepared to answer the questions he will probably be asked at trial. The questions asked at a deposition may also inadvertently reveal the strategy that is to be employed later in the litigation.

Procedure for Depositions

Unlike most forms of formal discovery, depositions can be used to obtain information from party and nonparty witnesses. This is an important distinction, because the procedure differs depending on the status of the deponent. To take the deposition of a party, a notice of deposition is sent to that party's attorney, giving notice of the date, time, and place of the deposition. A sample notice of deposition is at Exhibit 8–1. While courtesy and professionalism require that whenever possible the date, time, and place of the deposition be agreed upon in advance by all parties, the rules of discovery do not so require.

EXHIBIT 8–1   NOTICE OF DEPOSITION

IN THE SUPERIOR COURT OF _____ COUNTY
STATE OF_____

JEANNE CLAIRE MORRISON,

Plaintiff,

v.   CIVIL ACTION NO. _____

THOMAS JAMES MORRISON,

Defendant.

Notice of Deposition

To: Thomas James Morrison, and his attorney of record,

Peter A. Bair, Esq.
500 Main Street
City, State 12345

You are hereby notified that the attorney for the Plaintiff in the above-styled action will take the deposition of the Defendant, Thomas James Morrison, on the 24th day of April, 1996, at the offices of the attorney for the Defendant, 500 Main Street, City, State 12345, commencing at 10:00 a.m., and continuing day to day until concluded. The Defendant is further instructed to bring to the deposition all tax, income, and expense records for the period of time 1992 through and the time of the deposition.

This 1st day of April, 1996.

_____
Matthew S. Cornick

**subpoena;
subpoena duces
tecum**

Court order to a non-party requiring attendance at a deposition or court hearing. A subpoena duces tecum requires the nonparty to also provide access to specific documents or tangible things.

If the parties do agree to the details of the deposition, a formal notice of deposition should still be sent to all interested parties.

If the proposed deponent is a nonparty witness, a **subpoena** is required to give the court personal jurisdiction over the witness. A subpoena (literally, "under penalty") is a court order to a person to appear at a particular date, time, and place for the purpose of giving testimony on certain matters. No motions or hearings are required to obtain a subpoena. Usually, courts dispense blank subpoenas that can be filled in with the appropriate information and returned to the court to be issued much as a court issues a summons. A sample deposition subpoena is at Exhibit 8–2. A non-party deponent should be served with a subpoena and all other parties of record should be served with a notice of deposition, informing them of the deposition. *There are subpoena for depositions and subpoena compelling attendance at trial. You need to become familiar with the various forms, so that you will use the appropriate form at the proper time.*

Consider a case in which the divorce is filed in Kentucky and the nonparty witness lives in New York. Which is the appropriate court to issue the subpoena for the deposition? Barring extraordinary circumstances, the comparable court of the county or district in which the deponent then resides (in this example, the New York court) is the appropriate forum to obtain the subpoena. The reason is simply one of personal jurisdiction; the Kentucky court does not have personal jurisdiction over this deponent, the New York court does. Therefore, it may be necessary to request a foreign court to issue a deposition subpoena for a nonresident.

Often at a deposition, questions are asked that require the deponent to refer to certain documents or records to refresh her memory or to ascertain the answer. For example, a party may be asked, "What was your gross income in 1992?" But a deponent need not bring any documents or records to a deposition unless specifically requested to do so. The mechanism for requesting the production of the necessary documents at the deposition varies between parties and nonparty witnesses. For a party deponent, the notice of deposition should be combined with a request for the production of documents. (See later in this chapter for a discussion of the request for production of documents.)

For a nonparty witness, a **subpoena duces tecum** should be used. A subpoena duces tecum is a court order to a person having certain relevant documents or things in his possession to present them at a deposition or trial. This can also be used to merely obtain the documents without scheduling a deposition.

Paralegal Role before the Deposition

When either planning to take a deposition or when the client is to be deposed by the adverse party, preparation is the essential ingredient. There are several tasks that a paralegal must accomplish before a deposition, including the following.

Prepare and Serve Required Subpoena and/or Notices of Deposition

As noted above, the deponent must be formally notified of the impending

EXHIBIT 8–2   DEPOSITION SUBPOENA

_____   CASE NO. _____

VERSUS   SUPERIOR COURT
                                         _____ COUNTY, STATE OF_____
_____

                                         TO: _____

                                         _____

GREETINGS:

YOU ARE HEREBY COMMANDED, THAT YOU BE AND APPEAR AT _____

_____

_____ IN THE CITY OF

_____ ON _____ , 19 _____ , AT

_____ O'CLOCK A.M. P.M., THEN AND THERE TO BE EXAMINED ON

DEPOSITION FOR THE PURPOSE OF DISCOVERY AND FOR THE PRESERVATION OF

TESTIMONY BY THE_____ IN THE ABOVE-ENTITLED CASE, AND TO BRING

WITH YOU TO SAID DEPOSITION THE FOLLOWING DOCUMENTS, OBJECTS AND

THINGS:

_____

_____

_____

FAIL NOT UNDER PENALTY OF THE LAW.

THIS _____ DAY OF _____ , 19 ___ .

                           DEPUTY CLERK,_____ SUPERIOR COURT

deposition. Once issued, the deposition subpoena must be served upon the witness. This typically can be accomplished in a less formal manner than the service of a complaint and summons. A notice of deposition is served upon the adverse party's counsel.

Prepare Questions for Taking Attorney

Often an attorney asks a paralegal to prepare a preliminary list of questions to be asked at a deposition. Your first step is to determine the purpose(s) of the deposition. For example, it could be to determine an adverse party's financial status; to authenticate medical or employment records; to ascertain or corroborate the basis for an allegation of, or defense to, wrongdoing in a fault-based divorce, and so forth. The next step is to determine a logical progression for the questioning. Typically the deposition begins with basic questions about the deponent's background, including the deponent's name, address, age, social security number, etc. A deposition of an adverse party in a divorce action would then most likely entail the following topics:

— *History of the parties and the marriage*

— Prior marriages of deponent, including date and place, minor children, date of dissolution

— Date and place of wedding to the client (If it is a common-law marriage, then questioning should focus on the parties' mutual intent to be married and how that intent was manifested.)

— Each party's behavior during the marriage, especially how the behavior changed during the course of the marriage (How did each party contribute to the demise of the marriage?)

— *Employment history*

— A compilation of all jobs held, the dates of each, salary history, reasons for leaving, skills gained, etc.

— If deponent has not worked outside of the house recently, determine what skills the deponent has, and what if any impediments exist to prevent the deponent from earning a satisfactory salary.

— *Assets at the commencement of the marriage*—What property was owned by each spouse at the commencement of the marriage; its value at that time; its value now; the whereabouts of the property at present. If the property has been sold, what has happened to the proceeds of the sale?

— *Assets obtained by either party since the commencement of the marriage*—What property has been obtained by either party since the commencement of the marriage; how it was acquired; which party was originally responsible for the acquisition; what contributions or payments have been made by the party not originally responsible for the acquisition of the property; what was the value of the property at the time it was acquired; what is the present value of the property.

— *Retirement benefits of the deponent spouse*—In what retirement plans is the deponent a participant; what is the nature of each plan; what is the name and address of each plan administrator; to what extent is the deponent vested; when will the deponent be fully vested; whether the deponent is entitled to receive any military retirement benefits.

— *Standard of living during the marriage*—Number and description of vacations per year; ability to save and invest money; availability of domestic help.

— *Parenting skills of both parents*—Compliments and criticisms of both the deponent and the other spouse (the client) as parents; details and proof of any criticisms. This is especially important if custody of, or visitation with, the minor children is contested.

— *Financial affidavit*—Review every category of expense and income; determine how each amount was ascertained; what evidence the adverse party has to corroborate their calculations; the deponent's prioritization of the expenses, if there is not enough income to pay for everything.

(See the sample deposition, Appendix B, to see how some of these principles are put into practice.)

Prepare Deposition Materials

If the deponent is to be asked to identify or authenticate certain documents, records or things, the paralegal should arrange those items in the same order as the line of questioning for easy reference. The items to be used as exhibits at the deposition should be marked and numbered by the court reporter in advance of the deposition to save time and expense.

Prepare Client for the Deposition

Because a client must be prepared to answer almost any question, it is necessary to rehearse the deposition. It is critical to note that this rehearsal is not meant to put words in the client's mouth. The client needs to be cautioned that all answers must always be truthful and based on his own personal knowledge. But the client should not be confronted with any questions for the first time during the actual deposition. Therefore, a paralegal may assist the attorney in conducting a mock deposition.

Paralegal Role during and after the Deposition

At the deposition, the paralegal should, at a minimum, act as an additional set of ears, eyes, and hands for the attorney. Among the paralegal functions during the deposition are

— Taking accurate notes of the deponent's responses so that the attorney can review the testimony during a break in the deposition or immediately after it has concluded

— Evaluating the credibility of the deponent

— Organizing and handling the physical exhibits to be presented during the deposition (and if it is discovered that a necessary exhibit is missing, the paralegal may have to leave the deposition to retrieve it)

— Organizing, handling, and reviewing the physical exhibits brought to the deposition by the deponent

— Reminding the attorney of any particular questions or areas of inquiry that the attorney may have forgotten

Being present at the deposition also serves the paralegal well if he or she is called upon later to summarize the transcript of the deposition.

After the transcribed deposition is returned by the court reporter, the paralegal may be requested to do the following:

— *Review the deposition*—Once the transcribed deposition has been delivered by the court reporter, the paralegal should read the transcript to check for errors and misstatements. Additionally, when the deponent is the client or a friendly witness, the paralegal should be responsible for forwarding a copy of the transcript to the deponent so they can review it themselves. If either the deponent or paralegal discover any errors, typographical or otherwise, the corrections can be reported.

— *Prepare a summary of the deposition*—A deposition summary (also called a *deposition digest*) is essentially a detailed, organized summary of the relevant information obtained during a deposition. A deposition summary has several purposes, including (a) providing a concise synopsis of the deposition which can be used to review the results of the deposition quickly; and (b) allowing other legal professionals not present at the deposition to quickly acquaint themselves with information obtained at the deposition.

INTERROGATORIES

interrogatory
Written request for information which is responded to in writing and under oath.

Interrogatories are written requests for information, sent by one party to another party in litigation, that must be responded to in writing and under oath within a prescribed period of time.

Procedure

Either party can send interrogatories to another party at any time after litigation begins. Typically, the party upon whom the interrogatories are propounded has thirty days to respond (with an additional three days, if served by mail). To prevent the use of interrogatories to harass or annoy an adverse party, many jurisdictions have specific limitations on the number of interrogatories one party can send to another (i.e., no more than fifty interrogatories, not including subparts). This limitation can be exceeded upon a sufficient showing to the court that a need for additional interrogatories exists or when the parties voluntarily agree.

The primary advantage of interrogatories as compared to depositions is that interrogatories are more cost effective, since there is no additional cost for a court reporter. They are often served before a deposition to obtain basic, objective information upon which the questions for a deposition can be formulated. They may be used to discover the identity of persons who should be the subject of a deposition or to discover the existence of relevant documentary evidence. They are also effective for obtaining detailed information (i.e., financial information) that can be obtained only after a lengthy review by the responding party of the financial data available.

The primary disadvantages of interrogatories as opposed to depositions are the lack of immediacy of the responses and the opportunity for the responding party to carefully craft the responses. Additional disadvantages are that interrogatories usually can be served only upon parties to the litigation and not upon nonparty witnesses; the credibility of the witness cannot be fully ascertained as the interrogation occurs without the opportunity for a face-to-face meeting; it is easier for a reluctant party to provide evasive, vague, or incomplete answers; and, the actual responses, while based on the party's information, may not be in the party's own words.

Drafting Interrogatories

Interrogatories can be served upon a party all at one time or in several sets, as long as the total number of interrogatories propounded is within the limit permitted. Each interrogatory should be clear, concise, and request specific information. Here are some examples.

WRONG: "What is your current financial condition?"

This interrogatory is much too vague. There is no guidance as to what is meant by "current" or "financial condition." Does that include income, savings, property, or retirement benefits? The sought-after information can be obtained through a series of more detailed interrogatories, as noted below.

RIGHT: "State your present income from all sources. State if any changes in your income are anticipated within the next 12 months."

"List all real property in which you have an ownership interest, and state the nature and approximate value of that interest."

Additional examples of appropriate interrogatories are included in Exhibit 8–3.

EXHIBIT 8–3   SAMPLE INTERROGATORIES

IN THE SUPERIOR COURT OF ————— COUNTY
STATE OF —————

JEANNE CLAIRE MORRISON,

Plaintiff,

v.   CIVIL ACTION NO. ———————

THOMAS JAMES MORRISON,

Defendant.

<u>Plaintiff's First Interrogatories to Defendant</u>

To: Thomas James Morrison, and his attorney of record, Peter A. Bair

Pursuant to Rules 26 and 33 of the State Civil Practice Act, Plaintiff herewith serves upon you the following interrogatories. You must answer each interrogatory separately and fully in writing under oath, unless it is objected to, in which event the reasons for the objection shall be stated. The answers must be signed by the person making them, and the objections must be signed by the attorney making them. You must serve a copy of your answers, and objections if any, upon the undersigned attorney within thirty (30) days after the service of these interrogatories.

Seeks background infor-
mation regarding the
adverse party.

1.

State your full name, giving all previous names, if any, by which you have been known.

2.

What is the date of your birth?

3.

State the country, city, county, and state of your birth.

4.

State with respect to your current residence and all locations at which you have previously resided since the date of your marriage to the defendant:

a) Address (street or apartment number, state, city, county, and ZIP code)

b) Type of residence (apartment, duplex, condominium, single-family dwelling, etc.)

c) Size of residence (square feet, number and character of rooms)

d) Beginning and ending dates of your residence at each location

e) Other persons besides yourself, including relatives and children, who now reside or have resided with you at each location.

5.

State with respect to your educational background:

a) High school from which you graduated and year of graduation

b) Any college or university degrees that you now hold, giving the date you received each degree, the name of the college or university, and the field of concentration

c) Name of any educational or vocational training other than the above that you have received, giving the beginning and ending dates of your attendance as a student, and the field of concentration.

6.

State with respect to your present and past employment:

a) Present employer, stating name, address, and telephone number

b) Name and description of your present job or employment

c) Gross income or earnings received from your present employer on an annual and monthly basis

d) If self-employed, describe the nature of your work, providing the information requested in parts (a) through (c) above.

e) List all previous employers or periods of self-employment for the period since the inception of your marriage to defendant, providing the information requested in parts (a) through (d) above.

f) Do you plan to change your present employment in the foreseeable future?

g) Have you interviewed or consulted with anyone concerning a change in employment status within the last 6 months?

h) If not currently gainfully employed, list your skills and/or training that will enable you to obtain a job.

i) If not employed, list all attempts to obtain employment.

Seeks information regarding employment, including past employment and plans for future employment.

7.

Do you have the use or possession of any automobiles or other motor vehicles? If so, state the make, model and year of each vehicle and the name of the legal owner and any lienholders.

8.

Do you have need of an automobile for personal transportation?

Seeks information regarding responding party's ownership of automobiles. Part of determination of value of party's property.

9.

Are you a member of any civic or social organization? If so, state the name and address of each organization and the beginning and ending dates of membership.

Seeks information regarding any clubs. Can be used to locate witnesses who may be able to testify regarding adverse party's behavior.

10.

Are you a member of a professional or business organization or club? If so, state the name and address of the organization(s) or club(s) and the beginning and ending dates of membership.

Seeks information regarding children.

11.

Do you have children born of your marriage to the plaintiff? If so, state the:

a) Name of each child

b) Birthdate of each child

c) Birthplace of each child

d) School, kindergarten, or nursery attended by each child

12.

Do you have children born of previous marriage or relationship with a person other than the plaintiff? If so, state the name of such party and all information requested in Interrogatory No. 11 (a) through (d) above.

13.

Have any of your children ever attended a private school? If so, state the name and address of each school, and the beginning and ending dates of attendance, including tuition paid.

Seeks information regarding adverse party's spending habits.

14.

List all charge accounts and/or credit cards that are now in your control, custody, or possession. State the average monthly balance due for each of the listed accounts for the past year.

15.

Where do you buy the majority of clothing for yourself? For your children?

16.

How much did you spend on clothing in the past 12 months for yourself? For your children? For others? (If others, state the name and relationship with such person.)

17.

Have you taken any vacations or trips for pleasure within the past year? If so, state the location, any travelling companions, and the amount of your expenses.

18.

What percentage of your meals are taken in your home, and what percentage are taken outside your home?

19.

State with respect to your leisure time activities:

a) Your hobbies or recreational activities

b) The nature of any recreational equipment or vehicles that you own or have the use of

c) Whether you have any pets or animals. If so, describe and state your expenses for the last 12 months.

20.

State with respect to your physical and mental condition:

a) What is the current condition of your health?

b) Are you now under the care of a physician, psychologist, or other practitioner of the healing arts? If so, state the name of the care giver and the condition for which you are being treated.

c) When was the last time you consulted professionally with a physician, psychologist, or other practitioner of the healing arts?

d) Do you have an immediate need for medical attention?

e) What were your expenses for personal medical services within the last 12 months?

f) What were your expenses for medical services for the children of your marriage to the defendant, if any, within the last 12 months?

g) Do you have a foreseeable need for dental services?

h) What were your expenses for dental services in the last 12 months?

21.

List all real property in which you claim an interest, right, or title, providing complete legal descriptions, and state the nature of your interest.

Seeks information regarding real property owned by adverse party.

22.

If you claim an interest in your present residence (or that of the defendant), state:

a) The outstanding mortgage or debt on the property

b) The fair market value

c) The amount of any payment being made to reduce the mortgage or other indebtedness thereon

d) Who makes such payments?

23.

State whether, as of the date of answering these interrogatories, you have any interest in an option to acquire an interest in real property. If so, state the terms of the option(s), and describe the property subject to each option.

24.

List all transfers of property, real and personal, that you have made within the last 12 months to any individual or legal entity, describing the property transferred, the date of the transfer, to whom such property was transferred, the consideration paid by such transferee, and the consideration paid by you at the time of acquisition of the property.

Seeks information regard-ing adverse party's investments.

25.

List each corporation in which you own or claim an interest in stocks, bonds, franchises, or operating rights, or of which you may be the payee of any note. With respect to each corporation, state the following information:

a) As to any stocks owned, state the number of shares of each class outstanding and the number of shares of each class that you hold. List the total amount of dividends you have received in the last three years on each of these stocks.

b) As to any bonds owned, state the total number and denomination of bonds held. Also state the term of the bonds, including the maturity and annual interest or coupons.

c) As to any franchise or operating rights, state in detail the nature of each franchise or operating right, including when and where acquired.

d) As to any other type of claim you may have against any corporation, whether represented by note or otherwise, state the nature and amount of the claim.

e) If any of the stocks, bonds, notes, or other evidence of indebtedness listed in this answer is pledged as collateral, or otherwise used as security by you, state what is pledged, and the amount of the debt for which it is pledged or used as collateral, as well as the date of the pledgings.

26.

With respect to any business venture, whether a corporation, general or limited partnership, sole proprietorship, joint venture, trust, or otherwise, in which you claim a financial interest or from which you have received income, state the following:

a) The name and principal place of business, the financial interest you claim, the date(s) the interest was acquired, and the consideration paid

b) The names and addresses of all other persons having a substantial interest in such business and the ratio or proportion that your interest has to the interest of all others therein

c) If any such business has an interest in real property, list such holdings, giving the date of acquisition and acquisition price. Describe the improvements, if any, on such real property.

d) If you owned an interest in any business venture within the last five years, but no longer own said interest, state the information requested in subparts (a) through (c), and the date on which such interest terminated, whether by gift, sale, or otherwise, and the consideration received with respect to each business.

27.

State with respect to each of the last 3 years, the following information:

a) Each and every source of gross income and the amount of gross income derived from each source

b) Any expenses attributable to each source of income listed

c) The net income from each source listed

28.

State all current debts owed, including the name and description of each creditor, the amount, and the terms of payment.

29.

State the location and contents of all safe-deposit boxes, safes, vaults, or other places of safekeeping valuable papers over which you have possession, custody, or control; and provide an inventory of the contents of same.

Seeks information regarding personal property owned by adverse party.

30.

State the name(s) of any bank(s), savings and loan associations, brokerage firms, or other financial institution(s) in which you have an account, or have the right to withdraw funds. State the amount in each account as of the date of filing the answers to these Interrogatories.

31.

List any trust created by you, stating the date of its creation, the names of the trustees, the beneficiaries, the terms of the trust, including the date or event upon which it will terminate and the amount and source of the corpus of the trust.

32.

State any estate of which you have been a beneficiary, heir, devisee, legatee, or have in any way received property. With respect to each, state the following:

a) The name of the decedent, date of death, decedent's relation to you, and the name of the executor or administrator

b) A list of all property, real or personal, that was received by you, or to which you are entitled

c) The names of all other persons who have received, or will receive, property from said estates.

33.

State in detail what, if any, grounds you have for divorce against the plaintiff; and/or what, if any, complaints you have against the plaintiff as a spouse.

Seeks information regarding legal claims and defenses to be used by adverse party.

34.

State in detail what, if any, grounds you have for denying the plaintiff full custody of the minor child(ren) of the marriage; and/or what, if any, complaints you have against the plaintiff as a parent.

35.

State the name and address of the person who assisted you in the preparation of the answers to these interrogatories, the capacity in which he or she assisted, and the assistance given.

_____

Matthew S. Cornick
Attorney for Plaintiff

(A certificate of service is attached here.)

Responding to Interrogatories

Upon receipt of interrogatories, the paralegal carefully calculates the deadline for responding to the interrogatories and then records the date on all appropriate calendars. The paralegal then forwards a copy of the interrogatories to the client, along with a letter that instructs the client to review the interrogatories and to prepare a list of preliminary responses, along with any questions he might have; alerts the client to the impending deadline; and, requests that the client schedule an appointment within a week or so to meet with the paralegal and/or the attorney to formulate the responses to the interrogatories.

At the same time, the paralegal, in conjunction with the attorney, reviews the interrogatories to determine if any require the interjection of an objection (and if so, the basis for the objection) rather than an answer. When reviewing the interrogatories with the client, the paralegal must be careful to remain within proper ethical boundaries, referring those interrogatories calling for the imposition of legal judgment to the attorney. The client's precise answers are recorded by the paralegal. The paralegal then prepares the final responses, and while it is permissible to alter the language used by the client to answer the interrogatories, the factual content of the answers must remain inviolate. Once the responses are completed, the client reviews the final product. Assuming it accurately portrays his responses, the client signs a Verification. The responses are then signed by the attorney and served upon the opposing party. Most jurisdictions no longer require that discovery requests and/or responses be filed with the court.

REQUESTS FOR PRODUCTION OF DOCUMENTS AND THINGS

Documentary and other tangible evidence can be obtained by means of a request for **production of documents** and things. In divorce practice, the documents likely to be the subject of such a request are documents that tend to establish the financial status of a party, such as tax returns, year-to-date pay stubs, statements from banks and other financial institutions, financial statements, deeds to real property (including records of any encumbrances upon that property), insurance policies (life, health, disability, etc.), titles to personal property (automobiles, boats, etc.), and stock certificates or other documents evidencing an ownership interest in a corporation and/or partnership. (If an interest in a closely held corporation is an issue, production of the corporate minute book should be sought, since it contains and documents the complete history of the corporation.) A request for production of documents can also be made to either corroborate or attack a party's claim or defense relating to fault for the dissolution of the marriage, such as credit card records and receipts, photographs, diaries, letters, etc. Two sample sets of requests for the production of documents are at Exhibit 8–4.

> **production of documents**
> Written request for documents or other tangible things in the possession, custody, or control of an adverse party or non-party witness.

The rules of many states also permit a party in litigation to request the production of documents and things from a nonparty by means of a subpoena, or by sending a request for production of documents to the nonparty witness. Thus, it is possible to obtain documentary evidence not currently in the possession, custody, or control of a party, or that a party fails to produce as requested. For example:

— A spouse's travel history can be established by requesting that an airline produce copies of tickets.

— The equity in a parcel of real estate can be determined by requesting the production of a statement of the remaining mortgage balance (from the mortgage holder), as well as copies of any appraisals of the current property value (from the appraiser).

— Copies of jointly filed federal income tax returns can be obtained from the Internal Revenue Service.

— Joint financial statements can be obtained from the preparing accountants or attorneys.

— Copies of partnership agreements in which either spouse has an interest can be obtained from the partnership.

— Records of jointly held accounts can be obtained from banks, savings and loan institutions, and brokerage houses.

Drafting Requests

As with any discovery request, requests for production of documents should be drafted with as much specificity as possible. This specificity should be

EXHIBIT 8–4   SAMPLE REQUEST FOR PRODUCTION OF DOCUMENTS

IN THE SUPERIOR COURT OF _____ COUNTY
STATE OF _____

JEANNE CLAIRE MORRISON,

Plaintiff,

v.   CIVIL ACTION NO. _____

THOMAS JAMES MORRISON,

Defendant.

Plaintiff's Request for Production of Documents from Defendant

COMES NOW Plaintiff and requests that Defendant make production of documents and things, and permit Plaintiff to inspect and copy the same at the office of its counsel of record, all within thirty (30) days following service hereof and in accordance with Rule 34 of the State Civil Practice Act.

Seeks documentation relating to the adverse party's income.

1.

Copies of all income tax returns filed by you, individually and/or jointly with others, with the Federal and State governments for the years 19 ___ through and including 19___ .

2.

Copies of all declarations of estimated income tax filed by you, individually and/or with others, with the Federal and State governments for this current year, 19___ .

3.

All paycheck stubs or other documentation given to you by your employer showing your income for the period of time from January 1, 19___, to and including the date of any trial in the above-referenced matter.

Seeks documentation relating to the adverse party's account with financial institutions.

4.

All records of any accounts maintained in any bank, savings, or other financial institutions by you, individually and/or jointly, including, but not limited to, monthly statements, canceled statements, deposit slips for the period of time from January 1, 19 ___ to and including the time of any trial in the above-referenced matter.

Seeks documentation relating to adverse party's ownership of real and personal property.

5.

All evidence of property and or any interest in any property of any kind and character owned by you, individually and/or jointly with others, including, but not limited to, reversionary interests, notes, corporate agreements, partnership agreements, profit-sharing agreements, pension plan statements, and savings account passbooks.

6.

All warranty deeds, quit-claim deeds, and deeds to secure debt that name you as grantor, individually and/or jointly with any other person, relating to any property in which you have had or claimed an interest or equity from January 1, 19____ to and including the date of any trial in the above-referenced matter.

7.

All automobile registration certificates and automobile title certificates naming you, individually and/or jointly with others, as the owner.

8.

All stock certificates, bond certificates, mutual fund certificates, and any other evidence of ownership naming you, individually and/or jointly with others, as owner.

9.

All copies of all personal financial and/or net worth statements submitted by you to any bank or lending institution from January 1, 19____ to and including the date of any trial of the above-referenced matter.

Seeks documentation of any third-party appraisal of the value of real or personal property belonging to the responding party.

10.

All documents and/or letters received by you from January 1, 19____ to and including the date of any trial of the above-referenced matter, from any real estate agent, attorney, accountant, bank officer, stock broker, appraiser, or any other person, notifying you of the value of your interest in any corporation, trust, reversionary interest, or in any real or personal property.

11.

All life insurance policies and certificates on your life.

_____
Matthew S. Cornick
Attorney for Plaintiff

(A certificate of service is attached here.)

From: Nonparty Witness—Qualified Retirement Plan Administrator

(NOTE: *Depending on state rules, a request to a nonparty may require a subpoena.*)

IN THE SUPERIOR COURT OF_____ COUNTY
STATE OF _____

JEANNE CLAIRE MORRISON,

Plaintiff,

v.   CIVIL ACTION NO._____

THOMAS JAMES MORRISON,

Defendant.

Notice to Produce

To: Retirement Plan Administrator

You are requested to produce copies of the documents designated below, which are in your possession, custody, or control. You may do so by mailing copies of said documents to my paralegal, Pat Taylor, at the address noted below no later than June 11, 19___. You may also include a bill for any reasonable expenses incurred in copying the records and for your time.

Seeks general documentation regarding the adverse party's retirement benefits.

1.

Provide copies of documentation containing the exact names of all qualified plans and related trusts sponsored by participant's employer, including trust tax identification numbers and the date of the latest IRS determination letter for each plan.

2.

Provide copies of each plan and trust and amendments thereto, a Summary Plan Description (with modifications, if any) for each plan, and the appropriate benefit election and consent forms for the plan.

Seeks specific information regarding the adverse party's current entitlement to the plan benefits.

3.

Provide the participant's most recent benefit statement under each plan.

4.

Seeks documentation regarding whether the adverse party's retirement plans are "qualified" as defined by the Internal Revenue Service, and thus subject to the provisions of a Qualified Domestic Relations Order.

Provide a copy of any procedures used by the plan administrator to determine whether a Domestic Relations Order was to be considered "Qualified" as defined under the rules and regulations of the Internal Revenue Service.

_____
Matthew S. Cornick
Attorney for Plaintiff

(A certificate of service is attached here.)

applied to both the item required and the time period for which the item is requested. The documents requested must be described with sufficient particularity so that the person responding to the request can comply with it. For example, compare the two following requests for production:

WRONG: "Provide all financial records."

This request presents numerous problems. What is a financial record? Certainly this would include tax returns, bank account statements, and canceled checks. But would it also include receipts from automatic teller machines and credit card receipts? And would it require the responding party to provide such documentation for an indefinite period of time? Such a request would almost certainly result in an objection to its being vague and causing undue burden and expense. Instead of using ambiguous terms such as *medical records,* or *financial records,* the better practice is to specifically request the particular items required.

RIGHT: "Provide all paycheck stubs or other documentation given to you by your employer showing your income for the period of time from January 1, 1994, to and including the date of any trial in the above-referenced matter."

Responding to Requests

The procedure for responding to a request for production of documents is very similar to that employed in responding to interrogatories. Upon receipt of the request, the paralegal forwards a copy of the request to the client with instructions to assemble as many of the requested documents as possible. When meeting with the client to review the documents, the paralegal ensures that only those documents that were actually requested are forwarded to the adverse party. For example, if only "tax returns" are requested, it is not necessary to include bank account records, ledger sheets, or other similar documents. The paralegal must also ensure that all privileged documents are withheld. A typical privilege applied to documentary evidence is the **work product** rule, which provides that documents prepared by or for a party in anticipation of litigation are not discoverable unless the information contained within them is not otherwise discoverable without undue hardship to the party seeking the production. Examples of work product in divorce litigation are an individual financial statement prepared by a party's accountant, or an appraisal of any real property held individually by a party prepared in anticipation of divorce litigation.

work product
Documents or tangible things prepared in anticipation of litigation. Work product is not normally subject to discovery requests.

REQUESTS FOR ADMISSION

One party can request another party to admit or deny the truth of a fact at issue or the genuineness of a document relevant to the litigation. **Requests for admission** (also called *requests to admit*) are not phrased in the form of a question, but as statements of fact. While the time frame for propounding and responding to requests for admission is generally the same as that for both interrogatories and requests for production of documents, the distinguishing

request for admission
Written request to an adverse party for admission or denial of specific facts at issue in litigation.

FOCUS ON FEDERAL INCOME TAX RETURNS

It is axiomatic that an adverse party should be requested to produce recent federal tax returns (with all accompanying schedules) in divorce litigation. Once obtained, the returns should be examined carefully, since they can contain a treasure trove of information including, but by no means limited to salaries paid by owned corporations, dividend income, interest income, annuities, partnerships (income or losses; tax shelter investments), royalties, trust income, capital gains or losses, any miscellaneous income, property taxes paid (and then the existence of the property), interest paid, investment counsel fees, and legal and accounting fees. This same scrutiny should be applied to the client's own tax forms, since they can reveal information that adverse counsel may find advantageous.

If the adverse party either will not or cannot produce the requested tax returns, copies can be requested directly from the IRS.

To request these returns the taxpayer must execute IRS Form 8821. The Internal Revenue Service is exempt from most subpoenas or requests for production of documents. Note that if a copy of a joint tax return is requested, only one of the taxpayers needs to file Form 8821.

feature of a request for admission is that, if it is not responded to within the time permitted, *the matter is deemed to have been admitted.*

Requests for admission serve best to narrow the issues for litigation, to confirm suspicions and beliefs, and to clarify disputed issues. They are not especially useful for obtaining information known to another party or witness. They are usually continuing in nature, so should any additional information later become available, the necessary corrections should be promptly tendered.

Requests for admission are also useful to establish the authenticity (or genuineness) of any documentary evidence to be used at trial. Just as a live witness must swear to tell the truth and identify himself before testifying, documentary and physical evidence must be properly authenticated before a court will accept it as evidence. Authenticity should not be confused with accuracy; a document may be genuine (not a forgery), yet contain factual errors. Authenticity is established by the oral testimony of a person having personal knowledge as to the genuineness of the document.

The paralegal must, in assembling the documentary evidence to be used, consider how it is to be authenticated. For example, if financial statements are to be used at trial, the person responsible for creating the statement would authenticate it; a photographer would authenticate a photograph he had taken. Authenticity can also be stipulated to by the parties in advance of trial, thereby relieving the party seeking admission of the evidence of the burden of bringing a corroborating witness to court. Accordingly, it is common practice to attach copies of documents to a request for admission and to request that the adverse party admit the genuineness of the document.

Drafting Requests for Admission

Requests for admission should be drafted very narrowly, so that each request contains only one fact; the more facts in a request, the more likely it is to be denied. The paralegal prepares a list of all facts that either should be stipulated or that can be proven. That list is then broken down into as many individual requests as possible. For example, see how specific the requests are in Exhibit 8–5.

EXHIBIT 8-5   REQUEST FOR ADMISSION

IN THE SUPERIOR COURT OF _____ COUNTY
STATE OF _____

JEANNE CLAIRE MORRISON,

Plaintiff,

v.   CIVIL ACTION NO. _____

THOMAS JAMES MORRISON,

Defendant.

Defendant's First Requests for Admission from Plaintiff

COMES NOW, Defendant and, pursuant to Rule 36 of the State Civil Practice Act, requests the Plaintiff to admit the truthfulness of the following matters within thirty (30) days of service of this request.

1.

That Plaintiff has, since the separation of the parties, maintained a meretricious relationship with a member of the opposite sex.

Seeks admission of a meretricious relationship.

2.

The name of the individual referred to in Request No. 1 is Robert Andrews.

Seeks confirmation of the identity of the third party involved in the meretricious relationship.

3.

Robert Andrews remained in the residence of the Plaintiff until approximately 8:00 a.m. on the 15th day of March, 199__.

Seeks confirmation of a specific incident of infidelity.

4.

The Plaintiff and Robert Andrews slept in the same room on the occasion referred to in Request No. 3.

5.

The minor child of the parties was also present in the Plaintiff's residence at the time referred to in Request No. 3.

Seeks confirmation that the parties' minor child was a witness to the incident specified in Items 3 and 4.

Seeks an admission of the authenticity of documents that may tend to cast the adverse party in a negative light.

6.

The receipt from the Hotel D'Amour, dated March 22, 199——, and signed by Plaintiff, attached hereto as Exhibit A, is a true and genuine copy of the original.

7.

That the individuals depicted in the photographs attached hereto as Exhibits B through E are the Plaintiff and Robert Andrews.

8.

That the marriage between the parties is irretrievably broken and there is no hope of reconciliation.

_____
Peter A. Bair
Attorney for Defendant

(A certificate of service is attached here.)

Responding to Requests for Admission

The most important aspect of responding to requests for admission is to be certain to respond to all of the requests. The possible responses are

— Admit the matter.

— Deny the matter.

— State that the party does not have sufficient knowledge and information to form a belief as to the truthfulness of the matter.

— State an objection to the request.

— Respond using some kind of combination of the above.

The procedure is similar to that used for other discovery requests; the paralegal forwards the request to the client for review. The responses should be those of the client, but the paralegal and attorney may help the client craft the responses so that they do not inadvertently admit matters that are not to be admitted.

REQUESTS FOR PHYSICAL AND MENTAL EXAMINATIONS

When the physical and/or mental condition of a party, or of a third person in the custody of a party, is an issue in litigation, a party can request the court to issue an order for the physical or mental examination of the party or third person. In a family law practice, this request can pertain to:

— A dispute as to the paternity of a minor child (requiring a blood test of both parents and the child)

— A psychological or psychiatric examination of a parent or child when child custody is an issue

— A medical examination to confirm or dispute allegations of physical and/or sexual abuse by a spouse

Because this discovery tool is obviously more invasive than any other, a party generally must first file a motion for a physical (or mental) examination and obtain a court order to compel attendance at such an examination. Upon a showing of good cause, the court will grant such a motion. The costs of the examination must be borne by the party seeking the discovery, unless otherwise ordered by the court. The party against whom such an order is granted may obtain a copy of any report made by the examining physician by requesting it; however, by so doing, she must produce any similar reports she may have in her custody, control, or possession. A sample motion for a physical examination follows at Exhibit 8–6.

INFORMAL DISCOVERY

Much information is available through investigative techniques beyond the scope of the rules of civil procedure. This information can be obtained before initiating the litigation and can provide the basis for allegations of a fault-based divorce. It also can provide a glimpse at the finances of the adverse spouse before that spouse is able to secrete or exhaust marital property or funds. The most valuable source of such information is typically the client. It is a common practice to give the client a copy of the initial client interview checklist (see Chapter 2), so that the client knows precisely what information is required and has the opportunity to procure the necessary documents before litigation. Other methods of informal discovery follow.

Review of Courthouse Records

A quick trip to the courthouse can establish what, if any, real property is owned by a spouse, and what, if any, liens against the property exist. A list of all real and personal property on which taxes are paid can be obtained from the tax assessor's office. The criminal records clerk or docket can provide useful information, especially if you are seeking information to support your client's allegations of physical abuse, alcoholism, or drug abuse. (Remember to get a certified copy of any criminal conviction so it will be available for use at trial or an interlocutory hearing.) The civil filing docket will alert you to any other civil litigation in which the opposing party has been involved. If any such files exist, the pleadings and discovery should be reviewed by the paralegal for any relevant information.

Site Inspection and Photographing

If the client is seeking permanent alimony or there is a substantial amount of marital property subject to division, it may be worthwhile to photograph the

EXHIBIT 8–6   SAMPLE MOTION FOR PHYSICAL EXAMINATION (BLOOD TEST)

IN THE SUPERIOR COURT OF_____ COUNTY
STATE OF _____

DARLENE SIMPSON,

Plaintiff,

v.   CIVIL ACTION NO. _____

JOSEPH SUTTON,

Defendant.

<u>Plaintiff's Motion for Blood Test</u>

COMES NOW, Plaintiff in the above-styled action and moves this Court, pursuant to Rule 35 of the State Civil Practice Act, for an Order requiring Defendant to appear and submit to a blood-grouping test, with such restrictions and directions as this Court may deem proper, by one or more qualified physicians to be designated by this Court. It is further moved that the results of the aforedescribed blood-grouping tests be submitted to this Court in the form of a written report by the examining physician setting out his/her findings, including results of all tests made and resulting conclusions.

The Court should find that there is good cause for the granting of this motion in that Defendant disputes his paternity of Plaintiff's natural child, and that such issue is the basis of Plaintiff's Complaint for Paternity.

This____ day of _____ , 19___ .

(A certificate of service is attached here.)

Respectfully submitted,

_____
Attorney for Plaintiff

---

marital residence and furnishings. This allows the trier of fact to actually see the standard of living to which the client has been accustomed.

Witness Interviews

Depositions are not the only way information can be obtained from a nonparty witness. Whether before or during litigation, a paralegal or attorney can ask questions of any nonparty witness willing to be interviewed.

Private Investigators

In cases in which substantial property is at stake, it may prove beneficial to retain the services of a private investigator. Private investigators are especially adept at discovering information relating to (1) a determination of the assets held by an adverse party and (2) corroboration of allegations of marital misconduct (i.e., adultery). Private investigators are often former police officers or have other training as investigators.

WITNESSES

Paralegals work with two different types of witnesses—expert witnesses and lay witnesses. The significant distinctions between them are discussed below.

Expert Witness

An **expert witness** is a nonparty witness whose testimony is based on an analysis and examination of a set of facts in evidence, and who is permitted to state an opinion regarding a question of fact before the court. Experts are used to explain complicated issues to the court and to provide competent testimony concerning issues that only an expert can provide. In divorce litigation, some frequently used experts are

— Psychologists, to attempt to establish the emotional and mental fitness of a party as a parent

— Appraisers, to establish the value of a privately held business or other property owned by a spouse

— Economists, to establish the amount of money a party can be expected to earn within a certain time span

> **expert witness, lay witness**
> Expert witnesses review the facts of a case and give their opinion; lay witnesses testify to what they saw, heard, or did.

Unlike lay witnesses, experts are usually paid for their time. Most are paid by the hour, although it would also be ethical to pay a flat fee. It is, however, unethical to pay an expert witness a contingent fee based on the success achieved at trial. These costs must ultimately be borne by the client, regardless of the outcome. Divorce litigation is unique in that if one party cannot afford the services of an expert witness, a court can order the other party to pay for the expert.

Lay Witness

By contrast, a **lay witness** is typically someone who actually *witnessed* something (i.e., an act of domestic violence or infidelity). Lay witnesses are generally permitted to state only those facts that they know based on their personal knowledge and only those opinions that are based on common experience and having a rational basis (i.e., a lay witness may testify that a person was angry or happy, but only if they also relate the objective factors upon which they base this opinion).

REVIEW QUESTIONS

1. Which discovery tools may be used with non-party witnesses, and what is the procedure for using each?

2. What are the respective advantages and disadvantages of oral depositions and written interrogatories?

3. What is the difference between an expert witness and a lay witness? How are they treated differently during discovery?

4. What does *authentication* mean? What are the methods of authenticating documents, and how do each of them work?

5. What factors would be likely subjects of a discovery request when the issue at question is

   a) The ability to pay alimony and/or child support

   b) The right to have sole custody of any minor children

   c) The alleged infidelity of a spouse as the fault for the dissolution of the marriage

   d) The disposition of the parties' marital residence

   e) The future earning potential of each of the parties

6. Name three methods of informal investigation, and describe the information available from each.

7. How does the procedure for obtaining a physical or mental examination differ from other forms of formal discovery?

8. How is the failure to respond to a request for admission treated differently from a failure to respond to other discovery requests?

9. What is a subpoena duces tecum?

10. What does the phrase "scope of discovery" mean? Generally, what information falls within the scope of discovery?

KEY TERMS

admissible evidence
deposition

discovery
expert witness

hearsay
interrogatory
lay witness
privileged information
production of
   documents

relevance
request for admission
subpoena
subpoena duces tecum
testimony
work product

STATE RESEARCH PROBLEMS

Find the section in your state code and local rules of court relating to discovery in civil cases, and provide statutory authority for the following questions:

1. What specific discovery tools are available?

2. Is there a statutory duty to supplement responses to discovery?

3. What is the procedure for serving a deposition subpoena upon a nonparty witness in your state?

4. How long does a party have to respond to written interrogatories? Is there a limit to the number of interrogatories that one party can propound upon another party?

5. How long does a party have to respond to a request for production of documents? Is there a limit to the number of requests that one party can propound upon another party?

6. What is the procedure for obtaining documentary evidence from a nonparty witness?

ETHICAL PROBLEM

Your supervising attorney has received a telephone call from opposing counsel requesting an additional two weeks beyond the time permitted under the rules to prepare the responses to the interrogatories you had drafted. You and your attorney agree that the two-week delay in receiving the responses would not prejudice your client. But your client is adamant that his spouse not receive any extensions of time. What issues must be considered under these circumstances? What additional facts would you need to fully address these questions?

PRACTICE EXERCISES

1. Obtain a blank deposition subpoena from your local court.

2. Prepare a notice of deposition for Thomas James Morrison according to the rules of your state.

3. Read the deposition of Thomas James Morrison (Appendix B), and prepare the following:

   a) A list of additional questions that you believe should be asked of the deponent

   b) A list of additional documents in the possession, custody, or control of the deponent that he should produce

   c) A summary of the deposition (Spend the bulk of your time in choosing the categories used to organize the information, not in deciding which particular facts to include in the summary.)

4. Based on the deposition of Thomas James Morrison, prepare ten requests for admission that could be served on Jeanne Claire Morrison.

5. Go to your local courthouse and review the various public records available. What specific tools are available to determine whether a person owns any real or personal property?

Divorce—Alimony and Division of Property

In this chapter, we deal with one of the two issues at the heart of most divorce cases: money. (We discuss the other primary issue, children, in the next chapter.) The controversy over financial issues is summarized in these two questions:

— Is either spouse entitled to have some property (or an interest therein) that is currently in the possession of the other spouse?

— If so, what property is to be transferred between the spouses?

The three basic forms in which the transfer of assets can occur are alimony, child support, and property distribution. A general overview of the similarities and differences are presented in the accompanying chart.

	Alimony	Child Support	Property Distribution
—Duration	—Until death of either spouse or remarriage of receiving spouse	—Until emancipation of child	—Until paid
—Bankruptcy	—Not dischargeable	—Not dischargeable	—Dischargeable
—Tax Consequences	—Taxable income for payee; deductible for payor	—Not taxable for payee; not deductible for payor	—No tax consequences
—Modification	—Upon significant change of circumstances	—Upon significant change of circumstances	—Only upon a showing of fraud by one of the parties

The parties must divide their marital property—all property acquired since the inception of the marriage. This can pose intricate questions of valuation of assets such as pension benefits, professional degrees, and closely held corporations. The liabilities remaining after the termination of the marriage must also be apportioned between the parties. Additionally, the specter of bankruptcy often looms on the horizon, since divorce can cause severe economic problems for both spouses.

ALIMONY

Alimony (also called *maintenance* or *spousal support* in some jurisdictions) is the transfer of funds or other property from one party to a former spouse as a continuation of the spousal obligation of support. It is distinguishable from a division of the parties' property, which is not a form of continuing support or maintenance. Traditionally, alimony was solely an obligation of the husband, but two noticeable societal changes have occurred. First, alimony is no longer awarded as freely as it once was. Women are now recognized as being capable of providing for their own support. Second, payment of alimony is based on the relative requirements and assets of each party, so that husbands now have the same right to receive alimony as do wives. In the case of *Orr v. Orr,* 440 U.S. 268, 99 S.Ct. 1102, 59 L.Ed.2d 306 (1979), the United States Supreme Court held that an Alabama statute providing that only husbands could be required to pay alimony violated the Equal Protection Clause of the Fourteenth Amendment.

alimony; maintenance
Support payments made for the benefit of a former spouse.

Duration of Alimony

Unless otherwise provided in a final decree and judgment of divorce, the obligation to pay and the right to receive alimony may terminate upon the earliest of the following events:

— Death of the receiving spouse

— Death of the paying spouse (A minority of states would grant the receiving spouse a claim upon the estate of the paying spouse.)

— Upon the termination of a stated period of time (i.e., 2 years or 10 years)

— Remarriage of the receiving spouse

— Proof of a meretricious relationship on the part of the receiving spouse (Sometimes called the **"live-in lover" law,** it terminates the right to receive alimony when the recipient is engaged in a *de facto marriage.* This aspect of the law evolved in response to a trend in which an alimony recipient would live with a person of the opposite sex without benefit of marriage and thus claim continuing entitlement to receive alimony payments, all the while enjoying the benefits of a new "marriage.")

"live-in lover" laws
Laws that terminate the right to receive alimony upon a finding that the recipient is cohabitating with another person in a marriage-like relationship.

Naturally, the parties can mutually agree that alimony will be paid for a defined period of time (i.e., until the receiving spouse obtains gainful employment; for a period of two years following the date of the final decree, etc.), or that it will continue even after the remarriage of the receiving spouse or for whatever period of time is mutually satisfactory. This understanding should be made a part of the separation agreement, which is then incorporated into the court's final decree and judgment of divorce.

Types of Alimony

Alimony can be awarded in many different forms to meet the requirements of each case. Issues to be considered include (1) the duration and goals of the alimony payments; (2) the frequency of the payments; and (3) whether the payments should be made directly to the former spouse or indirectly to a third party, by paying one or more obligations of the receiving spouse.

Goals of Alimony

As we already noted, the obligation for *permanent alimony* may continue until the death of either party or until the remarriage of the receiving party. The trend in recent years is to award permanent alimony for a limited period of time or to award either rehabilitative or restitution alimony. *Rehabilitative alimony* is intended only to support the former spouse while he or she is actively engaged in training and education to obtain marketable skills, so that he or she will become self-supporting. *Restitution alimony* is intended to act as reimbursement for a party who had previously provided support for the family while the other spouse was training for a high-paying career. For example, restitution alimony might be appropriate for a wife who had worked to support her husband while he was attending medical school, only to see the marriage end in divorce soon after her "investment" in her husband's career was beginning to pay dividends.

Frequency of Payments

If alimony is to be paid in *periodic payments,* it can be paid in a predetermined amount every week or month (i.e., $200 every week or $1,000 every month) or a fluctuating percentage (i.e., 25 percent of gross pay) until the obligation for alimony is terminated. The advantage of using a predetermined sum is that, barring later modifications, each party has a degree of certainty as to the amount of future alimony obligations. The advantage of using a fluctuating percentage is that the alimony will increase or decrease as the income of the paying spouse changes. Alternatively, the total amount of alimony to be paid may be predetermined and paid in a lump sum (either a single payment or a series of payments).

Form of Payments

Alimony can be paid in a form of money (cash, check, etc.), or it can be paid to a third party to satisfy an obligation of the receiving spouse (i.e., where the husband pays his wife's monthly mortgage payment).

These alternatives can be combined to form innumerable potential remedies. *The party with the obligation to pay alimony (or child support, for that matter) should be advised to keep detailed records and corroborative evidence of all payments to protect against a later claim of contempt for nonpayment.*

PRACTICE
POINTER

Amount of Alimony

In the event that permanent or rehabilitative alimony is awarded, the court considers a number of factors in determining the appropriate amount of alimony. The Uniform Marriage and Divorce Act (UMDA) lists the following factors:

— The financial resources of the party seeking alimony, including marital property apportioned to him, including his ability to meet his needs independently, and the extent to which a provision for support of a child living with the party includes a sum for that party as custodian

— The time necessary to acquire sufficient education or training to enable the party seeking alimony to find appropriate employment

— The standard of living established during the marriage

— The duration of the marriage

— The age and the physical and emotional condition of the spouse seeking alimony

— The ability of the spouse from whom alimony is sought to meet her needs while meeting those of the spouse seeking alimony

Additional factors that may be considered are

— Whether the obligation to the minor children practically prevents the alimony recipient from returning to the work force (and similarly, the effect of the cost of any child care necessary so that the recipient can go to work)

— Any legal obligations of the provider of alimony to another family created by a prior divorce

— Any sacrifices made by the dependent spouse to assist the other spouse's career and ultimate earning potential

Marital fault (adultery, cruelty, etc.) is generally not a factor in determining entitlement to, or the amount of, alimony. But a minority of states hold that marital fault either acts as a complete bar to the recovery of alimony or may consider fault as a factor in the determination of alimony.

marital property
Property acquired by either spouse while married; opposite of separate property.

separate property
Property owned by a spouse before getting married; opposite of marital property.

community property; equitable distribution
The two theories regarding ownership of marital property. Under community property, each spouse has a one-half ownership in all marital property. Under equitable distribution, each spouse is entitled to an equitable distribution of all marital property between the spouses.

DIVISION OF MARITAL PROPERTY

The division of marital property is governed by several theories, which we describe in this section. But first we need to consider the difference between marital property and separate property. Generally, **marital property** is defined as property that was acquired by either spouse during the marriage, except gifts and property inherited by one of the spouses individually. **Separate property** is property acquired by a spouse before the marriage began and gifts and property inherited by one of the spouses individually. Generally, parties begin to acquire marital property with the commencement of the marriage and cease to do so at the time of the parties' separation, the filing of the divorce complaint, or the issuance of the final judgment and decree of divorce.

Equitable Distribution Theory

The majority of the states (currently forty-two) apportion the marital property according to the doctrine of **equitable distribution**, which provides that marital property should be divided according to the equities of each case, including

— Age and health of the parties

— Length of the marriage

— Income potential of each party

— Contribution of each party in acquiring the property

— Needs of the custodial parent and the minor children

— Amount and nature of the alimony awarded

SPERLING v. SPERLING

Supreme Court, Appellate Division,
Second Department
March 25, 1991.

. . . .

Before MANGANO, P. J., and KUNZEMAN, EIBER, and MILLER, JJ.

MILLER, Justice.

The sole issue on this appeal is whether or not the court improvidently awarded the plaintiff wife lifetime maintenance in the sum of $100 per week. For the reasons that follow, we find the award improvident.

This marriage lasted for approximately 20 years, during which the parties had two daughters. Both the husband and the wife worked and struggled to make ends meet. At the time of the trial the plaintiff wife Charlotte was 37 years old, the defendant husband Raymond was 39, and their daughters were 19 and 16 years old, respectively. Raymond, a truck maintenance supervisor, earned a gross annual salary of $30,000. Charlotte, a teacher's aide at a Lutheran school, grossed $9,500 per year. The oldest daughter attended college and received some financial aid while working part time, and received a subsidy from her mother. The younger daughter attended high school while working part time to pay for ballet lessons. The parties stipulated that the sole asset, the marital residence, would be sold no later than four years after the younger daughter graduated from high school, and the proceeds would be divided equally between them. They also agreed that Charlotte, as the children's custodial parent, would have exclusive possession of the marital residence until it is sold and would pay its maintenance (including mortgage and taxes) until that time.

Charlotte and the children enjoy good health. Raymond testified to being in "fairly decent health" and explained that although he works full time, he suffered two crushed discs in his back and a fractured heel and has been found to be partially permanently disabled. He receives disability benefits.

At the trial, the sole issues were child support and maintenance. The resulting judgment requires Raymond to pay $40 per week per child in support until each child reached the age of 21 years or is sooner emancipated, and $100 per week maintenance for Charlotte until the death of either party or Charlotte's remarriage.

In the challenging provision of the judgment, Raymond contends that Charlotte is an inappropriate candidate for lifetime maintenance since she is relatively young, healthy, a high school graduate with one year of college and additional training, and various work experience. Charlotte, on the other hand, contends that she devoted her married life (20 years) contributing to the good of the family as parent, homemaker, and part-time wage earner. She subordinated her personal ambitions and interests to family priorities and should not now, when approaching middle age, be penalized for the sacrifice that rebounded to her husband's benefit.

Notwithstanding our concern and awareness of the dire plight of many women who, after long-term marriages, are unrealistically expected to enter the competitive job market from which they have been separated, we find that Charlotte does not fit into that unfortunate category. The trial court's conclusion that "[i]t is doubtful she will ever become fully self-supporting" is simply not substantiated by the record or even consistent with other of the court's findings. Notably the court also found that "[w]ith time, plaintiff's clerical skills, should expand to include secretarial skills thereby increasing her earning capacity, although [she] may need to incur some relatively modest short term training expenses to achieve this goal". Entirely lacking is any basis for the court's ultimate pessimistic prediction that even with training she will never be able to sustain her needs.

That unsupported conclusion is further belied by her past history.

At age 37, Charlotte has demonstrated significant capability and industry. She not only raised two children (who appear to be ambitious and responsible) and maintained a home, but had also worked as a part-time school bus driver (starting when the youngest child was five), a sales person, a bank clerk, and teacher's aide. Since the family was chronically in debt notwithstanding its simple lifestyle, she was unable to complete her training in her chosen field of interpreting for the deaf. Nor was she able to hone her skills as a secretary or computer operator. Consequently, we view the limited nature of her earnings more as an indication of her limited opportunities than of any inherent limitations of her capabilities.

Based upon her age, mental and physical health, and past history, we find that Charlotte, given time and opportunity, will be capable of self support consistent with the parties' marital standard of living, and that, therefore, requiring Raymond to pay nondurational maintenance was improvident. On the other hand, we find the amount awarded insufficient to provide realistically for her rehabilitation.

. . . .

Clearly every case must be determined on its unique facts, and the resultant judicial authorities can provide no "bright-line test" clearly differentiating those cases where a spouse is found to be capable of future self-support, and therefore entitled only to durational maintenance, from those where the dependent spouse is found incapable of future self support and entitled to lifetime maintenance. However, the profile of the plaintiff in this case is clearly more identifiable with the former than the latter.

Where lifetime maintenance has been awarded, the recipient spouse has almost invariably been older than Charlotte, often in impaired health. Furthermore, the supporting spouse was in far better financial condition than Raymond. Thus, lifetime maintenance was directed in *Reingold v. Reingold*, 143 A.D.2d 126, 531 N.Y.S.2d 585 [wife, 52, never worked, husband earned over $100,000 per year], *Iacobucci v. Iacobucci*, 140 A.D.2d 412, 528 N.Y.S.2d 114 [husband owned a successful insurance business, wife had never worked], *Formato v. Formato*, 134 A.D.2d 564, 521 N.Y.S.2d 464 [wife, 46, had no business skills, husband earned $72,000 per year], *Jones v. Jones.* 133 A.D.2d 217, 519 N.Y.S. 2d 22 [wife 50, had psychiatric problems; husband earned $58,000 a year]. (Citations omitted.)

Where the spouse seeking support is relatively young and healthy, however, and is not required to care for young children, durational maintenance has more commonly been awarded (citations omitted).

. . . .

Having determined that Charlotte can be rehabilitated, we must next consider the appropriate time period and amount of financial support. Unfortunately, we cannot realistically hope to "rehabilitate" Charlotte in the dictionary definition of the term, i.e., to "restore to a former capacity" (Webster's Third International Dictionary, at 1914 [1965]), since the lost opportunities of youth are not likely to be recaptured. The more realistic function of durational maintenance is to allow the recipient spouse "an opportunity to achieve [economic] independence" (citation omitted). The maintenance award should therefore be in an amount and for a time period sufficient to give her "a reasonable period of time in which to learn or update [her] work skills and to enter the employment market with a view to becoming self-supporting" (citations omitted).

Statutory guidelines to determine the amount and duration of maintenance are set forth in Domestic Relations Law §236(B)(6), wherein the Legislature directed the courts to weigh and consider 11 factors. Analysis of those factors reveal two distinct legislative concerns relating first to the earning capacity of the parties and, second, to the equitable or meritorious nature of the application for maintenance. Impacting upon the parties' earning ability are their age, health, and the presence of children in the home. The tax consequences of maintenance must also be considered. The equitable factors to be considered include the duration of the marriage, the sacrifice made by the person seeking support in foregoing or delaying education, training, or career opportunities, and each party's contribution to the career or career potential of the other. Also to be considered are wasteful dissipation of marital assets or their transfer without fair consideration in contemplation of the marital action. Moreover, equity requires that the parties' marital standard of living must be considered in gauging the ability of the recipient spouse to become self-supporting, and the amount of maintenance to be awarded. For example, while a recipient spouse with earning capacity of $20,000 per year may be considered self-supporting in a given case, that same income may be deemed insufficient in the case of a spouse who had enjoyed a higher marital standard of living.

Keeping these guidelines in mind, we find that Charlotte requires substantially more financial assistance in the years immediately following the divorce than the $100 per week the court awarded. In order to compete with other applicants in secretarial or computer type employment, she requires substantial training, since she lacks basic secretarial skills, much less knowledge of word processing or computers. While obtaining this necessary training, she must continue working in order to defray her immediate expenses (including mortgage and taxes on the marital residence). Thus, it is reasonable to assume that her period of training may be considerable, that she may not find employment easily, while at the same time having no "nest egg" upon which to fall back. Therefore, we find that an award of $200 per week for the first four years, decreasing to $100 per week for an additional four years will more realistically enable her to rehabilitate herself than the $100 per week permanent maintenance awarded by the Supreme Court. We recognize that with Raymond's gross income of only $30,000 per year, the payment of such maintenance may well require financial sacrifice on his part. However, that sacrifice is justified by the 20 years Charlotte devoted to being primary parent and homemaker, while struggling to meet family obligations, working at one low-paying job after another, without planning for the economic independence she now lacks and did not anticipate she would require.

That two cannot live as cheaply as one in the context of divorce is exemplified by this family of modest means. The limited financial resources that caused financial strife during marriage commonly result, post-divorce, in circumstances more closely resembling actual economic suffering for both parties. In cases such as this, we can only seek to balance the level of their opportunity and deprivation.

Therefore, the judgment is reversed insofar as appealed from on the facts and as a matter of discretion, without costs or disbursements, the maintenance provision of the fourth decretal paragraph of the judgment is deleted, and a provision is substituted therefor directing the defendant to pay the plaintiff by check or money order drawn to her order and forwarded on Monday of each week commencing November 23, 1987, the sum of $200 per week as maintenance for four years, and the sum of $100 per week as maintenance for an additional four years, with all maintenance terminating in the event that either party dies or the plaintiff remarries.

DISCUSSION QUESTIONS

Based on the preceding case of *Sperling v. Sperling*, 567 N.Y.S.2d 538 (1991), answer the following questions:

1. What are the differing characteristics and requirements of what New York terms *lifetime maintenance* versus *durational maintenance*?

2. What form of alimony does the court award Mrs. Sperling, and what is the justification for that award?

Community Property Theory

The remaining eight states (Arizona, California, Idaho, Louisiana, New Mexico, Nevada, Texas, and Washington) use the theory of **community property**. Under this theory each spouse has an equal interest in all of the spouses' marital property, and all such property is to be divided equally (50–50) between the spouses. Usually, fault is not considered as a factor in apportioning marital property. But be aware that regardless of the theory of distribution in effect in any particular state, courts generally have wide discretion in fashioning an award of marital property that is fair and equitable to both parties in light of all the facts.

Commingled Property

To further complicate matters, married couples often pay for property over a lengthy period of time using both separate and marital property. For example, Marcia has owned her own house for five years. She married Greg and they live together in the house for seven years. They both contribute to the monthly mortgage payment. They then decide to terminate the marriage. How can they divide that property upon the termination of the marriage? As always, a number of theories abound, including but not limited to:

Inception of Title Theory
The **inception of title** theory holds that whichever party first had the right to acquire title to the property owns that property. Any later payments by the other spouse do not affect ownership but may create a right for reimbursement for the spouse making such payments.

inception of title theory; source of funds theory
Theories relating to ownership of property. Inception of title theory holds that whichever spouse first had the right to acquire title to the property owns it. Source of funds theory bases ownership on the parties' respective contribution toward the acquisition of the property.

DUGUE v. DUGUE

Supreme Court. Appellate Division,
Third Department.
April 11, 1991.

. . . .

Before CASEY, J. P., and MIKOLL, YESAWICH, MERCURE and CREW, JJ.

YESAWICH, Justice.

Appeals . . . (1) from a judgment of the Supreme Court, ordering, *inter alia,* equitable distribution of the parties' marital property, entered December 6, 1989 in Dutchess County, upon a decision of the court, and (2) from an order of said court, entered September 7, 1989 in Dutchess County, which denied plaintiff's motion for counsel fees.

The parties, both 29 years old at the time, were married on August 10, 1972. This divorce action was commenced on April 17, 1985. Although there were no issue from their union, the three children from plaintiff's previous marriage lived with the couple while they were still together. During the marriage, both parties obtained real estate licenses, and plaintiff also acquired a nursing license. In addition, they purchased a number of income-producing properties, several cars and other tangible items. In 1981, defendant started a real estate business, John Dugue, Inc., which he continues to operate.

Supreme Court granted mutual divorces, awarded the parties their identified separate property, ordered property it determined to be marital property sold and the proceeds therefrom equally divided, denied defendant any distributive award for plaintiff's nursing degree, credited plaintiff with one fourth of the value of John Dugue, Inc. and denied plaintiff's motion for counsel fees. Plaintiff appeals the denial of her request for counsel fees, while defendant challenges the court's distribution of the parties' real and personal property.

Examination of Supreme Court's comprehensive decision discloses that the court properly weighed all the relevant factors required to be considered in effecting equitable distribution, including the tax consequences and earning power of the parties (citation omitted), and then divided the property essentially equally. In view of the length of the marriage and the financial and other contributions of the parties, that division is fair (citation omitted).

Initially, we note that the bulk of defendant's criticism of Supreme Court's decision is directed at that court's resolution of credibility issues. To the extent that defendant claims that his witnesses' testimony should have been credited rather than plaintiff's, we find no reason to disturb the court's treatment of these issues (citation omitted). In any event, defendant's own testimony belies many of his challenges to the award's fairness. For example, he suggests that plaintiff's earning potential is greater than his own and that this fact, coupled with his alleged poor health, mandates that he be allotted more than a 50% share of the marital property. Defendant testified, however, that even though he has worn a pacemaker since 1976, at the time of trial he worked seven days a week, eight hours a day, and earned between $60,000 and $100,000 yearly. Plaintiff in contrast, though in good health, earned a maximum of only $29,000.

Equally uncompelling is defendant's contention that his property flow chart, which purportedly identifies the cash source for each real property purchase, was uncontroverted. The record is to the contrary; plaintiff testified at trial, and Supreme Court apparently accepted her testimony, that the money to attain these properties came from the parties' joint bank accounts.

Nor is defendant entitled to the entire proceeds from the sale of his Mercedes automobile. The vehicle was purchased before this action was commenced, the date Supreme Court chose as the valuation date; accordingly, it was rightly considered marital property (citation omitted). And as for defendant's assertion that he should be credited with an undocumented $30,000 loan advanced to him by his mother, which money was used by the parties to start-up the John Dugue, Inc. real estate agency, it suffices to note that this money was first deposited into the parties' joint account and then later withdrawn to begin the business. Given the presumption that the parties are equally entitled to deposits made to joint accounts (citation omitted), and that defendant's proof failed to overcome this presumption, the loan proceeds were thereby converted into marital property (citations omitted).

A number of defendant's other challenges which do not turn on the parties' credibility are simply unsupported by the record. There is no evidence to support defendant's charge that plaintiff secreted money in a bank account not listed on her statement of net worth to prevent Supreme Court from distributing it equitably. Nor is there any evidence buttressing defendant's claim that he earned the $70,000 in his bank account from commissions on his real estate transactions; hence, Supreme Court, cannot be faulted for distributing one half of this amount to plaintiff. And notwithstanding whether defendant's claim that his financial contribution to the marriage exceeded plaintiff's is accurate, the fact remains that it fails to appreciate the substantial contribution plaintiff made as wife, homemaker, and business associate (citations omitted).

There is little question that plaintiff's nursing degree, obtained during the marriage, is marital property (citation omitted), or that Supreme Court did not equitably apportion the nursing license's value because defendant's expert (and parenthetically plaintiff's as well) did not present an evaluation of it based on plaintiff's actual past and projected future earnings (cita-

tions omitted). There being no acceptable proof of the value of this property in the record, and bearing in mind that this trial, following an earlier mistrial, spanned more than a year, a remittal for additional hearings on this issue is, in our view, unjustified (citations omitted).

Nor is defendant entitled to a credit for the amount of temporary maintenance he paid plaintiff ($7,800 per year since 1986) in light of the fact that he received all the rental income from the jointly owned real estate since 1984. This net profit of $8,000 per year, which was in fact marital property, more than satisfied the maintenance obligation.

RAFIDI v. RAFIDI

Court of Appeals of Texas
Aug. 5, 1986.

. . . .

Before AKIN, HOWELL and HOLLINGSWORTH, JJ.

HOWELL, Justice.

This is a divorce case. Appellant Naim R. Rafidi appeals from the court's division of community property and award of child support. We find no reversible error and affirm the trial court's judgment.

In twenty-three points of error, Husband, Naim R. Rafidi, argues that the trial court's division of the community property constitutes an abuse of discretion. He asserts that the divorce decree awards some 85–90% of the community assets to Wife, Karima N. Rafidi, and that such a disproportionate division is unjustified.

The Family Code directs the trial court to divide the community estate in a just and right manner, giving due regard for the rights of each party and any children of the marriage. (Citation omitted). The trial court has broad discretion in dividing the property, and its judgment will be upheld absent a demonstration of abuse of discretion. (Citation omitted.) The court may consider many factors, including differences in earning capacity and business opportunities and probable future sup-

port. (Citations omitted.) The division need not be equal so long as there is a reasonable basis for an unequal division. (Citations omitted).

The evidence shows that Husband is a petroleum engineer with three college degrees. At the time of trial he was fifty-seven years old. There was no evidence of health problems. Wife, on the other hand, has only a high school education. She has had difficulty obtaining employment and is handicapped by a finger injury. The Rafidis' teen-aged daughter lives with Wife along with three adult children. The evidence permits the inference that Husband's earning capacity exceeds Wife's. An unequal division of the community estate is justified.

The trial court's division of the marital estate included certain property, the existence of which Husband disputes. The property consists of funds withdrawn from a $100,000 money market account, three commercial notes, and various securities. The trial court made the following findings with regard to this property:

> While working overseas for various oil companies during the period 1970 to 1979, Respondent [Husband] supported his family on the living allowance paid to him in addition to his salary and was able to save substantially all of his salary. A small portion of the period 1970 to 1979 was spent in the U.S. where he was not paid a living allowance. The accumulated savings for this period were substantial and are largely unaccounted for.

Petitioner [Wife] is a high school graduate who has been a housewife during the marriage. She is handicapped by the loss of a finger, has no specialized training or job skills, and has been unable to find employment despite good faith efforts to do so. Her earning ability is quite limited.

Respondent has kept meticulous financial records on a current basis and is in possession or control of such records. He has, however, failed to produce any such records.

Respondent has failed to account for the disposition and whereabouts of substantial funds and securities known to have been in his possession and subject to his control. The funds and securities unaccounted for are in addition to those awarded in the Decree of Divorce and are substantial in amount.

Respondent has failed to provide any documents for other substantiation which explain the origin or disposition of the substantial funds and securities which are unaccounted for.

Respondent has failed to provide material financial information or usual and customary documentation of his financial dealings. His explanation of various financial transactions lacks credibility.

Respondent has assets in an unknown but substantial amount that have not been disclosed to the Court and are unaccounted for.

It is evident that the trial court concluded that Husband was fraudulently concealing community assets. A similar case is *Arrington v. Arrington*, 613 S.W.2d 565. . . . The husband in *Arrington* withdrew a sum of money from a brokerage account during the pendency of his divorce suit in violation of a restraining order. The court of civil appeals ruled that "his concealing or disposing of the funds under such circumstances would sustain sufficiently the order of the trial court allowing him the . . . cash withdrawal as part of his share." *Id.* at 569.

In the case before us, the trial court's findings fully justified the property division. The court was free to include the concealed property in the pool of community assets. Once such assets are included, it is evident that the trial court's division was based on the exercise of sound discretion.

Husband argues that the evidence underlying the fraudulent concealment findings is factually and legally insufficient. He testified that the funds in the account represented money given to him by persons overseas to invest in the United States. Husband testified that he had returned the money to the investors. He also stated that some of the money had been used to repay loans that he had obtained from his father and brother. Husband presented no records to substantiate these claims.

The testimony of Wife and the Rafidis' adult daughter contradicted that of Husband. They testified that Husband was a meticulous record keeper even where small sums were involved. Husband took the financial records with him when he left the house upon the couple's separation. Wife stated that the couple had lived in several foreign countries. Husband's employer paid a living allowance to them while they were overseas which enabled the Rafidis to save most of Husband's salary and accumulate the substantial sums present in the accounts. Wife also presented certain handwritten notes of Husband detailing the family's assets and liabilities. The notes tend to show that Husband was a careful record keeper and indicate that he had loaned money to his brother and was not in debt to him.

The trial court's conclusion that the funds had been concealed is adequately supported by the evidence. Husband's version of the events lack credibility. Despite his habit of keeping detailed financial records, he was utterly unable to document the purported transactions that he contends that he conducted with his kin. The little documentary evidence that does exist tends to contradict his claims. The testimony provides an alternative version for the origin of the funds—that they represented salary saved from overseas employment.

Merely because Wife did not provide direct evidence that the property in question still existed does not mean that the trial court's findings are not supported by sufficient evidence. Rather, the record shows that 1) community funds existed; 2) Husband withdrew the money during the pendency of the divorce; and 3) Husband's explanation of the origin, purpose, and disposition of the fund lacks credibility. We conclude that the trial court's findings are supported by legally and factual sufficient evidence. Points of error one through twenty-three are overruled.

. . .

DISCUSSION QUESTIONS

To demonstrate the similarity between the two theories, compare the cases of *Rafidi v. Rafidi*,

718 S.W.2d 43 (1986, Tx.), from Texas, a community property state and *Dugue v. Dugue*, 568 N.Y.S.2d 244 (1991, N.Y.), from New York, an equitable distribution state. Notice how in both cases, the trial court seeks to use its discretion to balance the distribution between the parties. Answer the following questions:

1. In each case, what property does the court include as marital property, and what is the rationale?

2. What standard does each court use in reaching an adjudication of the marital property?

3. How are the two cases similar, and how do they differ?

Source of Funds Theory

According to the **source of funds** theory (also called *pro rata* theory), all contributions toward the acquisition of property by both parties are totaled, and the property is characterized according to the ratio of separate and marital contributions. Accordingly, ownership can vary over time as the ratio of contributions changes.

(NOTE—*A properly prepared antenuptial agreement may circumvent any dispute regarding the disposition of the parties' property. See Chapter 3 for a discussion of antenuptial agreements.*)

SPECIFIC TYPES OF PROPERTY

The particular types of property described below raise unique questions regarding the distribution of that property. Accordingly, each requires additional consideration.

Appreciation in Value of Separate Property

The value of separate property commonly appreciates. Consider a case in which one spouse purchases a residence before the marriage. During the marriage, the parties live together in the residence, make improvements to the property, and pay the mortgage obligation. To what degree, if any, is the nontitled spouse entitled to any appreciation in the value of the residence accrued during the marriage? Generally, appreciation of separate property (during the marriage) that is due to the inherent nature of the property or to market or other factors is considered separate property. But income derived during the marriage from separate property may well be considered marital property.

The different equitable distribution jurisdictions use two theories to resolve such issues. The first is the source of funds theory, in which the proportionate value of the party's separate property is returned to that spouse as separate property, and the remaining value of the property is treated in accordance with the laws of that state for the distribution of marital property. The second theory is the **transmutation of funds** theory, which holds that once separate and marital property are commingled, the entire property becomes marital property.

Pension and Retirement Benefits

A majority of the states hold that pension rights (vested or unvested, contributory or noncontributory, subject to one or more contingencies) constitute marital property that may be divided upon the dissolution of the marriage. As a matter of fact, very often—especially in marriages of long duration—pension and retirement benefits form the largest single asset owned by the parties. Pension rights may be considered as deferred payment for services rendered. What follows is intended as merely a general overview of the rules governing the distribution of such assets; the most important lesson you learn from this section should be knowing when a law firm should retain competent expert advice to analyze and place a specific dollar value on the benefits available.

Pension and retirement benefits pose several problems when distributing marital property. For example, the benefits may not be available for distribution for many years. Therefore, no one really knows what their value will be at the time of distribution. Additionally, as noted below, certain retirement benefits may legally be paid only to the employee unless a Qualified Domestic Relations Order is properly prepared.

Types of Retirement Plans

First, let's look at the retirement plans commonly available to private employees. **Qualified retirement plans** are those subject to Sec. 401–407 of the Internal Revenue Code, and include profit-sharing plans, 401(k) plans, employee stock option plans (ESOPs), and pensions. The cardinal rule of a qualified retirement plan is that it must not discriminate in favor of highly compensated employees. **Nonqualified retirement plans** are often created solely for management and other highly compensated employees, and include stock appreciation plans (also called *phantom stock plans*), stock option plans, and deferred compensation plans. Individual Retirement Accounts (IRAs) are considered nonqualified plans.

Qualified Domestic Relations Order

While nonqualified retirement plans are treated merely as contractual assets, qualified retirement plans can be controlled by a **Qualified Domestic Relations Order (QDRO).** The effect of this order is to make an ex-spouse or children of the marriage the alternative payee for a portion of all of the qualified retirement plans. (The QDRO is typically made in conjunction with a separate agreement or a final judgment and decree of divorce.) Prior to the Retirement Equity Act of 1984, such retirement plans were effectively exempt from marital property, since the proceeds could legally be paid directly only

transmutation of funds theory
The theory that holds once marital property and separate property are commingled, the entire property becomes marital property.

qualified retirement plan; nonqualified retirement plan
A qualified retirement plan does not discriminate in favor of highly compensated employees. A nonqualified retirement plan favors management and other highly compensated personnel.

QDRO (Qualified Domestic Relations Order)
A court order to an administrator of a qualified retirement plan to pay benefits to a person other than the participant in the plan.

to the employee. Even after the 1984 revisions, the retirement plan administrator is severely limited as to whom and at what time the proceeds of the
retirement plan may be paid. It is only through a valid QDRO that payments
may be made to a party other than the employee. Any award of retirement
proceeds pursuant to a QDRO must account for the following factors:

— The alternative payee will not be able to receive any benefits in
  excess of the participant's accrued benefits as of the date of distribution.

— The alternative payee may not receive a distribution from the plan
  until the participant's "earliest retirement age," which is defined as
  the date on which the participant is entitled to a distribution of
  benefits under the plan; or, the latter of (a) the date the participant
  attains the age of 50, or (b) the earliest date on which the participant could begin receiving benefits under the plan if he terminates
  his employment with the plan sponsor. Some plans do allow a participant to receive "in-service distributions," that is, a partial distribution of benefits while still in the employ of the plan sponsor.
  In such cases, distributions to the alternate payee may commence
  immediately, and the date of earliest retirement is considered to be
  the date of distribution.

— While the QDRO must ultimately be approved and signed by the
  presiding judge, it must also pass the review of the retirement plan
  administrator.

— The value of a participant's interest in a qualified plan (or a nonqualified plan) is usually not easily ascertainable without expert
  assistance. The reasons for this are: the funds in a retirement plan
  are placed in financial vehicles that are subject to the substantial
  price fluctuation (i.e., stocks, bonds, etc.), which creates difficulty
  in predicting their value at a date years in the future; it is difficult
  to accurately estimate the life expectancy of the participant; and
  the date when distributions are first made to the alternate payee
  may be uncertain. Should the entitlement to these funds be shroud-
  ed by any contingencies, those contingencies may affect the present
  value of those rights. A sample QDRO follows at Exhibit 9–1.

Professional Degrees

A spousal share in an ex-spouse's professional degree (M.D., J.D., Ph.D., etc.)
may be considered a form of alimony, an alternate to alimony, a part of property division, or not at all, depending upon the rule of the forum state.
Approximately one-third of the states have enacted statutes, and more than
one-half of the states now have appellate opinions regarding the division of a
professional degree.

A minority of the states treat the professional degree as a form of marital property, and accordingly the degree must be assigned a particular value.

EXHIBIT 9–1   SAMPLE QDRO

Judicial determination that the retirement benefits are marital property and that the non-employee spouse ("Alternative Payee") is entitled to a share of that property.

1

The court finds that certain interests of the Plaintiff in the retirement benefits provided by her employer, International Business Consultants, Inc., under a plan known as the "International Business Consultants, Inc. Retirement Plan" (the Plan), are marital property and that Defendant is entitled to share in these interests as recited below.

2

The court further finds that the parties were married on August 17, 1978, and were separated on November 4, 1993. The court further finds that the Plaintiff, who is a participant in the Plan, commenced her employment with International Business Consultants, Inc. on March 4, 1983 and became a member of the Plan on January 1, 1990. The current mailing address of the Plaintiff/Participant is 3414 Peach Road, Morristown, New Jersey 14994. The current mailing address of the Defendant, referred to herein as the "Alternative Payee," is 75 Palm Drive, Miami, Florida 33433. The Participant's early retirement age is 55 years old, which will occur on January 19, 2008.

Calculation of the precise amount due to the Alternative Payee.

3

The court further finds that the interest of the Defendant/Alternate Payee shall be determined as follows:

One-half of the product obtained by multiplying the amount of the benefit, payment, or refund due the Participant by a fraction whose numerator is the number of years the Participant was employed and a member of the Plan while married and still living with the Alternative Payee, and whose denominator is the total number of years employed while a member of The Plan.

*The Alternative Payee will not receive the full amount of the benefits immediately. Instead, the Plan is to create an **annuity** which is to be funded in the amount calculated in Paragraph 3 when the Participant either dies, retires, or when the Alternative Payee elects to receive benefits (after the Participant is eligible to receive benefits).*

4

It is ordered that the Plan establish an annuity for the Alternate Payee, and that the annuity be paid during the Alternate Payee's lifetime, commencing upon whichever of the following events occurs first: the Participant's death or retirement; or, upon the Alternative Payee's election when the Participant is eligible for retirement. The employer shall establish this annuity based upon a value at a time when any of the foregoing events occurs, whichever occurs first, using the formula set forth above.

5

This order does not require the Plan to provide any type or form of benefit or any option to the Alternative Payee not otherwise provided under the Plan.

The QDRO does not change the benefits available under the Plan.

6

This order does not require the Plan to provide increased benefits determined on the basis of actuarial value.

7

This order does not require the Plan to pay benefits to the Alternative Payee that are required to be paid to another alternative payee under another order previously determined to be a qualified domestic relations order.

8

This order is issued pursuant to state statutory law relating to marital property rights between spouses and former spouses in an action for divorce.

9

The court retains jurisdiction over this matter for the purpose of modifying this order, if necessary, to establish it as a "qualified domestic relations order" in the event that it is not accepted by The Plan Administrator, or for the purpose of entering alternative orders to provide the Defendant with a substantially similar property interest in the property of the Plaintiff in the event that this order, even if modified, cannot be established as a qualified domestic relations order.

If the QDRO does not meet the requirements of the Plan Administrator, the court may modify the QDRO, or alternatively, award the Alternative Payee other comparable property.

In this case, the Alternative Payee will receive payment pro-rated for the period of time the parties were (a) married to each other and (b) the Participant was employed and a member of the Plan. For example, suppose the Participant was employed and a member of the Plan from 1990 through 2001 (12 years) and the parties were married from 1978 until 1993. Thus, the parties were married for four years (1990–1993) while the Participant was employed and a member of the Plan. Therefore, the Alternative Payee is entitled to a 50% share of one-third ($\frac{4}{12}$) of the benefits.

(The services of an expert witness would be required in such cases.) The remaining states treat the professional degree as a factor to be considered when determining the amount and type of alimony to be awarded. Note that by using the degree as part of alimony, rather than property settlement, it may be susceptible to modification as circumstances change over the years and is not subject to the effect of a petition of bankruptcy filed by the paying party. Some courts use "reimbursement alimony" as a method of compensating a party who "invested" in a spouse by offering financial support while that spouse was free to engage in professional education.

Proceeds from Personal Injury Claims

How are the proceeds of a spouse's personal injury claim to be treated in divorce litigation? Generally, that portion of the judgment representing lost income (special damages) is marital property, as the income which this purports to replace would have been. That portion of the judgment that is paid to compensate the spouse for pain and suffering (general damages) is separate property and exempt from distribution by the divorce court.

VALUATION OF PROPERTY

When dividing property between spouses, it is a practical impossibility to divide each piece of property (real and personal) equally. Nor is it desirable to liquidate the spouses' property so that each can receive the cash equivalent. Rather, the court attempts to apportion the property in such a way that each party would receive different properties with the appropriate value. This requires the court to assess the value or price of such property; this process is called **valuation.**

valuation

The process of placing a specific monetary value on a piece of property.

Valuation is a question of fact, not a question of law. Each valuation case or issue is unique; even if the property is identical (which is unlikely), the parties in each case are different. Many values will change as general economic conditions change from "normal" to "boom" or "depression." Generally, there is no single "right" answer to a question of valuation, but rather, a range of possible values, supported by a convincing and logical rationale.

Each valuation case presents several issues to be determined:

— What is the date of valuation?

— What property must be subjected to valuation?

— How is the valuation to be conducted?

— Who is to conduct the valuation?

Date of Valuation

One of the first valuation issues to be determined is the date of valuation, that is, the effective date that the property will have the value assigned to it. Some courts use the date of separation, the date the action for divorce was filed or after formal discovery is completed. But a majority of the courts use either the date of the divorce trial or (more likely) the date of the final dissolution of the marriage. This issue is more critical in those cases in which the value of the property is likely to change significantly during the pendency of the divorce litigation, such as real estate or corporate stock. Along those same lines, it should be noted that there is often a considerable time delay between the time of the valuation and the time of trial. The factor most likely to distort such a valuation is the state of the economy in general.

Property to Be Valued

The foregoing discussion begs the question of how to place a specific value on marital property. This issue is most relevant to the effect of a significant asset, such as a spouse's business (either a sole proprietorship, or an interest in a partnership or closely held corporation) or professional practice, on the distribution equation. This is true whether the business was started before or after the commencement of the marriage, because the appreciation of the business may also be a marital asset. Normally, each side retains an independent appraiser to prepare an appraisal of the value of the asset. Since this can (and often does) result in contradictory opinions, the court then must decide which of the two valuations to accept as correct. Or the court may determine that the actual value is somewhere between the experts' stated valuations.

As to the valuation of a party's interest in an ongoing business, a distinction is to be made between publicly held and closely held corporations. The price of a share in a publicly traded corporation can be determined by doing nothing more than looking at the stock listings in the business section of your local paper. A more problematic situation arises when valuing a closely held corporation. Here are some factors to be considered when valuing a closely held corporation:

— Economic status of the nation in general and the industry in particular at the date of the valuation

— Book value of the stock and the condition and outlook of the specific industry in particular

— Earning capacity of the corporation

— Dividends paid and future dividend earning capacity

— Existence (or lack) of intangible value

— Sales of the corporation's stock and the size of the block of shares to be valued

— Selling price of comparable securities relative to their earnings, dividends, and asset values.

Methods of Valuation

The above referenced factors can be interpreted in a number of ways. Each of these approaches has its proponents and varies in acceptance depending on the jurisdiciton.

Book Value

The **book value** calculates the net assets (assets less liabilities) minus the **par value** of the shares of preferred stock outstanding. Although book value is relatively easy to compute, the value determined by this method rarely equals market value.

Liquidation Value

Liquidation value is the value if all the assets were sold and all liabilities paid; this method works best when the corporation owns a large amount of real estate, which may be worth more if sold and the proceeds invested elsewhere; a disadvantage is that when liquidating a business, property often sells for less than market value.

Return on Investment Value

Return on investment value considers the past earnings of a corporation as an indicator of what future earnings will be. This value is generally calculated by

book value; par value
Book value is the value of a corporation's net assets less the par value of its preferred stock. Par value is an arbitrary and nominal value assigned to a share of common stock (i.e, $1.00).

liquidation value
The value of a corporation remaining after all assets are sold and all liabilities are paid.

return on investment value
The value of a corporation based on the ability of that corporation to generate earnings.

reviewing the earnings over a period of five years. Once the level of earnings is established, then a comparison can be made with another company in the same industry having similar earning capacity that has recently been sold for a specific price. That price is the valuation of the corporation.

Example Valuation

Consider the effects of these various approaches on the following scenario. Here is the ABC Company's financial status:

— Assets worth $10,000,000

— Liabilities of $8,000,000

— 1,000,000 shares of preferred stock, with a par value of $1 per share

— Average earnings over the last five years of $1,000,000

Also consider that other companies in the same industry with similar earnings have recently sold for $1,500,000.

The book value of the ABC Co. is $1,000,000 (10,000,000–8,000,000–1,000,000 = 1,000,000). The liquidation value is $2,000,000 (10,000,000–8,000,000 = 2,000,000). The return on investment value is $1,500,000.

DIVISION OF LIABILITIES

Because financial problems are often stated as a chief cause for divorce, it is equally important that the obligation for the family's debts incurred during the marriage be apportioned in an equitable manner. These can include personal and business debts of either the husband or wife, or both. As a paralegal, your task is to compile a complete list of all outstanding debts incurred, noting the following: whether the husband or wife (or both) are legally responsible for the debt, the purpose of the debt, whether the debt is secured by any collateral (i.e., a mortgage), the monthly payment, and the duration of the obligation.

A court may first deduct any outstanding debts from the value of the marital property before apportioning the property between the parties. Other courts use the apportionment of the parties' debt as a piece of the financial puzzle, as well as alimony and property division. That is, in lieu of awarding one party a particular piece of property, the court may award a commensurate amount of debt to the adverse party. For example, rather than award a wife $5,000 of marital property, it could order the husband to pay $5,000 of marital debt. A court may also order that one spouse pay a specific debt, regardless of which spouse incurred the debt, while the benefits inure to the other spouse. For example, a husband may be ordered to make the payments on the wife's automobile.

Furthermore, the rights of third-party creditors are not limited in any way by a divorce decree or settlement agreement. They are free to seek collection of their debt from either spouse individually or both spouses jointly. This is especially important in those cases where one spouse files for personal bankruptcy, thus discharging his liability for any such debts—unless they are deemed to be in the nature of maintenance and support payments. A "hold harmless" clause (also called an *indemnity clause*) incorporated into the separation agreement may provide that the party apportioned the debt will reimburse the other party if a third-party creditor collects the debt from the other spouse.

EFFECT OF BANKRUPTCY

Often the devastating economic consequences of divorce eventually compel one or both parties to seek relief under the **bankruptcy** laws. (Bankruptcy is governed by Title 11 of the United States Code.) Bankruptcies may be categorized under Chapter 7, which is a liquidation of the debtor's assets and a discharge (or release) of all dischargeable debts; under Chapter 11, which is a reorganization typically used by businesses and individuals with income exceeding $100,000; and under Chapter 13, which is a wage earner plan wherein the debtor repays some or all of his creditors at least a portion of the debts owed to them over a period of several years. We next consider the primary functions of a petition for bankruptcy.

bankruptcy
A federal court procedure by which a debtor may be legally relieved of the requirement to pay certain debts.

Automatic Stay

The **automatic stay** (or prohibition) protects the petitioner against any attempt to seek collection of any existing debt from the debtor's estate effective from the time of filing the petition for relief, pursuant to 11 U.S.C.A. §362. However, Section 362(b)(2) lists those activities that are exempt from the automatic stay, including efforts to collect alimony, maintenance or support payments. When barred by the automatic stay, such collection efforts cannot be sought from the assets or property of the bankrupt estate (property owned by the debtor at the time of filing the bankruptcy petition), but rather can be had solely from the property claimed as exempt by the debtor and any later acquired property.

automatic stay
The requirement that creditors stop attempting to collect debts from a debtor immediately upon the filing of a petition for bankruptcy.

Dischargeable Debt

Bankruptcy laws provide for the ultimate discharge of the debtor's liabilities (pursuant to 11 U.S.C.A. §727). Debts constituting alimony, child support, or otherwise in the nature of support and maintenance pursuant to a court order *are not* dischargeable. (11 U.S.C.A. §523(a)(5)). Conversely, payments made pursuant to a division of property *are* dischargeable in bankruptcy.

When a party under a court-ordered obligation to make some payment on behalf of a former spouse petitions for bankruptcy, the United States Bankruptcy Court in which the petition was filed has sole jurisdiction to determine the **dischargeability** of that debt. In making such a determination, the bankruptcy court looks at the purpose of the debt owed: If it is in the

dischargeability
The quality of a debt that permits a bankruptcy court to discharge, or forgive, the debt. Alimony and child support are not dischargeable in bankruptcy.

nature of support or maintenance, it is not dischargeable; if it is in the nature of a property distribution, it is dischargeable.

The court is not necessarily bound by the categorization of the debt by the separation agreement or the final judgment and decree of divorce. Rather, it looks to the true nature and purpose of the debt. For example, a decree that gives the wife the marital residence while ordering the husband to make the mortgage payments may be construed as a payment in the nature of support or maintenance, if the decree makes clear that the mortgage payment is in lieu of alimony. That same provision could be construed as not being in the nature of support and maintenance if it appears to be nothing more than property distribution. Accordingly, it is wise practice to state specifically whether the debt is in the nature of support and maintenance, and whether the debt is to be dischargeable in any later bankruptcy proceeding.

REVIEW QUESTIONS

1. What are the different types of alimony? What are the goals and purposes of each?

2. What factors are most relevant in determining whether a party is entitled to receive alimony? How do the factors vary for each type of alimony?

3. How are the theories of community property and equitable distribution similar? How are the two theories different?

4. How do the court's obligation to determine the appropriate level of alimony and to ensure the appropriate distribution of marital property affect each other?

5. Why is the proper valuation of the parties' marital property an important concern in divorce litigation?

6. What is the effect of bankruptcy on the paying party upon an order for alimony and property distribution? Under what circumstances would bankruptcy cause a discharge of one party's responsibility to pay certain obligations under a divorce decree?

7. Name five types of property that may be subject to distribution upon divorce and the factors used by the court in making such a determination.

8. What is a QDRO, and what purpose does it serve in divorce litigation?

9. What are some of the methods used to assign a specific value to a parcel of property?

KEY TERMS

alimony	par value
annuity	return on investment
automatic stay	value
bankruptcy	QDRO (Qualified
book value	Domestic Relations
community property	Order)
dischargeability	qualified retirement
equitable distribution	plan
inception of title theory	separate property
	source of funds
liquidation value	theory
"live-in lover" laws	transmutation of funds
maintenance	theory
marital property	valuation
nonqualified retirement plan	

STATE RESEARCH PROBLEMS

Review the laws of your state and answer the following questions. Provide citations for the primary authority for your answers.

1. What are the forms in which alimony is available?

3. May marital fault be considered by the court when setting the amount of alimony to be paid?

4. Is your state a community property state or an equitable distribution state?

5. Does your state treat the following types of property as separate or marital property?

   a) Appreciation in the value of one spouse's separate property

   b) Pension and retirement benefits

   c) Professional degrees (Or is this a factor used in determining the amount of alimony to be paid?)

   d) Proceeds of one spouse's personal injury claim

6. Find a recent case from your state in which the appellate court upholds the use of a particular method of valuation. What property was valued? What was the method of valuation employed in that case? What was the court's rationale in supporting that particular method of valuation?

PRACTICE EXERCISES

1. A provision in a separation agreement states that the husband shall:

   a) Pay to the wife $500 per month until she remarries or either party dies

   b) Pay to First National Bank (holder of the wife's VISA card) $250 per month until the current balance on the wife's account is paid in full

   c) Pay to American Mortgage Co. (holder of the mortgage on the wife's house) the monthly mortgage payment of $1,000 for two years

   d) Transfer to the wife ownership of a certificate of deposit (CD) due to mature in one year with a face value of $10,000.

   Which of these transfers or payments qualifies as alimony? Why?

2. Using the sample QDRO in Exhibit 9–1, determine the percentage of the Participant's benefits to which the Alternative Payee would be entitled: The Participant was employed and a member of the Plan from 1990 through 1999 and the parties were married from 1978 until 1995.

Child Custody, Visitation, and Child Support

CHAPTER OBJECTIVES

In this chapter, you will learn:

- *The different forms child custody can take*

- *The criteria for determining which parent should have custody of the children*

- *How to determine the appropriate court to determine child custody disputes*

- *The parties entitled to visitation with the children*

- *The nature and criteria for an award of child support*

- *The specific benefits and limitations the law places on children*

The second major issue in divorce is determining which parent should be awarded physical and legal custody of any minor children of the marriage. The overriding criteria used by the courts is the "best interests of the child." Testimony of the parties and the minor children, as well as of lay and expert witnesses, provides the court with the evidence necessary to make the proper adjudication. Courts may consider factors such as the parties' religious preferences, life-style choices, and the ability of each parent to provide a stable environment for the minor child. When the parties are willing, joint custody may be awarded to both parties. When the parties reside in different states, the complex jurisdictional questions are addressed by statutes such as the Uniform Child Custody Jurisdiction Act (UCCJA) and the Parental Kidnapping Prevention Act (PKPA). The parent without custody of the minor child is usually awarded visitation privileges with the minor child. Visitation privileges may also be extended to the grandparents and stepparents of the minor child. The amount of child support is standardized by statutory guidelines that mandate a range of payments depending on the number of children and the income of the parents.

CHILD CUSTODY

Concurrent with the termination of the marriage, the court has jurisdiction to award temporary and permanent child custody to one parent (or to both parents jointly) and to award visitation rights to the other parent. The parent receiving exclusive legal and physical custody of the minor child is referred to as the custodial parent, and it should not be a surprise that the other parent is referred to as the non-custodial parent.

It is also necessary here to distinguish between two related but different concepts. **Physical custody** is the legal right to the actual possession of the children. **Legal custody** entails more than mere physical possession of the children. It encompasses the right to make decisions regarding the child's upbringing, education, and religious training. A court's decision to award one parent sole custody generally gives that parent the exclusive right to make all such decisions. While joint custody is gaining acceptance, sole custody is still the most commonly used remedy. Accordingly, child custody contests can be the most wrenching facet of divorce litigation. Also, because of the desirability for expert psychological testimony in such cases, child custody battles are often the most expensive element of divorce litigation.

physical custody
The legal right to the actual physical custody of a child.
legal custody
The legal right to make the most significant decisions regarding child rearing, such as religious training, education, medical treatment, and so forth.

Factors Determining the Award of Custody

Most states allow courts broad discretion in determining custody and do not disturb a trial court decision upon appeal unless there is a showing that the trial court abused its discretion and there are no facts supporting its conclusion. (This decision is made by the judge and is not left to the jury.)

State Laws

More than one-half of the states have specific criteria for an award of custody. The criteria applied are not necessarily which party is the best parent; the court attempts to do whatever is in the best interests of the child. As an example, the Uniform Marriage and Divorce Act (UMDA) lists the relevant factors as follows:

— The wishes of the child's parent or parents as to his custody

— The wishes of the child as to his custodian

— The interaction and interrelationship of the child with his parent or parents, his siblings, and any other person who may significantly affect the child's best interests

— The child's adjustment to his home, school, and community

— The mental and physical health of all individuals involved

As just noted, the wishes of the parents are given considerable weight. When the parents reach mutual agreement as to custody, that agreement is made a part of the court's final judgment and decree of divorce, barring any finding that the parties' agreement is not in the best interests of the child. In more than 40 states, once the minor child reaches the age of maturity (this varies among the states, but usually between 12 and 14 years of age), the child has the right to express her preference as to custodial parent. In certain states, the preference of the child at the age of maturity will be made the judgment of the court unless the court finds the parent of choice is unfit. Even a child who has not yet reached this age is usually asked her preference. This testimony may be elicited by the judge in chambers, outside the presence of the parents and counsel.

Court Testimony

The court also inquires as to which party is best equipped to attend to the needs of the child considering the ages and the physical and emotional health of the child and the parties. Barring evidence that one of the parents is blatantly unfit to raise the child, the court is typically left to award custody to one of two equally capable parents. Therefore, the determination is based on an evaluation of the details of the daily lives of the parties. The court examines the history of the relationship between the child and the respective parents. Such a determination is of course subjective, but it is determined with objective evidence. This can include the following kinds of testimonies:

— *Testimony of the parties*—The parties testify as to the nature of their relationship with the minor child. This testimony includes anecdotes about how that party has spent a great deal of "quality time" with the child, has been involved with the child's educational, athletic, and social life, and generally has provided the parental love, support, and guidance necessary. Each party also gives testimony as to how this relationship will continue in the future. Assuming the party receiving custody has to work outside the home, the court also inquires who will have custody of the child during working hours.

— *Testimony of lay witnesses*—To bolster their own testimony, each party typically calls upon several friends, neighbors, and family members to relate incidents manifesting that party's devotion to the minor child. A child's teacher can be called to testify to a parent's involvement with the child's education. The family physicians (or member of their staff) can relate how a parent looked after a child's medical needs.

— *Testimony of expert witnesses*—Due to the self-serving nature of the two preceding types of testimony, the court often requires an investigation and evaluation of the facts by an impartial third party. This can take the form of either a psychological examination of all the individuals involved or a "home study."

Psychological tests, diagnoses, and prognoses as to the emotional well-being of the parents and the child often form the basis for the court's decision; they also cause the lion's share of the extra costs incurred in a custody battle. The value of this testimony is in direct proportion to the credibility of the expert witness. (This is especially true in cases in which each side has its own expert and the case becomes a "battle of the psychologists.") The expert's professional credentials, as well as the objective basis for their opinions (i.e., did the expert spend 1 hour or 10 hours with each person involved?) must be detailed. In a home study, a court appointee (usually a case worker for the state department charged with the responsibility for children and families) visits each spouse at home, interviews friends and family members, meets with the child privately, and does whatever else is deemed appropriate to assess the fitness of each party as a parent and what would be in the best interests of the child. These reports contain the investigator's conclusions and the basis for those conclusions. The courts tend to give these reports significant weight when making the final decision about custody.

A growing trend is to provide a child who is the subject of a custody dispute with an independent advocate called a **guardian ad litem**. A minority of states have statutes that either require or permit the appointment of a guardian ad litem. This is especially useful in cases in which neither parent can be expected to adequately protect the best interests of the child.

guardian ad litem
A person appointed to represent the interests of another person in litigation.

Parents' Life-style

Another area of concern in awarding child custody is the life-style of the parents and how that life-style can affect the minor child. Here are some factors the court may consider:

— *Religion of the parents*—While it is unconstitutional for a court to base a decision about child custody on the religious preferences (or lack of preference) of either parent, religion is still cited as a factor in the decision-making process. This occurs when the religious preferences of a parent may adversely affect the child. For example, when a marriage dissolves because one spouse adopts a strict religious code, the court may consider whether the adoption of that religious code for the minor child would be detrimental (i.e., when religious practices would compel a parent to forgo medical treatment for a sick child). A court may also inquire into what religious practices were observed in the household before the divorce, and consider which parent is more likely to continue those practices.

— *Sexual preferences of the parents*—Perhaps of greater significance than the parties' sexual preferences is the manner in which these preferences manifest themselves. That is, the court is more likely to be concerned with whether these preferences are practiced behind "closed doors." In cases where one of the parties has a live-in lover (or more egregiously, a series of lovers), especially in communities in which such practices are frowned upon, it will be more difficult for such a parent to obtain sole custody. Note that an adulterous relationship charged as the fault for the termination of the marriage is not to be considered in determining child custody. The court considers future conduct, not any "past sins," in determining child custody. As to a party's sexual inclination, where one of the parties is homosexual or bisexual, while not necessarily authorized by law, such a preference is almost certain to be a factor in the court's award of child custody.

— *Morality*—While much of family law is subjective, the issue of morality is a real quagmire. For example, do either of the parties drink alcoholic beverages to excess (and what is "excess")? Do either of the parties use any controlled substances (i.e., marijuana, cocaine)? Do either of the parties smoke tobacco products (the concerns include providing a bad influence for the child as well as the potential dangers of secondhand smoke)? Do either of the parties have an eating disorder? Do either of the parties have a problem with gambling?

— *Race*—The United States Supreme Court has held that the race of the parents or child may not be used as the sole factor in determining what would be in the best interests of the child. [*Palmore v. Sidoti*, 466 U.S. 429, 104 S.Ct. 1879, 80 L.Ed.2d 421 (1984).] The potential ill effects of racial prejudice may not be used to deny a particular parent custody where that parent is an appropriate party to have custody.

— *Stable environment*—Often the parent having custody of the children at the time of the decision about permanent custody has an advantage in that if the child appears to be doing well, the court may be unwilling to disturb the existing living arrangements. (Of course, this is a two-edged sword; if there are problems, the other spouse can use that to bolster his or her claim for custody.) The court also looks to the respective work and social schedules of the parties. A parent who is a practicing obstetrician would have to show the court that the children will be cared for if she has to leave the house at 2:00 a.m. to deliver a baby.

Theories about Child Custody

tender years doctrine
Traditional theory of child custody that usually granted permanent child custody to a child's mother.

primary caretaker doctrine
Theory of child custody that grants permanent child custody to the parent who acted as child's primary caretaker.

Until recent years, courts adopted the **tender years doctrine**, which held that the mother is naturally better suited than the father to care for and raise a young child. While this doctrine no longer officially holds sway, and despite the fact that many fathers have successfully litigated for the custody of their minor children, many courts continue to favor the mother in questions of custody of minor children.

Part of the reason for this may be that courts have replaced the tender years doctrine with the **primary caretaker doctrine**, which holds that when both parents are fit to raise the children, the parent who has had primary responsibility for caring for the young child to that date should be awarded sole custody for the child. Factors thus considered include which parent had primary responsibility for planning and preparing meals, for bathing and dressing the children, for putting the children to bed at night and awakening them in the morning, for disciplining them, and so on. That role is still often played primarily by the mother. Therefore, whether it is fair or not, fathers may face an uphill battle when they desire child custody.

By the same token, fathers sometimes use child custody merely as a tool to obtain leverage in the divorce litigation. Especially in cases in which the mother is less sophisticated than the father, the father may convince the mother that unless she agrees to certain conditions, he will fight for, and win, custody. This is an aspect of family law that gives it an unseemly reputation. Such behavior cannot be tolerated ethically, and legal professionals must maintain a constant vigil to prevent either spouse from using the minor children as a pawn in the divorce.

Joint Custody

Although it was practically unheard of just twenty years ago, **joint custody** (also called *shared custody),* in which both parents share full legal and physical custodial rights to the child, has gained in popularity in recent years. The goal is to allow both parents to retain frequent and continuing contact with the child. Naturally, this type of arrangement is feasible only where the parties are able to work through their animosity for each other and cooperate to do whatever is in the best interests of the child. Accordingly, it is common for a court to require that both parties seek, or at least consent to, joint custody as a condition precedent for such an award.

One of the most important factors in such cases is to what extent the physical custody of the child is to be shared. Some courts oppose the practice of shifting the child between two homes, even when both residences are maintained in the same neighborhood or school district. Therefore, it is not uncommon for a court or separation agreement to award both parents joint legal custody (giving each an equal claim to the decision-making authority for the child), while awarding sole physical custody to one parent. Other factors considered by a court include the child's preference for joint custody; the nature of the relationship between the child and each parent; whether both parents are physically and psychologically fit; and whether adequate care can be provided in each home. The various states have differing attitudes and presumptions toward joint custody ranging from favorable to adverse, reflected in their statutory provisions concerning custody.

An award of joint custody can provide that the child spend alternating months or weeks with each parent. Joint custody should be distinguished from **split custody**, in which each parent has *exclusive* legal and physical custody of the child for extended periods of time. A common example of split custody is one in which the parents reside in different states, and one parent has physical custody while school is in session and the other parent has custody during the long summer vacation.

joint custody; split custody
Under joint custody, both parents share full legal and physical custody of the child. Under split custody, each parent has exclusive custody of the child for extended periods of time.

FOCUS ON CUSTODY OF HUMAN EMBRYOS

One of the most exciting aspects of family law is the opportunity to explore legal questions that have not been asked previously. One such question relates to the custody of frozen human embryos (fertilized human eggs) upon the termination of marriage. It has been estimated that human embryos are being frozen and stored (cryopreservation) in the United States at the rate of 10,000 per year.

To facilitate an understanding for the reasons behind this practice it is necessary to understand the biological factors. When an infertile couple seeks to attempt in vitro fertilization, the physician prescribes drugs that produce multiple ovulation, so that as many as eight to ten ova (female eggs) can be retrieved at one time. All these ova are typically fertilized immediately, since unfertilized ova do not survive freezing; fertilized ova do. Perhaps four or five fertilized ova are implanted in the female in the hopes that one will develop into a live birth. The remaining fertilized ova are then cryopreserved for possible future implantation, if necessary. Because these frozen embryos can survive at least two years, and may be able to survive for as long as two thousand years, the original intentions and desires of the biological partners can change, creating a new area for domestic conflict.

To say that the law in this area is unsettled would be an understatement. It is uncertain what right, if any, a party with any biological ties to the embryo has to force, or prevent, the implantation of the embryo and resulting pregnancy. It is uncertain what is the legal status of the frozen fertilized embryo. What is certain is that these issues can be made less volatile when the parties enter into a contract and agree to create, freeze, and store fertilized embryos. This contract is generally prepared by the medical facility conducting the in vitro fertilization procedure. Factors contemplated by such a contract include

— Under what circumstances fertilized embryos will be frozen and stored

— A declaration of intent to be a parent of the child resulting from the in vitro fertilization

— The duration of the cryopreservation (generally limited to the reproductive age of the woman in whom the embryo is to be implanted or the woman intending to be the mother)

— Whose consent is required for implantation

— Provisions for the termination of the marriage

See Chapter 16 for additional information concerning in vitro fertilization.

Jurisdictional Questions

While jurisdictional problems are minimal when all of the litigants are residents of the same state, there can be significant problems with interstate custody disputes. In years past, the problem was exacerbated by the variances among the jurisdictional requirements of the states. Today, however, every state has enacted the **Uniform Child Custody Jurisdiction Act (UCCJA)** or laws that mirror the UCCJA.

UCCJA (Uniform Child Custody Jurisdiction Act)
Uniform laws, adopted by the individual states, that set out the rules for determining venue in interstate child custody disputes.

Uniform Child Custody Jurisdiction Act
The stated goals of the UCCJA include

— To avoid jurisdictional conflicts among the states

— To assure that the litigation concerning the custody of a minor child occurs in the state having the closest connection to the child and his family

— To deter abductions to another state in an attempt to obtain custody

— To avoid relitigation of the decision having proper jurisdiction in other states

The UCCJA applies equally to the initial determination and later modification of child custody. (See Chapter 13 for a discussion of the jurisdictional questions peculiar to the modification of an interstate child custody decision and Chapter 16 for a discussion of the jurisdictional questions peculiar to an interstate adoption.)

Under Section 3 of the UCCJA, jurisdiction is conferred to a state if:

1. The state is the home state of the child *or* had been the home state of the child, and the child is absent from the state as the result of actions of a person claiming custody of the child *and* the other parent is still a resident of the home state.

2. It is in the best interests of the child that a state have jurisdiction to determine custody because the child and at least one of the parents have a significant connection with the state, *and* there is substantial evidence within that state concerning the child's present or future care, protection, training, and personal relationships.

3. The child is physically present in the state *and* the child has been abandoned, *or* it is necessary to protect the child because he has been subjected to or threatened with mistreatment or abuse.

4. It appears that no other state would have jurisdiction in accordance with the provision of paragraphs 1 through 3, *or* another state has declined to exercise jurisdiction *and* it is in the best interests of the child that that court assume jurisdiction.

It should be noted that the physical presence of the child, while preferable, it not a prerequisite for a state to obtain jurisdiction to determine custody. Other highlights of the UCCJA include

— Section 4 provides that before entering a custody decree, reasonable notice and an opportunity to be heard be provided to the litigants, any parent whose parental rights have not been previously terminated, and any person who has physical custody of the child.

— Section 7 permits a court having proper jurisdiction to decline to exercise its jurisdiction upon a finding that it is an inconvenient forum to make a custody determination and that another court is a more appropriate forum.

— Section 8 permits a court having proper jurisdiction to decline to exercise its jurisdiction upon a finding that the petitioner has wrongfully taken the child from another state or has engaged in other reprehensible conduct. (This is a codification of the equitable theory of "clean hands.")

— Section 13 provides for each state to afford full faith and credit to the child custody decrees of other states entered pursuant to the UCCJA. Accordingly, a judgment from one state is protected against a collateral attack from litigation in a second state initiated by the nonprevailing party.

— Section 15 provides that upon filing a certified copy of the custody decree of a foreign state, the court shall treat the decree as a custody decree of its own state.

(NOTE—*See Chapter 6 for an example of the affidavit that many states require to be filed in all divorce actions pursuant to the UCCJA, in which each litigant details the history of the child's custody for the 5 years prior to initiation of the litigation.)*

Parental Kidnapping Prevention Act

PKPA (Parental Kidnapping Prevention Act)
Federal laws designed to deter parents from unlawfully removing a minor child from a particular state.

On the federal side, in 1980, Congress enacted the **Parental Kidnapping Prevention Act (PKPA)**, 28 U.S.C.A. § 1738(A), which sought to implement the Full Faith and Credit clause of the Fourteenth Amendment to the U.S. Constitution to the custody decrees of the individual states. The goals and procedures of the PKPA mirror those enacted by the states in the UCCJA. Accordingly, under the PKPA, states are required to enforce the custody decrees of other states without modification, unless the original state did not have (or did not exercise) proper jurisdiction, or an emergency exists requiring immediate intervention to protect the child. The PKPA provides one of the rare opportunities for federal court intervention in family law. The federal courts may enforce compliance by state courts that have, in violation of the PKPA, asserted jurisdiction over a child custody case. It is not a prerequisite that a kidnapping occur to trigger the provisions of the PKPA. This federal law has preempted state law in the area of child custody jurisdiction. In other words, if state law conflicts with the federal law, the state law must yield to the PKPA.

Applying the Law

Consider the following applications of child custody jurisdictional problems:

— Child has lived with mother in California for more than six months prior to initiation of litigation. California is the "home state" and has jurisdiction.

— Child is moved from Florida to Massachusetts by mother without father's approval, and mother conceals their whereabouts. Father learns of their whereabouts and acquiesces to their presence in Massachusetts for over 1 year. Father then moves the child to Florida without the mother's permission. Massachusetts is the "home state" and has jurisdiction.

— Child has resided in Texas for her entire life. Father removes child to Kentucky. Four months later, a petition for divorce and custody is filed. Texas is the "home state" and has jurisdiction.

CASE

WESTNEAT v. WESTNEAT

Court of Appeals of North Carolina.
Jan. 4, 1994.

JOHNSON, Judge.

Pertinent facts to this appeal are as follows: Plaintiff father and defendant mother met in 1983 and were married in 1986; Brian Graham Westneat (the child herein) was born on 27 August 1987. The family lived in Florida before moving to North Carolina in June of 1989. During the child's early years, plaintiff father stayed home and cared for the child, while defendant mother worked full time. In February of 1990, the child started attending day care, and plaintiff began working in a position as an insurance agent.

In 1990, defendant mother went to New Hampshire to interview for a job with G. H. Bass Company. The child went with her on this trip. Defendant was offered a position with the company and accepted it, informing plaintiff father that she did not want plaintiff to move with her to New Hampshire. After much discussion, plaintiff agreed that defendant could take the child with her. Plaintiff and defendant separated on 1 August 1990, and defendant and the child moved to New Hampshire. In August of 1990, defendant mother re-established a personal relationship with an old boyfriend, David Kukla, who was in New Hampshire.

On 13 August 1990, plaintiff father removed the child from New Hampshire and returned the child to North Carolina. The child stayed with plaintiff until November of 1990, when the parties agreed to have the child return to defendant's home in New Hampshire, subject to certain conditions.

The weekend of 4 April 1992, plaintiff picked up the child from his day care in New Hampshire and brought him back to North Carolina. On 5 April 1991, plaintiff father filed a complaint for custody of the child in Mecklenburg County District Court. On 8 May 1991, defendant mother filed an action for child custody in New Hampshire and obtained an *ex parte* order allowing defendant temporary custody of the child. On 15 May 1991, defendant filed an answer and counterclaim for custody in Mecklenburg County District Court in addition to a motion that the North Carolina court decline jurisdiction.

By order entered on 25 June 1991, the Mecklenburg County District Court determined that the North Carolina court had jurisdiction and indicated that the North Carolina court would contact the New Hampshire court to determine if there was concurrent jurisdiction. On 5 August 1991, a further order was entered which provided that the New Hampshire court had been contacted and that the New Hampshire proceeding had been stayed pending resolution of the North Carolina action. In the order, the court noted that it would consider affidavits to determine the issue of convenient forum. On 23 August 1991, an order was entered, concluding that North Carolina was the most appropriate and convenient forum and denying defendant mother's motion to decline jurisdiction.

On 8 January 1992, plaintiff father filed a motion requesting that defendant mother allow him temporary visitation privileges pending a final disposition of the custody case. On 13 January 1992, order was entered granting plaintiff father's motion and awarding temporary visitation. A hearing was held on the custody issue from 11 February 1992 until 13 February 1992. On 23 April 1992, an order was entered awarding plaintiff primary care, custody and control of the child. From that order, defendant appeals to this Court.

The first issue defendant raises on appeal is that the trial court erred in failing to find facts and to reach appropriate conclusions of law regarding the best interest of the child when it entered and signed the child custody order awarding the father primary care, custody and control of the minor child born of the marriage. Defendant further argues that a child custody decree which is not supported by proper findings and conclusions of law which awards primary care, custody and control of a minor child to one of the parties but is not supported by competent evidence should be reversed.

We note:

It is clear beyond the need for multiple citation that the trial judge, sitting without a jury, has discretion as finder of fact with respect to the weight and credibility that attaches to the evidence. (Citation omitted.) The findings of fact made by the trial court are regarded as conclusive on appeal if they are supported by competent evidence. (Citation omitted.) In child custody cases, the paramount consideration of the court is the welfare of the child. (Citation omitted.) The welfare of the child is the "polar star" that guides the court in the exercise of its discretion. (Citation omitted.) The trial court's judge's discretion with regard to the weight and credibility of the evidence is bolstered by its responsibility for the welfare of the child. In child custody cases, where the trial judge has the opportunity to see and hear the parties and witnesses, the trial court has broad discretion and its findings of fact are accorded considerable deference on appeal. (Citation omitted.) So long as the trial judge's finding of fact are supported by competent evidence, they should not be upset on appeal.

Smithweick v. Frame, 62 N.C.App. 387, 392, 303 S.E.2d 217, 221 (1983). Defendant argues that several findings were conclusory in nature. We have reviewed defendant's contentions and find them to be without merit. Based on our review of the record, we find the trial judge's findings of fact are supported by competent evidence and should not be upset on appeal.

Defendant further argues that "the effect of the decree is to invoke a penalty upon the parent who had previously been the primary caretaker, the nurturing parent, and the person from whom custody should not be taken, absent some compelling evidence demonstrating sufficient reasons capsuled in the court's findings of ultimate fact and conclusions of law." We note once again that under North Carolina law, "the trial judge is entrusted with the delicate and difficult task of choosing an environment which will, in [the judge's] judgment, best encourage full development of the child's physical, mental, emotional, moral and spiritual faculties." (Citation omitted.) We find that the trial judge has properly performed this task.

We make reference to defendant's cite to *In re Kowalzek,* 37 N.C.App. 364, 367, 246 S.E.2d 45, 47 (1978) ("It is universally recognized that the mother is the natural custodian of her young . . . If she is a fit and proper person to have the custody of the children, other things being equal, the mother should be given their custody[.]") This "tender years" doctrine is no longer the law in North Carolina. *See* North Carolina General Statutes § 50-13.2(a) (1987) ("Between the mother and father, whether natural or adoptive, no presumption shall apply as to who will better promote the interest and welfare of the child.")

Defendant next argues the trial court erred when it failed to determine that New Hampshire was the more appropriate forum and therefore denied defendant's motion requesting the North Carolina court to decline jurisdiction. We are unpersuaded by defendant's argument.

The trial court, in determining which state was the most appropriate forum, made the following pertinent findings of fact:

1. On June 25, 1991, the Court entered an Order in this action after the presentation of evidence and argument of counsel which provided in pertinent part:
   a. North Carolina had jurisdiction for purposes of a custody determination pursuant to North Carolina General Statutes § 50A–3(a)(1)(i)(ii) and that this State is the home state of the minor child at the time . . . of the commencement of the North Carolina action.

. . . .

5. The Court finds that Plaintiff, Defendant and the minor child resided in Mecklenburg County, North Carolina, from on or about June 1, 1989, until on or about June 24, 1990, when the parties separated and the Defendant moved to the State of New Hampshire.

6. As between the States of North Carolina and New Hampshire, North Carolina is the only state where the parties and the minor child have lived as a family unit.

7. Although there are a number of witnesses Defendant may call that reside in New Hampshire that can testify about the present care, supervision and control of the minor child, there are numerous other witnesses who reside in the State of North Carolina who are in a position to testify about the qualifications of the parties and the care, custody and control of the minor child while all concerned lived as a family unit in the State of North Carolina.

8. The Court therefore finds that North Carolina is the more convenient forum for the determination of the custody issues raised in this case.

We find the district court's order that the state of North Carolina was the most appropriate and convenient forum for the trial of this case was supported by proper findings of fact and conclusions of law and was appropriate. Defendant's motion was properly denied.

. . .

The decision of the trial court is affirmed.
WYNN and JOHN, J., concur.

DISCUSSION QUESTIONS

Based on the preceding case of *Westneat v. Westneat*, 437 S.E.2d 899 (N.C. 1994), answer the following questions:

1. What is the status of the "tender years" doctrine in North Carolina?

2. Why did the court rule that North Carolina was the appropriate forum to determine child custody in this case?

VISITATION

Regardless of which parent gets permanent custody of the children, the court will also want to ensure that the non-custodial parent has sufficient opportunity to continue the parent-child relationship. Additionally, other parties may seek visitation with the children.

Visitation by the Noncustodial Parent

Where one parent is awarded sole custody of a minor child, the noncustodial parent is typically awarded visitation privileges. A finding that visitation would be detrimental, either physically or emotionally, to the child is required in order to deny or restrict the noncustodial parent's visitation privileges. Grounds for denying, or limiting, visitation can be upheld in cases demonstrating an adverse effect on the child due to one or more of the following: the threat of physical or emotional harm to the child, the mental illness of a parent, substance abuse by the parent, and infrequent past visitation.

In an attempt to foster and promote a continuing viable relationship between the noncustodial parent and the child, courts tend to award liberal visitation rights. Where logistics permit, courts may award the "usual" visitation privileges (i.e., alternate weekends, holidays, and birthdays, and an extended period of time during the summer). In cases where the parents do not reside in the same locality, it is common to award fewer but lengthier periods of visitation. Whether by agreement or court order, the provisions for child custody should also include guidance as to which party has the obligation for the transportation of the minor child, the costs of transportation, the precise times of visitation, and the requisite notice that specific visitation privileges are to be exercised or declined.

The use of the words *privileges* or *rights* in connection with a noncustodial parent's visitation with the minor child is something of a misnomer in that visitation is often treated by the courts as an obligation owed to the child. Therefore, visitation should not be viewed as an option that can be exercised when convenient for the noncustodial parent, but as a continuing right of the child to the support and companionship of both parents. However, it is highly unlikely that a court could, or would, compel a recalcitrant parent to fulfill the visitation privilege. Additionally, much as in cases of custody, older children (i.e., at least 12 to 14 years of age) are participants in determining visitation privileges.

Another factor the court must consider is whether any restrictions should be imposed on the custodial parent's ability to relocate to another state with the minor child. Generally, courts do not impose any such restrictions, notwithstanding the deleterious effect it will have on the noncustodial parent's visitation rights. Should the noncustodial parent challenge the move to another state, he will have the burden of proof to establish that the move is not in the best interests of the child. Factors considered by the court when faced with the issue of relocation include (1) the prospective advantages of the move for the child and custodial parent, (2) the motives of the custodial parent in seeking to relocate and of the noncustodial parent in opposing the relocation, and (3) the degree to which the noncustodial parent's visitation rights can be amended to preserve the relationship between parent and child.

Visitation by the Grandparents

The rights of grandparents to visitation with a child have been greatly expanded in recent years in most states. An obvious question, then, is which grandparents have rights to visitation? For these purposes, a *grandparent* may be defined as the parent of either parent of a minor child, whether or not the parent is presently living, and whether or not the parental rights have been terminated. For example, consider the scenario in which a child's biological parents are divorced and the child is adopted by her mother's (the custodial parent) new husband. There are now three sets of grandparents: the parents of both of the biological parents and those of the adopting father. This is an issue ancillary to actions other than just divorce, since a claim for visitation by a grandparent may result from the death of a parent and the later remarriage of the surviving spouse or whenever there has been a judicial termination of the parental rights of either parent.

All fifty states have statutes providing for grandparent visitation. Some states provide for visitation under any circumstances; others provide for it only upon the death of the parent related by blood to the grandparent, or only upon the separation or divorce of the parents. Factors considered by courts include the existence of a prior loving relationship between the grandparent and the child; the grandparent's physical and mental ability to cope with the child; the preference of the child; and, the effect, if any, on the time other family members will have with the child.

Visitation by Stepparents

Stepparent visitation is also permitted in some states, although it has yet to reach the level of acceptance of grandparent visitation. Such visitation, where provided by law, may be sought upon divorce or death of the spouse that was the natural parent of the child. The criteria for granting such a request are similar to that for grandparent visitation: the court examines the existing relationship between the stepparent and the child, noting whether the stepparent acted as a parent during the time he and the child lived in the same household.

CHILD SUPPORT

Non-custodial parents are obligated to continue to support their children. The amount payable and the duration of their payments is often a major issue in divorce litigation.

Entitlement

Whereas alimony is an obligation owed to the dependent spouse, **child support** is a right belonging to the minor children of the marriage for their maintenance. Accordingly, while a party can waive the right to receive alimony in an antenuptial or separation agreement, a court will not enforce a parent's waiver of the right to receive child support. Further, although the right to receive alimony may cease upon a party's remarriage, there is no similar effect on the right to receive child support. There are also significant tax differences between the two obligations, since the amount paid as child support is not considered taxable income to the receiving spouse and is not deductible for the paying spouse.

    The right to child support is generally enforceable until the child reaches the age of majority, graduates from secondary school, or is otherwise emancipated of the parents, regardless of the parent's marital status. In most states the age of majority is 18, and barring statutory authorization or an agreement of the parties to the contrary, the obligation for child support is terminated when the child reaches the age of majority. Some states continue the obligation for child support until the child graduates from college. (Note that where a child is physically or intellectually unable to care for himself, the obligation for child support may continue indefinitely.) Child support is similar to alimony in that it may not be discharged in bankruptcy.

child support
Payments made for the benefit of a minor child not in the permanent custody of the payor.

Emancipation

Emancipation is the legal recognition that an individual is independent of his parents and is legally responsible for his own actions. A minor can be emancipated by (1) marriage, (2) enlistment in one of the armed forces, or (3) some other manifestation that the minor has assumed responsibility for his own support (i.e., where a 16-year-old person leaves the parental home, gets a job, and pays her own bills). Notwithstanding reaching the age of majority or achieving emancipation, the obligation for child support is terminated by the death of either the parent or the child.

    It should be noted that most states will permit litigation to collect unpaid child support payments even after the child reaches the age of 18 or is otherwise emancipated, even though the current obligation to pay child support has been terminated. Traditionally, child support was the exclusive obligation of the father; however, in recent years, courts and legislatures have imposed this obligation upon both spouses equally.

emancipation
The process by which a person under the age of majority achieves the legal status of an adult.

Guidelines

The Child Support Enforcement Amendments of 1984 are a series of federal laws requiring every state to develop **child support guidelines** for the trial

child support guidelines
Statutes that set forth required levels of child support.

LANCLOS v. LANCLOS

Court of Appeal of Louisiana, Third Circuit. Feb. 3, 1993.

Before LABORDE, THIBODEAUX and WOODARD, JJ.

THIBODEAUX, Judge.

This is an action for child support involving a proper determination of support under LSA-R.S. 9:315 *et seq.* The defendant, Sandra Lanclos, appeals a trial court judgment which failed to award child support in the amount specified by the Louisiana Child Support Guidelines. . . . The trial court ordered Donald to pay $450.00 per month, or $225.00 per child for the two children of the marriage, April Marie and Shawn Wayne. . . .

FACTS

On August 29, 1991, Donald filed for divorce from Sandra. A hearing was fixed for and held on October 14, 1991 on various ancillary issues, including child support. The parties were awarded joint custody and Sandra was named the custodial parent by stipulation. Donald's child support obligation was set at $450.00 per month, or $225.00 per child. The trial judge calculated this amount on the basis of $7.50 per child per day and commented in his oral reasons for judgment that the application of the Louisiana Child Support Guidelines would result in an "excessive" award of $501.00.

. . .

Sandra contends . . . that the trial judge incorrectly deviated from the Louisiana Child Support Guidelines in awarding as child support $225.00 per month per child for a total of $450.00 per month and in failing to give a proper explanation for the deviation. The trial court was required to apply the child support guidelines in LSA-R.S. 9:315.14 since this statutory standard was in effect on the date this action was filed. Absent proper reasons for deviation, Sandra was entitled to the monthly amount specified in the schedule. Donald asserts that the deviation was proper because LSA-R.S. 9:315.1(C)6 allows the court to consider factors not listed in this section that would make the application of the guidelines inequitable.

The correct statutory provision is LSA-R.S. 9:315.1(C)7. Regardless of the factors considered by

the trial judge in determining Donald's child support obligation, the trial judge is required to articulate those factors. The issue on appeal is whether the trial court abused its discretion in deviating from the guidelines to award $450.00 per month in child support.

LSA-R.S. 9:315.1(A) creates a rebuttable presumption that the amount calculated under the guidelines is the proper amount of child support to be awarded. The court may deviate from the guidelines if their application would be inequitable to the parties or not in the best interests of the child or children. LSA-R.S. 9:315.1(B). This rule of deference to the guidelines is in accord with prior jurisprudence concerning the standard of review which an appellate court should exercise over a trial court's determinations regarding child support. We have previously defined this standard as leaving the trial court "much discretion." (Citation omitted.) Any deviation from the guidelines must be accompanied by the court's oral or written reasons and these reasons must be made a part of the record. LSA-R.S. 9:315.1(B).

LSA-RS. 9:315.1(C)(1–7) gives an illustrative list of factors which may be considered by a trial court in determining whether to deviate from the guidelines:

C. In determining whether to deviate from the guidelines, the court's considerations may include:

(1) That the combined adjusted gross income of the parties is not within the amounts shown on the schedule in R.S. 9:315.14. If the combined adjusted gross income of the parties is less than the lowest sum shown on the schedule, the court shall determine an amount of child support based on the facts of the case. If the combined adjusted gross income of the parties exceeds the highest sum shown on the schedule, the provisions of R.S. 9:315.10(B) shall apply.

(2) The legal obligation of a party to support dependents who are not the subject of the action before the court and who are in that party's household.

(3) The extraordinary medical expenses of a party, or extraordinary medical expenses for which a party may be responsible, not otherwise taken into consideration under the guidelines.

(4) An extraordinary community debt of the parties.

(5) The need for immediate and temporary support for a child when a full hearing on the issue of support is pending but cannot be timely held. In such cases, the court at the full hearing shall use the provisions of this Part and may redetermine support without the necessity of a change of cir-

cumstances being shown.

(6) The permanent or temporary total disability of a spouse to the extent such disability diminishes his present and future earning capacity, his need to save adequately for uninsurable future medical costs, and other additional costs associated with such disability, such as transportation and mobility costs, medical expenses, and higher insurance premiums.

(7) Any other consideration which would make application of the guidelines not in the best interest of the child or children or inequitable to the parties.

In the present case, the trial judge made the following statements regarding the award of child support:

"All right the Court's prepared to rule. Now first of all I want to rule on the question of child support, support for the two children, Uh the children are ages, aged as I understand 5 and 12, is that correct? . . .

The Court has Uh, listened very carefully to the testimony concerning Uh, the Uh wages or the income, let's say the income made by Uh, Mr. Lanclos and Uh, the Court believes that it would, if were to impose the schedule upon them that would be $501.00. The Court thinks that that would be excessive. . . .

Now for the two children I'm going to allow $15.00 a day, that's $450.00 a month . . . make it or each child, $225.00 per child. . . ."

As can be seen from this excerpt, the trial court did not apply the statutory guidelines. The trial court's reasons for deviating from the child support guidelines fail to establish that such deviation would be in the best interests of the children or would be inequitable to the parties. Contrary to what counsel for Donald argues in his brief—that the trial judge found adherence to the guidelines "onerous"—the trial judge merely stated that imposition of the guidelines would be "excessive."

The child support guidelines clearly establish that the trial court's discretion in the amount of child support to be awarded is now structured. Under the child support guidelines, a rebuttable presumption exists that the amount contained in the statutory tables, factoring in the number of children and the parents' income, is the proper amount to be awarded.

The guidelines would only allow a downward deviation, as in this case, where the guidelines amount would be inequitable to the parties since a deviation below the guidelines could never be in the best interests of the children. (Citation omitted.) When a perceived inequity exists, the court is required to explain orally or in writing its reasons for the deviation. Simply stating that imposing the guidelines is excessive is not a sufficient statement under the guidelines to support deviation.

Because of the failure of the trial court to give the required oral or written reasons for the deviation, the judgment is deficient. Not only must the court give its reasons for deviating from the guidelines, it must also provide an evidentiary basis for the deviation. (Citation omitted.) With clearly stated reasons, the reviewing court could more easily follow the trial court's reasoning in setting the basic support from the guidelines in considering any of the options allowed by LSA-R.S. 9:315.1(C).

Hogan v. Hogan, 549 So.2d 267 (La. 1989) mandates the appellate court, upon determining that the trial court abused its discretion in making a child support order, to assess the evidence anew from the record and render a judgment on the merits as if it were the trial court rather than to remand the case for further proceedings below. In cases where the record contains adequate information upon which to make a child support determination under the guidelines, pursuant to LSA-C.C.P. art. 2164, this court will apply the child support guidelines to the facts of the case rather than remand to the trial court. (Citation omitted.) In the present case, there is sufficient information upon which to apply the child support guidelines.

Sandra is unemployed due to serious health problems requiring surgery and the children are in need of at least the statutory amount of child support. Although the trial court's deviation is only $130.00 per month, there is no justification for depriving these children of the amount needed for their support without adequate reasons for deviation. Nor is Donald's prediction that his income will decrease due to depression in the oil industry a justification for deviation in this case. The record indicates that Donald's income for the year 1990 was $27,371.00. The guideline amount of support to be contributed by Donald is proportionate to the number of children and his income.

In brief before this court, Donald argues that a debt exists because he is required to pay the monthly automobile loan note of $189.00 until the loan is paid and the trial court failed to consider Sandra's earning potential. These may be proper factors for consideration under LSA-R.S. 9:315.1(C)(4) or (7), or 9:315.9 supra. However, we first note that the trial court made no finding that Donald's automobile note debt had any impact on the court's decision to deviate from the guidelines. Further, the record clearly shows that the court considered Donald's child support obligations and automobile note debt separately, one having nothing to do with the other. Moreover, the record supports the fact that Sandra is not voluntarily unemployed. Under these circumstances, Donald presents no justification for reduced child support payments.

The record does not support a finding that an award of $580.00 per month for these two children would be inequitable to the parties, nor did the trial court articulate sufficient reasons to justify its action in lowering the award below the minimum statutory guidelines.

Although we find that the trial court erred in this case, we do not hold that a trial court has no discretion in setting child support awards. The act provides for guidelines, and not rigid adherence. The trial court's judicial discretion should be protected in order to prevent inequities. The intended purpose of the guidelines is to provide consistency and certainty in child support awards. In order to serve that purpose, an evidentiary basis for deviation must be properly presented and, if accepted by the trial court, the reasons for deviation must be clearly stated. (Citation omitted.)

CONCLUSION

We find that the trial court erred in failing to apply the child support guidelines of LSA-R.S. 9:315 *et seq.* and in failing to provide sufficient reasons for the deviation. Accordingly, we reverse the judgment of the trial court as to the child support award and order that Donald pay to Sandra $580.00 per month for child support of their two children. The judgment is affirmed in all other respects. Costs of this appeal are to be divided equally between the parties.

REVERSED IN PART, AFFIRMED IN PART, AND RENDERED.

DISCUSSION QUESTIONS

Based on the preceding case of *Lanclos v. Lanclos,* 614 So.2d 170 (La. 1993), answer the following questions:

1. What are some of the factors a Louisiana court may consider in determining whether to deviate from the child support guidelines?

2. Why did the appellate court reverse the lower court's award of child support?

courts in determining child support levels. The purpose of these guidelines is to establish uniformity and equity in the award of child support. The genesis of these guidelines was not that individual judges discriminated among the parties appearing before the court, but that certain judges were generally more liberal in awarding child support than other judges. The courts are required to follow the statutory guidelines barring a finding that to do so would be inequitable to the parties or the minor child.

The states now have both a set of guidelines to determine the appropriate level of child support to be paid and a list of extenuating circumstances that would justify an award that deviates from the guidelines. But the format of the resulting guidelines varies widely from state to state. Some states have guidelines providing an exact computation for child support depending on such factors as the parties' respective incomes and the number of dependent children. Other states give courts greater latitude, in that they stipulate only an acceptable range of child support. Appendix C contains the child support guidelines for the states of Massachusetts and Texas. Notice how they vary in their approach to establishing uniform child support levels for the citizens of their respective states.

Medical Care

Both parties have a continuing obligation to provide adequate medical care for their children. The term "medical care" may also include dental, orthodontic, and psychological care, as well as any required medications. Accordingly, the non-custodial parent will usually be required to

— Provide medical coverage through the medical plan offered by the non-custodial parent's employer

— Reimburse the custodial parent for all or part of the expense of the child's medical coverage

— Reimburse the custodial parent for all or part of any medical expenses not covered by medical insurance

The Omnibus Budget Reconciliation Act of 1993 promulgated the Qualified Medical Child Support Order (QMCSO). The effect of a QMCSO is to compel a qualified employer-sponsored group health plan to provide coverage for children of a parent/employee. QMCSO's are similar in intent and form to QDRO's.

OTHER ISSUES RELATING TO CHILDREN

It is because of a child's natural vulnerability and inability to make informed decisions that the law extends to children significant benefits, as well as specific limitations. Generally, a child is any person under the age of 18. But this definition can vary depending upon the circumstances. For example, to purchase alcohol, a person must at least be 21 years of age. On the other hand, a person who would otherwise be considered a child may be entitled to be treated as an adult if she is emancipated. Following is a brief discussion of some of the benefits and limitations placed upon children.

Benefits Bestowed upon Children

Most of the benefits children receive have already been discussed, but here are two more.

Protection from Harm

In addition to the financial obligations (described earlier) owed to children, there is also an obligation to protect a child from physical harm. Parents are charged with the responsibility to protect their children from neglect and abuse. Neglect may be thought of as a passive harm or misfeasance—a failure to provide children with the necessities of life. Abuse may be thought of as an active harm or malfeasance—physical or mental damage. The remedies available to prevent abuse or neglect to children include imposing criminal penalties and terminating the parent-child relationship on either a temporary or permanent basis.

Protection from Criminal Liability

A prerequisite of a criminal act is the intent to commit a crime. States have statutes that generally presume children under a certain age (i.e., 17 or 18) do not have the ability to form criminal intent. Accordingly, if a child under the specified age is arrested for a criminal offense, they are not treated in the same manner as an adult. Rather, their case is adjudicated by a juvenile court that then determines whether the child acted in a delinquent manner. (You have probably read about cases in which the prosecuting attorney has attempted to prosecute a child as an adult. This typically occurs in cases in which the act was especially heinous, or when it can be proved that the child did in fact have the intent to commit the criminal act.) An adjudication of delinquency is not treated as a criminal conviction, and the penalties available range from probation to placement in a foster care or youth detention facility. In any event, the emphasis is placed on educating and rehabilitating the delinquent child.

Limitations Placed upon Children

There are also several limitations placed upon children including the following.

Contracts

Children do not possess the mental capacity to enter into a contract. Therefore, contracts entered into by children are generally voidable, and children are not legally obligated to perform any such contracts. Third parties who enter into an otherwise valid contract with a child may not escape liability under such a contract unless the child specifically rescinds the contract.

Compulsory Education

States generally require children up through a specified age (i.e., age 16 or sooner if high school is completed) to attend a public or private school. Schooling at home may also be permitted.

Decisions Regarding Medical Treatment

Any 4-year-old who has ever had an inoculation against their will can tell you that children have little right to refuse medical treatment mandated by parents. By the same token, children cannot demand medical treatment in the same manner as an adult. For example, a 12-year-old seeking plastic surgery must have the written permission of a parent.

REVIEW QUESTIONS

1. What are the most common factors used in determining the appropriate level of child support payments?

2. What are the most common factors used in determining which party should have permanent, sole custody of any minor children?

3. What is the effect of bankruptcy on the paying party upon an order for child support?

4. What persons other than parents may have a claim to visitation with a minor child, and under what circumstances will such visitation be permitted?

5. What are the purposes of the Uniform Child Custody Jurisdiction Act and the Parental Kidnapping Prevention Act?

6. What does emancipation mean? How does a child become emancipated? What is the relevance of emancipation to divorce litigation?

7. What is a guardian ad litem, and what is its relevance to divorce litigation?

8. How does the right to receive child support differ from the right to receive alimony?

9. What is cryopreservation? What potential problems are raised by this new process?

10. Why are children who participate in illegal activities treated differently than adults?

KEY TERMS

child support
child support guidelines
emancipation
guardian ad litem
joint custody
legal custody
physical custody
PKPA (Parental
  Kidnapping Prevention
  Act)

primary caretaker
  doctrine
split custody
tender years doctrine
UCCJA (Uniform Child
  Custody Jurisdiction
  Act)

STATE RESEARCH PROBLEMS

Review the laws of your jurisdiction and answer the following questions. Provide the citations for primary authority for your answers.

1. What are the guidelines for awarding child custody?

2. Is the preference of the minor child given any weight, and if so, what is the minimum age requirement for the court to inquire as to the child's preference?

3. Have the courts of your state adopted a particular theory regarding child custody (i.e., tender years or primary caretaker)?

4. Does your state permit, or encourage, joint custody?

5. Does your state permit grandparent and/or step-parent visitation with the minor child? If so, what are the requirements for establishing these rights?

6. What, if any, differences can you find between the child custody jurisdictional laws of your state and the description of the UCCJA as described in this chapter?

7. What are the guidelines in your state for the amount of child support to be paid?

8. Under what, if any, circumstances may a court deviate from the stated child support guidelines?

PRACTICE EXERCISES

1. Review the child support guidelines for Massachusetts and Texas in Appendix C and determine the amount of child support payable under the following circumstances: Mother (custodial parent) has monthly income of $2,000.00; Father (noncustodial parent) has monthly income of $3,000.00; there are two minor children, ages 6 and 9.

2. Using the UCCJA, determine which state has jurisdiction in the following scenarios:

   a) Child is moved from Georgia to North Carolina by father without mother's approval, and conceals the child's whereabouts. Four months later, a petition for divorce and custody is filed by father.

   b) Child runs aways from mother in Washington to his father in Arizona. After six months, mother seeks to bring the child back to Washington.

Divorce—Trial Preparation and Trial

CHAPTER OBJECTIVES

In this chapter, you will learn:

- *How a motion for summary judgment and a motion for judgment on the pleadings can be used in divorce litigation*

- *The unique elements of preparing for a divorce trial*

- *The unique elements of conducting a divorce trial*

While relatively few divorce actions actually result in a full trial of the issues, contested cases should be adequately prepared for the possibility of trial. This entails a series of tasks. Approximately one month before the trial, the court may command the parties to prepare a consolidated pretrial order. The pretrial order assists the litigants and the parties by detailing and clarifying the issues remaining to be decided by the court, both before and during the trial. A pretrial conference may be conducted by the court, at which time it attempts to resolve the remaining conflicts. During these last few days before trial, the paralegal prepares the trial notebook. The trial notebook contains all the information necessary for the attorneys and paralegals to try the case. The physical evidence that may be presented to the court (tax returns, receipts, bills, photographs, discovery responses, etc.) must be organized and indexed to allow for easy retrieval in court. Demonstrative evidence may be prepared to emphasize or to simplify a particular fact at issue. In addition to preparing the documentary evidence, paralegals must also ensure that the witnesses are able to appear and testify honestly and effectively at trial. At trial, a paralegal performs, among many other duties, as an additional set of ears and eyes for the attorney. The paralegal must be able to maintain, control, and retrieve the needed evidence, document, exhibit, or witness at a moment's notice. This requires thorough trial preparation and careful attention to trial events as they transpire.

JUDGMENT ON THE PLEADINGS/SUMMARY JUDGMENT

For cases in which the issue of whether the court should grant a divorce is itself in dispute, the issue may be resolved by means of a pretrial motion. This may be accomplished by either a motion for judgment on the pleadings or a motion for summary judgment. While the goals of these motions are essentially identical (to obtain a judgment without having a trial), there are several material differences.

First, a **motion for judgment on the pleadings** is essentially just that, a request that the court issue a final judgment of divorce based solely upon the complaint and answer. It is available only when the pleadings make it apparent that there are no genuine issues to be litigated and that the moving party is entitled to judgment. For example, a motion for judgment on the pleadings would be appropriate when the answer does not contest the plaintiff's allegations that the marriage is irretrievably broken and that the parties have entered into a separation agreement. A **motion for summary judgment** allows the court to consider also the facts contained in depositions, responses to other discovery requests, and affidavits. A motion for summary judgment typically occurs after the discovery phase in contested litigation, and a motion for judgment on the pleadings occurs after the filing of all the pleadings. Both motions attempt to establish that no genuine issue remains to be determined as to a particular material fact or facts, and that there is no need for a trial. A motion for judgment on the pleadings may be employed in uncontested divorces to quickly obtain a final decree of divorce.

When your firm is defending against a motion for summary judgment, it is not necessary to establish that the movant's statement of the facts is erroneous. Rather, all that is required is to establish that there is a genuine issue to be resolved regarding at least one material fact relevant to the litigation. A party may also file a motion for partial summary judgment, in which the moving party seeks the adjudication of one or more particular questions of fact at issue in the litigation. Here are some examples of motions for complete or partial motions for summary judgment in divorce cases:

— To enforce provisions of a divorce decree

— To collect attorney's fees awarded in a domestic relations case

— To determine questions of fact as to whether a particular piece of property is to be considered as separate or marital property

— To enforce a separation agreement signed prior to the final decree of divorce

motion for judgment on the pleadings
A motion in which a party seeks a final judgment immediately after the pleadings are filed because of the lack of any significant issue raised by the pleadings.

motion for summary judgment
A motion in which a party seeks a final judgment before trial because there are no material disputes about any significant issues.

GRIGSBY

v.

GRIGSBY

Court of Appeals of Texas,
San Antonio.
Aug. 31, 1988
. . . .
Before ESQUIVEL, BUTTS and CANTU, JJ.
  OPINION
  ESQUIVEL, Justice
  This is an appeal from a summary judgment in a divorce case. Olga Grigsby, appellant, sued Robert Grigsby, appellee, for divorce alleging a common law marriage. The parties had previously been married and divorced. The trial court granted appellee's motion for summary judgment on the basis that no marriage existed. Appellant's motion for new trial was denied. We reverse.
  Appellant raises four points of error, but we only need to address her first two points.
  Appellant contends that the trial court erred in granting the motion for summary judgment because material fact issues existed regarding whether the parties represented themselves to others as husband and wife, and whether they had a present agreement to be married.
  There are three elements of a common law marriage: (1) an agreement to be married, (2) cohabitation, and (3) representation to others that the couple are married. TEX.FAM.CODE ANN. § 1.91(a)(2) (Vernon 1975).
  Appellee's motion for summary judgment was based on the lack of an agreement to be married and the absence of any representation or holding out to others that they were married. Appellee did not seek to negate the cohabitation element.
  The standards for reviewing a motion for summary judgment are:

  1. The movant for summary judgment has the burden of showing that there is no genuine issue of material fact and that he is entitled to judgment as a matter of law.

  2. In deciding whether there is a disputed material fact issue precluding summary judg-

ment, evidence favorable to the non-movant will be taken as true.

  3. Every reasonable inference must be indulged in favor of the non-movant and any doubts resolved in her favor. (Citation omitted.)

  Once the movant has established his right to summary judgment, the non-movant's response should present to the trial court issues which would preclude summary judgment. (Citation omitted.) The question on appeal is not whether the summary judgment proof raises a fact issue, but whether the summary judgment proof establishes as a matter of law that there is no genuine fact issue. (Citation omitted.)
  We agree with appellant on her first point of error that a fact issue existed on the representation element. Appellant's affidavit attached to her response to the motion for summary judgment recites, "I named Robert as my spouse and beneficiary on my insurance. Robert continues to designate me as his spouse and beneficiary on his insurance." (Citation omitted.)
  Additionally, the affidavit stated that others addressed appellant as "Mrs. Grigsby" in appellee's presence. The affidavit of Ricardo Reyes showed that the parties cashed checks made payable to "Mr. and Mrs. Robert Grigsby."
  We conclude that the summary judgment evidence failed to conclusively establish that the parties did not represent themselves to others that they were married. Appellant's summary judgment evidence raises a material issue of fact as to the representation element. Accordingly, we hold that the summary judgment evidence does not establish as a matter of law that there is no genuine issue of fact as to representation. Appellant's first point of error is sustained.
  We also sustain appellant's second point of error and hold that appellant raised a fact issue concerning an agreement to be married.
  An agreement to be married need not be shown by direct evidence, but may be implied or inferred if it is established that the parties lived together as husband and wife and represented to others that they were married. (Citation omitted.)
  Appellee argues that appellant's own summary judgment evidence showed there was no agreement to be married. We disagree.
  Appellant's affidavit states, "During the time we were living together, Robert did ask me to participate in a ceremonial wedding for [our son's] sake, but I told him that we were already living together as husband

and wife and that [our son] had been born in wedlock [during the previous marriage] and would not carry any stigma."

Appellant's statement does not establish the lack of an agreement. The statement is distinguishable from those in the case cited by appellee. *See Leal v. Moreno,* 733 S.W.2d 322 (Tex.App.—Corpus Christi 1987, no writ). In *Leal,* the party seeking to establish a common law marriage stated in summary judgment evidence that she and a man were trying out the relationship before actually getting married. Her statements conclusively established that there was no present agreement to be married. *Id.* at 323. In the present case, appellant's statement in her affidavit does not preclude an inference that Robert Grigsby agreed to a common law marriage and additionally wanted a ceremonial marriage.

The summary judgment evidence did not conclusively establish that there was no agreement to be mar-

ried. A fact issue remains whether or not it can be inferred that such an agreement was present.

Having sustained appellant's first two points of error, we reverse the judgment and remand this case to the trial court.

DISCUSSION QUESTIONS

Based on the preceding case of *Grigsby v. Grigsby,* 757 S.W.2d 163 (Tx. 1988), answer the following questions:

1. What is the appropriate standard for an award of summary judgment?

2. What was the precise issue before the Court of Appeals?

3. Why did the Court of Appeals find that this was not an appropriate case for summary judgment?

PRETRIAL PROCEDURE

It should once again be noted that relatively few civil actions, regardless of subject matter, actually culminate in a trial. Sooner or later, the parties always seem to reach an agreement. In some cases, it becomes a matter of economics: The cost of additional litigation exceeds the potential value to be gained. In other cases, the parties ultimately learn to agree to disagree or simply tire of the fight. But as in any adversarial operation, the surest way of avoiding a confrontation is to be prepared for one. Hence, this brief primer on divorce trial preparation.

Prepare Pretrial Order and Conduct Conference

A **pretrial order** serves several functions:

— Compels the trial teams to prepare witness lists and exhibit lists in advance of trial

— Allows for resolution of any remaining issues (i.e., evidentiary questions, motions for summary judgment)

— Eliminates any opportunity for surprise at trial

Each party initially provides the information required by the order separately, and then the two individual responses are consolidated. Typically, the plaintiff has the responsibility for preparing the consolidated pretrial order and presenting it to the court. An important feature of a pretrial order is that,

pretrial order
An order prepared by the parties detailing the issues to be resolved at trial and the methods that will be employed in resolving them.

once it is signed by the judge, local rules may dictate that it supersedes the pleadings filed in the action. Accordingly, there is a paramount need to approach this task with caution.

Once a consolidated pretrial order is presented to the court, any conflicts requiring judicial intervention may be adjudicated at a **pretrial conference.** This conference usually occurs 3 to 4 weeks before the trial date. It is often an informal session, perhaps in the judge's chambers in which the judge attempts to resolve the remaining conflicts and urges the respective counsel to continue to work toward a mutually satisfactory negotiated settlement. Paralegals assist at such conferences by taking note of any significant deadlines imposed as well as any requests of the judge (i.e., that both counsel submit briefs on a particular point by a certain date).

pretrial conference

The court hearing in which the controversies raised by the pretrial order are resolved.

Prepare Trial Notebooks

At trial, the focus must be on the parties and witnesses; that is, the emphasis should be on the message, not the messengers. Accordingly, a successful trial is a fully prepared, well-choreographed trial. The script for such a trial is contained in the **trial notebook,** which holds the vital documents and information required for trial. Ideally, the information is organized in the same order as it will be presented in court. When preparing your first trial notebook, ask your supervising attorney for a copy of a trial notebook used successfully in a prior trial so you will have a useful sample to follow. In addition to those items contained in nondivorce pretrial notebooks, divorce litigation necessitates the inclusion of the following items:

trial notebook

The working notebook used by the trial team, containing all relevant information needed for trial.

— The financial affidavit filed by each party and documentary evidence to support the claims of income and expenses listed therein

— Detailed information as to each significant asset and liability to be awarded, including when and by whom it was acquired, the original cost and present value, its characterization as either separate or marital property and the facts supporting that claim, and cross-references to any discovery relating to the asset or liability

Organize Documents

It does little good to have acquired all the documents necessary to prevail at trial unless you can access them easily when needed. While in school, you will probably have the opportunity to attend trials in which the paralegals have carefully organized and indexed the documentary evidence. If so, observe the paralegal when the attorney needs a particular document. It will appear as though all the paralegal has to do is to pick it up and hand it to the attorney. In reality, that simple motion is the result of much pretrial planning.

The physical evidence may be organized in any number of ways, so long as the method chosen is logical and as uncomplicated as possible. One distinction to be made is between those items to be tendered as evidence at the trial (known as *trial exhibits*) and the material that is required only to assist the trial team. One common method is to organize the material by witness, so that all of the material relevant to each witness is in one location, available to support the claims of friendly witnesses and to impeach the credibility of hostile witnesses. For the primary witnesses in a divorce case—the litigants—additional subfiles are usually required. For example, there could be files for medical expenses, clothing, food, housing expenses, education expenses, and income, as well as many others.

Prepare Trial Charts and Other Demonstrative Evidence

Demonstrative evidence is often introduced at trial because, as the proverb goes, "one picture is worth a thousand words." A juror may not always pay close attention to everything a witness says, but effective demonstrative evidence always makes an impression on the trier of fact, especially a jury. Which do you think would have more impact, the testimony of a witness as to the infidelity of an adverse party, or an incriminating photograph or videotape?

While such a "smoking gun" is not always available, every case provides numerous facts that can be demonstrated in some tangible manner for the trier of fact. For example, a party's financial status can be established through tax returns, W-2 forms, titles to real property and automobiles, appraisals of businesses, jewelry, and photographs. The expert testimony of an economist may be difficult for a jury to comprehend or accurately recall during deliberations; however, a chart depicting the distribution of marital property between the parties can create a lasting image. Allegations of infidelity or deviancy can be established by playing audio and video recordings as well as by displaying enlarged copies of receipts for hotel rooms, meals, and gifts for the partners in an adverse party's meretricious relationship.

Some examples of the usefulness of demonstrative evidence in a divorce trial include providing photographs to show

— The parties in an earlier and happier time

— Injuries inflicted upon a spouse or child by the adverse party

— The marital residence with and without the furnishings

— A child's room, to present the environment in which the child is to be raised

(NOTE—*Before any photographs can be introduced into evidence, they must be authenticated. This can be accomplished by the testimony of the photographer as to the time, date, and place the photograph was taken.*)

Another effective use of demonstrative evidence is to present an enlargement of a calendar to show the dates and frequency of an adverse spouse's offensive conduct, absences from home, missed visitations, etc. This can be especially effective if the testimony begins with a blank calendar and it is filled in at trial as the testimony of the client progresses.

However, artistic ability is not a requirement for a paralegal; in most communities there are professionals trained in the production of trial evi-

demonstrative evidence
Audio or visual aids used during trial to emphasize or simplify specific issues in controversy.

dence. Further, these images can be presented in a variety of forms, including poster-size (4' × 6') charts or photograph enlargements (be certain that an easel will be available), slides, and opaque images, used with overhead projectors. A word of caution if electronic equipment is to be used: *Before trial, visit the courtroom to ensure that electric outlets are within reach, or bring extension cords to court. Also make sure that the windows have blinds or curtains that can be closed so that the jury can actually see the evidence. Any charts or enlarged photographs must be large enough to permit all members of the jury and the judge to view them comfortably.*

◀ PRACTICE POINTER ▶

All such demonstrative evidence must be otherwise admissible under the applicable rules of evidence, and a proper foundation for the evidence must be presented. For example, a chart indicating future expected earnings must be accompanied by the testimony of the economist upon whose calculations the chart was prepared.

Prepare Witnesses and Clients

witness preparation
The process of preparing a witness to testify.

The term **witness preparation** is often misunderstood by newcomers to the process of litigation. Witness preparation does not involve telling the witness what to say when they testify at trial. Rather, witness preparation is the process of acclimating the witness (either the actual litigant or a nonparty witness) to the procedure of testifying in court. A courtroom is designed to intimidate a witness with somber portraits of deceased judges upon the walls and a very much alive judge sitting high over the witness. A primary purpose of witness preparation is to relax the witness so the jury may see that witness as he really is, rather than as someone who is nervous, stammering, and perhaps less than credible. Accordingly, in preparing a witness to testify in court, at a minimum, it is necessary to make sure that the witness (1) knows what questions he will be asked in court, (2) how those questions will be posed, and (3) has an opportunity to answer the questions.

The best method of preparing a witness for court is to actually ask the witness the anticipated questions and require the witness to respond as he will in court. Additionally, the witness must be made aware of which questions will be asked on direct examination and which will most likely be asked on cross-examination. A witness must therefore be confident enough, and comfortable enough, to withstand the rigors of cross-examination. The witness must also be reminded not to become angry, belligerent, or rude for fear of alienating the jury or saying something that he will regret. This can be especially difficult in divorce trials in which the issues are much more emotionally charged than in more conventional litigation.

Subpoena Witnesses

All nonparty witnesses who may be required to testify at trial must be formally notified of their obligation to attend the trial, and this is accomplished by serving a subpoena upon them. Subpoenas to appear at trial are obtained and served in the same manner as subpoenas to appear at depositions.

Paralegals need to be aware of the appropriate methods of service of the subpoenas, including the requirement for and amount of any witness fees, since the subpoena is of no effect until it is served. Proof of the service must be obtained and maintained by the paralegal in the event service of the subpoena becomes an issue.

Prepare a Proposed Final Judgment and Decree of Divorce

Courts often allow (or order) the prevailing party in litigation to prepare the final order. By preparing and submitting the order in advance, you give the court another demonstration of your preparation as well as provide yet another reminder of the client's goals and desires.

DIVORCE TRIAL PROCEDURE

At trial, a paralegal acts as an additional set of hands, eyes, and ears for the attorney. A successful trial is the result of a team effort.

Present Evidence

Evidence takes one of two forms: oral testimony of witnesses or physical/documentary evidence. The paralegal is the choreographer of the evidence and as such has primary authority for organizing, maintaining, and retrieving the evidence while in the courtroom. This includes more than the physical evidence; it also includes the witnesses who are to testify in the case. One function of the paralegal at trial is to ensure that witnesses are available and ready when they are called to testify. As the evidence is presented, the paralegal must juggle a series of additional tasks simultaneously. Documentary evidence and exhibits must be ready to be handed to the attorney for introduction into evidence. The paralegal must take extensive notes of the proceedings for later review to assist in the preparation for the next day. This is especially important in lengthy trials, where the strategy employed on Thursday may be affected by what a witness said on Tuesday.

For example, suppose the husband testified on Tuesday that he has consistently spent his weekends with his children. On Thursday, a neighbor of the husband and wife is scheduled to testify. With accurate notes of the husband's testimony, the neighbor can be adequately questioned as to the husband's conduct with his children. Without accurate notes, the alternatives are to pay for a daily transcript of the trial or to rely on the trial team's collective memory. These notes can be recorded in the trial notebook. Furthermore, as the paralegal gains courtroom experience, his opinion concerning the progress of the trial will be invaluable to the attorney, who is often too involved with the battles of the moment to notice what impression the evidence is making upon the court. The paralegal should also record the objections made by each party, the grounds for each objection, the court's ruling and rationale for the ruling, if any is stated. *Bring a calculator to court to ensure that the opposing party's*

FOCUS ON MANAGING THE REST OF YOUR CASELOAD WHEN IN COURT

The good news about a trial is that it provides you with an incredible adrenalin boost, giving you additional energy. The bad news is that you are going to need every bit of that energy and more. A typical domestic trial takes from 2 to 4 days. Each trial day usually begins in the office, with members of the trial team conferring and making certain that all last-minute details have been completed. A full day in court is followed by a return to the office to review the events of the day and to prepare for tomorrow. At that time, you must review the day's mail and telephone messages for any action that is required in any other case.

Paralegals are responsible for more than one case at any given time. Active divorce law offices may have dozens of files pending, all with deadlines of their own. How to balance that workload is one of the most difficult tasks a paralegal (or attorney) ever has to learn. As with any other task, it begins

with adequate preparation and time management. Common sense dictates that a paralegal prepare for the worst-case scenario and hope for the best.

As the trial date approaches, make a list of all deadlines that must be met during the anticipated time of the trial, and arrange for other staff members to attend to these needs. Alert clients with whom you are in frequent contact that you will be out of the office and unavailable for an extended period of time. Take care, however, to assure those clients that their case is being monitored by the office, and give the name of the staff member having direct responsibility for that case during your absence. It is often helpful to remind such clients that the time may come when it will be necessary to spend a similar amount of time exclusively on their case. It will also be necessary for you to call the office regularly to check on your other cases.

PRACTICE POINTER

evidence is supported by correct arithmetic and to be able to follow the applicable testimony of the expert financial witnesses.

Submit Application for Attorney's Fees

At the conclusion of the trial, the financially dependent spouse may make an application to the court for the payment of reasonable attorney's fees. The court will inquire as to whether the fees requested are reasonable according to the standards of that community, the amount of time expended, the difficulty of the issues presented, the ability of the financially superior party to pay, and the degree of the financially dependent party's need. The application for attorney's fees may be supported by presenting the court with records of the time spent by the attorneys and paralegals on behalf of their client. In addition, the testimony of other local attorneys may be used to determine whether the fees requested are reasonable.

REVIEW QUESTIONS

1. What are the paralegal's responsibilities during the presentation of the evidence? How do these responsibilities change, if at all, during direct examination as opposed to cross-examination?

2. What is summary judgment, and how is it applicable to divorce litigation?

3. What is demonstrative evidence, and what is its utility at trial?

4. What is a trial notebook, and how is it used before and at trial?

5. List at least five items that should be brought to court for a divorce trial.

KEY TERMS

demonstrative evidence	pretrial conference
motion for judgment on the pleadings	pretrial order
	trial notebook
motion for summary judgment	witness preparation

STATE RESEARCH PROBLEMS

Review the laws of your jurisdiction and answer the following questions. Provide primary authority for your answers.

1. Are jury trials permitted in divorce litigation in your jurisdiction? If so, what specific issues may a jury determine?

2. What is the procedure for obtaining subpoenas to compel the attendance of nonparty witnesses at trial?

3. Do your local courts permit paralegals to sit with the attorneys during trial?

PRACTICE EXERCISE

Based on the deposition of Thomas James Morrison (Appendix B), what demonstrative evidence should be prepared for the trial of his divorce?

Divorce—Enforcement of Divorce Decrees

CHAPTER OBJECTIVES

In this chapter, you will learn:

- *How to discover the existence and location of assets available for support payments*

- *How federal and uniform state laws enforce court orders for support*

- *How a judgment for alimony and child support from one state*

may be domesticated so collection may occur in a second state

- *How normal collection techniques may be used to collect alimony and child support payments*

- *How civil contempt may be used against a delinquent payor*

The judgments and decrees made in a divorce case, like those in any case, are capable of being enforced through the auspices of the court. What distinguishes divorce actions are the tools available to enforce the decrees and the nature of the orders to be enforced. While several of the enforcement tools available are applicable to all aspects of a divorce case, a few are available only for the collection of unpaid alimony and child support (for example, URESA—the Uniform Reciprocal Enforcement of Support Act). When the party obligated to make payments fails to do so, the receiving party may use postjudgment discovery to inquire into the nature and location of any assets held by the paying party. Some jurisdictions require that a party seeking to enforce provisions of a divorce decree obtain a final judgment for the specific amount in arrears. Other jurisdictions permit the immediate use of enforcement tools. Generally, the states requiring a final judgment also provide for retroactive modification of the divorce decree. Common enforcement vehicles include

— Garnishment, in which the amount in arrears is collected directly from third parties having possession of the delinquent party's property (i.e., employers and financial institutions)

— Levy and sale, in which the delinquent party's property is seized by the sheriff or marshall and sold at auction, with proceeds going toward the arrearage

— Civil contempt, in which the court directly orders the delinquent party to comply with the provisions of the divorce decree under penalty of incarceration for the willful failure to comply

Finally, if the delinquent party resides in a state other than the one that issued the divorce decree, it is necessary to domesticate the divorce decree in the delinquent party's state of residence.

POSTJUDGMENT DISCOVERY

The primary issue in any case involving enforcement of a court order for payment of alimony, maintenance, and support is whether the debtor party has assets to pay the debt owed, and if so, where the assets are located. Often, the debtor claims to be either completely or partially judgment proof, that is, without sufficient assets to pay the claim. When the litigation extends beyond the time of the final judgment, the parties may engage in postjudgment discovery. (The enforcement proceedings must be initiated before commencing postjudgment discovery.) Thus, it is common for the party seeking to collect **arrearages** of alimony, maintenance, or support to submit interrogatories to— or take the deposition of—the delinquent party. The same procedures and rules used with regular discovery apply to postjudgment discovery, including the authority to order compliance, and hold recalcitrant parties in contempt, in response to proper discovery requests. *When attempting to collect support arrearages, review discovery responses made during the original divorce litigation. You may find information concerning the existence or location of the debtor's property.*

In postjudgment discovery related to the collection of an arrearage of alimony and child support, the scope of discovery includes all the financial issues typical in prejudgment divorce litigation. It also includes investigating the existence, nature, and amount of any financial obligations owed by the debtor to a new family (especially whether any such debts are legal commitments, such as support of a new spouse, or merely voluntary payments, such as support of a stepchild); and determining whether the delinquent party has disposed of any property, by gift or sale, in an attempt to establish an inability to comply with the court order for maintenance. It may not be necessary to inquire into more mundane areas such as current income and expenses if the court requires the filing of a financial affidavit similar to the one used in divorce litigation.

An additional investigatory tool available to parents seeking unpaid child support balances is the Federal Parent Locator Service [42 U.S.C.

arrearages
Unpaid past due balances of alimony and/or child support.

PRACTICE POINTER

653(b)], which provides inquiry into federal records to determine the last known address for a delinquent parent. For a nominal fee, this service provides access to tax, criminal, driving, military, unemployment insurance, and postal records. It takes at least two to three weeks for a response, and the information thus obtained is likely to be at least two to three months old.

An informal investigation similar to the one conducted at the outset of the litigation can be useful. Another tool available to your client as a judgment

---

INTERVIEW CHECKLIST

(The following questions are to be answered by the client in conjunction with the basic interview checklist provided in Chapter 2.)

In what state was the original divorce decree obtained?

What is the date of the original divorce decree?

Has the original divorce decree been amended or modified, and if so, what is the date of such amendment or modification?

What specific provision(s) of the divorce decree has your former spouse failed to obey?

Have you filed any prior motions to enforce provisions of the divorce decree?_____ If so, provide details.

If you are seeking to collect unpaid alimony and/or child support, answer the following questions:

What is the amount of alimony and/or child support that is to be paid? _____ How often is that payment due?

When did you last receive an alimony and/or child support payment? _____ What is the current total amount of the arrearages?

How have prior payments been tendered to you (cash, check, etc.)?

Amount   Date

Have you or your children received other goods (food, clothing) in lieu of alimony and/or child support? _____ If so, provide details.

Item   Date

Describe any prior efforts made to collect the arrearage, including the date of the attempt and the result obtained.

What, if any, records do you have in your custody that document the status of the arrearage?

Have you ever denied the party owing alimony and/or child support visitation privileges with the minor children? _____ If so, provide details.

Has your income changed since the time of the divorce decree? _____ If so, provide details.

Has the other party's income changed since the time of the divorce decree? _____ If so, provide details.

If you are seeking to enforce visitation privileges with a minor child, answer the following questions:

What are the specific provisions of the divorce decree relating to visitation with the minor child(ren)?

_____

How have you been denied visitation privileges with your minor child(ren)? Provide specific details.

_____

Provide the names of any witnesses who can testify on your behalf as to the denial of visitation privileges.

_____

When was the last time you visited with your minor child(ren)?

_____

At what location is the visitation to occur?

_____

Who is responsible for the transportation of the minor child(ren) to and from the visitation?

_____

Have you ever failed to make a regularly scheduled visitation with your minor child(ren)? If so, provide details and the reason for the failure to visit.

_____

Has your former spouse ever claimed that you pose any threat, either physically or emotionally, to the welfare of the minor child(ren)? If so, provide details.

_____

Have you ever been arrested? _____ If so, provide details.

_____

Are you current with your alimony and/or child support payments? _____ If not, provide details.

_____

creditor (as opposed to being merely a litigant) is the delinquent party's credit report, which can be acquired from a credit reporting service. A credit report reveals the existence and status of the delinquent party's debts (i.e., whether any are in arrears, and if so, to what extent). It may include information about some of the delinquent party's purchases, such as real property, automobiles, appliances, etc. It may also reveal the delinquent party's employment history and the location of bank accounts.

COLLECTION OF ARREARAGES

There are legal remedies available to a person seeking to collect support payment arrearages. As discussed below, these remedies can be found in both federal and state law, as well as in both civil and criminal law.

Federal and Uniform Laws

While some collection tools are unique to a particular state, others are more generally available. Typically, these take the form of either federal laws or uniform state laws.

Title IV-D

In 1975, federal legislation enacted Title IV-D of the Social Security Act in an effort to provide custodial parents with a low-cost (or no-cost) means of collecting child support. Although based on federal guidelines, the IV-D program is administered by the individual states. Under these programs, the custodial parents are represented by state-employed attorneys in hearings to establish or enforce support orders. In addition, Title IV-D programs require that the individual states enact the following procedures, among others, to assist support recipients:

— Income tax refund intercept programs

— Reporting of child support arrearages exceeding $1,000.00 to credit bureaus

— Immediate wage withholding (in all child support orders issued since January 1, 1994, as well as all other child support orders modified since January 1, 1990)

— Promulgation and revision—at least every 4 years—of child support guidelines

— The "Bradley Amendment," which requires states to enact laws making each installment of court-ordered child support a final judgment upon accrual. (In the next section of this chapter, we discuss the importance of having a final judgment when attempting to collect support arrearages.)

URESA and RURESA

URESA; RURESA
Uniform state laws authorizing state action to recover arrearages of alimony and child support owed by an out-of-state debtor.

The difficulties in collecting support arrearages are greatly magnified when the delinquent party resides in a different state than the dependent party. Over the years, a series of uniform laws have been promulgated and revised in an attempt to address this issue. **The Uniform Reciprocal Enforcement of Support Act (URESA)** was originally enacted in 1950. It has since been adopted in approximately one-third of the states. **The Revised Uniform Reciprocal Enforcement of Support Act (RURESA)** has since been adopted by the remaining two-thirds of the states. The two acts are largely the same, except that RURESA provides for establishment of paternity and uses a simplified method of enforcing existing support orders. The stated goal of these acts is to provide a relatively uncomplicated and inexpensive means of recovering unpaid support from both resident and nonresident debtors.

Although it is a civil proceeding, a URESA claim is initiated by filing a verified petition with a prosecuting attorney of the state of the petitioner's residence (the initiating state). The petition should contain, at a minimum, the name and address of the defendant, and information relating to the nature and amount of the default. A copy of a petition under URESA is at Exhibit 12–1. The initiating court reviews the petition to determine whether the plaintiff is entitled to the relief sought, and whether the responding court has personal jurisdiction over the debtor. The papers are then forwarded to the prosecuting attorney of the state and county in which the delinquent party resides

EXHIBIT 12-1 SAMPLE URESA ORDER

IN THE SUPERIOR COURT OF_____ COUNTY,
STATE OF_____

UNIFORM SUPPORT PETITION

PLAINTIFF/PETITIONER

☐ IV-D NON AFDC
☐ IV-D AFDC/IV-E FOSTER CARE
☐ NON IV-D
INITITATING CASE/DOCKET NO.

COUNTY/STATE

FILE STAMP

DEFENDANT/RESPONDENT

OTHER REFERENCE NO.

RESPONDING CASE/DOCKET NO.   COUNTY/STATE

OTHER REFERENCE NO.

This petition of Plaintiff/Petitioner respectfully shows the court that:

1. This is a petition for:

☐ ESTABLISHMENT OF PATERNITY (URESA)

☐ ESTABLISHMENT OF AN ORDER (URESA) FOR:
   ☐ CHILD SUPPORT
   ☐ SPOUSAL SUPPORT (NON-IV-D)
   ☐ UNREIMBURSED PUBLIC ASSISTANCE (IN IV-D CASES
      THE AMOUNT MUST BE REDUCED TO A CHILD SUPPORT
      JUDGMENT)
   ☐ MEDICAL COVERAGE
   ☐ OTHER COSTS (e.g. DELIVERY, OTHER MEDICAL,
      GENETIC TESTING, ATTORNEYS' FEES)

☐ MODIFICATION OF EXISTING RESPONDING STATE ORDER
(URESA)

☐ COLLECTION OF ARREARAGE (URESA OR UEFJA)

☐ ENFORCEMENT OF EXISTING ORDER

☐ REGISTRATION OF FOREIGN SUPPORT ORDER

☐ OTHER

☐ THE GENERAL TESTIMONY FOR URESA IS ATTACHED AND
INCORPORATED BY REFERENCE

☐ A PATERNITY AFFIDAVIT IS ATTACHED AND INCORPORATED
BY REFERENCE

2. _____ resides in _____
      (NAME AND RELATIONSHIP)   (CITY, COUNTY, STATE)

and has custody of the following dependents of Defendant/Respondent:

(DEPENDENTS' NAMES (FIRST, MI, LAST)   SOCIAL SECURITY NUMBER   DATE OF BIRTH

                                ADDITIONAL
                                NAMES ATTACHED
                                ☐

3. _____ and Defendant/Respondent were:

☐ NEVER MARRIED TO EACH OTHER
☐ MARRIED BY COMMON LAW FOR THE PERIOD_____
                          DATES
☐ SEPARATED ON _____
               DATE
☐ LEGALLY SEPARATED ON _____ IN _____
                  DATE   COUNTY/STATE
☐ DIVORCED PENDING IN _____
                  COUNTY/STATE

☐ MARRIED ON_____ IN_____
          DATE   COUNTY/STATE
                      IN_____
                      COUNTY/STATE
☐ DIVORCED ON_____ IN_____
         DATE   COUNTY/STATE
☐ OTHER_____

4. Defendant/Respondent resides in _____
                          CITY/COUNTY/STATE

Defendant/Respondent's last known employer is_____
                                    NAME AND ADDRESS

UNIFORM SUPPORT PETITION, PAGE 2

INITIATING CASE NO.

5. The dependents are entitled to support and/or medical coverage from Defendant/Respondent, who has an obligation to pay support pursuant to the laws of the initiating jurisdiction, which is enforceable under the reciprocal support statute which is _____ . The responding state may obtain jurisdiction of Defendant/Respondent or his/her property.

6. Defendant/Respondent has refused to provide reasonable support for the above named dependents.

7. Defendant/Respondent:

a. ☐ IS THE FATHER OF THE DEPENDENT CHILD(REN) AS ALLEGED IN THE ATTACHED PATERNITY AFFIDAVIT(S)

b. ☐ SHOULD PAY AN AMOUNT OF CURRENT SUPPORT FOR THE DEPENDENTS AS REQUIRED BY THE LAW (GUIDELINES) OF THE RESPONDING STATE

c. ☐ IS NOT UNDER A CURRENT ORDER TO PROVIDE SUPPORT. HOWEVER (AGENCY) _____
IS ENTITLED TO REIMBURSEMENT FOR UNREIMBURSED PUBLIC ASSISTANCE AS STATED IN THE TESTIMONY ATTACHED AND INCORPORATED BY REFERENCE IN THE AMOUNT OF

REIMBURSEMENT AMOUNT $_____ AS OF (DATE) _____

d. ☐ SHOULD PROVIDE MEDICAL COVERAGE AS PERMITTED BY THE LAW OF THE RESPONDING STATE

e. ☐ SHOULD BE ORDERED TO PAY OTHER COSTS INCLUDING BUT NOT LIMITED TO GENETIC TESTING COSTS AS APPLICABLE. SPECIFY

_____ $ _____

_____ $ _____

_____ $ _____

f. ☐ IS UNDER A COURT/ADMINISTRATIVE ORDER TO PROVIDE SUPPORT (A CERTIFIED COPY OF THE ORDER IS ATTACHED AND INCORPORATED BY REFERENCE)

g. ☐ HAS FAILED TO COMPLY WITH THE SUPPORT ORDER. THIS HAS RESULTED IN AN ARREARAGE OF ARREARAGE AMOUNT $ _____

AS OF DATE _____ (INCLUDES AFDC, NON-AFDC, PRINCIPAL AND INTEREST)

8. (Name) _____

☐ HAS MADE AN ASSIGNMENT OF RIGHTS: AND/OR

☐ HAS GIVEN AUTHORITY TO THE FOLLOWING AGENCY TO COLLECT SUPPORT FOR THE ABOVE NAMED DEPENDENTS:

WHEREFORE, Plaintiff/Respondent requests an order for:

☐ PATERNITY

☐ CHILD SUPPORT

☐ SPOUSAL SUPPORT (NON IV-D)

☐ UNREIMBURSED PUBLIC ASSISTANCE (NON IV-D)

☐ CHILD SUPPORT JUDGMENT FOR UNREIMBURSED PUBLIC ASSISTANCE

☐ MEDICAL COVERAGE

☐ MODIFICATION

☐ PAYMENT OF ARREARAGE

☐ ENFORCEMENT OF THE CURRENT SUPPORT ORDER

☐ REGISTRATION OF FOREIGN SUPPORT ORDER

☐ PAYMENT OF COSTS AND ATTORNEYS' FEES BY THE DEFENDANT/RESPONDENT (SEE INSTRUCTIONS)

☐ OTHER:

☐ COMMENTS ATTACHED

Under penalties of perjury, all information and facts stated in this petition are true to the best of my knowledge and belief.

_____   X _____
DATE   SIGNATURE OF PLAINTIFF/PETITIONER OR REPRESENTATIVE

_____   _____
DATE   SIGNATURE OF ATTORNEY (OPTIONAL)

_____   _____   _____
SWORN TO AND SIGNED BEFORE ME   NOTARY PUBLIC, COURT/AGENCY OFFICIAL AND TITLE   COMMISSION EXPIRES
THIS DATE, COUNTY, STATE

(the responding state). A copy of the petition and a Notice to Appear are then formally served upon the defendant. The defendant may file a responsive pleading to the petition.

At the court hearing, the defendant must establish that he is not indebted to the plaintiff as alleged in the petition. Should the court enter an order for payment of the arrearage, payments are made to the court that forwards it to the plaintiff (less a surcharge for the court's services). Failure to pay the arrearage can result in the imposition of any of the enforcement remedies available in the forum state.

A significant disadvantage of using URESA is that it tends to be a low priority on the agenda of most prosecuting attorneys. A little-known aspect of URESA is that it allows private attorneys to act as prosecuting attorneys. Also note that if a private attorney initiates the process, arrangements must be made for a private attorney to continue the representation in the forum state.

Criminal Laws

The esteem that society places on the obligation to pay family debts is evidenced by the existence of criminal sanctions for the failure to do so. Many states recognize the criminal offense of abandonment, which is the failure of a person to provide financial support for a specific period of time for his minor children. (Note that criminal abandonment does not usually apply to adults, such as former spouses.) Thus, where available, an arrearage of child support may be remedied by seeking a criminal warrant against the delinquent party. This may be a viable remedy for a client who does not have the resources to hire a private attorney to collect the arrearage. Often, the criminal charges are dropped when the child support payments are made current. (Be careful not to confuse criminal abandonment with "abandonment" as a ground for divorce.)

FINAL JUDGMENT

As discussed below, the unique nature of support payment requires a final judgment be issued by a court within the state in which the collection is to be attempted.

Reducing the Arrearage to a Final Judgment

Collecting money owed pursuant to a court judgment, including divorce decrees, requires a **final judgment**. A final judgment (also called a *money judgment*) is one that completely resolves the issues between the parties and is not subject to retroactive modification or reversal. This is especially important in family law because of the peculiar nature of alimony and child support payments. Alimony and child support are debts that are payable over an extended period of time, and are subject to later modification. The states differ in their determination as to when these postmarital debts become final judgments. Some states consider each alimony or child support payment a separate final judgment as soon as the payment accrues. Other states require a formal adjudication as a prerequisite for a final judgment.

final judgment
A court judgment that is not subject to further modification.

In states in which each accrued unpaid alimony and child support installment is treated as a final judgment, the filing of an affidavit by the party to whom the debt is owed is sufficient to trigger collection procedures such as garnishment and levy and sale. The law in these states provides that the divorce decree itself is a final judgment, and that the judgment cannot be retroactively modified. As each payment accrues, it becomes a separate and final money judgment. In a second and fewer number of states, the first step in any action to recover arrearages of alimony, support, and maintenance is to seek a money judgment for the specific amount owed at that time. In this second category of states (including New York, New Jersey, and Arizona), the court maintains the continuing jurisdiction to modify the amount of alimony, support, and maintenance until such time as the court officially sets the amount of the arrearages. In other words, the absolute right to receive such payments does not "vest" until sanctioned by the court. In such states, a court may retroactively modify, upward or downward, alimony and child support payments. Therefore, a final judgment may be sought only for those payments that are already past due.

By whatever means created, a final judgment has the following effects:

— Provides the claimant with a lien on the debtor's property

— Protects the claimant against a defense that collection of the arrearage is barred by the statute of limitations

— Ensures that the arrearage is afforded full faith and credit by all foreign jurisdictions

Before initiating any of the collection devices described later in this chapter, the creditor party must generally obtain a writ of execution from the court issuing the divorce. A writ of execution is an order from the court to the marshals, sheriffs, constables, etc. of the state, authorizing them to seize property of the delinquent party, sell it at public auction if necessary, and pay the proceeds to the creditor party. This writ should then be entered in the appropriate public records of that county for the recordation of debts. By doing so, a lien is placed on all the delinquent party's personal property as well as all of his or her real property located in that county. This acts as notice to the world of the creditor's claim. Thus, even if the property is later transferred to a third party in an attempt to avoid payment, the lien permits attachment of the property from the third party.

Domestication of Foreign Judgments

foreign judgment
A judgment issued by a court in one state, upon which collection is sought in another state.

domestication
The process of officially recognizing the validity and authority of a foreign judgment.

A **foreign judgment** is one rendered in a state other than the one in which it is to be enforced. Should a party seek to enforce a foreign judgment, the first requirement is to domesticate the foreign judgment. Generally, a court order is effective in the state in which it was issued. **Domestication** is the process of creating a domestic judgment to correspond with a foreign judgment. Pursuant to the United States Constitution, each state must afford "full faith and credit" to the judgments of its sister states. With our increasingly mobile society, domestication of a foreign judgment is a common and relatively simple procedure. It is an especially simple procedure in states that have adopted the Uniform Domestication of Foreign Judgments Act. In such states, the filing of a petition for domestication and a certified copy of the original final judgment is sufficient for domestication. A sample petition for domestication and collection of a foreign judgment is at Exhibit 12–2.

A final judgment from the foreign state is required for domestication. This is especially important when the judgment to be domesticated is issued from a state that permits alimony and child support to be modified retroactively.

METHODS OF COLLECTION

State laws provide various methods of collecting support arrearages. Following are the most commonly used collection techniques.

(NOTE: *Each method of collection may not be available in each state.*)

Civil Contempt

The obligation to pay alimony and child support is an obligation to society as well as to the particular recipients, and as such the failure to make timely payments is punishable by civil contempt. (Other private debts are not generally enforceable by contempt.) **Civil contempt** is the willful disobedience of a court order.

(NOTE: *Civil contempt is not in the nature of a criminal proceeding, and any ensuing penalties are not intended as punitive; rather, they are designed to coerce from the defendant the desired behavior. Unlike a criminal action, the "penalties" in civil contempt can be terminated by complying with the court order.*)

civil contempt
A judicial remedy available when a person intentionally disobeys an existing court order.

The operative element of contempt is willfulness. It must be established that the delinquent party *could* comply with the court order to pay alimony and/or child support, but *will not* do so. For example, a delinquent party is not found to be in contempt of court if the failure to pay court-ordered alimony and/or child support on a timely basis is due to a physical or mental incapacitation. A party defending against a claim of civil contempt will attempt to establish either (1) that he has complied with the court order, or (2) that he is unable to do so through no fault of his own. This second alternative requires a showing that the delinquent party has exhausted all available remedies, and that the inability to pay the monies owed is not due to any deliberate action on the part of the delinquent party (i.e., voluntarily leaving gainful employment). The court must first determine whether the required payments have been made, and if not, whether the failure to do so has been willful. The court must then determine the amount of payments that are in arrears, the timetable for payment, and if necessary the sanctions that will be levied if payment is not forthcoming. Most courts do not impose the relatively harsh sanctions of contempt unless the petitioning party can establish that all other available remedies have been attempted without success.

EXHIBIT 12–2
SAMPLE COMPLAINT FOR DOMESTICATION
OF FOREIGN JUDGMENT

IN THE SUPERIOR COURT OF _____ COUNTY
STATE OF _____

KIMBERLY PETERSON,

Plaintiff,

v.   CIVIL ACTION NO. _____

SEAN PETERSON,

Defendant.

<u>Complaint For Domestication of Foreign Judgment</u>

COMES NOW, the Plaintiff in the above-referenced action and for her Complaint shows the Court as follows:

1.

The Defendant is subject to the jurisdiction of this Court and may be served with a copy of this complaint and summons at 550 Capitol Avenue, Atlanta, Fulton County, Georgia.

2.

On the 24th day of April, 1987, the District Court of Dallas County, in the State of Texas, issued a Final Judgment and Decree of Divorce, a duly authenticated copy of which is attached hereto as Exhibit A. This judgment provided in its pertinent part that Defendant is to pay to Plaintiff the sum of Five Hundred Dollars ($500.00) per month as child support for the support of the parties' minor child.

3.

The Defendant is in default of the foreign judgment and owes the sum of Two Thousand Dollars ($2,000.00) to Plaintiff.

4.

The amount sought by Plaintiff is a final and enforceable judgment under the laws of the State of Texas.

WHEREFORE, Plaintiff demands:

a) That the foreign judgment annexed hereto as Exhibit A be made the judgment of this Court; and

b) That the Plaintiff have judgment against the Defendant for Two Thousand Dollars ($2,000.00), plus interest and costs as provided by law.

Respectfully Submittted,

_____
Attorney for Plaintiff

Jurisdiction and Venue

Once a court has obtained personal jurisdiction over the parties, and the proper venue has been established in a divorce action, that court retains permanent jurisdiction to enforce its rulings and orders. This is true even if the defendant has since relocated to another county in the same state or to another state, assuming that the forum state has a domestic relations long-arm statute. The court may also require a showing by the party seeking the imposition of contempt that all other available remedies have been exhausted, and that a finding of contempt is required to compel payment of the owed sums.

Procedure for Initiating and Defending

Consider the following example: Father has been ordered to pay Mother child support payments of $500.00 per month. From January 1994 through and including June 1994, Father paid Mother child support totaling $1,000.00, creating an arrearage of $2,000.00. In an attempt to collect the arrearage, Mother could file and serve a motion for contempt, with an accompanying brief in support of the motion, and a request for a hearing at which the court could cite Father for contempt. (This request for a court hearing is similar to the request that is made for a temporary hearing.) Since failure to respond may result in incarceration, personal service of these documents is required to satisfy due process. Father would have to promptly file and serve a brief in opposition to the motion for contempt, arguing that a finding of contempt is inappropriate. (A sample motion for contempt is at Exhibit 12–3.)

At the court hearing, Mother first has the burden of proof to make a *prima facie* case for the imposition of civil contempt. This requires (1) proof of the amount of child support owed for each time period and (2) proof that the requisite amounts have not been fully paid. She may also testify as to Father's history of compliance (to prove Father's awareness of the order) and about the consequences of the default (emotional, financial, etc.). The attorney for Mother may also wish to introduce the testimony of third parties to further establish the ability of Father to pay the support (testimony about his recent purchases, life-style, etc.).

The burden of proof then shifts to Father to prove that he has not willfully disobeyed the court order. Since it is not possible for mother to conclusively prove a negative (that the monies have not been paid), Father must affirmatively prove that the monies have been paid. To do so, Father will have to produce canceled checks, receipts, or other corroborative evidence. Alternatively, should Father attempt to prove that the reasons for nonpayment were not willful, he must do more than merely establish that he does not currently have possession of sufficient assets to pay Mother. Father must show that he does not have control or dominion over any assets not titled in his own name (i.e., that he has transferred title to any of his property to a new spouse or other third party). Additionally, Father must prove that he is unable to obtain the necessary funds through additional employment, loans, or other means.

(NOTE: *It is generally an insufficient response for Father to allege that the amount of alimony and/or child support support is excessive. All such allegations are more prop-*

EXHIBIT 12-3
SAMPLE MOTION FOR CONTEMPT

IN THE SUPERIOR COURT OF _____ COUNTY
STATE OF _____

HARRIET P. SINGER,

Plaintiff,

v.   CIVIL ACTION NO. _____

ROBERT D. SINGER,

Defendant.

<u>Motion for Contempt</u>

COMES NOW, the Plaintiff in the above-referenced Motion for Contempt and shows the Court as follows:

1.

The Defendant is subject to the jurisdiction of this Court and may be served with a copy of this Motion for Contempt at his residence.

2.

On February 29, 1992, this Court issued a Final Judgment and Decree of Divorce which provided in its relevant part that Defendant was to pay for the support of the parties' minor child in the amount of Five Hundred Dollars ($500.00) per month.

3.

Notwithstanding such judgment, Defendant has willfully failed or refused to make said court-ordered support payments.

4.

To date the amount of the support in arrears totals no less than Two Thousand Dollars ($2,000.00) and barring court intervention, Plaintiff anticipates that the arrearages will continue to increase.

5.

Additionally, Defendant's actions have necessitated Plaintiff to retain legal counsel and incur substantial attorney's fees and other costs of litigation to enforce the judgment of this Court.

WHEREFORE, Plaintiff prays as follows:

a) that a court hearing be scheduled requiring Defendant to appear and show cause why he should not be held in contempt of court;

b) that Defendant be required to immediately pay to Plaintiff an amount not less than Two Thousand Dollars ($2,000.00);

c) that Defendant pay for Plaintiff's reasonable attorney's fees and costs of litigation; and

d) that Plaintiff have all other relief deemed proper by this Court.

Respectfully Submittted,

_____
Attorney for Plaintiff

(A Certificate of Service is attached here.)

erly presented in a separate motion to modify or amend the amount of alimony and/or child support.)

Additional issues for the defense to consider in determining civil contempt include

— Whether the underlying action is void due to lack of proper personal jurisdiction or venue

— Cohabitation or common-law marriage of the receiving party

— A change in child custody, irrespective of whether a court so ordered (can be a valid defense to contempt if the receiving party consented to the change in custody)

— Substantial compliance with the court order

— Whether the child who is the beneficiary of the child support has since reached the age of majority

— If the party owed the payment has established a custom of accepting, without objection, a lesser amount of alimony, support, and maintenance

Should the court determine that Father has willfully refused to obey the court order, it has several options to choose from:

— Father can be held in contempt of court and immediately incarcerated until such time as he **purges** (relieves) himself of the contempt; that is, until he makes arrangements satisfactory to the court to pay the arrearages.

— The court can allow Father a specific period of time to purge himself of the contempt under penalty of incarceration.

— The court can order Father to pay an additional sum to reduce the amount of the arrearage with each subsequent regularly scheduled payment.

Naturally, the court can fashion any other remedy deemed appropriate to afford the parties the necessary relief. Additionally, Mother can be awarded reimbursement of any reasonable attorney's fees and costs of litigating the motion for contempt. Accordingly, it is essential that complete and accurate

purge
To take actions that relieve a person of a court order for civil contempt.

time records be maintained to properly establish and justify the award of appropriate attorney's fees.

While civil contempt is used most often in divorce litigation to collect financial arrearages, that is not its only possible use. All other rights and obligations contained in the court's final decree and judgment of divorce are susceptible of a motion for civil contempt. These include the obligation to pay for insurance, to transfer title to property, and visitation with the minor children. For example, suppose Father alleged that Mother was denying him access to their child for visitation, in violation of the court order. The same procedure used to collect money would be employed in this case. After Father proved his entitlement to visitation and the Mother's refusal to cooperate, the burden of proof would shift to Mother, who would have to establish that either she had not refused to cooperate with visitation or that Father's lack of visitation was not due to any willful disobedience by Mother (i.e., that the child was sick at the time of the attempted visit).

It is questionable whether an allegation that Father posed a physical or emotional danger to the child would be sufficient to defuse such a motion for contempt. That issue is more properly addressed by a separate motion to modify or amend visitation. A violation of the noncustodial parent's visitation rights may result in jailing the custodial parent or in a change of custody. Additionally, a minority of courts will suspend the child support obligations upon a violation of visitation rights. In states that provide for retroactive modification of child support, denial of visitation rights may augur a reduction or elimination of the claimed arrearages.

Occasionally a violation of the divorce decree, whether real or perceived, by one party triggers a retaliatory violation by the other party. A common example would be where the failure to pay child support in a timely fashion results in the denial of visitation rights with the minor children. Such conduct is not uncommon in cases with former spouses who maintain feelings of bitterness and ill will long after the ink is dry on the divorce decree. But since the provisions of a divorce decree are generally held to be independent of each other, the refusal of one party does not justify the refusal of another.

As always, litigation should be resorted to only after all reasonable attempts to settle the dispute have failed. Issues relating to the enforcement of support and visitation rank at the bottom of most courts' lists of favorite litigation. Accordingly, it is always the best practice to show the court that the client tried to settle the dispute voluntarily, but that the adverse party would not cooperate. These efforts should be reduced to writing and should be available to present to the court if necessary. This approach is especially helpful when petitioning the court for attorney's fees.

Other Methods of Collection

Garnishment

garnishment
A court order to a person holding property that belongs to a debtor, requiring that some or all of that property be transferred to the court for payment to a creditor.

In states that permit it, garnishment is one the most effective methods of obtaining payment of a judgment from a reluctant debtor. **Garnishment** is an action, separate and independent from the divorce action, filed after obtaining a final judgment for a sum certain against the debtor, filed against a third party having possession of some property for the account, use, or benefit of the defendant/debtor. The most common third parties are employers (having possession of earned but yet unpaid wages) and banks (having possession of monies in savings, checking accounts, etc.), although the process can be applied with any third party having possession of the debtor's property.

Garnishment is governed by the law of the state in which the third-party garnishee resides. The plaintiff is entitled only to property or wages that are not exempt from garnishment (a statutorily prescribed percentage, i.e., 25 percent or 50 percent), and such nonexempt property or wages are withheld by the garnishee and paid to the court in which the garnishment was filed. Under federal law, the maximum amount subject to garnishment is 60 percent of the debtor's disposable income if the debtor does not have a second family to support and 50 percent if he does.

(NOTE: *Statutes may dictate that a smaller than ordinary percentage can be exempted from garnishment by the defendant/debtor when the garnishment is for the collection of an arrearage of alimony and/or child support.*)

In addition to garnishment, states have procedures for automatic income withholding of support payments directly from the debtor's employer. This is accomplished by an Income Deduction Order issued by the court. These procedures result from amendments to Title IV-D of the Social Security Act (42 U.S.C. 651–662) requiring their establishment by the individual states. While income withholding is similar to garnishment, a distinguishing feature is that it is used to collect current installments.

Levy and Sale

It is possible for a judgment creditor to have the property of a judgment debtor levied (or "seized") by a sheriff or marshall of the state and sold at auction, and to receive the proceeds. (In practice, **levy and sale** is a seldom-used collection tool. This is because few people have much property worth seizing.) A writ of execution specifying the property to be seized by the sheriff or marshall is required to commence levy and sale. The posting of a bond is often required by the sheriff's office to protect against any potential liability caused by the seizure of the property, such as the possibility of seizing property not actually owned by the debtor. If the property to be seized is encumbered, the amount of the debtor's equity in the property must be determined and arrangements must be made to satisfy the debt secured by the property.

Certain property may be exempt from levy and sale, such as a debtor's homestead or any tools of the trade necessary for the debtor to continue to earn income. After the property is seized, an advertisement informing the public as to the nature of the property and the date of the auction must be published in the legal newspaper. Once the property is sold, the creditor receives any proceeds, less the sheriff's expenses, up to the full amount of the debt owed. Any amount collected in excess of the debt is returned to the debtor. The properties most often subjected to levy and sale are automobiles, boats, collectibles, real estate, and jewelry.

levy and sale
Court-authorized process of seizing a debtor's property, selling it, and paying the proceeds to a creditor.

Posting Security

A court may require the party with the obligation to pay alimony or child support (or both) to provide the court with some collateral, or security, as a guarantee of compliance with the court's order. This remedy is especially useful when there is reason to believe that the obligated party may be preparing to leave the state or to dissipate assets. It may or may not be necessary to demonstrate to the court that there have been past violations of the court's orders, or that future violations are likely. Courts vary widely as to the circumstances under which they require the posting of security, the nature and amount of the property to be used as security, the circumstances under which the security will be seized by the court, and alternatively, when the secured property will be returned.

Sequestration

The court has the authority to seize property of the delinquent party until compliance with the court's orders is achieved. The property is held and maintained by a third-party receiver during this interim period. Sequestration differs from posting security in that security is posted prior to default, and sequestration occurs as a remedy to cure an existing default. This remedy is most efficient in cases with significant assets to justify the expenses incurred by the receiver while maintaining the property.

APPLE
v.
APPLE

Court of Appeals of Georgia.
March 11, 1988.

. . . .

BEASLEY, Judge.

Mrs. Apple brought suit against Mr. Apple to domesticate the parties' 1975 New York divorce decree, as amended in 1975 and 1978, and to attach Mr. Apple for contempt because he was $52,000 in arrears for alimony and child support payments. He moved to dismiss the complaint because the New York decrees were not final, being subject to retroactive modification, and thus not entitled to full faith and credit and domestication by this State. The trial court denied Mr. Apple's motion, domesticated the New York decrees and set a hearing date on the contempt issues. We granted Mr. Apple's application for interlocutory review and now consider his appeal.

The parties were divorced in July 1975 by a New York decree which awarded custody of two minor children to Mrs. Apple as well as $150 per week alimony and $50 per week for each child. The decree was technically amended in November 1975 and then substantially in March 1978 when the alimony payments were reduced to $75 per week and Mr. Apple was relieved of child support payments as to one of the two children. Upon Mr. Apple's failure to make timely payments of alimony and child support, Mrs. Apple initiated proceedings in New York which reduced the arrearages to money judgments in April 1977 for $2,725, in August 1978 for $15,000, in June 1979 for $675, and in November 1983 for $15,500. These judgments are not part of the record.

In 1984 Mrs. Apple brought an action to domesticate the four money judgments in DeKalb State Court. She then brought the present suit to domesticate the New York divorce decrees in DeKalb Superior Court and dismissed the state court action. Mr. Apple contends that the trial court erred in concluding it had jurisdiction over the enforcement of arrearages under the New York divorce decree prior to its domestication in Georgia and in denying his motion to dismiss.

Final divorce decrees of other states are recognized under the full faith and credit clause. Even those which may be prospectively modified are properly domesticated and enforced in this state under principles of comity. (Citations omitted.) Nevertheless, judgments of other states which may be modified retroactively lack the requisite finality to be entitled to full faith and credit. (Citations omitted.) The cited cases follow the principles enunciated in *Sistare v. Sistare*, 218 U.S. 1, 17, 30 S.Ct. 682, 54 L.Ed. 905 (1910), which held that a judgment loses the protection of the full faith and credit clause "where by the law of the State in which a judgment for future alimony is rendered the right to demand and receive such future alimony is discretionary with the court which rendered the decree, to such an extent that no absolute or vested right attaches to receive the installments ordered by the decree to be paid, even although no application to annul or modify the decree in respect to alimony had been made prior to the installments becoming due."

Traditionally, New York decrees involving alimony and child support were not final. An "alimony and support order was no more than a direction for the payment of sums of money from time to time in the future." (Citation omitted.) The support awarded in a matrimonial decree did not become a judgment debt enforceable by execution until the award was reduced to a money judgment pursuant to N.Y. Domestic Relations Law §244, *Gaines v. Gaines,* 487 N.Y.S.2d 61, 63, 109 A.D.2d 866 (1985), because the original decree was subject to retroactive modification in the discretion of the trial court. (Citations omitted.) Thus, a judgment for arrearage, not the divorce decree itself, was enforced under D.R.L. §244 in the "manner provided by law for the collection of money judgments." (Citation omitted.)

In 1986, effective August 5, D.R.L. §244 was amended to provide that child support payments could not be changed retroactively and that, on application, judgment for amounts past due must be entered. As amended, the section was intended to supply summary relief for nonpayment of support. (Citation omitted.) No change was made as to alimony, which remained under a two-part test: in response to an application for past due alimony a defendant could seek retroactive downward revision upon a showing 1) of a change of circumstances of the parties warranting a retroactive reduction in the support obligation and 2) "good cause" on the part of the obligated party for the failure to move to reduce the obligation prior to the accrual of arrearages (with emphasis on the necessity of petitioning the court for modification prior to resorting to a "self-help" solution). (Citations omitted.)

Yet, either with regard to child support where the imposition is virtually automatic or to alimony where discretion still remains, a judgment must be entered before execution. Under D.R.L. §245 one must have an

order directing payment before attempting enforcement by contempt. Further, under that section contempt does not lie until it appears presumptively that payment cannot be enforced pursuant to sections relating to garnishment and seizure of property, sequestration, or a wage deduction order. "Such a finding by the court and the exhaustion of those other remedies are a prerequisite to a contempt order for violation of an order requiring payments of money in matrimonial actions." (Citation omitted.) It is apparent that in New York contempt is not the readily available remedy that it is in Georgia support actions.

Based on the foregoing cases, our interpretation of the relevant authority in Georgia is that while decrees which are not final in the sense that they may be prospectively modified in the state of origin will be domesticated and enforced in this state, decrees which are susceptible to retrospective amendment and enforcement, while they may be domesticated under principles of comity, are not enforceable in Georgia as to amounts due prior to domestication. Otherwise, we would be giving rights to the parties and powers to the courts not available in the state of origin. "It is fundamental that under the Full Faith and Credit Clause the courts of this State are required to give only such effect to a judgment of a sister State as it would have in that State." (Citation omitted.)

Therefore, while it was not error to domesticate the 1975 and 1978 New York decrees, there was no basis to enforce an action for contempt based on unpaid sums allegedly owed under those decrees because, absent a reduction of the sums owed to judgment, they were not enforceable in New York. Furthermore, a determination of the status of the four money judgments was premature since they were not properly before the court and their domestication was not sought by Mrs. Apple.

Judgment affirmed in part and reversed in part.

McMURRAY, P.J., and SOGNIER, J., concur.

DISCUSSION QUESTIONS

Based on the preceding case of *Apple v. Apple,* 367 S.E.2d 109 (Ga. 1988), answer the following questions:

1. What is the status in Georgia of Mrs. Apple's New York arrearage of alimony and child support?

2. After this opinion, what should Mrs. Apple do to enforce her claim against Mr. Apple in Georgia?

REVIEW QUESTIONS

1. What portions of a divorce decree are susceptible to court-ordered enforcement?

2. How does postjudgment discovery differ from regular discovery?

3. What is a final judgment or money judgment, and what is its relevance to the enforcement of divorce decrees?

4. How can a party purge himself of civil contempt issued due to his failure to pay child support?

5. List at least two distinguishing features of a debt for support payments as opposed to other debts.

6. What types of assets are subject to a suit for garnishment? What is the procedure for garnishment?

7. What types of assets are subject to levy and sale? What are the prerequisites for it?

8. What does *domestication* mean? What is its relevance to the enforcement of divorce decrees?

9. What criminal law penalties may be assessed against a noncomplying party? Under what circumstances are they available?

10. What are the goals of a URESA case? What procedure is used?

KEY TERMS

arrearages	levy and sale
civil contempt	purge
domestication	RURESA
final judgment	Title IV-D
foreign judgment	URESA
garnishment	

STATE RESEARCH PROBLEMS

Review the laws of your state and answer the following questions:

1. What methods are available to collect arrearages of child support and/or alimony?

2. What forms of postjudgment discovery are available. Which are available for collecting arrearages of child support and/or alimony?

3. What procedure, if any, is required to convert arrearages of alimony and/or child support to a final judgment?

PRACTICE EXERCISE

Using the facts of the *Apple* case, prepare a Motion for Domestication and a Motion for Contempt.

Divorce—Modification and Appeals of Divorce Decrees

CHAPTER OBJECTIVES

In this chapter, you will learn:

- *The difference between modification and appeals*

- *What elements of a final decree and judgment of divorce may be modified, and under what circumstances modification is appropriate*

- *The procedural requirements for modification*

- *The peculiar requirements of appealing a final decree and judgment of divorce*

The end result of divorce litigation is a final judgment and decree of divorce. Unlike other forms of litigation, however, a final decree and judgment of divorce does not necessarily terminate the relationship between the parties. Among other things, there may be support to be paid, as well as custody of—and visitation with—minor children. As the circumstances under which the parties live change, the divorce decree may require modification to conform to the parties' changed circumstances. There must be a significant change of circumstances to justify the modification of the divorce decree. Here are some of the provisions most frequently subjected to modification:

— Amount or form of alimony to be paid

— Amount or form of child support to be paid

— Permanent physical and legal custody of the parties' minor children

— Visitation permitted to the noncustodial parent

While modifications generally result from a change in the parties' circumstances, an appeal results from the immediate dissatisfaction of one or both of the parties with the court's rulings. Appeals are petitions to a higher court seeking a partial or complete reversal of the lower court's rulings. Only final judgments and orders having the effect of a final judgment are immediately appealable.

MODIFICATION

modification
The process of revising an existing court order.

As a preface to the discussion of **modification,** it should be noted that the parties may, and often do, voluntarily and mutually agree to alter the terms of their original divorce decree to conform to changed circumstances. But while the parties are generally free to voluntarily agree to whatever terms they find satisfactory, they must obtain judicial approval of the changes. This can be accomplished by presenting the court with a proposed consent order setting forth the desired modifications, signed by the parties and their attorneys. The judge reviews the changes, especially those affecting the welfare of any minor children. If the modifications meet with the judge's approval, she signs the consent order, thus incorporating the changes into the existing divorce decree.

Before filing a petition for modification of a divorce decree, the party seeking modification should attempt to obtain the adverse party's consent to the proposed changes. This request should be made in writing to demonstrate to the court that an attempt was made to reach an out-of-court agreement. This written request can prove helpful later in the litigation process if a claim for attorney's fees is to be made.

Modification of Alimony

Whether as a result of a court decree or the parties' separation agreement, courts generally retain jurisdiction to modify, upward or downward, the amount of spousal support paid.

Payments Which Can Be Modified

A court's power to modify spousal payments is generally limited to the payment of periodic alimony, not a lump-sum payment of alimony. The rationale for this distinction is a simple one. A significant change in circumstances over time may make the modification of a continuing obligation necessary. But a lump-sum payment by definition does not occur over a long period of time. For the same reason, courts generally do not permit modification of a prior division and distribution of marital property. (However, where there is a showing that one party participated in a fraud to the detriment of the other party, a corrective modification remains possible.)

Unfortunately, the distinction between alimony and property distribution can be a muddled one. For example, consider the case in which Wife is awarded the marital residence and Husband is ordered to pay Wife's mortgage until she should remarry or die. Should this payment be treated as alimony or part of a property distribution?

Courts typically consider more than the mere appellation used in the divorce decree to describe the transfer. Rather, the court considers all of the factors and determines whether the payment is in the nature of maintenance and support, much as a bankruptcy court does when considering the issue of dischargeability. For example, does the obligation terminate upon the death or remarriage of the dependent spouse? If so, it is more likely to be treated as support. If not, it is more likely to be treated as a property distribution. Even in cases in which the parties entered into a separation agreement in which they voluntarily agreed that there would be no modification without the written agreement of the parties (see the separation agreement on page 130), under certain circumstances, the court may still modify the agreement. Certain states permit court-ordered modification of alimony in spite of the parties' prior waiver of same.

Appropriate Time for Modification

Due to the traumatic nature of divorce litigation, it is to be expected that the party receiving alimony (the payee) usually feels entitled to more alimony than is due under the court order. Similarly, the party paying alimony (the payor) usually believes that the amount due under the court is more than necessary or appropriate. But such feelings are not a sufficient legal basis for modification. The general rule is that the party seeking modification, whether upward or downward, must establish that there has been a "significant" change of circumstances since the time of either the original divorce decree or the last attempt to modify the divorce decree.

The first issue to be determined is, what is a "significant" change of circumstances? One factor is the length of time the existing decree has been in effect. For example, it may well be significant that the party paying support has enjoyed a 50 percent increase in gross income if that increase has occurred in the last two years. It would be considerably less significant if that increase occurred over a period of 20 years, especially if the income of the party receiving support has increased correspondingly.

In some states, courts may require that the alleged change of circumstances be of a kind that could not have been anticipated by the parties. Additionally, courts will inquire into the ability of the payor to pay, as opposed to the amount actually earned. Accordingly, a party cannot voluntarily induce a decrease in income as a means of lessening the obligation to pay support. Consider the example of a doctor earning $250,000 per year and paying support of $6,000 a month. He decides to reduce his practice by 80 percent, so that he can write the great American novel. He then files a motion to reduce the amount of alimony payable by 80 percent. The court may rule that since his ability to earn has not changed significantly, his obligation to pay alimony should not be modified. But if the doctor's decision to abandon his medical practice was not based on a desire to injure his former wife, a minority of courts might permit a modification decreasing the amount of alimony.

When a client seeks to modify alimony or is defending against an attempted modification, the paralegal must obtain a copy of the final judgment and decree of divorce and any separation agreement entered into by the parties. These documents provide the necessary data about the amount and nature of the payments that are owed, and they also reveal whether either or both of the parties have voluntarily agreed to waive the right to seek modification. Generally, such waiver provisions are enforced and effectively bar future modification. But a minority of courts will act on a motion for modification in spite of a waiver if the failure to do so would cause an unconscionable result for the party seeking modification. For example, if Wife currently suffers from multiple sclerosis and is no longer able to support herself, a court might modify the award of alimony, even in the face of a written waiver of modification. In certain jurisdictions, courts are reluctant to modify an award of alimony *unless* the parties have previously agreed that future modifications are permissible.

Some states have laws that permit the reduction or elimination of periodic alimony payments upon a finding that the party receiving alimony is engaging in an ongoing, meretricious (meaning "notorious" and "illicit") relationship. Such laws are commonly called "live-in lover" laws. These laws arose in response to a trend that has developed in recent years in which the party receiving alimony lives with, but does not marry, a person of the opposite sex, thus preserving the legal right to receive alimony. The rationale supporting the "live-in lover" laws is that it is not equitable to permit one party to continue to receive alimony while also enjoying many of the benefits of a de facto marriage with a third party. To prevail on such a motion, it is necessary to establish that the dependent party is cohabiting on a continuing basis with a person of the opposite sex with whom he has a sexual relationship. Some jurisdictions also require a showing that the cohabitation effectively lessens the dependent party's financial obligations before the amount of alimony can be modified downward. Note that the "live-in lover" laws apply to the modification of alimony, not child support.

To prevent abuse by litigious parties, states may establish statutory time limitations for the filing of petitions for modification. For example, a state's statutes may prohibit the filing of a petition for modification within two or four years of the date of the original divorce decree or the time of the last attempt at modification. Similarly, a state may have a prohibition against the filing of a motion for modification as a counterclaim to a motion for contempt or other attempt to enforce the existing court decree. Without such legal restraints, some domestic relations cases would perpetually be in court as the parties endlessly attempt to modify the various provisions of the divorce decree.

Procedure for Modification

The process of modification may, depending on the state's procedural rules, be initiated by the filing of a complaint, motion, petition, or claim. It is often considered a continuation of the prior divorce action, and as such it may have the same civil action number as the original divorce litigation. Notwithstanding its status as the continuation of existing litigation, formal service of process is usually required. Service of process upon a party's attorney may not be sufficient. The motion must state with specificity the basis for the modification. (A sample motion for modification is at Exhibit 13–1.) An updated financial affidavit may also be required if the motion is based upon a change in financial circumstances. In addition, as with most motions in most jurisdictions, a brief in support of the motion, providing the appropriate legal authority, is also required.

EXHIBIT 13-1   MOTION FOR MODIFICATION OF ALIMONY

IN THE SUPERIOR COURT OF _____ COUNTY
STATE OF _____

JEANNE CLAIRE MORRISON,

Plaintiff/Respondent,

v.   CIVIL ACTION NO. _____

THOMAS JAMES MORRISON,

Defendant/Movant.

Motion for Modification and Reduction of Alimony

COMES NOW, Thomas James Morrison, by and through his attorney of record, files this Motion for Modification and Reduction of Alimony, and shows the Court as follows:

1.

Respondent, Jeanne Claire Morrison, is subject to the jurisdiction of this Court, and may be served with a copy of this motion at her residence.

Allegation of personal jurisdiction.

2.

On September 11, 1994, this Court issued a Final Judgment and Decree of Divorce awarding permanent alimony to the Respondent in the amount of One Thousand Dollars ($1,000.00) per month.

Details of existing divorce decree requiring modification.

3.

Since that date, Respondent has voluntarily cohabited with a member of the opposite sex and has engaged in a meretricious relationship. Such behavior is in violation of this state's "Live-in Lover" statute and is sufficient to deny her any further payment of alimony.

   Additionally, since that date, the income of the Respondent has increased, which has had the effect of reducing the Respondent's need for permanent alimony.

Legal basis for modification.

*Factual details support-
ing modification.*

4.

Specifically, at the time of the Final Judgment and Decree, the Respondent was earning Two Thousand Dollars ($2,000.00) gross income per month; and, as of November 10, 1998, Respondent's gross income had increased to Three Thousand Dollars ($3,000.00) per month.

*Allegation that no prior
attempt at modification
has been made within
the time mandated by
state law.*

5.

There have not been any attempts to modify any provisions of the Final Judgment and Decree of Divorce within the previous two years.

WHEREFORE, Movant seeks a modification of the Final Judgment and Decree of Divorce reducing the amount of alimony payable to Respondent commensurate with Respondent's changed financial status.

Respectfully Submittted,

_____
Attorney for Defendant/Movant

(A Certificate of Service and Brief in Support of the Motion would be attached here.)

In some jurisdictions, a court hearing to adjudicate the issue is scheduled when the motion is filed with the court. In others, especially those that treat modification as a complaint rather than a motion, the issue is placed on the regular domestic trial calendar. In any event, it may be possible to obtain an interlocutory modification of alimony pending a final determination of the issue. (This is analogous to the award of temporary alimony pending trial.) The party seeking modification must bear the burden of proof to show that a significant change of circumstances has occurred warranting a modification of the final judgment and decree of divorce. In some states, counterclaims to a petition for modification are not permitted in order to discourage frivolous or spiteful claims. For example, a petition seeking an upward modification of child support could not be met with a counterclaim for a change in child custody.

The parties may engage in discovery, the scope of which is limited to the parties' claims and defenses regarding the proposed modification. The focus of the discovery in an alimony or child support modification action will be on the parties' financial status, and any significant changes that have occurred within the relevant time period. This will require the production of documents, from the litigants or third parties, that support or rebut the alleged change of circumstances (i.e., tax returns, bank statements, financial statements, applications for credit, etc.). Depositions and interrogatories are also used to prepare for the court hearing.

Obtaining personal jurisdiction over the defendant/respondent is generally elementary, because the court issuing the divorce will retain personal jurisdiction over both parties, even when a party moves to another state. The appropriate venue for modification depends on the laws of the state. Generally, venue properly lies in the county in which the original divorce was issued. Alternatively, venue may lie in the county of the respondent's residence. What if the respondent has moved to a different state? Is modification possible in the new state? The answer is yes, if the decree is properly domesticated in the foreign state. (See Chapter 12 for a discussion of domestication of foreign judgments.) The next question is which state's laws shall apply to the modification. Generally speaking, the court in the foreign state cannot take any action that would not be permissible under the laws of the state issuing the divorce.

Factors Influencing the Decision to Modify Alimony

The issue of modifying alimony ultimately depends on changes in the parties' respective need for support, as well as on their own ability to provide support. For example, to prevail on a request for modification, it is necessary to prove one or more of the following:

— Increased need of the dependent spouse (i.e., deteriorating physical or mental health; a genuine inability to find or retain gainful employment; inflation; increased maintenance of home; return of a previously emancipated child)

— Increased ability to provide support (i.e., assets obtained by inheritance; assets and income made available by the declaration of personal bankruptcy; discharging other unrelated obligations; increased income and bonuses received from employment; remarriage and access to a second income)

— Decreased need of the dependent spouse (i.e., emancipation of child; increased income from employment; move to a less expensive home)

— Decreased ability to provide support (i.e., a genuine, current, and involuntary loss of income due to loss of employment; deteriorating physical or mental health; remarriage and obligations to new family)

Modification of Child Support

Because the process of modifying child support is essentially the same as that for modifying alimony, in this section we highlight the material distinctions between the two. The standard generally used by the courts in determining whether child support should be modified is whether there has been an increase or decrease in the financial, educational, or emotional requirements of the minor child. The court also considers any increases or decreases in the income, assets, or needs of either the custodial or noncustodial parent. As with modification of alimony, changes to child support must be relatively significant and continuing. Unlike modification of alimony, in the modification of child support process the party receiving child support may not waive the right to seek modification of child support in a separation agreement. This is because the right to receive it belongs to the child, not to the parent who actually receives it.

The following factors are considered when the issue of modifying child support arises: inflation; increased educational or health requirements of the child; emancipation; and perhaps the most important factor of all, the statutory guidelines for payment of child support. As of October 1993, federal law mandates that, upon request of a parent, child support orders are to be reviewed once every 36 months to ensure that they are still in accordance with the statutory child support guidelines. As these guidelines base the child support payments on the amount of the payor's gross income, and the amount of income earned tends to change over time, this requirement will have an immediate and continuing impact on the amount of child support that is payable.

Modification of Child Custody and Visitation

After issuing a court order for the physical and legal custody of minor children, it is also possible for the appropriate court to exercise its jurisdiction and modify its order as to custody and visitation. Typically, the party seeking modification of custody or visitation must prove two elements: that there has been a substantial change in circumstances since the issuance of the existing custody order, and that modification is in the best interests of the child.

Procedure

The procedure and standards for modifying child custody and visitation are similar to those for modifying either alimony or child support. Here, we shall highlight the differences between them. As always with minor children, the stated goal is the best interests of the child. The party seeking to modify child custody must establish that a significant change of circumstances affecting the welfare of the child has occurred since the time of the divorce decree (or the last attempt to modify that decree), and that modification of custody is thus required to meet the best interests of the child. The issues of personal jurisdiction and venue are governed by the Uniform Child Custody Jurisdiction Act (UCCJA), which we discussed fully in Chapter 10. But it is worth noting that according to the UCCJA, a state has jurisdiction to modify child custody if:

— It is the home state of the minor child.

— It has been the child's home state within the past six months before commencement of the modification proceeding, and the child is absent from the state because of his removal or retention by a person claiming his custody; and a parent or person acting as parent continues to reside in the state.

— It is in the best interests of the child that a court of the state assume jurisdiction because the child and at least one parent have a significant connection with the state; and there is available in the state substantial evidence concerning the child's present or future care, protection, training, and personal relationships.

— The child is physically present in the state and has been abandoned, or it is necessary in an emergency to protect the child.

— It appears that no other state would have jurisdiction under the foregoing requirements, or another state has declined to exercise its jurisdiction.

Unlike alimony and child support, for child custody the court issuing the original divorce does not automatically retain jurisdiction to modify child custody. Rather, venue for modification of child custody generally lies with the court of the county in which the legal custodian of the minor child resides, unless the party opposing modification agrees to waive the jurisdictional requirements.

As with the original determination of custody, a child who has reached the statutorily prescribed age of discretion may play a role in determining future custody and visitation. For example, a boy of 14 who has been living with his mother may elect to move in with his father.

Considerations

Some of the factors considered by a court when modification of child custody is sought include

— Remarriage of either the custodial or noncustodial parent, which may provide the child with a more stable environment

— Conversely, the presence of a stepparent who poses a threat to the child's physical or emotional well-being

— The preference of a child who has reached the statutorily prescribed age of discretion (or is deemed capable of giving a preference, regardless of age, in some jurisdictions)

— Change in the child's age

— The custodial parent's frequent changes of residences

— Violence, or the threat of violence

— Use of illegal drugs by the custodial parent

— Refusal by the custodial parent to permit visitation by the noncustodial parent

— Sexual activities or cohabitation of the custodial parent

Following in Exhibit 13–2 are several sample clauses which could be used in a Motion to Modify Child Custody.

Modification of visitation with minor children may also be appropriate if a significant change of circumstances affects the viability of the existing visitation schedule. Once again, the stated goal of the court is to do whatever is

EXHIBIT 13-2   SAMPLE CLAUSES FOR MODIFICATION OF CHILD CUSTODY

1.

Since the date of the original Final Decree and Judgment for Divorce, there has been a significant change in circumstances affecting the welfare of the minor child of the parties, to wit: Defendant has been convicted of a crime involving moral turpitude; or, Defendant is now a habitual user of narcotics, alcohol, and other mind-altering substances; or Defendant is suffering from a physically debilitating disease that prevents Defendant from attending to the needs of the minor child; or other facts justifying a modification of child custody.

(NOTE: *It is generally not necessary to provide explicit details in this pleading.*)

2.

As a result of the aforesaid change in circumstances, the Defendant is now an unfit parent and should not be permitted to retain custody of the minor child.

3.

The Plaintiff is a fit parent and is capable and desirous of assuming the role of custodial parent of the minor child.

in the best interests of the child. Common circumstances requiring modification of visitation with minor children include a relocation by either parent (in this case, weekend visitation might be replaced with extended visits during the summer and at Christmas) and allegations that the noncustodial parent is molesting or otherwise posing a physical or emotional danger to the child (in this case, visitation might be terminated completely, or it might occur only under the supervision of a third party). These circumstances mirror those contemplated by a court when making the initial determination of child custody. The difference is that for modification, it is necessary to show that the acts complained of have occurred since either the time of the divorce decree or the most recent attempt to modify child custody.

Modification of Property Distribution

As already noted, those provisions of the divorce decree relating to the distribution of property are generally not subject to modification. One notable exception to this general rule is the marital residence. It is a common practice in divorce cases to award exclusive possession of the marital residence to one party while maintaining joint ownership of the real property. This arrangement allows one party to remain in the residence while both parties ultimately profit from the additional equity that accrues. This possession is typically limited in duration (i.e., until the party in possession remarries, or until all of the minor children reach the age of majority).

GRIGGS

v.

GRIGGS

Court of Civil Appeals of Alabama. May 13, 1994

THIGPEN, Judge.

This modification case involves child support.

Patricia Ann Staton Griggs (mother) and Joe Rayburn Griggs (father) divorced in 1991, and, pursuant to an agreement incorporated into the divorce judgment, the mother was awarded custody of the parties' two minor children, and the father was ordered to pay child support of $375 per month per child, to maintain life insurance naming the children as beneficiaries, and to pay one-half of each child's college educational expenses. Pursuant to an agreement apparently made in January 1993, the divorce judgment was modified in March 1993, ordering the father to continue paying $375 per month child support for the parties' younger child, and clarifying the college expenses for which the father was required to pay one-half for the older child.

In February 1993, prior to the entry of the above-mentioned modification order, the father filed a petition for modification of the judgment, alleging that he was unemployed and that he was unable to meet his child support obligations. After ore tenus proceedings, the trial court entered an order in August 1993, reducing child support to $118.80 for the younger child; requiring the father to pay $1,485 for post-minority expenses for the 1993–94 school term for the older child; terminating the father's future obligation to pay post-minority educational expenses, but reserving the right to award such expenses upon future petitions; and terminating the father's obligation to maintain life insurance. The court further required the father to file copies of his 1993 tax returns with the court and to notify the court regarding any future employment. The mother appeals.

The issues on appeal are whether the trial court abused its discretion in reducing child support and whether the trial court abused its discretion in terminating the father's obligation to pay future post-minority educational expenses.

The mother first contends that the trial court abused its discretion by reducing child support. A prior child support order may be modified only upon a showing of a material change in circumstances that is substantial and continuing, and the burden is on the party seeking the modification. (Citations omitted.) The modification of child support because of changed circumstances is a matter within the trial court's discretion, and its decision will not be disturbed absent a clear abuse of discretion. (Citation omitted.)

The record reveals that at the time of the divorce, the father was employed at SCI Systems in Huntsville, and his gross monthly income was $3,000. The father testified that due to a reduction in force, he was laid off in February 1993, and from that time until June 1993, he received $165 per week in unemployment compensation, and he continued to seek employment. He testified that he had distributed approximately 90 resumes since being laid off, and that he had been on three job interviews, but that he had not received any employment offers. He further testified that his present wife purchased some tools for him, and that he began "doing odd jobs in construction, whatever I [could] find to do." Child support income forms indicate that the father's monthly income was $866 in July 1993.

This evidence supports a finding of changed circumstances. Once a change in circumstances is proven, Rule 32(A), Ala.R.Jud.Admin., etablishes a rebuttable presumption that the correct amount of child support results from the application of the guidelines. (Citation omitted.) The court considered the child support guidelines in this case and awarded support accordingly; however, the mother argues that the trial court should have imputed income to the father because, she says, he was voluntarily unemployed.

Prior to the amendment effective October 4, 1993, rule 32(B)(5), Ala.R.Jud.Admin., stated:

> "If the court finds that either parent is voluntarily unemployed or underemployed, it shall impute that parent's income and calculate child support based on that parent's potential income which would otherwise ordinarily be available."

The trial court must determine that the paying parent is "voluntarily" unemployed or underemployed before it may impute income to that parent, and this determination is discretionary with the trial court. (Citation omitted.)

In the case sub judice, the record reveals conflicting evidence regarding whether the father requested to be laid off from his position or whether he was laid off simply due to a reduction in force. The father's supervisor testified that in January or February 1993, the father made an informal request to be laid off. On cross-examination, the supervisor testified that after the layoff occurred, he was informed that the father had been laid off due to a reduction in force and that SCI did not hire a replacement but consolidated the father's position with another position.

The mother testified that before the January agreement between the parties, she and the father had several telephone conversations in which the father threatened to ask to be laid off from SCI to escape paying child support. She further stated that a few days after the agreement was entered into, he called her and said he would ask to be laid off in order to avoid paying support "and that he would fix a construction company up and the books would show . . . that he was in the hole."

The father testified that he had never requested that he be laid off. He stated that "everybody was always worred about their job" and that he had said, "Well, if it's my turn and they are going to lay me off, I just wish they would go ahead and do it; I'm tired of worrying about it."

Where the trial court considers conflicting ore tenus evidence, its judgment is entitled to a presumption of correctness, and we are not permitted to substitute our judgment for that of the trial court. (Citation omitted.) It is our duty to affirm the trial court's judgment if it is fairly supported by credible evidence, "regardless of our own view of that evidence or whether we would have reached a different result had we been the trial judge." (Citation omitted.) There was evidence to support a finding that the father was not voluntarily unemployed or underemployed; therefore, the trial court's judgment will not be disturbed.

The mother also contends that the trial court abused its discretion by terminating the father's obligation to pay post-minority support. At the time of the current petition, the older child had completed her freshman year in college. The father testified that he had "cashed out" $1485 in retirement benefits from SCI which he would give to the older child for college expenses, but that he had no other money or assets with which he could pay for college expenses the next year. The trial court ordered the father to pay $1485 towards

the college expenses for the next school year, but otherwise terminated his obligation regarding post-minority support, subject to an express reservation regarding any future petition for post-minority support.

Where evidence is presented ore tenus in post-minority cases, the trial court's judgment is presumed to be correct and will be reversed only upon a showing that the trial court abused its discretion, or that its determination is plainly and palpably wrong. (Citation omitted.) Furthermore, the general principles concerning child support are equally applicable to a motion for post-minority college support. (Citation omitted.) Therefore, the father had the burden of showing a change of circumstances since the previous judgment. Our review of the record reveals support for a finding of changed circumstances, and we find no error.

Based upon the foregoing, the judgment of the trial court is due to be, and it is hereby, affirmed. We note that the trial court ordered the father to file 1993 income tax returns with the court and to notify the court regarding any future employment he obtains, and that the trial court expressly reserved modification rights regarding future petititons for post-minority education expenses. We further note that the trial court has continuing jurisdiction over matters of child support, and its judgment may be modified in the future as the result of changed circumstances.

AFFIRMED.

ROBERTSON, P.J., and Yates, J., concur.

DISCUSSION QUESTIONS

Based on the preceding case of *Griggs v. Griggs,* 638 So.2d 916 (Al. 1994), answer the following questions:

1. What are ore tenus proceedings?

2. What were the issues before the court?

3. What provisions of the divorce decree did the court modify? What was the court's rationale for its rulings?

Attorney's Fees

It may be possible for the prevailing party to recover some or all of her attorney's fees from the losing party, whether the prevailing party was seeking or opposing the modification. To do so, it will be necessary for the prevailing party to establish that the losing party acted in bad faith or was stubbornly litigious. An award of attorney's fees requires that the losing party either sought or fought modification of the divorce decree without any justification for so doing. For example, a father seeking a change in custody of the minor children in retaliation for the mother's new boyfriend; or a former wife seeking additional alimony after voluntarily leaving her gainful employment. The amount of attorney's fees awarded by the court is affected by the amount of time spent by both the attorneys and paralegals, the results achieved by the legal team, the fees charged and how they compare with the legal community at large, and the parties' respective financial positions.

APPELLATE PROCESS

While modification remedies the inequities that may result in a relationship that extends over many years, the appropriate remedy for significant and prejudicial errors of the trial court is an **appeal**. In general, appellate procedure for a divorce case is no different than that for any other subject matter.

appeal
A process by which a higher court reviews the decisions of a lower court.

What Is Appealable?

The title of this section is somewhat misleading, since eventually every decision of the court is subject to appellate review. But as a general rule, only final judgments and orders are immediately appealable. For example, an order of the court either granting or denying a motion for a protective order is interlocutory in nature and therefore not appealable. An order granting a motion for summary judgment is final, and therefore appealable; an order denying the same motion for summary judgment is not final, and accordingly, is not appealable at that time.

Of course, every general rule has its exceptions, and this general rule has significant exceptions. The first is that an interlocutory order that has an immediate and material effect on the parties may be immediately appealable. For example, a court order awarding, denying, or modifying temporary alimony, child custody, or support may be immediately appealable. Such an order has the effect of a final judgment, albeit for a limited period of time. Second, in cases in which the interlocutory order appears erroneous and is likely to produce error at trial, or when the establishment of a new precedent is desirable, the appellate court may review the interlocutory order.

In addition, a party may seek court permission to appeal an order not otherwise appealable. Depending on state rules, this permission may be sought from the trial court, the appellate court, or both. With such discretionary appeals, the court considers the potential prejudice to the party seeking the appeal, the desirability of any resulting precedent the appeal would create, and the extent to which the order would dispose the issues to be determined at trial. The application to appeal the interlocutory order is usually initiated via motion, filed with a brief in support of the appeal, and accompanied by an affidavit from the attorney, the client, or both. This affidavit should demonstrate the compelling reason for the immediate appeal. Finally, the application should contain copies of all pertinent documentation including,

INTERVIEW CHECKLIST

(To be used in conjunction with the basic interview checklist provided in Chapter 2.)

Did you and your former spouse enter into a Separation Agreement? _____ If so, was it incorporated into the Final Judgment and Decree of Divorce?

Have either you or your former spouse previously attempted to modify any provisions of the divorce decree?

If so, provide details, including the party seeking modification, the provisions sought to be modified, and the court's order. Also, please attach copies of all papers filed in any such modifications.

If the separation agreement was not incorporated into the Final Judgment and Decree of Divorce, explain why not.

For Modification of Alimony and Child Support

What amount of alimony is currently due under the existing divorce decree? $_____ per _____
Child support? $_____ per _____

Does the separation agreement have any provisions relating to modification? If so, provide details.

What was your income from all sources, other than your former spouse, at the time of the existing divorce decree? Provide documentation.

Where are you currently employed?

If you are not currently employed, state the reason; provide the dates and location of your most recent employment.

To the best of your knowledge, what was your former spouse's income from all sources at the time of the existing divorce decree? Provide any documentation.

Have either you or your former spouse suffered a decline in the ability to earn income because of an adverse change in physical or mental health?_____ If so, provide details and documentation.

Have your expenses increased since the time of the existing divorce decree? If so, provide specific details and documentation.

Have your former spouse's expenses decreased since the time of the existing divorce decree? If so, provide specific details and documentation.

Have either you or your former spouse remarried? _____ If so, state the date and location of the marriage, and the (maiden) name of the new spouse.

Does your former spouse currently reside with a person of the opposite sex?_____ If yes, state the third party's name, address, age, and the duration of the relationship.

Is the new spouse (if any) gainfully employed? If so, provide details and documentation.

Have the physical, educational, or emotional needs of any or all of the minor children increased since the time of the existing divorce decree? _____ If so, provide specific details and documentation.

Have any minor children become emancipated by marriage or otherwise begun living independently of the custodial parent? _____ If so, provide details and documentation.

continued on page 279

continued from page 278

For Modification of Child Custody and Visitation

Which party has custody of the minor children?

_____

What conduct, if any, has the custodial parent engaged in that you believe justifies the modification of child custody? Provide details, documentation, and the names of any corroborating witnesses.

_____

What is the child's preference as to custodial parent?

_____

What are the provisions for visitation in the existing divorce decree?

_____

Is either parent moving a distance of greater than fifty miles? _____ If so, provide details.

_____

What conduct, if any, justifies a modification of visitation?

_____

Provide details, documentation, and the names of any corroborating witness.

_____

but not limited to, the pleadings, the motions, and of course the order from which an appeal is sought. *In some jurisdictions, all or some appeals from the final decisions of domestic cases may be discretionary; that is, the appellate court has the authority to determine whether the case merits appellate review. In these states, appellate procedure becomes a two-step process: first, permission to appeal must be obtained from the appropriate court; second, if permission to appeal is granted, then the regular appellate process commences.*

PRACTICE POINTER

Stay Pending Appeal

In certain extraordinary cases, the party filing the appeal (called an *appellant* or *petitioner*) may seek a stay of the trial court's judgment pending the determination of the appeal. The criterion for a stay pending appeal is similar to that for a temporary restraining order; there must be evidence that the order or judgment complained of constitutes an injustice to the appellant and is going to cause an immediate and irreparable injury. This evidence may be presented by means of an affidavit by the attorney, the client, or both. Here are some examples of circumstances that might require a stay pending appeal:

— A court-ordered sale of the parties' marital residence

— An order granting custody to a party with intentions of removing the minor child to another state, thus causing a cessation, or at least a severe interruption, of visitation with the noncustodial parent

— Where the appellant seeks to reduce an excessive temporary order for support, in cases in which the excess payment could not be recouped, even if the appeal were to be successful

The posting of a bond, or some form of collateral, may be a prerequisite for imposing a stay pending appeal. If the stay is granted, it may be granted conditionally. For example, the appellate court may stay the trial court's judgment ordering the father to pay $1,000 per month, if the father agrees to pay support of $750 per month.

REVIEW QUESTIONS

1. How do modification and appellate procedure differ as to the appropriate grounds and goals for each?

2. Which provisions of a separation agreement or divorce decree are subject to modification, and which provisions are not? What is the rationale for the different treatment?

3. What are the respective general standards for modifying (a) alimony, (b) child support, (c) child custody, and (d) visitation with the minor children?

4. How does federal law affect the modification of any provisions of a separation agreement or divorce decree?

5. Under what circumstances will a particular state have jurisdiction to modify child custody?

6. What is the process for initiating an appeal of an order or judgment of a trial court?

7. What is a "stay" pending the determination of an appeal, and under what circumstances is a court likely to issue one?

KEY TERMS

appeal
modification

STATE RESEARCH PROBLEMS

Review the law of your state and answer the following questions:

1. What parts of a divorce decree are modifiable?

2. Is modification treated as a continuation of the original divorce litigation or as a separate action?

3. What are the standards for modifying alimony, child support, and child custody?

4. Which issues in a divorce case are immediately appealable?

5. Are there any provisions for the immediate appeal of those orders of the court that are not ordinarily appealable, and if so, what are they? Does your state employ discretionary appeals? If so, what issues are subject to the appellate court's discretion?

6. Under what circumstances is a stay pending appeal of the court's order or judgment granted?

PRACTICE EXERCISE

Review the separation agreement of Thomas and Jeanne Morrison (Exhibit 6–7). Thomas Morrison is moving to California, and therefore the existing visitation schedule will require modification. Prepare a Motion for Modification of Visitation.

Divorce—Tax Considerations

CHAPTER OBJECTIVES

In this chapter you will learn:

- *The fundamentals of income tax law*

- *Whether payments between former spouses are includable and/or deductible for income tax purposes*

- *Which party may claim the dependency exemption*

- *How transfers of property are treated under the tax code*

Family law practitioners can be certain of two things: Tax laws will continue to change, and tax laws will always have a significant influence on the ultimate economic impact of a divorce. In cases involving significant sums, tax professionals may be required to lead the way through the tax maze. But all family law professionals must be familiar with the essentials of tax law and the areas in which the taxes are most likely to have an impact. In this chapter, we examine the effect of the current tax laws on the following issues:

— The distinction between alimony, which is deductible from the income of the payor and includable in the income of the payee, and child support, which is neither deductible from the income of the payor nor includable in the income of the payee

— Which parent is to be permitted to claim the children as dependents, and thus claim the resulting dependency exemptions

— The ability to transfer property between divorcing spouses without incurring any tax liability

— The use, possession, or transfer of the marital residence

— Miscellaneous issues, such as attorney's fees and the liability of spouses signing joint tax returns

A brief introduction to some basic tax principles is necessary to understand the implications of the issues discussed herein. If you have never studied any tax law, don't panic. It is not as bad as you might think.

TAX LAW BASICS

All family law professionals must have at least a basic understanding of tax law as it affects parties to a divorce. Accordingly, following is a very general sketch of income tax law. (Note that this chapter details *federal* income tax; many states and cities impose their own income taxes.)

All United States citizens and resident aliens with income in excess of a specific minimum are required to file tax returns. The individual filing a tax return may file under one of four statuses:

— Single

— Married filing jointly

— Married filing separately

— Head of household (This status applies to unmarried or legally separated individuals contributing at least one-half the costs of providing a residence for the taxpayer and at least one dependent. The cost of providing a residence includes rent, mortgage interest, property taxes, utilities, insurance, maintenance, repairs, and food. It does not include clothing, education, medical expenses, vacations, or transportation.)

gross income; adjusted gross income; taxable income
Generally, gross income is all income from whatever source derived. Adjusted gross income is gross income less necessary business expenses, payments to qualified retirement accounts, and flexible spending accounts for child care or health care. Taxable income is adjusted gross income less personal exemptions and itemized deductions or the standard deduction, whichever is greater.

Each status has its own tax rates. To be eligible to file a joint return for a given year, a couple must still be married to each other as of December 31 of that year, because a person's tax status is determined on that date for each tax year. The income tax paid by an individual is based on a percentage of taxable income. The percentage paid increases incrementally as taxable income increases (thus there are varying progressive "tax brackets").

(NOTE: *Because this is a family law text, and not a tax law text, be aware that the definitions provided in this chapter tend to be somewhat generalized.*)

Gross income is defined as all income from whatever source derived, including wages, interest, dividends, tips, bonuses, gains from the sale of property, and prizes; and excludes only income specifically exempted by law, such as workers' compensation. **Adjusted gross income** is gross income less payments to qualified retirement accounts, and *payments of alimony*. **Taxable income** (the amount upon which the income tax is computed) is adjusted gross income less itemized deductions or the standard deduction, whichever is greater, and personal exemptions. The **personal exemption** is a specified amount that each person may deduct from their adjusted gross income. A married couple filing a joint tax return may claim a single, albeit greater, exemption. Additional exemptions may be claimed for other resident family members (i.e., the taxpayer's children). Specific itemized deductions include mortgage interest; certain taxes paid; charitable contributions; medical expenses incurred in excess of a specific minimum percentage of adjusted gross income; losses resulting from theft, accidents, and fire; and numerous others.

Capital assets are all items of property held for a period of at least one year, other than inventory, receivables, and property used in connection with a trade or business. The sale or transfer of such assets results in either capital gains (if a profit is realized) or capital losses (if a loss is realized). To determine whether there is a gain or loss, deduct the property's basis from the sale price received. If acquired by purchase, a property's **basis** is its acquisition cost. For example, real estate purchased for $10,000 and sold for $15,000 yields a taxable profit of $5,000. When sold, the real estate has a new basis of $15,000.

INCLUDABLE/DEDUCTIBLE DISTINCTION

For purposes of individual income taxes, payments of temporary and permanent alimony are generally **deductible** from the gross income of the payor and **includable** as gross income of the payee. Payments of temporary and permanent child support are neither deductible from the gross income of the payor nor includable in the gross income of the payee. The Tax Reform Acts of 1984 and 1986 made significant changes in the treatment of alimony and child support. For all separation agreements and divorce decrees made after January 1, 1984, as well as those made before that date but modified after January 1, 1984, payments of alimony will be deductible from the gross income of the payor and includable in the gross income of the payee, if all of the following prerequisites are satisfied:

— *The payments must be made in cash,* check, or money order, as opposed to the transfer of services or property. As noted below, the payments need not be made directly to the payee spouse, but may be made to third parties on behalf of the payee.

— If there is a final decree and judgment of divorce, *the parties may not live together in the same residence,* even if they do not maintain marital relations. If the parties are operating under a separation agreement or an order for temporary alimony, this requirement does not apply.

— Liability for such *payments must terminate upon the death of the payee spouse.* If the obligation continues after the death of the payee, *none* of the payments (including those made before the payee's death) will be treated as alimony. They can, however, continue beyond the remarriage of the payee.

---

personal exemption
A specific amount that may be deducted from adjusted gross income.

capital assets
Generally, property held for a period of at least one year.

basis
Basis is an amount assigned to an asset (often acquisition cost) used to determine gain or loss upon its sale or transfer.

deductible
A payment that results in a deduction from the payor's taxable income by a like amount.

includable
A payment by a person that results in an addition to the taxable income of the recipient.

— The *payment must be made pursuant to a divorce or separation instrument* (i.e., final decree of divorce, separation agreement, or temporary order for alimony). Therefore, payments made before the execution of a divorce or separation instrument cannot serve as alimony for tax purposes, nor can voluntary payments.

— The parties *may not file a joint tax return* for the year in which the payments were made.

— The *payments may not be specifically designated as payments for child support.*

— The divorce instrument *must not designate alimony payments as nondeductible to the payor* and nonincludable to the payee.

— Any payments in excess of $15,000 during the first three postseparation calendar years must comply with special (and even more complex) **recapture** rules designed to prevent any transfers of marital property under the guise of alimony.

recapture
Recovery by the IRS of a tax benefit previously taken by a taxpayer.

For tax purposes, these prerequisites for alimony apply regardless of how alimony is defined under state law. The parties may mutually elect in any given year(s) to provide that payments that would otherwise qualify as alimony will not be deductible from the gross income of the payor nor includable in the gross income of the payee. This provision gives the parties a degree of flexibility. Any such agreement must be in writing, and a copy of it must be attached to the payee spouse's filed tax return.

Cash payments to a third party on behalf of the payee spouse by the payor spouse may be treated as qualifying alimony if the payment is required by the separation agreement or divorce decree, and if it is not specifically designated as nondeductible to the payor spouse; or if it is made pursuant to a later written agreement entered into by the parties. For example, it is possible that mortgage payments or rent, utilities, real estate taxes, home and life insurance premiums, and medical expenses can be treated as deductible alimony by the payor spouse.

When payments are clearly designated as child support, they are not deductible from the payor's gross income nor includable in the payee spouse's gross income. This distinction is somewhat more problematic when the designation is less specific. Until the Tax Reform Act of 1984, any payments not specifically designated as either alimony or child support were treated as alimony. Until 1984 it was common practice for parties to allow all such payments to be treated as alimony, which allowed the payor (who usually was in a higher tax bracket) to deduct a greater sum from adjusted gross income. Accordingly, the payor saved a greater amount on taxes, which in turn made more money available to pay the payee spouse.

While any unspecified payments are still generally treated as alimony, the current tax laws specify that if any amount to be paid is to be reduced either on the happening of a contingency relating to the minor children specified in the separation agreement or divorce decree or at a time that can be clearly associated with such a contingency, it shall not be deductible by the payor. Possible contingencies include the child attaining a specific age, marrying, dying, or leaving school. As a matter of fact, if the amount paid is reduced within a six month period before or after the date on which a minor child reaches the age of majority, it shall be assumed that that portion of the payment is child support. For example, consider a clause in a separation agreement stating that "Husband shall pay to Wife the sum of $1,000 per month, which shall be reduced by $500 per month when the parties' minor child shall either reach the age of 18, marry, or otherwise become emancipated." In that case, $500 would be treated as alimony, and $500 would be treated as child support for tax purposes. Clearly, the better practice is to specify in the divorce instrument precisely what sums are to be allocated as alimony or child support.

The term *recapture* refers to the ability of the IRS to recover a tax benefit or deduction previously taken by a taxpayer (Internal Revenue Code Section 71(f)). In the context of alimony, it refers to circumstances in which the payor must pay taxes on "alimony" paid in prior years due to a significant discrepancy (i.e., greater than $15,000) in the amount of payment during the first three years in which alimony is paid. This discrepancy is often referred to as "front loading"—the distribution of marital property disguised as alimony payments (i.e., disproportionately large payments in the first postseparation years, followed by much smaller payments once the transfer has been effected).

DEPENDENCY EXEMPTIONS

The general rule (Internal Revenue Code Section 152) is that the custodial parent shall have the right to the dependency exemption, and the resulting tax benefits, if the following requirements are met:

— The parents are either divorced, legally separated pursuant to a separation agreement, or have lived apart for the last 6 months of the calendar year.

— The dependent has gross income less than the current exemption amount, or is less than 19 years of age or less than 24 years of age and a full-time student.

— The dependent is a citizen or resident of the United States, or a resident of Canada or Mexico for some portion of the year in which the exemption is claimed.

— Both parents together provide over one-half of the support for the child, and both parents have custody of the child for more than one-half of the year.

(Note that there are additional, more detailed requirements beyond the scope of this text.) The exceptions to the general rule include (a) when the custodial parent signs an agreement releasing her rights to the dependency exemption, and (b) when the parties are governed by a pre-1985 divorce decree or separation agreement specifying that the noncustodial parent shall have the dependency exemption and the noncustodial parent pays at least $600 in support of that child in that year. When the payor spouse is in a higher tax bracket, it might be mutually beneficial for that party to have the dependency exemption, thus providing for a greater tax savings and more money available to both parties. (But note that these exemptions are phased out for persons with income over a certain amount, that is $150,000. In such cases, it would be of mutual benefit to allow the spouse earning less to use the exemptions.) The spouse waiving the dependency exemption must then execute and file IRS Form 8332 with the IRS for each year that the exemption is to be waived. A sample of IRS Form 8332 is at Exhibit 14–1.

TRANSFERS OF PROPERTY BETWEEN PARTIES

There is a significant distinction between a transfer of property and payments of alimony and child support. The division of property between parties pursuant to divorce is a division of wealth. Pursuant to Section 1041 of the

---

EXHIBIT 14–1   IRS FORM 8332
WAIVER OF DEPENDENCY EXEMPTION

Form **8332**
(Rev December 1987)

Department of the Treasury
Internal Revenue Service

Release of Claim to Exemption
for Child of Divorced or Separated Parents

▶ **Attach to Tax Return of Parent Claiming Exemption**

OMB No 1545-0915
Expires 10-31-90

Attachment
Sequence No. **51**

Name(s) of parent claiming exemption as shown on tax return

Social security number

Part I Release of Claim to Exemption for Current Year

I agree not to claim an exemption for _____

Name(s) of child (or children)

for the calendar year 19 ___

Signature of parent releasing claim to exemption   Social security number   Date

If you choose not to claim an exemption for this child (or children) for future tax years, complete Part II, as explained in the instructions below.

Part II Release of Claim to Exemption for Future Years

I agree not to claim an exemption for _____

Name(s) of child (or children)

for tax year(s) _____

(Specify. See instructions.)

Signature of parent releasing claim to exemption   Social security number   Date

Internal Revenue Code, effective in 1984, the transfer of property incident to a divorce is not treated as a taxable event. "Incident to divorce" means either within one year of the cessation of the marriage or, alternatively, if made pursuant to a divorce or separation instrument, within 6 years after the cessation of the marriage. (Note that these provisions could also apply to a marriage ending in annulment.)

The effect of this rule is that all such transfers are treated as though they were gifts, whether or not they were intended as such. The transferee acquires the property with the transferor's adjusted basis in the property at the time of the exchange. (Note that the term *carryover basis* is used to describe such a basis in property that is transferred from one party to another.) Thus, any gain or loss realized by the transferee is computed based on the carryover basis, and not necessarily the fair market value of the property at the time of the transfer. This means that when the transferee ultimately sells or disposes of the property, she will recognize a taxable gain or loss using the carryover basis from the transferor. The transferor must provide sufficient documentation to establish the carryover basis so that the net gain or loss can be accurately computed upon any later transfer of the property. For example, Husband transfers to Wife 100 shares of Acme Explosives, Inc. The purchase price of the shares was $10 per share. Each share now has a fair market value of $20. In a Section 1041 transfer, Husband does not incur any tax liability, even though he realized a gain of $1,000 in the transaction. Furthermore, if Wife later sells the shares for $30 per share, she will be liable for the taxes owed on her gain of $2,000 ($3,000 selling price less $1,000 basis).

Section 1041 also applies to cases in which the transfer of property is made to a third party if that transfer is made for the benefit of the other spouse and is made pursuant to the divorce instrument or is pursuant to the written request of the other spouse.

MARITAL RESIDENCE

The most significant asset owned by many couples is the marital residence. A divorce often causes one or both parties to relinquish their ownership of the marital residence, so it is important to be aware of the various tax provisions relating to the transfer or sale of a home. Internal Revenue Code Section 1034 allows all taxpayers to defer the payment of taxes on any net profit realized from the sale of a primary residence when the net gain of the sale is "rolled over" into the purchase of another primary residence, which costs at least as much as the sale price of the home sold, and is to be used as a primary residence. In addition, Internal Revenue Code Section 121 provides for a one-time deduction to a person who has reached the age of 55, of up to $125,000 from the proceeds of real estate used as a primary or secondary residence. The Section 121 exclusion is typically used upon the sale of a long-time residence having a significant amount of equity, where the seller either does not intend to purchase another home or plans to purchase a smaller, less expensive home. It is important to note that once this exclusion has been used by an individual, that person *and his or her spouse* are forever barred from using it again. For example, if the marital residence is sold prior to the date of the final decree of divorce, only one exclusion can be used. But if the property is sold after the final dissolution, each party may use the exclusion. Obviously, this would be especially important in cases in which the marital residence has more than $125,000 in equity. Additionally, if a party uses the exclusion when selling the marital residence pursuant to a divorce decree or separation agreement and marries again, the new spouse would be prohibited from taking this deduction, even if she had not done so before the remarriage.

To qualify for the Section 121 one-time exclusion, the seller must actually have reached the age of 55 before the date of the sale and must have owned the property and used it as his or her principal residence for at least three of the last five years.

MISCELLANEOUS TAX CONSIDERATIONS

In addition to the tax issues discussed earlier, there are several other issues that merit brief mention.

Deductibility of Attorney's Fees

Attorney's fees paid in connection with divorce litigation are generally not deductible (Internal Revenue Code Section 262). But attorney's fees may be deductible to the extent that they relate to: (1) the production of income; (2) the management, conservation, or maintenance of property held for the production of income; or (3) the determination, collection, or refund of any tax (Internal Revenue Code Section 212). Therefore, for example, where the attorney advises the client about the potential tax consequences of the divorce and drafts instruments seeking to minimize the tax liability, the fees so generated may be deductible. The bill for attorney's fees should clearly substantiate and specifically allocate the fees generated for tax matters as opposed to those generated by nontax matters. Note that this deduction is currently permitted only to the extent that it (along with other miscellaneous deductions) exceeds two percent of the taxpayer's adjusted gross income.

Deductibility of Medical Expenses

Either parent may deduct any medical expenses actually incurred on behalf of the dependent child. (Note that current tax laws provide for this deduction only to the extent that all medical expenses exceed 7.5 percent of the taxpayer's adjusted gross income.)

Joint Returns and "Innocent Spouses"

When a husband and wife both sign and file a joint return, they are jointly and severally liable for any taxes, penalties, and interest due thereon. In the course of divorce litigation, however, it is possible to discover that one spouse either concealed income or claimed fraudulent deductions (or did both) without so informing the other spouse. The Internal Revenue Service may then seek the collection of any unpaid taxes as well as the resulting penalties and interest from either or both of the taxpayers. An exception to this rule exists for an "innocent spouse" under Internal Revenue Code Section 6013(e). To obtain relief as an innocent spouse, it must be established that (1) a joint return was filed for the year in question; (2) there is an understatement of the taxes owed of at least $500 due to grossly erroneous items of the other spouse on the return; (3) the innocent spouse did not actually know, nor have any reason to know, of the substantial understatement when signing the return; and (4) considering all the facts and circumstances, it would be inequitable to hold the innocent spouse responsible for the deficiency caused by the erroneous return. This last prerequisite includes consideration of whether the innocent spouse benefited from the understatement of taxes owed, and if so, what was the degree of benefit.

INTERVIEW CHECKLIST

(Use this checklist in conjunction with the basic interview checklist provided in Chapter 2.)

What filing status(es) did you use when filing Federal Income Tax returns while you were married?

_____

Who was responsible for preparation of the tax returns while you were married?

_____

In what manner of ownership do you and/or your spouse own any real property?

_____

What was the purchase price of the property referred to in the preceding question?

_____

List all improvements made to the property, including the date and cost of the improvements.

_____

Who paid for these improvements?   _____

_____

Do either you and/or your spouse wish to remain in the marital residence, or do you both desire to sell the residence at this time?

_____

Have either you or your spouse ever sold a primary residence? _____ If yes, provide details.

_____

REVIEW QUESTIONS

1. Under what circumstances is a payment between former spouses treated as alimony for income tax purposes?

2. What is the importance of the "basis" in property, and how is it calculated?

3. What is *recapture,* and under what general circumstances is it applicable?

4. What is the "innocent spouse" doctrine, and under what circumstances is it applicable?

5. Under what circumstances is the payment of attorney's fees tax deductible?

6. What are the prerequisites for a custodial parent to claim a dependency exemption for a minor child? What are the prerequisites for a noncustodial parent?

7. Under what circumstances is the transfer of property between parties to divorce litigation not considered a taxable event? When is it considered a taxable event?

8. When an individual sells a primary residence, what provisions are available for the deferral of taxes on the gain realized in the transaction?

9. Under what circumstances is the transfer of cash or property to a third party treated as alimony or as a tax-free transfer of property?

10. What is the difference between gross income and adjusted gross income? Between adjusted gross income and taxable income?

KEY TERMS

adjusted gross income
basis
capital assets
deductible
gross income

includable
personal exemption
recapture
taxable income

STATE RESEARCH PROBLEMS

Review the laws of your state and answer the following questions:

1. Do the tax laws of your state treat married persons differently than unmarried persons? If so, state the nature of the difference.

2. What are the tax rates in your state and the respective income brackets for each tax rate?

PRACTICE EXERCISES

1. Determine whether the following payments would be treated as alimony, either partially or completely, and explain your answer. What other facts might you need to know to better answer these questions? Why?

   a. Where Husband and Wife have no children, the final divorce decree orders Husband to transfer to Wife every month: $500 by check, Wife's $500 mortgage payment, and $500 worth of Husband's stock in ABC Corp. What if Husband made these transfers voluntarily?

   b. Husband and Wife enter into a separation agreement wherein Husband agrees to pay Wife $10,000 a year for 10 years or until Wife's death, whichever occurs first. But if Wife dies before the tenth year, Husband must pay her estate an amount equal to the difference between $100,000 and the total amount actually paid to Wife. What difference does it make if Wife survives the full 10 years?

2. Determine whether the following transfers result in any taxes due, and if so, the amount of the gain upon which taxes would be realized, and the party responsible for paying such taxes:

   a. Where Husband transfers his interest in a parcel of real property (valued at $20,000) to a third party, and the third party releases Wife from a debt of $20,000. What if Wife is obligated to the third party in the amount of $10,000? Of $30,000?

   b. Where, incident to a divorce, Wife pays Husband $5,000 in exchange for Husband's interest in a closely held corporation, having a fair market value of $20,000.

Paternity and Legitimation

Historically, a child born out of wedlock was denied many legal rights afforded legitimate children. Today, while such discrimination is not permitted, paternity must still be formally established to create the obligation to provide support. The process of establishing parentage and creating the legal obligation to provide support is called a paternity action. A paternity action can be initiated by the mother of the child, by the putative father, by the child, or by the state.

A complaint to establish paternity is filed and served upon the putative father; the burden of proof is on the party claiming the child is illegitimate. As in any form of litigation, the parties may engage in discovery. The most important elements of discovery are the results of blood tests of the mother, child, and putative father. While these tests cannot affirmatively establish parentage, they can absolutely rule out a particular person's genetic linkage to the minor child. At the trial of a paternity action, other evidence including physical similarities (or dissimilarities) between the child and putative father and expressions of parentage by the putative father may be introduced. Once paternity is established, the amount of child support is determined in the same way it is determined in divorce litigation, and the statutory support guidelines will apply.

In some jurisdictions, paternity actions confer only the obligations and none of the benefits of parenthood upon the father. In those states, if a father of a child born out of wedlock desires the right to visit with the child, he must legitimate the child. This can be accomplished in a number of ways, including making a public declaration of parentage, signing the child's birth certificate, taking the child into his household, and initiating litigation to confer legitimation.

ILLEGITIMACY AS STATUS

legitimacy; illegitimacy
Legitimacy is the legal status that results from being born to parents who are legally married to each other. Illegitimacy is the legal status that results from being born to parents who are not legally married to each other.

Legitimacy has been defined as the condition of being born in wedlock; it is a legal status, as is "married" or "single." The opposite of legitimacy is **illegitimacy,** the condition of being born out of wedlock. Historically, a child born out of wedlock has been called a "bastard." When a woman who is lawfully married gives birth, there is a presumption of legitimacy; that is, the husband is presumed to be the father of the child. This is true even if the child is born so soon after the marriage that it is certain the child is the product of a prenuptial conception, or if the child is born after the termination of the marriage. While this presumption is rebuttable, it requires convincing proof of the husband's nonparentage, such as results of a blood test. Generally, children born as issue of a void marriage are considered illegitimate, whereas children born as a result of a voidable marriage are legitimate, even if the marriage is later annulled. (See Chapter 5 for a discussion of the distinctions between void and voidable marriages.)

When a child is born out of wedlock, legal action may be initiated to establish the identity of the child's father. If the mother seeks to have the putative father established as the legal father of the child, the process is called a **paternity action.** (Such a proceeding may also be called a "bastardy" action.) It is also possible for the **putative father** to file an action of legitimation to establish himself as the lawfully recognized father of the child.

paternity action
Litigation initiated to establish the legal identity of a person's father.

putative father
An alleged father.

At common law, illegitimate children had none of the rights afforded legitimate children (i.e., the right to receive support from their parents, as well the right to make a claim upon their father's estate upon his death). But the United States Supreme Court, in a series of cases, found no rational basis to treat illegitimate children differently than those born in wedlock. Further, the Court held that such discriminatory laws violate the Equal Protection Clause of the Fourteenth Amendment to the U.S. Constitution. Illegitimacy is not considered (once paternity has been legally established) in areas such as a child's right to receive support from the father and the right to make a wrongful death claim should the father die as a result of the negligence of a third party.

The Uniform Parentage Act (UPA) has been enacted in approximately one-third of the states. The primary purpose of the UPA is to establish procedures for the identification of the person against whom the rights of the illegitimate child may be asserted. The act also provides details for conducting pretrial procedures; performing blood tests; and establishing custody, visitation, and child support; as well as for enforcing and modifying the judgments issued as a result of the UPA.

PATERNITY ACTIONS

Paternity actions are civil actions filed to legally establish the identity of an illegitimate child's father and to create the father's legal obligation of support for the child. The following parties may initiate a paternity action:

— An unmarried woman seeking to legally establish the identity of her child's father may file a paternity action.

— The child may file for paternity; if a minor, she will normally have a guardian ad litem appointed to represent and assist her in the litigation. In some states, the statute of limitations for paternity extends several years beyond the child's age of majority. (Under the UPA, the child is a necessary party and must be joined in a paternity action, and a guardian other than the child's parents is appointed for the benefit of the child.)

— A third party providing support for the child, such as a grandparent, may file for paternity.

— A state agency may file a paternity action seeking to recover monies paid on behalf of the child necessitated by the failure of the father to pay for the support of the child.

— The father may file for paternity.

— A married woman may file a paternity action against a man other than her husband.

Although a civil action, paternity litigation may invoke certain elements of criminal litigation, such as the use of a warrant (as opposed to a complaint) to initiate the action, as well as the use of the term *guilty* as opposed to *liable*. In a minority of states, the court may also require the defendant to post security (or "bail") if there is fear that the defendant will flee the jurisdiction.

Jurisdictional Issues

States vary as to which court has subject matter jurisdiction for paternity litigation. Such litigation might be filed in the civil court of general jurisdiction, or in a family or juvenile court. Because paternity imposes the personal obligation to provide support, it is an action *in personam* and thus requires personal jurisdiction over the defendant.

Venue is usually proper in the county of the defendant's residence. The statute of limitations for paternity tends to be longer than for most causes of action. States vary, but the statute of limitations is typically the child's age of majority or a certain number of years beyond the age of majority. States may permit a paternity action to be filed before the birth of the child, but will issue no order until the child has been born alive.

Procedure

The petition or complaint must set forth the jurisdictional requirements and allege that:

— The plaintiff has not been married to the defendant during all relevant times.

— The parties engaged in sexual intercourse during the time period surrounding conception of the child.

— The defendant is the father of the child.

— The child is entitled to receive support from the defendant.

The plaintiff may demand future financial support for the child, as well as accrued support from the time of the child's birth, expenses of pregnancy, and attorney's fees. The complaint must be served personally upon the defendant. A sample petition to establish paternity is at Exhibit 15–1. The parties may engage in discovery prior to trial of the issues, and the usual sanctions are

---

EXHIBIT 15–1   COMPLAINT TO ESTABLISH PATERNITY

IN THE SUPERIOR COURT OF _____ COUNTY
STATE OF _____

DARLENE SIMPSON,

Plaintiff,

v.   CIVIL ACTION NO. _____

JOSEPH SUTTON,

Defendant.

Complaint to Establish Paternity

COMES NOW, Plaintiff in the above-styled action, and shows the Court as follows:

1.

Jurisdictional allegations.

Plaintiff and her minor child, known as Thomas Simpson, are residents of the State of _____.

2.

Defendant is a resident of Smith County, State of _____ , where he may be served with process.

3.

Plaintiff is the mother of said minor child known as Thomas Simpson, born on October 10, 1992.

4.

Plaintiff and Defendant engaged in sexual intercourse resulting in birth of the aforesaid child. At no time have Plaintiff and Defendant been married to each other.

Allegation of Defendant's paternity and that the parties have never been married to each other.

5.

Plaintiff is entitled to custody of said child.

6.

Plaintiff is entitled to receive child support from Defendant for the future support, education, and maintenance of said minor child. In addition, Plaintiff is entitled to receive from Defendant a lump sum representing all arrearages of child support owed from the time of the minor child's birth until the issuance of a court order formally establishing Defendant's paternity.

Allegation of entitlement of child support, both prospectively and retroactively.

7.

Plaintiff is entitled to receive reimbursement of her reasonable prenatal medical expenses and loss of income caused by her pregnancy with Defendant's child.

Allegation of entitlement to reimbursement of medical expenses resulting from pregnancy with Defendant's child.

8.

If the Court deems necessary, said child should be made a party to this litigation, and a guardian ad litem should be appointed to represent the interests of the child.

9.

In the event Defendant disputes his paternity of the child, the Court should order the taking of blood tests to establish paternity.

Allegation of entitlement to blood test to determine paternity.

10.

Plaintiff is entitled to reasonable attorneys' fees and other expenses of this proceeding.

Allegation of entitlement to reimbursement of attorneys' fees.

WHEREFORE, Plaintiff prays as follows:

a) that the paternity of Thomas Simpson be established, declaring Joseph Simpson to be the father of said minor child;

b) that Plaintiff be awarded permanent custody of said minor child;

c) that Plaintiff be awarded future child support from Defendant for the support, education, and maintenance of said minor child; in addition, that Plaintiff receive a lump sum representing the arrearage of child support owed to Plaintiff from the time of the minor child's birth until the issuance of the court order formally establishing Defendant's paternity;

d) that Plaintiff be awarded reasonable prenatal medical expenses and loss of income caused by her pregnancy with Defendant's child;

e) that Plaintiff be awarded reasonable attorneys' fees and litigation expenses associated with this proceeding;

f) that the minor child be made a party to this litigation, and that a guardian ad litem be appointed to represent the child's interests;

g) that blood tests be required to establish paternity; and,

h) that Plaintiff have other such relief as deemed proper by this Court.

Respectfully Submitted,

_____
Attorney for Plaintiff

(A Verification should be prepared and attached.)

available to coerce reticent parties to comply. Once paternity has been established, the obligation to provide support can be imposed on the father.

Because the obligation to provide support begins when the child is born, it may be possible to obtain retroactive child support for the period from the child's birth to the date of the paternity order. The authority to recover retroactive child support varies among the states. A minority of states have statutes that permit a court to order retroactive child support for the period from the birth of the child until the institution of the order of paternity. Other states permit retroactive child support for a defined period of time. For example, a mother might be entitled to child support for a period of four years before the initiation date of the paternity action. Still other states leave the issue of retroactive child support to the discretion of the trial court. To successfully obtain an award of retroactive child support, appropriate evidence must be presented to the court (for example, documentation of the actual expenses incurred on behalf of the minor child as well as the income earned by both parties). In addition, all written attempts (and such attempts should *always* be reduced to writing) to secure child support should be presented to the court to demonstrate that resorting to the court was the fault of the putative father.

In states that have adopted the UPA, paternity actions are to be tried by the court without a jury; other jurisdictions may treat this as an issue for a jury. At trial, the court considers all relevant evidence, including the testimony of the parties. The testimony will probably delve into the sexual relationship, or lack of same, between the parties, during the period of time that approximates the date of the child's conception. A remnant from the English common law, Lord Mansfield's rule, remains in a number of states. This rule of law states that neither spouse can testify that they had not engaged in sexual intercourse at the time of the child's conception, if such evidence would tend to illegitimate the child. Such a scenario is most likely when a husband is denying paternity of his wife's child. As noted earlier, there is a strong legal presumption in favor of finding legitimate a child born to parents married to each other. Before the development of blood tests to scientifically determine parentage, Lord Mansfield's rule made it all but impossible for a husband to deny parentage of his wife's child.

While scientific blood tests are certainly a well accepted and highly accurate method of establishing paternity, the traditional theories used before the advent of blood tests are still viable. One such theory is *res judicata* (Latin for "the thing has been decided"), which may be used when there has been a prior court determination of the father's paternity. For example: An unmarried woman gives birth to a child. Several months after the child is born, the woman marries the defendant. During the marriage, the defendant supports the child financially and emotionally. A year later, the couple divorces, and in the separation agreement, the defendant agrees to pay child support and is awarded specific visitation with the child. A year after the divorce, the defendant cannot pay the child support and claims that he is not the child's father. The mother initiates paternity proceedings against the defendant. The prevailing view is that the divorce judgment, which established the defendant as the father, is controlling and that no further judicial inquiry is required. This may still be the result even when blood tests conclusively establish the defendant's nonparentage. The rationale for this holding is that once established, the determination of legitimacy is not to be disturbed.

Similarly, the equitable theory of estoppel may be used when, although there has been no judicial determination of paternity, a party's conduct toward the child over an extended period of time is determinative of paternity. For example, when the defendant holds himself out to be the father of a child, such representations (or misrepresentations, as the case may be) may preclude further judicial proceedings regarding paternity.

res judicata
A legal holding that a particular set of circumstances has been fully adjudicated and that no further related litigation will be entertained.

Blood Tests

Where the complaint for paternity is contested by the putative father, and an answer denying the allegations has been filed, the next step is generally to conduct blood tests of the mother, child, and putative father. Courts have the power to order blood tests where a party fails to submit to one voluntarily. A putative father who refuses to participate in the blood tests can be held in contempt; a mother's refusal may result in dismissal of her paternity action. Additionally, since this is a civil litigation, the failure of the father to submit to blood tests can be used to implicate the father at trial. These tests are usually conducted simultaneously for all three parties, to verify the identification of all parties. Otherwise, the father might send another man to take the blood test for him. The cost for these tests, which can be significant, is typically borne by the putative father, although they may be apportioned by the court between the parties, and payment may be required in advance by the testing facility. In cases in which the parties are indigent, the state bears the cost for the tests. The results of properly administered blood tests are admissible in a court of law. While the test results alone are not conclusive, they are often the single most important piece of evidence available in a contested paternity case.

These blood tests are more complex than the standard blood tests conducted for a routine medical examination. The phrase "blood tests" really refers to a battery of possible tests that may be conducted. There are three levels of blood testing:

— *Level I*—examines only red blood cell antigens; also examines twenty genetic markers.

— *Level II*—examines red blood cell antigens, enzymes, and serum proteins; examines sixty genetic markers.

— *Level III*—the human leukocyte antigen (HLA) test examines all materials included in Levels I and II, plus the white blood cell (leukocyte) antigens; examines ninety genetic markers. The HLA test has been shown to establish paternity within a 99.95% probability. It is generally accepted in both legal and scientific circles as a reliable indicator of paternity. The HLA test is actually a tissue typing test, as opposed to the less sophisticated blood grouping tests.

Many other blood tests are available, including DNA testing, and it is advisable to know which tests may be performed by the testing facility. The paralegal may be required to make the necessary arrangements for the blood test, including assuring that the mother, father, and child all appear for the blood tests.

It must be remembered that blood tests cannot affirmatively prove paternity. They can only exclude paternity or establish a probability of paternity. Paternity may be excluded if a genetic marker found in the child is not found in either parent, or if the father has a genetic marker that could have been passed to the child but is not found in the child's blood. If paternity is not excluded, a **paternity index** is calculated. The paternity index states in percentage terms (i.e., 12.27%, 99.87%) how much more likely it is that the putative father is the actual father than a random male in the population. Under the UPA, the results of blood tests are admissible at trial.

Where the results of the blood tests are consistent and indicate that the putative father genetically *cannot* be the father of the child, and the court believes that the expert witnesses presenting the test results testified truthfully and that the tests were conducted properly, the court may find that the putative father is not the true parent of the child in question.

paternity index
A percentage of probability that a particular male is the biological father of a particular child, based on the results of blood matching tests.

Trial of a Paternity Case

There are several issues peculiar to the trial of a paternity action.

— The burden of proof is on the party claiming that the child is illegitimate; therefore, a putative father denying parentage has the burden of proof, as does a married woman asserting that a man other than her husband is the father of her child.

— Blood tests are generally admissible in court, but the proper foundation must be laid during the direct examination of the expert witness presenting the test results. This requires the expert witness to testify as to her expertise and competence in this particular field.

— Evidence of the mother's sexual history is not admissible except as it relates to the period of time surrounding conception and as it tends to show that a man other than the defendant could be the actual father.

— States are divided in permitting a jury to view the child and consider to what degree, if at all, the child physically resembles the putative father.

— The court may also consider any conduct or document tending to establish or preclude the defendant's parentage, such as admissions or denials of paternity, letters to the mother or child, proof of support, etc.

— Some states will permit an award of medical and hospital expenses incurred as a result of the plaintiff's pregnancy with the defendant's child. This usually requires corroboration of the expenses. The plaintiff may also be able to recover income lost due to her pregnancy.

Defenses to Paternity Actions

A putative father may have available several defenses to a paternity action. Perhaps the most effective defense is proof of the putative father's sterility at the time the child was conceived. Another effective defense is a result of the blood tests, tending to show that the defendant is not the child's father. In cases in which the mother has knowledge of the true father's identity but fails to initiate litigation for a number of years, the claim may be barred by either the applicable statute of limitations or the equitable doctrine of laches. Before the advent of accurate blood tests, the most effective defense was evidence that the mother had engaged in sexual liaisons with men other than the putative father. Defenses vary among jurisdictions; consider the following:

— In some jurisdictions, when a pregnant woman marries a man other than the defendant, and that man has full knowledge of her condition, it is presumed that the new husband, rather than the defendant, is the father of the child.

— Age and insanity are typically *not* available as defenses.

Third parties may make a defense to a paternity case if they claim an interest in the child. For example, estoppel may be used as a defense to paternity actions in cases in which the mother has previously claimed that a third party was the father and at a later time alleges that the defendant is the true father of the child. This may be true even if blood tests reveal the defendant to be the child's father. In such cases, the court may find that the child and the third-party "father" have formed a father-child relationship, and that it is in the best interests of the child for the third party to retain all legal rights to the child.

Once paternity has been legally established, the amount of child support due is determined using much the same method as in divorce litigation. The statutory child support guidelines are used. An award of attorneys' fees may be appropriate in favor of the prevailing party, so both the attorneys and paralegals should keep accurate and complete time records to corroborate the claim for attorneys' fees. The award of attorneys' fees is based on factors similar to those used in divorce actions, including the results obtained, the amount of time spent, and the usual and customary fees charged in similar actions.

As with any form of litigation, a mutually acceptable compromise and settlement is desirable over a court-imposed adjudication. A mother and putative father can enter into a contractual release under court auspices. Any such agreement must adequately provide for the child's welfare. Under the UPA, no such settlement between the parties is enforceable until it has been approved by the court. Notwithstanding any such agreement, if the agreement does not provide an admission of the father's paternity, the mother may later initiate a paternity action to recover any additional sums of support.

LEGITIMATION ACTIONS

A child is considered to be legitimate when, among other things, she is born in wedlock, she is lawfully adopted by her parents, or when she is born to an unwed mother and the father legally recognizes her as his own. A child is also legitimate if the biological parents of the child ultimately marry after the birth of the child. Failing any of the above, in a minority of states, a father may legitimate his child:

— By publicly acknowledging the child as his own

— By signing the birth certificate or certificate of baptism

— By openly receiving the child into his home

— By acknowledging the child as his own to a public official or notary public (Note that the laws of the state of the father's domicile, not the child's, will be controlling.)

In addition, in several states, the father may initiate formal legal action to legitimate the child. Upon legitimation, the child is legally entitled to receive support and maintenance from her father, as well as to make a claim upon her father's estate upon his death. Similarly, the father is then entitled to seek visitation privileges with the child, as well as to seek legal and physical custody of the child. (Note that the father does not typically enjoy such rights in a paternity action.) Unlike paternity actions, legitimation actions are not usually contested, because the mother is only too happy to allow the father to legally obligate himself to support the child. Legitimation may be opposed, however (for example, when the mother denies that the plaintiff is the father of the child, or when the mother does not want the "father" to be granted visitation privileges).

An action for legitimation is usually brought in the county of either the child's or father's residence. Unless waived, service of process must be effected upon the mother of the child. Since these actions are often welcomed by the mother, they may be presented to the court in the form of a nonadversarial proceeding. In such cases, after the petition to legitimate is filed, both parties would sign a consent order, which would contemplate several issues, including an agreement relating to the support of and visitation with the parties' child.

COMINO

v.

KELLEY

Court of Appeal, Fourth District, Division 3.
June 3, 1994.

. . . .

OPINION

SONENSHINE, Associate Justice.

Stephanie Lynne Kelley appeals from a judgment of paternity in favor of Paul Henry Comino in his action to establish a parental relationship with Joshua Paul. We conclude the court properly (1) refused to apply the conclusive presumption of Evidence Code section 621 to establish the paternity of Stephanie's husband, and (2) found Paul to be a presumed father under Civil Code section 7004 (footnotes omitted).

Factual Background (Footnote omitted.)

Stephanie met Jeffrey Moyer at a wedding in May 1987. At the time, Stephanie lived in a two-bedroom apartment with a roommate, and Jeffrey, a sergeant in the Marine Corps, lived in barracks on a military base. Stephanie and Jeffrey did not date one another, but in July, when Stephanie's roommate moved out, the two agreed to marry for the sake of mutual convenience or economic advantages. Jeffrey called the marriage a "business relationship" which made it possible for him to receive a married man's "privileges through the military." Stephanie had a "replacement" roommate to share rent payments, and she qualified for medical insurance available to dependents of military personnel.

After their July meeting, Stephanie and Jeffrey did not see each other again until August 12, when they were married at the Orange County courthouse. Following the ceremony, which none of their friends or relatives attended, they went their separate ways until September, when Jeffrey moved from the barracks into Stephanie's apartment, occupying the bedroom vacated by her former roommate. Jeffrey and Stephanie each paid one-half of the rent and their respective long-distance telephone charges; Stephanie paid the utility bills. They had no joint bank accounts. They opened a joint credit card account, but each paid his or her own charges. They did not have a sexual relationship. Jeffrey dated another woman, and Stephanie dated other men, including Paul Comino.

When Paul met Jeffrey, he had no knowledge of the marriage, probably because Stephanie introduced Jeffrey as her roommate. In April 1988, Stephanie and Paul were sexually involved and, at about that time, Stephanie became pregnant. In June, she told Paul about the pregnancy and said he was the father (footnote omitted). In July, Jeffrey moved out of the apartment he and Stephanie had shared for 11 months.

A few weeks before the birth of the child, Stephanie moved into Paul's home, and they attended at least one La Maze childbirth class together. On Christmas Eve, Paul was with her when she delivered the baby; he cut the umbilical cord. With his knowledge and consent, the child was named Joshua Paul Comino. Paul was identified as the father on the birth certificate, which was signed by Stephanie (footnote omitted).

Stephanie and Paul took Joshua to the home they shared and treated him as Paul's natural son. Stephanie sent out birth announcements to Paul's family and friends, identifying Paul as the father. She sent photographs identifying Joshua as a member of the Comino family (footnote omitted). For the next two-and-a-half years, except for one or two brief interludes of separation, Paul, Stephanie and Joshua lived together as a family unit. Paul supported Joshua and shared care-giving responsibilities with Stephanie. When Stephanie returned to work, and until Joshua began attending preschool, Paul's mother provided day care. According to a court-appointed mental health care expert, Joshua and Paul became "well bonded."

Nonetheless, in April 1991, Stephanie moved out of the family residence and into Jeffrey's home (footnote omitted). Without identifying any other man as Joshua's father, she told Paul, for the first time, that he might not be the biological father. When she threatened to restrict his access to the child, Paul filed the underlying action against Stephanie and Jeffrey to establish his parental relationship. He also sought and was granted pendente lite custody orders awarding him joint legal and physical custody of Joshua, and 50 percent physical custodial time with the minor.

In his answer to the complaint, Jeffrey denied he was the child's biological or adoptive father, but Stephanie's answer asserted his paternity as a matter of law, based on their marriage and cohabitation. Stephanie denied her sexual relations with Paul had resulted in Joshua's conception. Her motion for an order compelling Paul to submit to paternity blood tests was denied. After a two-day trial of the matter, the court adjudged Paul to be the father of Joshua, ordered him to pay child support to Stephanie, and continued joint legal and physical custody.

On appeal, Stephanie contends the court erred in failing to apply the conclusive presumption of Evidence Code section 621 to establish Jeffrey's paternity as a matter of law. She further contends the doctrine of equitable estoppel cannot be invoked to bar her from contesting Paul's paternity because he failed to carry his burden of establishing a biological link with Joshua.

Discussion

I

Evidence Code section 621, subdivision (a) sets forth a conclusive presumption regarding paternity. It states: "Except as provided in subdivision (b), the issue of a wife cohabitating with her husband, who is not impotent or sterile, is conclusively presumed to be a child of the marriage" (footnote omitted). However, as

another panel of this court recently observed, in *County of Orange v. Leslie B.* (citation omitted), "courts have refused to apply [the conclusive presumption of section 621] when its underlying policies are not furthered." [Citations omitted.]

In *Leslie B.,* the Orange County District Attorney filed a complaint against two men to establish paternity and provide support for a minor. The first man, Gregory, was married to and lived with the minor's mother, Catherine, when the child, Jennifer, was conceived, but they later separated and divorced. Blood tests conclusively showed he was not the biological father. The second man, Leslie, was having sexual relations with Catherine at the relevant time period. Blood tests established the virtual certainty of Leslie's paternity, and Catherine had told Jennifer he was her father. The trial court concluded Leslie was Jennifer's biological and legal father, and Leslie appealed, contending, as does Stephanie, that the court had an absolute obligation to apply the conclusive presumption of Evidence Code section 621.

Rejecting the contention, this court first noted Leslie was attempting to use the conclusive presumption to protect himself from responsibility rather than achieve involvement in the life of the child he had fathered. (Citation omitted.) It then discussed the balancing test of *In re Lisa R.* (citation omitted) and its progeny, a test under which competing state and private interests are weighed to determine whether the presumption should be applied in a given case. (Citation omitted.) It found the traditional policies underlying the presumption—"to preserve the integrity of the family unit, protect children from the legal and social stigma of illegitimacy, and promote individual rather than state responsibility for child support" (citation omitted)—would not be served by application of the presumption under the circumstances (footnote omitted). "If Leslie prevailed Jennifer would be 'given' a father [Gregory] whom she knows is not her natural father, to preserve the integrity of a family unit that never existed. Catherine, Gregory and Jennifer have never lived together as a family, they share no ties other than those that exist due to a long-ago failed marriage of brief duration. . . . [T]o apply the presumption will not remove 'the stigma of illegitimacy' from Jennifer. She knows Gregory is not her father. She has never been held out as his daughter. She believes Leslie is her father and blood tests have confirmed it. Finally, the state's interest in establishing a source of child support is completely served by declaring Leslie to be the legal father." (Citation and footnote omitted.)

The *Leslie B.* court also noted how well-served Jennifer's interests would be by avoidance of the conclusive presumption regarding Gregory's paternity. "To name Leslie as her legal father entitles her to benefits she is currently unable to receive. She will be entitled to financial assistance from him and will finally have a legal as well as a biological father. While Leslie may suffer some financial hardship as a result of his being declared Jennifer's legal father, this is far outweighed by the benefits to her." (Citation omitted.)

We find Leslie B.'s analysis and conclusion abundantly apt here, where none of the policies underlying the presumption of paternity would be served by its application. (1) There is neither a marital union nor a family unit to preserve: The so-called marriage was one in name only and Joshua never lived in a family unit with Stephanie and Jeffrey. (2) To the extent there is a recognizable societal concern for Joshua to have a father, that concern is served by avoiding the presumption that would prevent Joshua from enjoying a parental relationship with the only man he has ever known as a father. And (3), the state's interest in making sure Joshua has a source of child support is furthered by the court's order rejecting the presumption and awarding to Paul the responsibility he seeks to assume.

In *Leslie B.*, the reviewing court cited as "apt" the observation of the "learned trial judge" who stated: "'[A]pplying the [presumption] leads to an absurd result that defies reason and common sense. To apply the [presumption] is to rely upon a fiction to establish a legal fact which we know to be untrue, in order to protect policies which in this case do not exist." (Citation omitted.) We heartily agree. Here, the court properly refused to apply the paternity presumption of Evidence Code section 621.

II

In its statement of decision, the trial court determined Paul was Joshua's presumed father under section 7004, subdivision (a)(4), which provides for such paternity when a man "receives the child into his home and openly holds out the child as his natural child." There was uncontradicted evidence Paul received Joshua into his home, lived with him, held him out as his own and supported him for nearly two-and-a-half years. In the absence of rebuttal evidence, Paul was unquestionably entitled to the benefit of the statutory presumption.

Stephanie initially contends it was Paul's burden to present evidence of biological paternity to take advantage of the presumed father status of section 7004. This contention is ridiculous. By its very terms, the statute creates the presumption of natural fatherhood, arising out of a man's acceptance of a child into his home and acknowledgement of it as his own. Paul had no burden to present evidence establishing his biological link with the child. Rather, it was Stephanie's burden to rebut the presumption of natural fatherhood with clear and convincing evidence. . . . She claims blood tests eliminated the probability of Paul's paternity (footnote omitted). But she failed to introduce any blood test results into evidence, thus she may not raise the issue on appeal. . . .

The judgment is affirmed. Comino shall recover his costs on appeal.

SILLS, P.J., and WALLIN, J., concur.

DISCUSSION QUESTIONS

Based on the preceding case of *Comino v. Kelley*, 30 Cal.Rptr.2d 728 (Cal. 1994), answer the following questions:

1. How does the presumption of paternity affect the holding of this case?

2. How did the case of *County of Orange v. Leslie B.* affect the court's holding in this case?

INTERVIEW CHECKLIST

For Paternity

State the name and date of birth of the minor child(ren).

_____

State the name, address, telephone number, date of birth, and Social Security Number (if known) of the putative father of the above-referenced child(ren).

_____

Does the child resemble the father? _____ If yes, provide relevant details.

_____

_____

State the period of time during which you were engaged in a sexual relationship with the father.

_____

_____

State the frequency of sexual contact with the father.

_____

Did you use birth control? _____ If yes, provide details.

_____

If not, explain why not.

_____

Where did you reside during the time you were engaged in a sexual relationship with the father?

_____

In whose name(s) was the above-referenced property owned or rented?

_____

Where and when was the child conceived?

_____

Within the period of time commencing three months before you became pregnant and ending three months after you became pregnant, did you have sexual intercourse with any men other than the father of your child? _____ If yes, provide their name, address, and telephone number.

_____

When did the father learn that you were pregnant?

_____

What was his reaction upon learning that you were pregnant?

_____

Describe the nature of your relationship with the father at the time your child was conceived.

_____

Has the father at any time acknowledged the child(ren) as his own? _____ If so, provide details and state the names and addresses of any witnesses to such acknowledgments.

_____

Has the father written anything in which he acknowledges that he is the child's father (i.e., a letter)?

_____

Is the father named as the father on the birth certificate?

_____

If yes, did he also sign the birth certificate as the child's father? _____ If not, explain why not.

_____

Has the father at any time provided for the support and maintenance of the child(ren)? _____ If so, provide details, including the nature and amount of the support and the date(s) on which it was provided.

_____

Are you currently married? _____ If yes, state your husband's name and the date and location of your marriage.

_____

(NOTE—*The questions relating to a claim for child support from Chapter 10 would also be employed here.*)

continued on page 305

continued from page 304

For Legitimation

State the name and date of birth of your child(ren) you seek to legitimate.

_____

State the name, address, telephone number, date of birth, and Social Security Number (if known) of the mother of the child(ren) named above.

_____

Are you currently married?_____ If yes, state your wife's name, and the date and location of your marriage.

_____

Has the mother acknowledged that you are the father of the child(ren) named herein? _____
If so, provide details, including the names and addresses of any witnesses to such an acknowledgment.

_____

Will the mother oppose this action to legitimate the child?

_____

If yes, explain her reasons for opposing the legitimation.

_____

Have you at any time provided for the support and maintenance of the child? _____ If so, provide details, including the nature and amount of such support and the date(s) on which it was provided.

_____

If no such support has been furnished, provide details explaining the lack of support.

_____

State the period of time in which you were engaged in a sexual relationship with the mother.

_____

How would you describe your relationship with the mother at the time the child(ren) was conceived?

_____

Do you seek custody of the child? _____
If so, provide details as to why you believe that it would be in the best interests of the child if he or she were in your custody.

_____

Do you seek visitation privileges with the child? _____ If so, do you believe that the mother will oppose visitation?

_____

If so, explain.

_____

Describe the nature of the relationship you currently have with the child.

_____

Describe the nature of the relationship you currently have with the mother.

_____

Are you aware that by legitimating this child you are legally obligating yourself to support the child until the age of 18, and that upon your death the child will be legally entitled to make a claim upon your estate?

_____

REVIEW QUESTIONS

1. What are the different goals of paternity and legitimation actions?

2. How do successful actions for paternity and legitimation affect the rights of the father regarding his child? What is the effect upon the rights of the child regarding her father?

3. What blood tests are available to parties in paternity? What is the procedure used when blood tests are required? How do the results of blood tests affect the ultimate determination of the case?

4. What are two of the traditional defenses to a paternity action? Describe them and the circumstances under which they might be employed.

5. What is the appropriate venue in a paternity action? What is the appropriate venue in a legitimation action?

6. What is the possible effect of *res judicata* in paternity litigation?

7. How does the HLA blood test differ from less sophisticated blood tests?

8. What can a blood test conclusively establish? What is it unable to prove conclusively?

9. What is the significance of the paternity index?

10. What types of damage may a successful paternity plaintiff recover?

KEY TERMS

legitimacy   putative father
paternity action   *res judicata*
paternity index

STATE RESEARCH PROBLEMS

Answer the following questions, based on the law of your jurisdiction:

1. What are the prerequisites for a paternity action? Who may initiate a paternity action? What is the applicable statute of limitations? What rights are afforded a child who is the subject of a successful paternity action?

2. What defenses to a paternity action are available? What, if any, presumptions are maintained regarding the legitimacy of a child born in wedlock, and how may those presumptions be adequately rebutted?

3. What legal procedure(s) are available to legitimate a child? In addition, what conduct on the part of the putative father may legally establish him as the actual father of an otherwise illegitimate child? Provide the specific details and appropriate citations.

PRACTICE EXERCISES

1. Contact a local laboratory that is authorized to conduct court-ordered blood tests. What is the fee for the tests? What type(s) of blood tests are available?

2. Based on the facts of *Comino v. Kelley,* assume the mother of the child wants to establish the putative father's paternity. Draft an appropriate motion for paternity.

Adoption

Adoption is a legal proceeding in which the legal relation of parent and child is created between parents and a child who are not naturally so related. There are several legal methods of adoption: adoption through private agency; adoption through independent placement; adoption through a state child welfare agency; adoption by a stepparent or relative; and adoption of an adult. Adoption is really a two-step procedure: the first step, in which the existing parent-child relationship is terminated; and the second, in which the new parent-child relationship is created. The birth parents may voluntarily consent to the termination of their legal rights to the child, or the parental rights may be judicially terminated. As with any determination of child custody, the guiding principle of adoption is the best interests of the child. With few exceptions, once the adoption is final, the child is as much a part of her new family as a child born as issue to those parents. A new wrinkle has been added to the area of adoption by the advent of artificial reproduction. Such procedures involve the use of the ovum, sperm, and/or uterus of a person other than one of the future parents of the child.

TERMINATION OF EXISTING PARENT-CHILD RELATIONSHIP

Adoption
The creation of the legal relationship of parent and child.

Adoption is the creation of a parent-child relationship. But if either of the parents of the child who is to be adopted are alive, that legal relationship must first be terminated. The parent-child relationship is protected as a fundamental right under the United States Constitution; a court cannot end the relationship unless the natural parent voluntarily surrenders her rights to the child or there is convincing evidence that the natural parent is either unwilling or unable to adequately provide for the child. If the child is legitimate, both parents must consent to the adoption, or a court must terminate their legal relation to the child. If the natural parents voluntarily agree to the adoption, this requires nothing more than the execution by both parents of formal docu-

---

EXHIBIT 16–1   CONSENT TO ADOPTION AND TERMINATION OF PARENTAL RIGHTS

IN THE SUPERIOR COURT OF _____ COUNTY
STATE OF _____

IN RE: ROBERT DALE MURCER, A MINOR

ARTHUR GIBBONS AND DOROTHY GIBBONS,
Petitioners.

CIVIL ACTION NO. _____

Mother's Consent to Adoption and Termination of Parental Rights

1.

I, Maureen Anna Murcer, the mother of Robert Dale Murcer, a male child, reside at 733 Briarcliff Drive, _____ County, State of _____ .

2.

I am older than 18 years of age.

3.

I hereby consent to the adoption of my above-referenced child.

4.

I acknowledge and understand that by signing this consent that I do permanently and irrevocably waive all custody and other personal rights I have to this child.

5.

I acknowledge and understand that this child will be placed for adoption and I cannot, under any circumstances, after signing this document change my mind and revoke or cancel this consent.

6.

I am signing this document freely and voluntarily, and I understand the consequences of doing so. I have not been threatened or coerced to sign this consent. Furthermore, I am not now under the influence of alcohol or drugs.

7.

I acknowledge that I have been encouraged to obtain legal counsel prior to my signing this consent.

This ___ day of _____, 199 ___.

_____
Maureen Anna Murcer

Unofficial witness _____

Sworn to and subscribed before me this ___day of _____, 199 ___.

_____
Notary Public

My commission expires _____

---

ments relinquishing parental rights to the child. See Exhibit 16–1 for a sample of a consent to adoption.

If the child is illegitimate, the mother and possibly the putative father must relinquish their rights to the child. At common law, the biological father had no standing to intervene in an adoption of his illegitimate child. But a series of U.S. Supreme Court cases have essentially provided that under the Equal Protection and Due Process clauses of the Fourteenth Amendment, the putative father may be entitled to a degree of due process before his legal relationship with the child can be forever severed. The degree of the unwed father's rights is directly related to the existence and nature of his relationship with his children.

If the putative father is unwilling to agree to the adoption, the court may terminate his parental rights. State laws will dictate the conditions precedent for termination, but typically a court may deem that a parent has relinquished any rights he may have to the child if the parent has failed to support the child or to visit with the child for a prescribed period of time (i.e., one year), or has otherwise abandoned the child. Typically, the mother provides an affidavit establishing the father's abandonment of the child. A sample affidavit is provided below at Exhibit 16–2. In addition, consent to adoption may not be nec-

---

EXHIBIT 16–2   AFFIDAVIT REGARDING PATERNITY OF CHILD

IN THE SUPERIOR COURT OF _____ COUNTY
STATE OF _____

IN RE: ROBERT DALE MURCER, A MINOR

ARTHUR GIBBONS AND DOROTHY GIBBONS,
Petitioners.

CIVIL ACTION NO. _____

Mother's Affidavit Regarding Paternity of Child

Personally appeared before me, the undersigned officer, duly authorized to administer oaths, MAUREEN ANNA MURCER, who, after being duly sworn, deposes and states as follows:

1.

My name is Maureen Anna Murcer, and I am the natural mother of a minor child, Robert Dale Murcer, currently two years of age. My address is 733 Briarcliff Drive, _____ County, State of _____ .

2.

The natural father of the child is James T. Garvey, and his address is 2774 College Avenue, East Point, State of _____ . At no time have I been married to the father of the aforesaid child.

3.

That the natural father of the child has not lived with the child since his birth on September 30, 1994, and has not provided any support for the benefit of the child, nor has he made any attempt to legitimate the child.

4.

I have not received or been promised any financial compensation for surrendering my parental rights to my child to the Petitioners.

_____
Maureen Anna Murcer

Sworn to and subscribed before me this ___ day of _____, 199 ___ .

_____
Notary Public

My commission expires _____

essary in cases in which the parent is legally adjudicated incompetent to give consent, or where his parental rights have previously been terminated. Generally speaking, if an unwed father has in any way provided support for or visited with the child, his consent is required for the adoption to proceed.

Each state has specific laws regarding the nature of the consent that must be given by the parents. These laws attempt to balance the rights of the birth parents, ensuring that their rights are not infringed upon, while also providing for a degree of finality and certainty for the adoptive parents. The following issues governing consent to adoption should be considered. *The procedures for termination of parental rights and adoption must be followed precisely. The failure to do so could allow a natural parent to seek to recover custody of the "adopted" child.*

PRACTICE
POINTER

When Can Consent Be Given?

Some states permit the parents to give their consent before the birth of the child; others require that consent be given only after the birth of the child and then only after a specific time period after birth.

How Is Consent Given?

It is universally required that a parent's consent to adoption must be in writing, impartially witnessed, and notarized. It must clearly identify the child and state that the parent voluntarily and permanently terminates all his or her rights to the child. It should contain a recitation of the rights afforded parents relinquishing custody of their children.

When and How Can Consent Be Revoked?

Some states do not permit revocation of consent to adoption given freely, knowingly, and intelligently. Other states require court approval to revoke such consent, and then only upon a showing that the revocation is in the best interests of the child or that the consent was procured by means of fraud, duress, or undue influence. Still other states permit consent to adoption to be withdrawn either within a specific period of time or until the adoption is final. Revocation of consent should be in writing and signed by the party revoking consent.

CREATION OF NEW PARENT-CHILD RELATIONSHIP

A number of preliminary matters must now be addressed including who may adopt; who may be adopted; and which laws are to be applied.

Who May Adopt?

As with any decisions regarding the custody of a child, the controlling issue is the best interests of the child. Generally, any competent adult may file a petition for adoption. But the states have codified certain requirements for potential adoptive parents, which usually include the following:

— *Marital status.* Single persons, as well as married couples, may be considered as adoptive parents. Married couples are usually favored, because they would be better able to provide the child with an "ideal" family. However, courts usually require both spouses to participate when a married couple adopts a child.

— *Age.* Adoption statutes typically require that the adoptive parents have reached a certain minimum age (i.e., 21 years of age), or that each adoptive parent be at least a certain minimum number of years older than the person being adopted.

— *Ability to care for child in the home.* While no court expects adoptive parents to be perfect, they must establish their ability to care for the child physically, emotionally, and financially. The environment of the adoptive home also comes under the court's scrutiny. The same issues that would complicate a claim for child custody will diminish the chances of prospective adoptive parents (i.e., problems with alcohol, drugs, gambling, violence, etc.).

— *Religion.* It is not unconstitutional to attempt to place a child in a home in which the child will be able to continue her established religious practices. As a matter of fact, some state statutes provide that whenever possible or practicable, a child should be placed in a home of her own religious affiliation. This is a greater concern with older children who have already formed basic religious beliefs.

— *Race.* Unlike religion, the race of the adoptive parents or the child cannot be used by the court as the sole factor in denying a petition for adoption; doing so is unconstitutional. But courts most certainly consider race in adoption cases when determining the best interests of the child. The extent to which race can or should be considered is not clearly delineated. The primary concern once was whether a child could be properly raised in a multiracial home.

— *Sexual preference of adoptive parents.* Historically, it would have been impossible for a homosexual individual or couple to successfully adopt a child. While it is now possible, it is still highly unlikely that a homosexual person or couple could adopt a child.

Who May Be Adopted?

In most states, both children and adults may be adopted. Adoption of adults is usually based on the desire to establish a legally recognized heir. Of course, whether child or adult, any person who seeks to be adopted can not presently have legally recognized parents. Adoptions of competent adults are subjected to less scrutiny than those involving children. But in cases in which adult homosexuals seek to create a legally recognized relationship between themselves by adoption, they may well fail since such relationships are generally not recognized.

What Form May Adoptions Take?

Adoption takes many forms: The adoptive parents may be related to the child by blood or marriage, they may have no legal relationship to the child, or the child may be adopted by the new spouse of her custodial parent. Adoptions may be contested by one or more parents or by a third party, or they may be uncontested. Adoptions may be transacted through a licensed child placement agency, by a state child welfare agency, or by private attorneys. Finally, they may be conducted legally or illegally ("baby selling"). Of course, many combinations of the above are possible. Because each has its own considerations we shall discuss each form individually.

Agency Adoptions

In an agency adoption, the birth parents relinquish legal custody of the child to the licensed adoption agency, which in turn ultimately places the child in a permanent adoptive home. Agency adoptions are permitted in all states. The agency screens potential adoptive parents and seeks to make the best possible match between parent and child. The screening process includes an investigation of the potential adoptive home. All members of the household are interviewed, as well as nonresident family members, neighbors, employers, etc. The home is visited and inspected to ensure a clean, healthy, and loving environment for the child.

The agency must secure the proper termination of parental rights, and pending final placement, the agency has the legal custody of the child. Physical custody may lie with the agency, foster parents, or (pending finalization of the adoption) the potential adoptive parents.

Frequently cited disadvantages of agency adoptions include the limited number of "desirable" or "adoptable" (healthy, infant, Caucasian) children available to be adopted, and the lengthy delays encountered by many prospective parents.

State Child Welfare Agency Adoptions

If a family is either unwilling or unable to properly care for their child, the state may seek to terminate all parental rights. The state child welfare agency will claim temporary custody of the child. It will then seek to place the child in a foster home until a permanent placement can be found.

Private Adoptions

In a private, or "independent," adoption, the birth parents transfer custody of the child directly to the adoptive parents. Due to the lower degree of regulation possible in a private adoption, the practice is not permitted in all states. Private placements are often sought by potential parents seeking to avoid the lengthy delays often found in agency adoptions. The role of the law office is more prominent in this form of adoption, since the attorney must attend to all the details otherwise handled by the agency in addition to shepherding the case through the legal process.

Disadvantages of private adoptions include the risk that the birth mother will not actually release the child to the adoptive parents; decreased privacy for the adoptive parents because the natural mother knows their identity; and a greater possibility that the child and adoptive parents will not be a suitable match due to the less stringent screening process employed.

Illegal Adoptions—"Baby Selling"

Illegal adoptions usually involve a mother releasing her child to adoptive parents for a fee. These transactions are commonly organized by an intermediary, who also collects a hefty fee for his services. While a surrogate may legally receive reimbursement of her reasonable medical expenses incurred in bearing a child, the fees paid in an illegal adoption are far more than "reasonable expenses." Thus, the term *baby selling* is an apt one. Many states require adoptive parents to file an affidavit detailing the expenses incurred. Accordingly, the paralegal should be certain to maintain adequate documentation of all payments made to the birth mother.

Remarriage and Adoption—Stepparent Adoptions

At one time, most adoptions involved the transfer of responsibility for a child from a married couple (or an unmarried woman) to another married couple. But many adoptions currently occur as a result of either a divorce and remarriage of the custodial birth parent or the marriage of a mother of an illegitimate child. In such cases, the child retains a legal relationship with one natural parent and is adopted by that natural parent's new spouse. While these adoptions still require the termination or release of the other parent's parental rights, if such an adoption is uncontested, courts are far less likely to subject a stepparent adoption to significant scrutiny.

Equitable Adoptions

Equitable adoption (also called *adoption by estoppel*) is something of a misnomer, because it is not really an adoption. Rather, it provides the "adopted" child only the right of inheritance from the "adoptive" parents. It typically occurs when, pursuant to a contract between the birth parents and the adoptive parents, a child is taken into the adoptive parents' home, where she is raised as their own child. But the contract is not completely fulfilled and the adoption is not finalized. Should the adoptive parents die intestate, the question of the child's right to inherit from the adoptive parents arises.

In some states, a court may find that the child's right to inherit should not be prejudiced because of the adoptive parents' failure to consummate the adoption process. Hence, the equitable adoption, where, for purposes of inheritance, the child is treated as though the adoption had been completed, and the estate is estopped from claiming that the child is not entitled to a claim for inheritance. Note that in other states, a child under identical circumstances would not be entitled to make a claim upon the parents' estate. In those jurisdictions, the courts have ruled that strict adherence to the statutory guidelines for adoption is required for such a child to make a valid claim for inheritance.

International Adoptions

The adoption of children born and residing outside the United States is possible via either agencies or private placement. But in such cases, care must be taken to ensure compliance with the laws of the United States and the birth country of the child, as well as with the rules of the U.S. Immigration and Naturalization Service. Additionally, such children must go through the naturalization process if they are to be U.S. citizens. And while not an international question, caution must be exercised when a Native American child is to be adopted by non–Native American parents. Many Native American tribes have tribal rules and rights.

ADOPTION PROCEDURE

An adoption must be filed in a court having the necessary subject matter jurisdiction. Depending on the state, that may be the court of general jurisdiction, such as a Superior or District Court, or a court of limited jurisdiction, such as a Family or Juvenile Court. The court selected must also have personal jurisdiction over the child to be adopted. While personal service of the petition to terminate the father's right to the child is always preferable, state law may permit service by publication. Venue is typically proper in the county of the residence of either the child or the adoptive parents. Adoption is typically commenced by a Petition for Adoption filed in the name of the child to be adopted, by the prospective parents or the adoption agency. A sample petition for adoption is at Exhibit 16–3. The birth parents must be afforded notice of the impending adoption, requiring formal service of the adoption petition upon the natural parents.

Once the petition is properly filed and served, an interlocutory order is entered scheduling a court hearing (at which time the adoption may be finalized) and granting the petitioners temporary custody of the child. At some time before the final order of the court is issued, a court-ordered home study takes place. This involves an investigation of the prospective home by a state agency. Barring unforeseen circumstances, at the time of the court hearing, the judge signs the final decree of adoption. A sample final decree of adoption is at Exhibit 16–4.

Interstate Compact on the Placement of Children

Any adoption (other than a stepparent or relative adoption) involving the movement of a child from one state to another must comply with the Interstate Compact on the Placement of Children (ICPC). All fifty states have adopted these rules. The ICPC prohibits the movement of a child to be adopted from his home state (the "sending state") to the adoptive parents' state of residence (the "receiving state") until permission has been received from the

EXHIBIT 16–3 PETITION FOR ADOPTION

IN THE SUPERIOR COURT OF _____ COUNTY

STATE OF _____

IN RE: ROBERT DALE MURCER, A MINOR CHILD

ARTHUR GIBBONS AND DOROTHY GIBBONS,
Petitioners.

CIVIL ACTION NO. _____

Petition for Adoption

COMES NOW, Arthur and Dorothy Gibbons, Petitioners in the above-referenced proceeding, and show the Court the following:

1.

That the above-referenced child is eligible for adoption and currently does not maintain a legal parent-child relationship.

2.

That all parties statutorily entitled to receive notice to this proceeding have been so notified.

3.

That the consents of all parties necessary to the adoption of this child have been obtained, and/or that documentation establishing the grounds for the involuntary termination of the father's parental rights are attached as exhibits to this petition.

4.

That the child was born in the State of _____ , County of _____ , on or about September 30, 1994.

5.

That as far as petitioners are able to ascertain, the child is the owner of or is entitled to personal property of the value of $10,000.00, and real property of the value is $0.00.

6.

That the petitioners were married to each other on or about February 19, 1989, in Brooklyn, New York, as evidenced by a certified copy of their marriage license, attached hereto as an exhibit to this petition.

7.

That the petitioners, and each of them, are fit to assume responsibility for the care, custody, supervision, education, and training of the child, and are financially able to provide for the child.

Because adoptions are not initiated as adversarial proceedings, they are not couched in terms of plaintiff v. defendant. In addition, in some states, the full name of the adoptee is not used; rather, the child is identified by his or her initials.

Compliance with due process requirement for notice to natural parents.

Allegation that the relationship between the adoptee and the birth parent(s) has been properly severed.

Allegation of the adoptee's property; courts will conduct further inquiry when child has significant assets to ensure that petitioners' desire to adopt the child is not based on the measure of the child's property.

Allegations that petitioners are married; some courts may require proof of the marriage (i.e., marriage license).

Allegation of the petitioners' fitness to adopt the child.

8.

That the petitioners are of the Jewish faith, and upon information and belief, the child is of the Jewish faith, as are his natural parents.

Allegation of the parties' religious beliefs.

9.

That the name by which the child will be known is Robert Dale Gibbons.

10.

No previous application has been made to any court for the relief sought herein.

Allegation that the instant case is the only such attempted proceeding; res judicata would prevent relitigation of a failed adoption.

WHEREFORE, Petitioners pray for an order:

a) approving the above petition for adoption;

b) directing that the child shall be treated in all respects as the natural child of the petitioners;

c) further directing that the name of the child shall be changed to Robert Dale Gibbons; and,

d) for all such other relief as deemed proper by this Court.

Respectfully submitted,

_____
Attorney
Address, City, State, ZIP
Telephone Number

VERIFICATION

We, Arthur and Dorothy Gibbons, having been duly sworn, declare that we have read the foregoing Petition for Adoption, and state under oath that the facts contained therein are all true and correct.

All allegations are presented under oath by the petitioners.

_____
Arthur Gibbons

_____
Dorothy Gibbons

Sworn to and subscribed before me this___ day of_____ , 199___ .

Sworn to and subscribed before me this___ day of_____ , 199___ .

Notary Public_____
My commission expires_____

Notary Public _____
My commission expires _____

EXHIBIT 16–4   FINAL DECREE OF ADOPTION

IN THE SUPERIOR COURT OF_____ COUNTY
STATE OF_____

IN RE: THE ADOPTION OF ROBERT DALE MURCER, A MINOR CHILD

ARTHUR GIBBONS AND DOROTHY GIBBONS,
Petitioners.

CIVIL ACTION NO. _____

Final Decree of Adoption

This Court, after hearing evidence and otherwise considering the pleadings, makes the following order and Decree of Adoption:

1.

That the Petition was properly filed in the Superior Court of_____County, and the Petition for Adoption was in the form required by law.

2.

The petitioners, Arthur and Dorothy Gibbons, are qualified to petition for adoption and are fit to assume the responsibility for the care, custody, supervision, education, and training of the child, and are financially able to provide for the child.

3.

The child, Robert Dale Murcer, is the owner of or is entitled to personal property of the value of $10,000.00, and real property of the value of $0.00.

4.

The natural mother of the child, Maureen Anna Murcer, has surrendered her rights to the child in accordance with state law.

The natural father of the child, James T. Garvey, has not surrendered his rights to the child, but has abandoned the child and has significantly failed to communicate with and/or provide support for the child for more than twelve (12) consecutive months prior to the filing of the petition for adoption.

5.

The adoption is in the best interests of the child.

6.

All formalities, including service, notice, surrender, and termination have been complied with in accordance with state law.

ACCORDINGLY, IT IS DECREED that the adoption of Robert Dale Murcer by the Petitioners in this cause be and is hereby made permanent. The parent-child relationship between the natural parents and the child is hereby terminated, and a new parent-child relationship is hereby created between the Petitioners and the child.

IT IS FURTHER DECREED that the name of the child shall be Robert Dale
Gibbons henceforth, and that a new birth certificate be issued incorporating the
new information resulting from this adoption.

SO DECREED, this ___ day of _____ , 199___ .

Judge, _____ Superior Court

receiving state for the entry of that child. Accordingly, it is critical that provisions of the ICPC be satisfied as soon as possible. Otherwise, the adoptive parents will not be permitted to bring the child home.

Therefore, in an interstate adoption, the appropriate ICPC forms must be completed and filed with the ICPC Administrator of the sending state. This person typically works for the state child welfare agency. The ICPC Administrator then forwards the forms to the ICPC Administrator of the receiving state. The receiving state Administrator then makes arrangements for an investigation (home study) of the prospective adoptive family's home. If satisfied that a suitable environment exists for the child, the ICPC Administrator of the receiving state notifies the ICPC Administrator of the sending state that approval for the entry of the child in that state has been granted.

OTHER ADOPTION CONSIDERATIONS

There are several collateral issues regarding adoption which require a brief discussion.

Confidentiality

The traditional view has held that once finalized, all adoption records were permanently sealed, thus effectively preventing the adoptee from discovering the identity of her birth parents. The rationale for this confidentiality includes the privacy rights of the birth mother and the fear (unfounded or not) of the adoptive parents that any contact with the birth parents would threaten their relationship with their child. To ensure that this veil of privacy remains intact, concurrent with the order for adoption, the court also orders that the child's birth certificate be changed to incorporate the changes effected by the adoption.

While the traditional view still prevails, courts and legislatures in several states have opened small cracks in this once impenetrable wall. One of these cracks is an exception for medical reasons; for example, where the adoptee requires information about any diseases or medical conditions that might be hereditary in her family (i.e., diabetes, high blood pressure, allergies, etc.). The records could also be accessed if the adoptee required a transplant of an organ, bone marrow, etc. from a close blood relative. Finally, this exception also applies when the now-adult adopted child has children of her own and requires such information. Note that there is no exception for the adult adoptee who seeks to find her roots or to ease her emotional anguish.

Open Adoption

The other exceptions to confidentiality requirements result from the consent of the birth parent(s) to meet the adoptee. One such exception is the so-called open adoption, a private adoption in which the birth parents meet the adoptive parents and relinquish the child to them in a ceremony celebrating the adoption. In such adoptions, the birth parents often remain in contact with the adoptive parents and the child. Another exception can be found in "adoption registries," state agencies that permit adoptees to attempt contact with their natural parents. The procedure used allows the adoptee to contact the adoption registry, which in turn attempts contact with one or both of the birth parents. If the birth parent consents to meet with the adoptee, the necessary arrangements are made. If the birth parent refuses, no further contact is made. These "adoption registries" may also be used by adoptees to locate their siblings. Adoption registries are available in several states including California, Colorado, Florida, and Georgia.

Effect of Adoption

With the finalization of the adoption, the relationship between the child and her adoptive parents is identical to that between a child and her natural parents. Among the items the adopted child is entitled to receive from her new parents are the adopted parents' surname, financial and emotional support, and inheritance rights. In addition, if an adoptive parent is injured or killed through the negligence of a third party or a work-related incident, the adopted child is entitled to claim damages as would a natural child. Note that in some states, however, an adopted child is not entitled to claim a statutory share if an adopted parent dies intestate (without a valid will).

ARTIFICIAL REPRODUCTION

artificial reproduction
The general term for all medical procedures by which a child is conceived.

It has been estimated that as many as 10 to 20 percent of couples of child-bearing age are unable to conceive and bring a child to term. Adoption was once the only solution available to such couples. But today there is a shortage of "adoptable" children, and the wait to adopt can be long. The good news is that science and technology have in a few short years turned science fiction into fact. **Artificial reproduction** has significantly increased the options for childless couples. The bad news is that the law has not always kept up with the latest medical developments. Accordingly, this is an area of the law subject to constant change and modification. The primary issue raised by the advances in scientifically assisted reproduction is, who is the legal parent of the child so produced? The candidates include those with a genetic connection with the child (the donors of the ovum and sperm), the spouses of the donors, and the woman who actually bore the child. Be aware that absolutes are few and far between in this field, and today's precedent may tomorrow be a foot-note in history. In the following sections, we consider the various methods of artificial reproduction.

Artificial Insemination

Artificial insemination is a medical procedure through which a woman's ovum is fertilized by sperm directly inserted into the woman by artificial means. There are two types of artificial insemination:

— Artificial insemination homologous (AIH), in which the sperm is that of the woman's husband or partner

— Artificial insemination donor (AID), in which the sperm is that of a man other than the woman's husband or partner (The sperm is usually obtained from a sperm bank.)

Historically, the child born of a union with an AID donor was consid-ered a bastard. Today it is widely accepted that when the husband gives his informed consent to the procedure, a child of artificial insemination is legiti-mate and the husband is legally treated as the child's father. Under these cir-cumstances, the sperm donor has neither any obligations nor any rights to the child, the child is treated as legitimate from birth, and no adoption is neces-sary. If the mother is not married, then there is no presumptive father. If the donor is known, he may attempt to assert his parental rights; it is not certain what rights, if any, an anonymous donor might have.

In Vitro Fertilization

Unlike artificial insemination, **in vitro fertilization** is a process in which the sperm and ovum are brought together outside of the woman's body. The fer-tilized egg, or "zygote," is then implanted into either the donor of the ovum or into a surrogate, who will carry the so-called test-tube baby to term. The ovum may be that of the birth mother or it may be that of a surrogate; the sperm may be that of the husband or of a third-party donor.

Where the birth mother and her husband contribute the ovum and sperm, they are accepted as the natural parents of the child. Where a third party has contributed either the ovum or sperm, the issue is not settled quite so easily. If a man other than the mother's husband supplies the sperm, the offspring is treated as one conceived through AID. If the mother's fertilized zygote is implanted in the uterus of another woman, a full and complete release of all parental rights should be obtained from the child bearer. But today it is uncertain what effect a court would give such a release, and it may still be possible for the child bearer to make a claim to the child.

In Vivo Fertilization

In vivo fertilization is a medical procedure in which a woman is impregnated via artificial insemination, followed by a "lavage" (the introduction of a spe-

artificial insemination
The medical proce-dure by which a woman is impregnat-ed through artificial means.

in vitro fertilization
A medical process in which the sperm and ovum are brought together outside of the woman's body, and then implanted in the uterus.

in vivo fertilization
A medical procedure in which a woman is impregnated via artifi-cial insemination. The zygote is later implanted in the uterus of a second woman.

cial fluid into the uterus, by catheter, which carries the embryo, not yet attached to the uterine wall, into the catheter). Five days later, the zygote is implanted in the uterus of another woman, where it usually attaches itself to the uterine wall. The recipient then carries the embryo to term. This procedure is relatively new and has produced little case law.

Surrogate Mothers

Pursuant to express agreement, a surrogate mother is artificially impregnated with the sperm of either the husband of an infertile woman or of a third-party donor. The agreement and the surrogate's release of all parental rights is typically obtained prior to conception. The child is the genetic offspring of the surrogate and the father. The surrogate carries the embryo to term, and upon the birth of the child, is supposed to relinquish all rights and claims to the child in favor of the parent(s) who have sought the child. The operative phrase here is "supposed to." *If* the surrogate honors the contract and renounces all rights to the child, then the wife of the father may formally adopt the child. But if the surrogate renounces the contract, the legal consequences are less certain. Because a child conceived via a surrogate mother is essentially a child born out of wedlock, both parents have equal claim to the child.

surrogacy
A process in which one woman bears a child for another woman. The child may or may not be biologically related to either woman.

Many states are loathe to enforce a **surrogacy** contract against a reluctant birth mother, especially where the surrogate signed the release before the birth of the child. (Such agreements may have the appearance of "baby selling.") Effectively, the surrogate then has the option of contesting custody of the child at any time prior to the finalization of the adoption by the father's wife. It is highly unlikely at this time that a court will enforce a surrogacy contract in favor of terminating the surrogate's parental rights when she has a genetic connection with the child.

The best-known case on this point remains *In re: Baby M*, 109 N.J. 396, 537 A.2d 1227 (N.J.1988), in which a surrogate claimed custody of the child artificially conceived with the sperm of a husband of an infertile wife. The married couple, unable to bear their own child, had contracted with the surrogate to carry the husband's child. The court awarded custody of the child to the husband, but acknowledged the surrogate's parental rights and granted the surrogate visitation privileges.

REPRODUCTIVE RIGHTS

abortion
A medical procedure intended to terminate pregnancy.

Few, if any, topics of interest today are as emotionally charged as abortion. For purposes of this discussion, **abortion** is defined as a medical procedure that causes the termination of pregnancy. It is commonly believed that modern abortion law began with *Roe v. Wade*, 410 U.S. 113, 93 S.Ct. 705, 35 L.Ed.2d 147 (1973). But *Roe v. Wade* is really an extension of legal reasoning that began with *Griswold v. Connecticut*, 381 U.S. 479, 85 S.Ct. 1678, 14 L.Ed.2d 510 (1965). *Griswold* held that the state could not prohibit a married couple from using contraceptives. The United States Supreme Court held

DOE
v.
ATTORNEY GENERAL

Court of Appeals of Michigan.
Decided June 1, 1992.

. . . .

Before HOLBROOK, P.J., and MURPHY and JANSEN, JJ.

HOLBROOK, Presiding Judge.

In this action for a declaratory interpretation of the Surrogate Parenting Act, M.C.L. §722.851 et seq.; M.S.A. §25.248(151) et seq., plaintiffs appeal as of right from an order of the Wayne Circuit Court granting defendant's motion for summary disposition for failure to state a claim. We affirm in part and reverse in part.

Plaintiffs are infertile couples and prospective surrogate mothers. In their suit, filed on August 4, 1988, plaintiffs assert that if the Surrogate Parenting Act were interpreted as being an outright ban on surrogacy contracts for pay, the statute would deny them their constitutionally protected privacy rights and would offend the Due Process and Equal Protection Clauses of the state and federal constitutions. Plaintiffs maintain that, to avoid unconstitutionality, the statute must be read as permitting such contracts as long as payment to the birth mother is not contingent upon the relinquishment of her parental rights.

In response to plaintiffs' motion for a preliminary injunction, defendant moved for summary disposition for failure to state a claim. At the hearing on the motions, counsel for plaintiffs stated on the record that if the court were to interpret the statute in accordance with defendant's interpretation, plaintiffs would be satisfied with regard to the constitutionality of the statute. Upon this representation, the trial court found the statute to be constitutional and stated that it would issue a declaratory judgment within sixty days.

On October 4, 1988, defendant moved for reconsideration of the court's oral ruling that a declaratory opinion was to follow, arguing that in light of the agreement of plaintiffs and defendant with regard to the controlling issue, there was no longer a case or controversy and the court had no jurisdiction. Plaintiffs' response, in essence, was that it had become clear that the alleged agreement was a misunderstanding and controversy remained. In an opinion and order issued on November 9, 1988, the court held that the statute prohibited surrogacy contracts where the surrogate mother receives compensation and agrees to voluntarily relinquish her parental rights. The court held that it was still permissible to enter into a surrogacy contract where no compensation, other than medical expenses, is paid to the mother. The court then went on to rule that because the parties were in agreement concerning the constitutionality of the statute, there was no actual controversy.

Plaintiffs' subsequent motion for reconsideration was denied, and this appeal followed.

. . . .

. . . Plaintiffs' contend that the statute violates the due process guarantee of freedom from government interference in matters of marriage, family, procreation, and intimate association. They maintain that the state has no compelling interest in intervening in this conduct. We disagree.

We agree with plaintiffs that the Due Process Clauses of the state and federal constitutions, together with the penumbral rights emanating from the specific guarantees of the Bill of Rights, protect "individual decisions in matters of childbearing from unjustified intrusion by the State." (Citation omitted.) Government can, however, justify the abridgment of a fundamental right by demonstrating that a countervailing compelling state interest is thereby promoted and that the means are closely tailored to the end sought to be achieved. (Citation omitted.)

The question before us, then, is, Did the Legislature have a compelling government interest sufficient to justify intrusion into plaintiffs' right to procreate in the surrogacy context? We answer that question in the affirmative.

The first interest is that of preventing children from becoming mere commodities.

As overwhelmingly repugnant as the thought may be, unbridled surrogacy for profit could encourage the treatment of babies as commodities. Whatever sense of idealism that may motivate a fertile woman into hosting a pregnancy for an infertile couple is rent asunder by the introduction of the profit motive. It could be only a matter of time before desirable, healthy babies would come to be "viewed quantitatively, as merchandise that can be acquired, at market or discount rates." (Citation omitted.) As the New Jersey Supreme Court commented in *In re Baby M*, (citation omitted): "In a

324 Chapter 16 Adoption

civilized society, there are some things that money should not be able to buy." In our opinion, babies ought to be one of those things.

The best interest of the child is also an interest that is sufficiently compelling to justify government intrusion.

Surrogacy arrangements focus exclusively on the parents' desires and interests, and, accordingly, the parties are apt to be insensitive to what would be in the children's best interests. That position is in direct opposition to the child custody law in this state, the guiding principle of which is the best interests of the child. (Citations omitted.)

As the New Jersey Supreme Court in *Baby M* (citation omitted) commented: "The long-term effects of surrogacy contracts are unknown, but feared." It is almost impossible to imagine the emotional anguish that could result to children who learn that they, in effect, were bought and paid for and that their mothers gave birth as a means of obtaining money.

The long-term effects are by no means limited to the emotional trauma that might result from knowing of the purchase and sale aspect of one's birth. The custody battles that in all likelihood will occur where one of the parties to a surrogacy contract has a change of heart, no doubt, will inflict grievous wounds upon the child regardless of who prevails.

A third compelling state interest is that of preventing the exploitation of women.

Surrogacy-for-profit arrangements have the potential for demeaning women by reducing them to the status of "breeding machines." The plaintiffs before us validate this fear with their argument that the compensation given surrogate mothers is to be looked upon as compensation for their "gestation services" only.

Surrogacy contracts, no matter how they are cast, contemplate, indeed logically dictate, that there be no connection between the birth mother and the baby after the delivery. Were surrogacy contracts to be validated, every surrogate mother would soon be cast in the role of an "unfeeling, emotionless machine whose purpose is to create a life and then disappear." (Citation omitted.)

The potential for such exploitation is much broader than being just gender-based, it is economic-based as well. Women in the lower economic strata could well become "breeding machines" for infertile couples of the upper economic brackets. Accordingly, it is the surrogate who bears the brunt of the contractual obligations, for it is her health that is at risk and her conduct

that is restricted. The contracting couple, on the other hand, need to supply only the sperm and the compensation. While the surrogate endures the nine-month gestation period and all the attendant physical burdens and risks, the contracting couple are free to go about their lives, anticipating the delivery of their baby.

This is not to say that all surrogate mothers will feel exploited; we can conceive of instances where the surrogate may derive a great deal of satisfaction from being able to assist an infertile couple in having a child. The fact remains, however, that there is a danger of women being exploited by these surrogacy-for-profit arrangements, and the protection of women from that danger warrant government intrusion.

Having thus concluded that there are compelling interests sufficient to warrant governmental intrusion into the otherwise protected area of privacy in the matter of procreation, we next address plaintiffs' argument that the statute is so vague and indefinite in meaning that it is incapable of giving fair warning of what conduct is prohibited by the statute.

A statute may be challenged for vagueness on three grounds: (1) it does not provide fair notice of the conduct proscribed; (2) it confers on the trier of fact unstructured and unlimited discretion to determine whether an offense has been committed; and (3) its coverage is overly broad and impinges on First Amendment freedoms. (Citations omitted.)

In testing a statute for vagueness, a court should give the words of the statute their ordinary meaning. (Citations omitted.)

Plaintiffs' argument focuses on the use of the conjunctive "and" in the definition of "surrogate parentage contract" found M.C.L. §722.853(i); M.S.A. §25.248(153)(i). Plaintiffs maintain that the phrase "and to voluntarily relinquish her parental rights to the child" means that only those arrangements that link conception and surrogate gestation services to the relinquishment of parental rights are prohibited. The plaintiffs assign error to the trial court's interpretation that the act prohibits all arrangements where surrogacy is undertaken for compensation.

We affirm the lower court's ruling to the extent it holds that the Legislature intended to make void and unenforceable those arrangements that provide both for conception or surrogate gestation services and for the relinquishment of parental rights. The statutory language clearly defines "a surrogate parentage contract" as consisting of two elements: (1) conception, through either natural or artificial insemination, of, or surrogate gestation by a female and (2) her voluntary relinquishment of her parental rights to the child (footnote omitted). Only a contract, agreement, or arrangement combining these two elements constitutes a "surrogate parentage contract" that is void and unenforceable under the act (footnote omitted).

Section 9 of the act provides that a "surrogate parentage contract" for compensation is unlawful and prohibited (footnote omitted). Hence, a contract, agreement, or arrangement providing compensation solely for conception or surrogate gestation services is not unlawful and prohibited, because the element of "relinquishment of parental rights" is lacking.

We therefore reverse that portion of the lower court's ruling that holds that all surrogate arrangements for compensation are unlawful. Such a reading of the statute is a strained one, because it overlooks the linkage of the elements required to qualify a surrogate arrangement as a "surrogate parentage contract." Our role is to interpret the act as written by the Legislature and to give effect to the legislative intent as expressed in the language of the act. If the Legislature intended to prohibit surrogate contracts solely on the basis of the existence of compensation for conception or surrogate gestation services, it failed to do so.

To summarize, we hold:

(1) A surrogate parentage contract is void and unenforceable under §5;

(2) A surrogate parentage contract entered into for compensation is unlawful and prohibited by §9;

(3) For a surrogate parentage contract to exist there must be present the elements of (1) conception, through either natural or artificial insemination, of, or surrogate gestation by a female and (2) the voluntary relinquishment of her parental rights to the child; and

(4) A contract, agreement, or arrangement that does not contain both elements set forth in (3) above is neither void and unenforceable under §5 nor unlawful and prohibited by §9, even when entered into for compensation (footnote omitted).

Lastly, plaintiffs argue that because the state permits surrogacy-for-compensation arrangements where the husband is infertile, the state may not, consistent with equal protection, make it a criminal offense for a married couple, where the wife is infertile, to enter into a surrogacy arrangement that provides for the payment of compensation to the surrogate for conception or surrogate gestation services. Given our holding that the act does not prohibit surrogate contracts that provide compensation solely for conception or surrogate gestation services, there is no need to reach plaintiffs' equal protection argument.

We note that the Legislature has recently passed amendatory language that creates a presumption that every surrogacy contract includes a provision that the surrogate agrees to relinquish her parental rights. 1990 P.A. 190 amends §3(i) of the act to read:

"Surrogate parentage contract" means a contract, agreement, or arrangement in which a female agrees to conceive a child through natural or artificial insemination, or in which a female agrees to surrogate gestation, and to voluntarily relinquish her parental or *custodial* rights to the child. *It is presumed that a contract, agreement, or arrangement in which a female agrees to conceive a child through natural or artificial insemination by a person other than her husband, or in which a female agrees to surrogate gestation, includes a provision, whether or not express, that the female will relinquish her parental or custodial rights to the child.* [Amendatory language emphasized.]

Obviously, we do not render an opinion concerning the effect of this amendatory language, and nothing in this opinion should be read or construed as doing so.

Affirmed in part and reversed in part.

DISCUSSION QUESTIONS

Based on the preceding case of *Doe v. Attorney General*, 194 Mich. App. 432, 487 N.W.2d 484 (Mich. 1992), answer the following questions:

1. What is the effect of this case on the validity of surrogacy contracts in Michigan?

2. Are there any circumstances under which residents of Michigan may now enter into a contract for surrogacy, and if so, what are they?

that the Bill of Rights to the U.S. Constitution guarantees personal privacy and creates a penumbra, or zone, or privacy. Thus, the concept of privacy was created and the foundation was laid for *Roe v. Wade.*

Roe v. Wade

Prior to 1973, abortion was permitted only when the health of the woman made it a medical necessity. *Roe v. Wade* established the extent to which a state could restrict a woman's right to an abortion. This was accomplished by propounding a trimester approach to the termination of pregnancy.

— In the *first trimester,* the decision whether to have an abortion is left entirely to the discretion of the individual woman and her physician. The Court's rationale was that at this early stage of pregnancy, the mortality rate for women having abortions is lower than for women having full-term pregnancies. Thus, the state does not have a compelling reason to regulate abortion.

— In the *second trimester,* the state may regulate abortion procedures only for the purposes of protecting the pregnant woman's health. For example, a state could require that abortions occur in hospitals, as opposed to clinics.

— In the *third trimester,* the state is permitted to regulate, or prohibit, abortion, except when the life or health of the woman requires an abortion. The Court held that during this last trimester, the fetus became **viable** (capable of living apart from its mother) and accordingly, the state has a compelling interest in protecting the fetus.

viability
The ability of a fetus to live outside the uterus.

The Court reasoned that as the fetus develops during the pregnancy, so should a state's ability to regulate, or even abolish, abortion. *Roe v. Wade* did not end the abortion debate. Many subsequent cases have further defined this area of law:

— A married woman does not have to obtain her husband's permission for an abortion.

— A state is not required to provide public funding for abortions that are not required to protect the life or health of the mother (nontherapeutic abortions).

Recent Abortion Cases

Two relatively recent abortion cases also merit discussion.

— Webster v. Reproductive Health Services, 492 U.S. 490, 109 S.Ct. 3040, 106 L.Ed.2d 410 (1989). *Webster* shook the foundations laid by *Roe v. Wade* in a number of ways. First, the Supreme Court appeared to move away from the strict trimester approach of *Roe v. Wade.* The Supreme Court held that it would consider state regulations of abortion on a case-by-case basis, and that all such regulations are not necessarily unconstitutional.

— Planned Parenthood of Southeastern Pennsylvania v. Casey, ___ U.S. ___, 112 S.Ct. 2791, 120 L.Ed.2d 674 (1992). After the *Webster* decision, Pennsylvania enacted laws that limited nontherapeutic abortions to the first 24 weeks of pregnancy; required physicians to inform patients about the physical and emotional consequences of abortion, the availability of adoption services, and child support; required a 24-hour waiting period between the receipt of this information and the effectuation of the abortion; established reporting and public disclosure regulations for physicians; required that minors obtain parental consent before an abortion; and required that wives give their husbands notice before an abortion. The United States Supreme Court issued a plurality decision in which it reaffirmed the right to the woman to choose to have an abortion before viability and to obtain it without undue influence from the State. It also upheld all of the challenged provisions except the requirement that a wife notify her husband before obtaining an abortion.

INTERVIEW CHECKLIST

Checklist for Adoptive Parents

	Father	Mother
Hair color	_____	_____
Eye color	_____	_____
Height	_____	_____
Weight	_____	_____
Complexion	_____	_____
Age	_____	_____
National ancestry	_____	_____
Religion	_____	_____
Occupation	_____	_____
Social Security No.	_____	_____
College attended/years	_____	_____

Degree awarded _____ _____

Advanced degrees _____ _____

State the date and place of your marriage.

_____

Has either spouse ever filed for divorce or separation of this marriage? _____ If so, provide details.

_____

State the name and age of any children living in your household.

Were any such children adopted? _____ If so, state where and when.

_____

Does any member of the household have any health problems?

If so, provide details.

_____

continued on page 328

continued from page 327

What is the average household income for the last three years?_____ From what sources is it derived?

_____

Do you own or rent your residence? _____
Monthly cost?

_____

If you own your own home, what is the amount of equity?

_____

How many bedrooms does your residence have?

_____

How many automobiles are owned by your household?

_____

State the amount of all savings, excluding pension and retirement accounts. _____ State your net worth.

_____

Has either petitioner ever been married before?

_____

If yes, state the full name of former spouse, date and place of marriage, the names of any children born as issue of that marriage, and the reasons and date of the termination of the marriage.

_____

_____

Has either petitioner ever filed for bankruptcy?

_____

If so, provide details.

_____

Has either petitioner been institutionalized in a mental hospital or undergone psychological treatment?_____ If so, provide details.

_____

Has either spouse ever been arrested? If so, provide details.

_____

Has either spouse ever been turned down by an adoption agency? _____ If so, provide details.

_____

Has either spouse ever placed a child for adoption?

_____

If so, provide details.

_____

Do you have preference as to the gender, race, religion, and/or national ancestry of the child?_____
_____ If so, would you insist on such preferences?

_____

Would you be willing to meet with the natural parents?

_____

Checklist for Birth Parents

	Birth Mother	Birth Father
Hair color	_____	_____
Eye color	_____	_____
Height	_____	_____
Weight	_____	_____
Complexion	_____	_____
Age	_____	_____
National ancestry	_____	_____
Religion	_____	_____
Occupation	_____	_____
Social Security No.	_____	_____
College attended/years	_____	_____

continued on page 329

continued from page 328

Degree
awarded   _____   _____

Advanced
degrees   _____   _____

Health
problems   _____   _____

Allergies   _____   _____

Aptitudes   _____   _____

Indicate whether any of the birth parents or your
blood relatives have ever had any of the following
conditions:

Muscular dystrophy   _____

Multiple sclerosis   _____

Cerebral palsy   _____

Epilepsy   _____

Cystic fibrosis   _____

Parkinson's disease   _____

Tuberculosis   _____

Cancer   _____

Heart attack   _____

Stroke   _____

Hypertension   _____

Angina   _____

Blindness   _____

Deafness   _____

Asthma   _____

Hay fever   _____

Hemophilia   _____

Leukemia   _____

Sickle cell disease   _____

Tay-Sachs disease   _____

Speech problems   _____

Learning difficulties _____

Mental retardation   _____

Spina bifida   _____

Schizophrenia   _____

Mental illness   _____

Have the birth parents ever been married to each
other? _____ If yes, provide details.

_____

Has either birth parent ever used any illegal drugs?
If yes, provide details.

_____

Does either parent (   ) drink alcohol socially
(   ) have a drinking problem (   ) not drink alcohol? Provide details.

_____

Does the birth mother smoke cigarettes?_____
If yes, when did you start, how many cigarettes do
you smoke each day, and did you continue to
smoke during the pregnancy?

_____

List the employment history of both parents.

_____

_____

What is the child's (anticipated) birthdate?

_____

Name and address of your obstetrician.

_____

Name and address of the child's doctor.

_____

continued on page 330

continued from page 329

Where was (or will) the child be delivered?

_____

If child is not a newborn when relinquished, state the place, date, and exact time of child's birth.

_____

If child is not a newborn when relinquished, describe child's health and level of development.

_____

Describe the ideal parents for your child.

_____

Do you have a religious preference for your child?

_____ If yes, state your preference.

_____

Do you want to meet the adoptive parents?

_____

Would you refuse to meet the adoptive parents?

_____

Are you willing to place your names in a registry that would allow your child to meet you someday in the future?

_____

REVIEW QUESTIONS

1. How may a court terminate the parental rights of a parent who does not voluntarily waive parental rights?

2. How do courts consider the race and religion of the child and prospective parents in the adoptive process?

3. What is the difference between artificial insemination homologous and artificial insemination donor?

4. How do the rights, relating to a child artificially conceived, of a surrogate differ from those of a donor of a sperm or an ovum?

5. How does in vitro fertilization differ from in vivo fertilization?

6. What is an equitable adoption? Provide an example of an equitable adoption.

7. How do agency adoptions differ from private adoptions in procedure?

8. What rights does a putative father have when his child is the subject of an adoption proceeding? How do these rights vary given the nature of the putative father's relationship with the child?

9. What is the Interstate Compact on the Placement of Children and what purpose does it seek to accomplish?

10. In the following forms of artificial reproduction, what parts of the reproductive process are contributed by a third party?

    a) artificial insemination donor

    b) in vitro fertilization

    c) in vivo fertilization

    d) surrogacy

KEY TERMS

abortion
adoption
artificial insemination
artificial reproduction
in vitro fertilization
in vivo fertilization
surrogacy
viability

STATE RESEARCH PROBLEMS

Review the laws of your state and answer the following questions:

1. What are the prerequisites for a valid waiver of parental rights and consent to adoption? Under what conditions, if any, may the consent so given be withdrawn? Under what circumstances, if any, may a parent have his or her parental rights terminated by a court?

2. Are there any prerequisites to adoption? If so, what are they? May adults be adopted? If so, detail any specific circumstances under which adult adoption would not be permitted.

3. Are private adoptions permitted? If so, are there any restrictions regarding their use?

4. Are adult adoptees permitted to contact their natural parents? If so, under what circumstances may the identity of the natural parents be revealed?

PRACTICE EXERCISES

1. Contact a local adoption agency and request a copy of the questionnaire they use. Ask them how long the wait is to adopt a newborn child. What is the waiting period to adopt a five-year-old child?

2. Based on the case of *Doe v. Attorney General*, assume that all parties had agreed upon the terms of adoption. What documents would have to be prepared? Draft the necessary documents.

Appendix A
Family Law Legal Research

Your education in the law is not designed to provide you with all of the answers to all of the questions you will encounter during your career. Rather, the goals are to train you 1) to ask the right questions at the right time and 2) to find the right answers. The ability to ask the right questions has been emphasized throughout the text. Generally, although the questions remain the same from state to state, the answers may differ considerably. This appendix concerns finding the right answers to your questions in your jurisdiction.

Remember that this is not a legal research textbook, and that what follows is not a substitute for the study of legal research. Rather, this appendix is intended to demonstrate how the basic concepts of legal research specifically apply to family law and to highlight certain points of legal research unique to family law.

BACKGROUND SOURCES

Before you can find the right answer, you must be certain that you are asking the right question. Accordingly, you must have a full understanding of the subject area of the law you wish to research. A background source is a legal research tool that provides a general overview of an area of the law. It is also referred to as secondary authority, because it is a compilation of various cases and statutes. The original cases and statutes referred to in the background source are called primary authority. For example, this text is a background source on the topic of family law. You would not use this book as authority for a claim of what the law is on a particular topic.

A background source affords the researcher a broad overview of the topic and helps the researcher determine what precise questions require further research. Following are some examples of background sources applicable to family law.

Legal Encyclopedias

Legal encyclopedias can be further divided into national encyclopedias and state encyclopedias. National encyclopedias include *Corpus Juris Secundum* (CJS) and *American Jurisprudence*, 2d (Am. Jur.2d). These are arranged just like the traditional encyclopedias we all used in grade school: The law is divided into various topics and arranged in alphabetical order. Each topic is then further divided into a series of shorter subtopics. Both encyclopedias are updated annually by pocket parts.

Here are some topics in CJS that most directly relate to the subject of family law:

— Abortion and Birth Control
— Adoption
— Adultery
— Bigamy
— Breach of Marriage Promise
— Children Out of Wedlock
— Divorce
— Husband and Wife
— Incest
— Marriage
— Parent and Child

Additionally, many states have their own encyclopedias, which document only the law of that particular state. If your state has an encyclopedia, you may find it preferable to a national one because it provides the law of your jurisdiction.

American Law Reports (ALR)

The ALR is a series of annotations, or articles, that discuss precise questions of law in great detail. In this regard, using ALR is an all-or-nothing proposition—you may not find an annotation on the topic you are researching. But if you do find an annotation, you will probably find an exhaustive discussion of all the relevant case law and statutes in all of the states that have addressed that question. It is updated by pocket parts that are published annually.

Form Books

See discussion at the end of this appendix.

Legal Periodicals

Numerous magazines, newsletters, and law reviews provide a good source of background material. A major advantage of these periodicals is the speed with which they can report on the impact of a new statute or of a new trend in the law. Here are some of the different types of periodicals:

— *Law Reviews*. These are scholarly magazines usually published or sponsored by law schools. Typically, the articles contained in these reviews comment on current trends in the law or speculate as to what direction the law may next take. While most law reviews cover all areas of the law, a few choose to specialize in one specific area. Examples of law reviews that specialize in family law are the *Journal of Family Law* and the *Family Law Quarterly*.

— *Bar section magazines and newsletters.* State and national bar associations maintain specialized subgroups (sections). For example, many attorneys who specialize in family law choose to join the Family Law section of their bar associations. These sections may publish magazines and newsletters that provide practical day-to-day advice on topics of interest to family law practitioners. For example, the American Bar Association Family Law Section publishes *The Family Advocate.*

— *Other periodicals.* There are several newsletters that may be of value in a family law office. *Fair$hare* emphasizes the tax and financial consequences of divorce. *The Matrimonial Strategist* offers up-to-the-minute advice on the latest trends in family law. Additionally, *The Practical Lawyer,* while addressing all fields of the law, often has practical articles concerning family law.

Hornbooks and Treatises

A hornbook is a book that presents a summary of the law in a specific area of the law. Hornbooks are national in scope. The leading hornbook in the area of family law is *The Law of Domestic Relations,* by H. Clark (published by West Publishing Company). A treatise is also a summary of a single area of the law, but it differs from a hornbook in several ways. While hornbooks are more like traditional textbooks, treatises are more practical in their orientation. For example, a treatise is often published in looseleaf form so that it can be updated simply by adding and deleting new pages as the law changes. It also usually contains sample forms that a researcher can adapt.

STATUTORY RESOURCES

Family law is almost completely controlled by the laws of the individual states. Federal law applies in only a very few specific areas, that is, federal taxation, parental kidnapping, and issues concerning the United States Constitution (due process, equal protection, etc.). This greatly simplifies your research because you can practically ignore the federal portion of your law library.

Family law can generally be found in one or two volumes of your state code. Open the first volume on family law in your state code and look at the subtopics listed.

The law exists not in a single statute but in a series of statutes. This series of statutes is called a statutory scheme. The law is similar to a novel, each statute adding another wrinkle to the story. Just as you cannot get a clear picture of a novel by reading a single paragraph, you cannot get a clear picture of the law in a particular area by reading a single statute. Many times a general rule is stated in one statute, and the exceptions or defenses are stated in one or more other statutes. This means that when you find a statute that you believe answers your question, you cannot stop your research just yet. You must continue researching the question until you have the complete statutory scheme.

Many of the questions you will be researching will be procedural questions (How is a complaint for divorce served? When can discovery commence? What are the requirements for a valid notice of appeal?). These questions and more are usually answered with a statutory scheme that contains a set of prerequisites that must be satisfied before the desired result can be obtained. For example:

Question: What are the requirements for a valid marriage in Georgia?
Answer: Official Code of Georgia Annotated (O.C.G.A.) 19–3–1 states:

To constitute a valid marriage in this state there must be:
1) Parties able to contract;
2) An actual contract; and
3) Consummation according to law

But appearances to the contrary, this single statute does *not* answer the question completely. Consider:

— O.C.G.A. 19–3–2 details the prerequisites to be able to contract for marriage (age, health, etc.).
— O.C.G.A. 19–3–3 details those family relationships in which persons may not marry.
— O.C.G.A. 19–3–4 details the nature of the consent that a person must give to marry.

As you can see, the answer to the example question, and to most legal questions, is not found within the confines of a single statute. Always seek out the statutory scheme.

FOCUS ON USING AN INDEX

State codes, like all other legal reference tools, are indexed according to topic. But the same topic may be indexed differently by different publishers of different resources. For example, one reference source may list divorce under "Divorce," which seems easy enough. Others, however, may list divorce under "Family Law" or "Domestic Relations" or "Marriage, Termination of" or "Matrimonial Law." The point here is that you should not become discouraged if you think you have the right topic but cannot find it in the digest. Instead, think of other topic headings that may lead you to the answer you seek.

CASE LAW AND THE KEY NUMBER SYSTEM

The *West Key Number Topics* include several topics that are of interest to family law practitioners. Of the numerous types of digests, the one most likely to yield relevant answers to family law questions is the individual state digest (i.e., New York Digest, Texas Digest, etc.) for the state in which the question is pending. For broader research results, consult a regional digest, general digest, or decennial digest. The *Modern Federal Practice Digest* may be helpful if the issue involves an aspect of federal law.

The Key Number Topics that relate most directly to the subject matter of this text are largely identical to the topics listed earlier for encyclopedias.

FORM BOOKS

A basic tenet of being a legal professional is to avoid reinventing the wheel. Much of the practice of family law, such as divorce pleadings, discovery, and motions, is very similar in all cases. And if a particular document worked in one case, there is no reason why, with necessary modifications, it will not work again. A *form* is a sample document (i.e., complaint, motion, notice of deposition, etc.) that can be adapted for use in many different cases. A *form book* is a collection of forms that usually have been time tested and are acceptable to the courts in a particular jurisdiction. Form books provide a foundation upon which to draft the appropriate papers for any particular case. The job of the paralegal or attorney is to choose the appropriate form and adapt it to the needs of the particular client and case. It is vital to remember that the forms provided are only a starting point. It is not sufficient just to fill in the names and dates. The form must be tailored to fit the precise specifications of the particular case. This means deleting some parts of the form and adding others. This textbook is replete with forms (i.e., see Chapter 8 for an example of discovery forms).

By the same token, some of the most useful forms you will use are located in the form files of your law firm. Every time a law firm files a particular pleading, motion, etc. for the first time, a copy of that document is usually placed in a form file. The firm can then use and adapt that document for any later cases that require it. One of your first tasks in a law office is to locate the form file and to understand how it is organized. Later, it is a typical paralegal responsibility to maintain and update the form file.

Appendix B
Sample Divorce Deposition

```
 1        IN THE      COURT FOR THE COUNTY OF
 2                    STATE OF

 3   THOMAS JAMES MORRISON,    )
 4              Plaintiff,     )
 5         vs.                 )        CIVIL ACTION
 6                             )
     JEANNE CLAIRE MORRISON,   )        FILE NO.96102183
 7                             )
 8              Defendant.     )
     _____

 9                    DEPOSITION OF

10              THOMAS JAMES MORRISON

11               April 25, 199__,

12                   9:30 a.m.

13

14

15

16

17

18

19      Connie Starr, Certified Court Reporter

20

21

22

23

24

25
```

2

<u>APPEARANCES OF COUNSEL</u>

1   On behalf of the Plaintiff:

2
    MATTHEW S. CORNICK, Esq.
3   Law Offices of Matthew S. Cornick
    City, State ZIP
4

5   On behalf of the Defendant:

6   PETER A. BAIR, Esq.
    Law Offices of Peter A. Bair
7   City, State, ZIP

8
Also Present:
9   Mrs. Jeanne Claire Morrison

10   – – –

11

12

13

14

15

16

17

18

19

20

21

22

23

24

25

3

1   INDEX TO EXHIBITS

2

3

4

5   Defendant's

6   Exhibit   Description   Page

7   1   Stock Dividend

8   Reinvestment Plan   17

9   2   401(k) Summary   20

10   3   ESOP Distribution Form   23

11   4   Statement of Pension   23

12   5   1990 Tax Return   29

13   6   1991 Tax Return   30

14   7   1992 Tax Return   31

15   8   1993 Tax Return   31

16

17

18

19

20

21

22

23

24

25

4

1   MR. BAIR: This will be the deposition

2   of Thomas James Morrison. It's take in the

3   Civil Action File No. 96102183, in the Fulton

4   County Superior Court. It's taken on

5   cross-examination, pursuant to agreement of

6   counsel, for discovery and any and all other

7   uses allowed by law.

8   I propose all objections other than as

9   to the form of the question and the

10   responsiveness of the answer will be reserved

11   until use of the deposition.

12   MR. CORNICK: That's agreeable.

13   MR. BAIR: Have you discussed signature

14   with Mr. Morrison?

15   MR. CORNICK: We'll reserve signature.

16   THOMAS JAMES MORRISON,

17   having been first duly sworn, was examined and

18   testified as follows:

19   CROSS-EXAMINATION

20   BY MR. BAIR:

21   Q.   Mr. Morrison, would you state your full

22   name for the record?

23   A.   Thomas James Morrison.

24   Q.   What is your age?

25   A.   47.

1   Q.   How would you describe your current

2 health?

3   A.   Excellent.

4   Q.   Have you had any health problems in the

5 last, say, five years?

6   A.   No.

7   Q.   You and Mrs. Morrison married on or about

8 June 6, 1978?

9   A.   Correct.

10   Q.   And when did you say that you were

11 separated?

12   A.   November 15, 1993.

13   Q.   Is that when you moved out of the house?

14   A.   Yes.

15   Q.   Have you all had any sexual relations

16 since that date?

17   A.   No.

18   Q.   And what is your current address?

19   A.   2610 Brook Valley Drive.

20   Q.   Brook Valley?

21   A.   Uh-huh.

22   Q.   Where is that?

23   A.   Cumming, Georgia.

24   Q.   Is that a house or apartment?

25   A.   House.

1   Q.   How big a house is it?

2   A.   It's a two-story house.

3   Q.   How many bedrooms?

4   A.   Four.

5   Q.   How long have you resided there?

6   A.   Since about April 10th.

7   Q.   Where did you go when you first moved out

8   of the marital residence?

9   A.   To a trailer.

10   Q.   Where was that?

11   A.   In Duluth.

12   Q.   Who owned the trailer?

13   A.   I don't know. I just rented it.

14   Q.   You were renting that?

15   A.   Yes.

16   Q.   And you said you were renting this house?

17   A.   No.

18   Q.   Have you bought—

19   A.   I am just a resident in the house.

20   Q.   Who owns the house?

21   A.   Dave Thomas.

22   Q.   Is this a friend of yours?

23   A.   Yes.

24   Q.   Are you paying him any rent or anything

25   at this time?

7

1   A.   Yes.

2   Q.   What are you paying?

3   A.   About a hundred dollars a month.

4   Q.   Do you have any written agreement on

5 that?

6   A.   No.

7   Q.   You pay any other expenses on the house?

8   A.   No.

9   Q.   Is Mr. Thomas married?

10   A.   Yes, he is.

11   Q.   So who is living there at this time?

12   A.   He, his wife and four children.

13   Q.   Anyone else?

14   A.   No.

15   Q.   Have you taken any furniture out of the marital

16 residence to this house?

17   A.   No.

18   Q.   So you're just basically living with his

19 furniture?

20   A.   That's right.

21   MR. CORNICK: Let him ask the whole

22   question before you answer it. Helps the

23   court reporter, too.

24   Q.   (By Mr. Bair) What are your intentions

25 as far as your living there at this point?

8

1   A.   Oh, it's just temporary.

2   Q.   Have you looked into renting another

3 place or purchasing another residence?

4   A.   Yes.

5   Q.   And then you have a daughter, Tiffany

6 Crystal?

7   A.   Yes.

8   Q.   Daughter, she's 12?

9   A.   Correct.

10   Q.   And where is she currently in school?

11   A.   All Saints High School.

12   Q.   And that's a private school?

13   A.   Yes, it is.

14   Q.   Do you know what that runs?

15   A.   Yes. About $5300 a year.

16   Q.   What year is she?

17   A.   She's a seventh grader. She will be

18 entering Cobb County High in Cobb County next year.

19   Q.   Is this an agreement? Have you discussed

20 this with Mrs. Morrison?

21   A.   Yes, those are our intentions.

22   Q.   You discussed with Mrs. Morrison she

23 would go to Cobb County High?

24   A.   Yes. That's agreeable to her last time I

25 discussed it with her as far as I know.

9

1   Q.   So you will not have the $5300 the
2   beginning of September; is that correct?

3   A.   Correct.

4   Q.   Mrs. Morrison is asking for custody of
5   Tiffany. Do you have any objections to that?

6   A.   No problem at all.

7   Q.   Have you been visiting with her since the
8   separation?

9   A.   Yes, I have.

10   MR. CORNICK: Let him finish the whole
11   question. We want to be sure you know what
12   he is asking.

13   Q.   (By Mr. Bair) Has that been going okay?

14   A.   Yes.

15   Q.   Been no problems with visitation as far
16   as what Mrs. Morrison has done or you and Tiffany
17   seeing each other?

18   A.   No.

19   Q.   What has been visitation, regularly
20   scheduled each week or—

21   A.   No, it isn't. It was and then she was
22   playing soccer. I was picking her up after school
23   every day—

24   Q.   Anything else?

25   A.   —and taking her home.

10

1   No. I have taken her shopping for shoes.

2   Q.   So you just see her on an irregular

3   basis?

4   A.   Right, and I will be seeing her this

5   afternoon.

6   Q.   But you're satisfied with the way it's

7   working as far as visitation?

8   A.   Yes, at the present time.

9   Q.   That's good. Since you moved out in

10   November, have you provided any financial funds for

11   the benefit of the family?

12   A.   Yes.

13   Q.   What amount?

14   A.   Approximately $750 a month.

15   Q.   Does Tiffany have any health problems?

16   A.   No.

17   Q.   Does she have any learning disabilities?

18   A.   No.

19   Q.   How does she do in school?

20   A.   Tiffany is doing well, all except for

21   social studies.

22   Q.   After college graduation in 1976, you

23   went to law school?

24   A.   Yes.

25   Q.   Did you go straight to law school?

11

1   A.   Straight to law school.

2   Q.   Where did you go?

3   A.   Northwestern University in Chicago.

4   Q.   When did you graduate?

5   A.   January of 1979, 2-1/2 years. I went to

6   summer school two summers.

7   Q.   When did you marry in relation to your

8   schooling?

9   A.   In June of 1978.

10   Q.   And did your parents pay for your

11   schooling?

12   A.   Yes.

13   Q.   Did you have any assets or liabilities of

14   significance at the time of the marriage?

15   A.   No, no liabilities, no particular assets.

16   Q.   Did Mrs. Morrison?

17   A.   No. She was teaching. She was teaching

18   at the time.

19   Q.   So she had started teaching prior to your

20   marriage?

21   A.   Yes.

22   Q.   Then after you graduated from law school

23   in January of 1979, what did you do?

24   A.   I was accepted into the FBI as a special

25   agent, and I did not report until May 1979.

12

1   Q.   So in May of '79 you went with the FBI.

2   Tell me just briefly what your history through the

3   FBI was.

4   A.   I was assigned to the Atlanta office of

5   the FBI first, from '79 to '80; and then New York

6   City from '80 through 1982.

7   Q.   Now, when did you leave the FBI?

8   A.   In April of 1982 to accept a position as

9   security representative with Southeastern Bell.

10   Q.   Why did you decide to leave the FBI at

11   that point?

12   A.   My wife and I had both agreed that New

13   York was not the place to raise a child and our son

14   was born while we were up there. And we just

15   decided that we enjoyed Atlanta very much.

16   Q.   What was your income at the time you left

17   the FBI?

18   A.   I had gotten incremental raises. I think

19   it was 23,000, something like that.

20   Q.   Did you have any other benefits through

21   them?

22   A.   No. Our retirement was deducted from our

23   salary and then, of course, we had health benefits,

24   which were also deducted from our salary.

25   Q.   Did you have any other benefits through

13

1 them?

2   A.   No.

3   Q.   Did you have any vested retirement at the

4 time that you left?

5   A.   Yes, I did.

6   Q.   Was that paid out to you?

7   A.   Yes. It was paid out to me in a lump

8 sum.

9   Q.   Do you recall how much?

10   A.   It was about $3600, somewhere in that

11 range.

12   Q.   Was there any other benefits of any other

13 cash payouts at the time you left?

14   A.   No, that was it.

15   Q.   Do you recall what you did with that

16 money?

17   A.   Yes. That went into joint savings and

18 was ultimately used to make a down payment on our

19 current residence.

20   Q.   What was your position with Southeastern

21 Bell?

22   A.   I was initially a security representative

23 in the Atlanta area, and in August 1993 I was

24 promoted to the staff manager at corporate

25 headquarters in Southeastern Bell Center.

14

1   Q.   As a security representative, what did

2   that entail?

3   A.   It entailed investigating criminal and

4   quasi-criminal matters against the telephone

5   company.

6   Q.   Did this involve people using the

7   telephone for criminal matters, or give me some

8   examples?

9   A.   Well, 75 percent of the case load was

10   telephone fraud and the rest was internal matters

11   involving employee misconduct.

12   Q.   Do you recall what your starting salary

13   with Southeastern Bell was?

14   A.   25,000.

15   Q.   You get incremental raises throughout?

16   A.   Right.

17   Q.   In 1993 when you were staff manager, was

18   that a promotion?

19   A.   Yes, it was.

20   Q.   With a significant raise at that point?

21   A.   About 6,000 that year.

22   Q.   What were you making by that point?

23   A.   Forty-five two, I believe.

24   Q.   So did you stay in that position until

25   when?

15

1   A.   Until July of 1993.

2   Q.   And what happened then?

3   A.   I resigned from Southeastern Bell.

4   Q.   And at the time you resigned in 1993,

5 what was your salary?

6   A.   Forty-six three, plus a bonus of about

7 $3300, so approximately $50,000 a year.

8   Q.   And what benefits were you receiving at

9 that time?

10   A.   At the time of my resignation?

11   Q.   Right.

12   A.   I got health benefits, retirement

13 benefits.

14   Q.   Coverage?

15   A.   Yes, family benefits.

16   Q.   Do you have any life insurance through

17 Southeastern Bell?

18   A.   Yes. I had basic plus supplementary.

19   Q.   Do you know how much it was?

20   A.   Yes. It was a total of $284,000.

21   Q.   Did all of that immediately stop upon

22 resignation?

23   A.   Yes, and, of course, under COBRA you have

24 the option to continue.

25   Q.   Have you done that?

16

1   A.   No.

2   Q.   Do you currently have any health

3   insurance?

4   A.   No, I do not, except family through

5   Jeanne's employment as a substitute teacher with the

6   Cobb County School System.

7   Q.   Now, you had some retirement

8   benefits, pension, profit sharing at the time?

9   A.   Right.

10   Q.   Let's go through that. Mr. Morrison, at

11   the time that you left Southeastern Bell, did you

12   receive any severance pay or anything at that time?

13   A.   No, I did not.

14   Q.   Your salary immediately stopped the date

15   you left?

16   A.   Yes. I was paid for any unused vacation

17   and that was about $3200, in addition to my

18   last paycheck.

19   Q.   What had been your monthly net take home?

20   A.   2600 a month.

21   Q.   What did you withhold from that?

22   A.   I had a 401(k) plan, and that was about

23    $103 a month. That was savings.

24   Q.   Right.

25   A.   In addition to pension.

17

1   Q.   Anything else?

2   A.   Yes. Supplementary life insurance, which

3 I believe was about $36 a month.

4   Q.   Anything else besides your taxes and

5 FICA?

6   A.   No.

7   (Document was marked for identification

8 as Defendant's Exhibit 1.)

9   Q.   I am going to just hand you a few

10 documents and get them on the record and understand

11 what we have here. The first one has been marked

12 Defendant's Exhibit 1 and I think it is Southeastern

13 Bell stock dividend reinvestment plan?

14   A.   Yes.

15   Q.   How is that one titled? Whose name is

16 that in?

17   A.   Thomas James Morrison.

18   Q.   Is that something through your employment

19 at Southeastern Bell?

20   A.   No. This was purchased outside. I

21 purchased these shares from a fellow employee who

22 once had to sell some shares to get cash to help pay

23 for his son's college education.

24   Q.   So this is not something through your

25 employer?

18

1   A.   No, it is not. This was beyond

2   employment.

3   Q.   That statement is as of January of 1993,

4   I believe.

5   A.   Correct.

6   Q.   And how many shares did you have at that

7   point?

8   A.   According to this, 208.891.

9   Q.   Since purchasing that, have you made

10   any financial contributions other than having

11   the dividend reinvested and purchasing additional

12   stock?

13   A.   No, I have not.

14   Q.   And when did you purchase that stock?

15   A.   I think it was about 1986.

16   Q.   Do you remember what the original

17   purchase price was?

18   A.   2,238, somewhere around there.

19   Q.   Do you know the source of those funds

20   that purchased that?

21   A.   Yeah, our joint accounts.

22   Q.   Joint savings?

23   A.   Right.

24   Q.   In which both of your incomes were going

25   at the time?

19

1 A. Yes.

2 Q. And Mrs. Morrison was working at that

3 time?

4 A. Yes. She was by that time teaching part

5 time.

6 Q. Have you since then made any withdrawal

7 from this account?

8 A. No, I have not.

9 Q. Have you made any withdrawals since

10 February of 1993?

11 A. No, I have not.

12 Q. Do you know what the current value is?

13 A. I think it is about 57 a share.

14 Q. You've got 280 shares?

15 A. Yes.

16 Q. Approximately $12,000?

17 A. Correct.

18 MR. CORNICK: Don't agree on his math

19 unless you're that good in your head.

20 (Document was marked for identification

21 as Defendant's Exhibit 2.)

22 Q. Then Defendant's Exhibit 2, would you

23 identify that document, please, sir?

24 A. Yes. This is a statement dated 3/20/93

25 for the Southeastern Bell long-term savings plan for

20

1   management employees and that is the 401(k) form

2   that I made reference, which is my savings plan at

3   Southeastern Bell.

4   Q.   And what as of March 20th was the value

5   of that account?

6   A. $25,998.73.

7   Q.   Is that 100 percent vested?

8   A.   Yes.

9   Q.   And is that still in that account at this

10   date?

11   A.   Yes. It is frozen in that account until

12   such time as I decide to roll it over.

13   Q.   Now, under the plan, to your knowledge

14   you could roll it over into an IRA?

15   A.   Yes.

16   Q.   Without incurring any taxes or penalty?

17   A.   Correct.

18   Q.   Otherwise, can you withdraw any of those

19   funds without incurring expenses or—

20   A.   No. I would pay a 10 percent penalty.

21   Q.   Do you have any plans at this time to

22   take it out of the 401(k) plan?

23   A.   No, I do not.

24   Q.   And obviously there's no further

25   contribution being made to that plan?

21

1   A.   Right.

2   Q.   Other than accrued interest?

3   A.   Right.

4   Q.   And all of that Southeastern Bell

5 long-term savings plan accrued during the marriage?

6   A.   Yes.

7   Q.   And you have been funding it and it was

8 being matched by Southeastern Bell?

9   A.   Yes.

10   Q.   Do you know when you first got into that

11 plan?

12   A.   Yes. Went into it in 1986. That's when

13 the company started the 401(k) plan.

14   Q.   And you've made no withdrawals from that

15 since 1986?

16   A.   No.

17   (Document was marked for identification

18 as Defendant's Exhibit 3.)

19   Q.   And Defendant's Exhibit 3, would you

20 identify that, please?

21   A.   Yes. That is a lump sum distribution

22 from my employee stock ownership plan, which I

23 requested in February of 1993.

24   Q.   And I believe attached to it is a

25 statement indicating how much that was?

22

1   A.   Correct.

2   Q.   And what does the statement indicate?

3   A.   It shows that I had accumulated 160.281

4   shares of Southeastern Bell.

5   Q.   Does the letter indicate how much you

6   will be paid out?

7   A.   No, it does not. What happens, in June

8   over a ten-day period they will start selling those

9   2306 shares at whatever the price is on those dates

10   and at the latter part of June you will be given a

11   distribution.

12   Q.   Do you know right now what the

13   Southeastern Bell is selling for?

14   A. $38 a share.

15   Q.   Will they withhold taxes or anything from

16   that?

17   A.   No, they will not. I will have to pay

18   taxes on it.

19   Q.   But you're expecting to pay out, then, in

20   the latter part of June approximately $6,000 or

21   something in that range?

22   A.   Correct.

23   (Document was marked for identification

24   as Defendant's Exhibit 4.)

25   Q.   And then Defendant's Exhibit 4, would you

23

1   identify that?

2   A.   Yes. This is the statement that I

3   received from Southeastern Bell on March 12, 1993,

4   setting forth my monthly deferred vested pension of

5   $1,379.76 per month at the time that I reach my 65th

6   birthday.

7   Q.   So that's still in effect, and you will

8   still receive that?

9   A.   That is locked in stone. That is exactly

10 the amount that I will receive on March the 18th,

11 2013, when I turn 65.

12   Q.   Do you know if there is any type of

13 survivor's annuity along with that? In fact, it

14 does say that.

15   A.   Yes, there is.

16   Q.   Have you declined that coverage?

17   A.   I have not set forth any direction for it

18 at this time.

19   Q.   Do you know when that would have to have

20 been done, or can it be done at any point?

21   A.   It can be done at any time.

22   Q.   And apparently unless you get the consent

23 of your spouse, it is going to be there?

24   A.   Yes.

25   Q.   I presume then, the amount includes that

24

1   survivor annuity?

2   A.   Yes, right. In other words, what would

3   happen if I elected the survivor annuity, it would

4   reduce this amount by a certain number of dollars.

5   Q.   You think it would reduce that?

6   A.   Yes, it will reduce it. It will reduce

7   that amount.

8   Q.   What have you done in the way of

9   employment since — was it July of 1993 that you

10   resigned?

11   A.   Right.

12   Q.   What have you done employment wise since

13   then?

14   A.   I have sent out resumes to about 14 major

15   corporations; and most recently I sent one to

16   Holiday Inn Worldwide, who has moved their worldwide

17   corporate headquarters from Memphis to Atlanta.

18   Q.   Have you had any interviews with any of

19   these organizations?

20   A.   No, I have not. I have received several

21   negative responses from four corporations, and I

22   have got some encouraging invitations from others;

23   but they are not interviewing at this time.

24   Q.   What do you think is your income

25   potential if you could find a job?

25

A.   About 60,000 a year.

Q.   Is that what you're asking?

A.   Yes. And I will take anywhere from 40 to 60 and possibly 80 if I get a corporate director's security position.

Q.   Are you looking only in the Atlanta area?

A.   No. I've applied in Chicago and in New York.

Q.   You're willing to relocate if necessary?

A.   Yes.

Q.   Have you considered any other types of positions?

A.   Yes. I have also been in touch with the director of human resources for Southeastern Bell for a labor relations job.

Q.   What's come of that?

A.   They are in the process of offering an early retirement plan to 3,000 managers; and I was told within the last week and a half that after those 3,000 are gone, his words were, there is a possibility a job might be open for you.

Q.   Do you have any time frame of when that might be?

A.   Fall. Because the offering has not yet been made to those people and then they will be

1 given an X period of time to exercise the option of

2 early retirement.

3   Q.   Do you know how much this would pay?

4   A.   Approximately $50,000 a year.

5   Q.   Have you had any other income come to you

6 since you left Southeastern Bell?

7   A.   No.

8   Q.   Let's talk a little about the dispute

9 regarding the estate of your parents or your mother?

10   A.   No, my aunt and uncle.

11   Q.   Aunt and uncle?

12   A.   Yes, on my father's side.

13   Q.   Has that been resolved.

14   A.   Yes, it has.

15   Q.   What is the status of that estate at this

16 time.

17   A.   They are in the process of making a

18 partial distribution to all beneficiaries.

19   Q.   Do you know how much that will be?

20   A. $10,000.

21   Q.   To each?

22   A.   Each initially.

23   Q.   And do you know when you expect to

24 receive that?

25   A.   Friday.

27

1   Q.   Have you already earmarked that money?

2   A.   No.

3   Q.   What further distributions do you

4   anticipate?

5   A.   Let's see. $78,000.

6   Q.   When do you anticipate receiving that?

7   A.   As soon as all expenses and federal,

8   state and gift taxes have been paid.

9   Q.   End of the summer?

10   A.   Oh, sooner than that.

11   Q.   Within the next couple of weeks?

12   A.   Maybe within the next month and a half.

13   Q.   At the rate the bank has been moving?

14   A.   Yes.

15   Q.   Is there any inheritance that you're

16   receiving under this estate?

17   A.   No.

18   Q.   Have you received any other inheritance

19   during the marriage.

20   A.   No.

21   Q.   Are you the beneficiary of any other

22   wills?

23   A.   Yes.

24   Q.   Whose will is that?

25   A.   My mother's.

1 Q.   How old is she?

2 A.   She's 85. She will be 85 on August 29th

3 of this year.

4 Q.   Is she in good health?

5 A.   No.

6 Q.   Do you have any idea as to the value of

7 her estate?

8 A.   Yes. Approximately 700,000.

9 Q.   Are you the sole beneficiary?

10 A.   Of hers, yes. And then I will share in a

11 family trust that was set up by my father during her

12 lifetime. She is receiving all income from both the

13 family trust and the R. Morrison trust.

14 Q.   Do you know what the income is?

15 A.   No, I do not. She is distributed a

16 certain amount per month by the trust department of

17 the bank, and I don't know what that sum is.

18 Q.   Would you be the income beneficiary?

19 Will you receive the corpus of that trust?

20 A.   I will receive the corpus.

21 Q.   Do you have any idea what the corpus is?

22 A.   I told you about 700,000.

23 Q.   That's included in her estate?

24 A.   Right.

25 Q.   Who would you share that with?

29

1   A.   I will share with a half brother and my

2   sister.

3   Q.   Have you received any gifts from any

4   third parties during the marriage?

5   A.   No.

6   Q.   At this point do you have any business

7   interests at all?

8   A.   No, I do not.

9   (Document was marked for identification

10   as Defendant's Exhibit 5.)

11   Q.   Defendant's Exhibit 5, is that your 1990

12   return?

13   A.   Yes, joint return.

14   MR. CORNICK: Flip through it and make

15   sure it looks like it.

16   Q.   (By Mr. Bair) Is that true and correct to the best

17   of your knowledge?

18   A.   Correct.

19   Q.   And what was your total income that year

20   in 1990?

21   A.   Total joint income was $66,315.

22   Q.   And there's some 50,000 odd wages?

23   A.   Yes, that was all mine.

24   Q.   That was all of yours?

25   A.   Yes.

30

1   Q.   And then there's the dividend and

2   interest income. The majority of that, would it be

3   safe to say, is from Mrs. Morrison's inherited

4   assets?

5   A.   No. The joint savings and so on, some of

6   it was definitely from her inherited assets.

7   Q.   And then there's also some business

8   income. That is from Mrs. Morrison's teaching?

9   A.   Yes.

10   Q.   That's basically what we have throughout

11   these sources of income on all of them?

12   A.   Yes.

13   (Document was marked for identification

14   as Defendant's Exhibit 6.)

15   Q.   (By Mr. Bair) Defendant's Exhibit 6,

16   1991 return.

17   What was your total income that year?

18   A.   63,228.

19   Q.   Did Mrs. Morrison have any wages that

20   year that are reflected there?

21   A.   Yes, 6,204.

22   Q.   Is that the business income?

23   A.   Yes.

24   Q.   On the first line, is that all your

25   income?

31

1   A.   That's correct.

2   (Document was marked for identification

3   as Defendant's Exhibit 7.)

4   Q.   (By Mr. Bair) And Defendant's Exhibit 7

5   is the 1992 return. What was the total on that one?

6   A.   68,820.

7   Q.   And again the income on the first line,

8   does that all reflect your income only?

9   A.   Yes.

10   Q.   And there was some business income again?

11   A.   Yes, 8,436.

12   (Document was marked for identification

13   as Defendant's Exhibit 8.)

14   Q.   (By Mr. Bair) And Defendant's Exhibit 8,

15   the 1993 return, what was the total on that one?

16   A.   74,136.

17   Q.   Does that reflect at that point Mrs.

18   Morrison was teaching school, or is that 74,000 all

19   your income?

20   A.   No. 49,893 was my income.

21   Q.   I am sorry. I misspoke. And then was

22   there some business income from the teaching?

23   A.   Yes, 10,777.

24   Q.   And then interest and dividends also?

25   A.   Right.

32

1   Q.   And all of those returns are true and

2   correct to the best of your knowledge?

3   A.   Correct.

4   Q.   Have you prepared any net worth

5   statements in the last year?

6   A.   No.

7   Q.   Is the current residence at 2881 Canton

8   Hills Drive, is that the first home you all have

9   purchased?

10   A.   Yes.

11   Q.   That was purchased in 1982?

12   A.   Correct.

13   Q.   Do you recall what the purchase price was?

14   A. $41,500.

15   Q.   And do you recall your down payment?

16   A.   Approximately 8,000 something.

17   Q.   And what was the source of that, do you

18   recall?

19   A.   Yeah. The distribution that I received

20   on my FBI retirement plus joint savings.

21   Q.   Do you know the current balance on that

22   mortgage?

23   A.   It is $21,000.

24   Q.   What is the monthly note payment?

25

33

1   A. $370, something like that.

2   A.   That does not include taxes and

3   insurance?

4   A.   Yeah, it does. That includes the escrow

5   which covers taxes and insurance.

6   Q.   Do you know what the taxes are on it?

7   A.   I believe last year they were about

8    $1,000, property tax.

9   Q.   Could you briefly describe the house for me?

10   A.   Yes. It is a two-story, aluminum siding,

11   four bedrooms on a half acre lot.

12   Q.   What is its current condition?

13   A.   Excellent.

14   Q.   Does it need anything to your knowledge?

15   A.   No.

16   Q.   And how is that titled?

17   A.   In my name.

18   Q.   Alone?

19   A.   Yes.

20   Q.   Do you have any opinion as to the current

21   fair market value of this residence?

22   A.   103,000.

23   Q.   What is that based on?

24   A.   Just the sales prices of houses in the

25

34

1   area.

2   Q.   Have you had it appraised?

3   A.   Not recently.

4   Q.   How would you describe the furniture and

5   furnishings in the house?

6   A.   Excellent.

7   Q.   Have they all been acquired during the

8   marriage?

9   A.   Yes, and some of them are antiques that

10   came from her parents' residence and some of the

11   furniture is from my dad's office and a game table

12   in the breezeway that was given to us by my mother.

13   Q.   Do you want any of the marital furniture?

14   A.   Only the two chairs and the table and the

15   four chairs in the breezeway.

16   Q.   Do you own any other real estate?

17   A.   No.

18   Q.   You have a car?

19   A.   Yes.

20   Q.   What are you currently driving?

21   A.   1991 Toyota Cressida.

22   Q.   Does that have a debt on it?

23   A.   Yes, it does. 6,138, I believe.

24   Q.   Who is that payable to?

25   A.   First National Bank.

35

1   Q.   Who is making the payments on that equity

2   loan?

3   A.   I am.

4   Q.   Do you know what the monthly note is?

5   A.   About $200 a month.

6   Q.   What does Mrs. Morrison drive?

7   A.   A 1990 Grand Prix.

8   Q.   And it is paid for?

9   A.   Yes. A gift from my mother.

10   Q.   Do you know the condition of that car?

11   A.   Yes. Excellent.

12   Q.   Do you know how many miles it has on it?

13   A.   I would say 53,000.

14   Q.   Do you have any credit card debt at this

15   time?

16   A.   Yes.

17   Q.   What credit cards are you currently —

18   A.   A Visa card. That's the only one.

19   Q.   What do you currently owe on that?

20   A.   About $1100.

21   Q.   When did you open that account?

22   A.   It was a joint account that Jeanne and I

23   had and she suspended it. I thought about it, then

24   I decided I would reactivate it and she's either

25   getting her own card or has gotten another credit

36

1   card.

2   Q.   When has the $1100 accrued on that

3   account, since when?

4   A.   Since I left the house.

5   Q.   So since November of 1993.

6   A.   Right.

7   Q.   What have you charged on it?

8   A.   I don't recall all the exact charges.

9   Q.   Have you produced the statements on that

10 credit card?

11   MR. CORNICK: I think so. I don't have

12 a specific recollection of it.

13   THE WITNESS: I don't believe we have

14 because she got the last statement that would

15 have come and I only recently reactivated the

16 account in the last two weeks.

17   Q.   (By Mr. Bair) But you have charged $1100

18 in the last two weeks?

19   A.   Right. No, not the last two weeks.

20 There was an outstanding balance on the account when

21 it was transferred to me from Jeanne.

22   Q.   So $1100 includes an outstanding balance that

23 accrued prior to your moving out?

24   A.   Right.

25   Q.   Can I get a copy of whatever statement

1 you have on that?

2   A.   Jeanne will have a statement and then I

3 should be getting a statement any time now from

4 them.

5   Q.   You have not gotten a statement at this

6 time?

7   A.   No, not since I reactivated the account.

8   Q.   Briefly you've mentioned that Mrs.

9 Morrison taught school in the early part of the

10 marriage, right?

11   A.   Right.

12   Q.   When did she stop teaching school?

13   A.   With the birth of our daughter Tiffany.

14   Q.   Which was some 12 years ago.

15   A.   Right.

16   Q.   Did she work outside the home after that?

17   A.   Yes, she did. As soon as Tiffany was

18 starting to attend nursery school, she began

19 substitute teaching.

20   Q.   And so she has been a substitute teacher

21 since then?

22   A.   That's correct.

23   Q.   So for the last 12 years, something like

24 that?

25   A.   Yes, right.

Q.   What kind of income has she received from that?

A.   Eight to $10,000. I think at one time it was six. It has gotten increasingly greater. Tiffany has gotten older and gotten involved in more activities.

Q.   Has your wife had any health problems over the years?

A.   Yes. She had a hysterectomy in February of 1991.

Q.   Does she have any side effects of that, any problems with it out of the ordinary?

A.   She did have a chemical imbalance which she has regulated now.

Q.   What do you think is her ability to earn at this time?

A.   Well, if she taught school full time, about 22,000.

Q.   Do you feel that teaching is the best way for her to earn an income?

A.   Yes.

Q.   How would you describe Mrs. Morrison's contribution as a mother to your child?

A.   Fantastic.

Q.   Fantastic mother?

39

1   A.   Yes, she's a fantastic mother.

2   Q.   Have no complaints about that?

3   A.   None.

4   Q.   Has she been a good wife?

5   A.   No.

6   MR. BAIR: We won't go into that any

7   further. We will reserve on conduct and stop

8   at that point.

9   MR. CORNICK: All right.

10   Q.   (By Mr. Bair) Are you willing to pay

11   some child support for the support of your minor

12   child?

13   A.   Yes.

14   Q.   Do you feel like child support should be

15   paid in addition to using marital assets?

16   A.   Yes, correct.

17   Q.   So you feel like that once you get the

18   70,000 you will be able to live pretty comfortably

19   to tide you over until you get a job?

20   A.   Right.

21   Q.   So that was good timing?

22   A.   Right.

23   MR. BAIR: That's all I have.

24   No, let me go on the record and say

25   that we at this time are going to reserve any

40

1   questions concerning conduct or the causes of

2   the separation; and if need be, we will

3   reconvene and get into those issues.

4   MR. CORNICK: I have got no problem

5   with that and I reserve the right to take you

6   up on your offer to depose Jeanne in the future

7   if circumstances require.

8   (Deposition concluded.)

9

10

11

12

13

14

15

16

17

18

19

20

21

22

23

24

25

Appendix C
Child Support Guidelines

TEXAS CHILD SUPPORT GUIDELINES

Tex. Rev. Civ. Stat. Ann.

§14.054 Evidentiary Factors

In applying the guidelines for the support of a child in this chapter, the court shall be guided by the guidelines for the support of a child in this chapter. However, the court may, in rendering its final determination of the amount of support, set the amount of child support either within or outside the range recommended in Section 14.055 of this code if relevant factors other than the guidelines justify a variance from the guidelines. In making its final determination, the court shall consider all relevant factors, including, but not limited to:

(1) the amount of the obligee's net resources, including the earning potential of the obligee if the actual income of the obligee is significantly less than what the obligee could earn because the obligee is intentionally unemployed or underemployed and including, as provided by Section 14.053(e) of this code, any increase or decrease in the income of the obligee or income that may be attributed to the property and assets of the obligee;

(2) the age and needs of the child;

(3) child care expenses incurred by either party in order to maintain gainful employment;

(4) whether either party has the managing conservatorship or actual physical custody of another child;

(5) the amount of child support actually and currently being paid or received by either party under another child support order;

(6) the amount of alimony or spousal maintenance actually and currently being paid or received by a party;

(7) the expenses of a son or daughter for education beyond secondary school;

(8) whether the obligor or obligee has an automobile, housing, or other benefits furnished by his or her employer, another person, or a business entity;

(9) the amount of other deductions from the wage or salary income and from other compensation for personal services of the parties;

(10) provision for health care insurance and payment of uninsured medical expenses;

(11) special or extraordinary educational, health care, or other expenses of the parties or of the child;

(12) the cost of travel in order to exercise access to or possession of a child;

(13) positive or negative cash flow from any real and personal property and assets, including a business and investments;

(14) debts or debt service assumed by either party; and

(15) any other reason or reasons consistent with the best interest of the child, taking into consideration the circumstances of the parents.

§ 14.055. Guidelines: Amount Ordered

(a) Rebuttable Presumption.   The guidelines for the support of a child in this chapter are specifically designed to apply to situations in which the obligor's monthly net resources are $6,000 or less. In any suit affecting the parent-child relationship, there is a rebuttable presumption that an order containing the amount of periodic child support payments established by the schedule provided in this section is reasonable and that the order is in the best interest of the child. A court may determine that the application of the guidelines would be unjust or inappropriate under the circumstances.

(b) Schedule.   In rendering an order of child support under circumstances in which the obligor's monthly net resources are less than the amount specified in Subsection (a) of this section, the court shall presumptively apply the following schedule:

CHILD   SUPPORT   GUIDELINES
BASED   ON   THE   MONTHLY   NET
RESOURCES   OF   THE   OBLIGOR

1 child	20% of Obligor's Net Resources
2 children	25% of Obligor's Net Resources
3 children	30% of Obligor's Net Resources
4 children	35% of Obligor's Net Resources
5 children	40% of Obligor's Net Resources
6+ children	Not less than the amount for 5 children

(c) More than $6,000 Monthly Net Resources. In situations in which the obligor's net resources exceed $6,000 per month, the court shall presumptively apply the percentage guidelines in Subsection (b) of this section to the first $6,000 of the obligor's net resources. Without further reference to the percentage recommended by these guidelines, the court may order additional amounts of child support as appropriate depending on the income of the parties and the proven needs of the child. The proper calculation of a child support order that exceeds the presumptive amount established for the first $6,000 of the obligor's net resources requires that the entire amount of the presumptive award be subtracted from the proven total needs of the child. After the presumptive award is subtracted, the court shall allocate between the parties the responsibility to meet the additional needs of the child according to the circumstances of the parties. However, in no event may the obligor be required to pay more than an amount equal to 100 percent of the proven needs of the child as child support.

(d) Partial Termination of Support Obligation.   A child support order that provides for the termination of the support for one child because the child reaches the age of majority, graduates from high school, or for some other reason, but continues the support order for another child must establish a level of support for the remaining child or children in accordance with these guidelines.

(e) Temporary Orders.   The rebuttable presumption established in this section is applicable to temporary orders for the support of a child. This subsection does not impair the authority of the court to enter other temporary orders under this code.

(f) Children in More Than One Household.   In applying the child support guidelines for an obligor who has children in more than one household, the court shall apply the percentage guidelines in this section by making the following computation:

(1) determine the amount of child support that would be ordered if all children, both before the court and not before the court, whom the obligor has the legal duty to support lived in one household by applying the schedule in Subsection (b) of this section;

(2) compute a child support credit for the obligor's children who are not before the court by dividing the amount determined under Subdivision (1) of this subsection by the total number of children whom the obligor is obligated to support and multiplying that number by the number of the obligor's children who are not before the court;

(3) determine the adjusted net resources of the obligor by subtracting the child support credit computed under Subdivision (2) of this subsection from the net resources of the obligor; and

(4) determine the child support amount for the children before the court by applying the percentage guidelines from Subsection (b) of this section for the number of children of the obligor before the court to the obligor's adjusted net resources.

(g) Child Support Credit.   For the purpose of determining a child support credit under Subsection (f)(2) of this section, the total number of an obligor's children includes the children before the court for the establishment or modification of a support order and any other children, including children residing with the obligor, whom the obligor has the legal duty of support.

(h) Child Support Paid by Obligor.   The child support credit under Subsection (f)(2) of this section with respect to children for whom the obligor is obligated by a court order to pay support is computed, regardless of whether the obligor is delinquent in child support payments, without regard to the amount of the order.

(i) Child Support Received by Obligor.   Child support received by an obligor who is obligated to support children in more than one household shall be added to the net resources of the obligor to compute the net resources of an obligor before determining the child support credit under Subsection (f)(2) of this section or applying the percentages in the table in Subsection (j) of this section.

(j) Alternative Method of Computing Support for Children in More Than One Household. In lieu of performing the computation under Subsection (f) of this section, the court may determine the child support amount for the children before the court by applying the percentages in the table below to the obligor's net resources.

Multiple Family adjusted guidelines (% of net resources)		Number of children before the court						
		1	2	3	4	5	6	7
Number of	0	20.00	25.00	30.00	35.00	40.00	40.00	40.00
other	1	17.50	22.50	27.38	32.20	37.33	37.71	38.00
children for	2	16.00	20.63	25.20	30.33	35.43	36.00	36.44
whom the	3	14.75	19.00	24.00	29.00	34.00	34.67	35.20
obligor has a	4	13.60	18.33	23.14	28.00	32.89	33.60	34.18
duty of support:	5	13.33	17.86	22.50	27.22	32.00	32.73	33.33
	6	13.14	17.50	22.00	26.60	31.27	32.00	32.62
	7	13.00	17.22	21.60	26.09	30.67	31.38	32.00

MASSACHUSETTS CHILD SUPPORT GUIDELINES

COMMONWEALTH OF MASSACHUSETTS

OFFICE OF CHIEF ADMINISTRATIVE JUSTICE

CHILD SUPPORT GUIDELINES

I. Income Definition

A. For purposes of these guidelines, income is defined as gross income from whatever source. Those sources include but are not limited to the following:

1) salaries and wages (including overtime and tips) and income from self-employment (except in certain instances, see B, below)

2) commissions

3) severance pay

4) royalties

5) bonuses

6) interest and dividends

7) income derived from businesses/partnerships

8) social security

9) veteran's benefits

10) insurance benefits (including those received for disability and personal injury)

11) worker's compensation

12) unemployment compensation

13) pensions

14) annuities

15) income from trusts

16) capital gains in real and personal property transactions to the extent that they represent a regular source of income

17) spousal support received from a person not a party to the order

18) contractual agreements

19) perquisites or in kind compensation to the extent that they represent a regular source of income

20) unearned income of children (in court's discretion)

21) income from life insurance or endowment contracts

22) income from interest in an estate (direct or through a trust)

23) lottery or gambling winnings received either in a lump sum or in the form of an annuity

24) prizes or awards

25) net rental income

B. In individual cases, the court may choose to disregard overtime income or income derived from a second job. However, consideration of such income may be appropriate in certain instances such as those where such income constituted a regular source of income when the family was intact.

II. Factors to be Considered in Setting the Child Support Order

A. RELATIONSHIP TO ALIMONY OR SEPARATE MAINTENANCE PAYMENTS

So long as the standard of living of the children is not diminished, these guidelines do not preclude the court from deciding that any order be denominated in whole or in part as alimony or a separate maintenance payment. It is the responsibility of counsel representing the parties to present the tax consequences of proposed orders to the court.

B. CLAIMS OF PERSONAL EXEMPTIONS FOR CHILD DEPENDENTS

In setting a support order, the court may make an order regarding the claims of personal exemption for child dependents between the parties to the extent permitted by law.

C. MINIMUM AND MAXIMUM LEVELS

The guidelines recognize the principle that, in many instances, to maintain a domicile and a reasonable standard of living for the minor children, the custodial parent will choose to work. In those cases, a disregard of gross income of the custodial parent is to be applied up to a maximum of $15,000. The formula in these guidelines is intended to be adjusted where the income of the custodial parent exceeds the $15,000 disregard after consideration of day care expenses.

These guidelines are also intended to ensure a minimum subsistence level for those non-custodial parents whose income is less than $200 per week. However, it is the obligation of all parents to contribute to the support of their children. To that end, in all cases, a minimum order of $50.00 per month should be set. This minimum order corresponds to the $50.00 disregard of support payments that is passed through to families receiving Aid to Families With Dependent Children mandated by Federal law. This minimum should not be construed as limiting the court's ability to set a higher order, should circumstances permit.

Where the court makes a determination that either or both of the parties is either purposely unemployed or underemployed, the section of this guideline entitled ATTRIBUTION OF INCOME should be consulted.

These guidelines are not meant to apply where the combined gross income of the parties exceeds $100,000 or where the gross income of the non-custodial parent exceeds $75,000. In cases where income exceeds these limits, the court should consider the award of support at the $75,000/$100,000 level as a minimum presumptive level of support to be awarded. Additional amounts of child support may be awarded at the judge's discretion.

D. CUSTODY AND VISITATION

1) Custody.   These guidelines are based upon traditional custody and visitation arrangements. Where the parties agree to shared physical custody or the court determines that shared physical custody is in the best interests of the children, these guidelines are not applicable. The guidelines are also not meant to apply for cases in which there is split physical custody, i.e., each parent has physical custody of one or more children.

2) Visitation.   These guidelines recognize that children must be allowed to enjoy the society and companionship of both parents to the greatest extent possible. The court may adjust the amount of child support beyond the 2 percent range (see Basic Order, Section III A.) after taking into consideration the parties' actual time sharing with the children and the relative resources, expenses, and living standards of the two households.

In some instances, the non-custodial parent may incur extraordinary travel-related expenses in order to exercise court ordered visitation rights. To foster parental involvement with the children, the court may wish to consider such extraordinary expenses in determining the support order.

E. CHILD CARE AS DEFINED BY INTERNAL REVENUE CODE SECTION 21

The basic child support obligation set out in the guidelines includes the non-custodial parent's share of day care expenses. Child care expenses are not seen as a separate support item and responsibility for them resides with the custodial parent.

The reasonable cost of day care actually paid is to be subtracted from the custodial parent's gross income before the disregard formula is applied.

F. AGE OF CHILDREN

To reflect the costs of raising children, age has been broken down into four groups: 0–6, 7–12, 13–18, and over 18. A single adjustment to the basic order should be made based on the age of the oldest child for whom support is ordered. The support order where the oldest child is six or under should be the basic support order according to the schedule. Where the oldest child is 7–12, the order should be increased by 10 percent of the basic order amount. Where the oldest child is 13 or older, the order should be increased by 15 percent of the basic order amount. For cases involving children between the ages of 18 and 21, the amount of the order, if any, will be left to the court's discretion.

Where the parties file an agreement with the court that allows for the private payment between the parties, it is suggested that the incremental age issue be addressed in the agreement.

G. HEALTH INSURANCE, UNINSURED, AND EXTRAORDINARY MEDICAL EXPENSES

1) Health insurance.   When the court makes an order for child support, the court shall determine whether the obligor under the order has health

insurance on a group plan available to him/her through an employer or organization or has health insurance or other health coverage available to him/her at reasonable cost that may be extended to cover the child for whom support is ordered. When the court makes a determination that the obligor has such coverage, the court shall include in the support order a requirement that the obligor exercise the option of additional coverage in favor of such child, unless the obligee has already provided such coverage for the child at a lesser cost (except for health insurance funded under public assistance programs), or has and prefers to continue such coverage irrespective of cost.

If insurance is to be provided by the obligor, the support order should be reduced by the full amount of the obligor's actual cost of group health insurance, and not the difference between an individual and family policy. However, there shall be no reduction if the obligor has a preexisting family health insurance policy which could be amended to name the additional dependents to the policy at no cost to the obligor. Should health insurance not be provided for any period for which it is ordered, the credit for the premium payment shall be revoked and the order shall be increased by the amount of the credit during the period of noncompliance.

2) Routine Uninsured Medical and Dental Expenses.   The custodial parent shall be responsible for the payment of the first $100 per child per year for routine medical and dental expenses. For amounts above that limit, the court shall allocate costs on a case by case basis. No reduction in the child support order should be allowed.

3) Uninsured Extraordinary Medical and Dental Expenses.   The payment of uninsured extraordinary medical and dental expenses incurred by the minor children, absent agreement of the parties, shall be treated on a case by case basis. (Example: orthodontia, psychological/psychiatric counseling, etc.) In such cases, where the court makes a determination that such medical and dental services are necessary and are in the best interests of the child, consideration toward a reduction in the child support order should be given.

H. ATTRIBUTION OF INCOME
If the court makes a determination that either or both parties is earning substantially less than he or she could through reasonable effort, the court may consider potential earning capacity rather than actual earnings. In making this determination, the court shall take into consideration the education, training, and past employment history of the party. These standards are intended to be applied where a finding has been made that the party is capable of working and is unemployed, working part-time or is working a job, trade, or profession other than that for which he/she has been trained.

This determination is not intended to apply to a custodial parent with children who are under the age of six living in the home.

I. PRIOR ORDERS FOR SUPPORT
To the extent that prior orders for spousal and child support are actually being paid, the court should deduct those payments from the gross income

before applying the formula to determine the child support order. This section applies only to orders for child support for children other than the one who is the subject of the pending action.

J. EXPENSES OF SUBSEQUENT FAMILIES

In instances where the non-custodial parent has remarried and has children by a subsequent marriage, the court should examine such circumstances closely to determine in the allocation of available resources whether consideration beyond Part II Section I (Prior Orders of Support) should be given when the custodial parent of children borne of the first marriage, or subsequent marriages appears before the court seeking a modification of the existing child support order. In actions pursuant to G.L. c.209C, this paragraph shall be construed to apply equally to children born out of wedlock.

III. Child Support Obligation Schedule

A. BASIC ORDER

The basic child support obligation, based upon the income of the non-custodial parent is as follows.

GROSS WEEKLY INCOME	NUMBER OF CHILDREN		
	1	2	3
$0–$200	Discretion of the court, but not less than $50.00 per month		
$201–$500	25%(±2%)	28%(±2%)	31%(±2%)
$501–max.	27%(±2%)	30%(±2%)	33%(±2%)

Within the discretion of the court, and in consideration of the totality of the circumstances of the parties, the order may be either increased or decreased by 2 percent. Where the court must set a support order where there are more than three children, the minimum order is to be no less than that contained in this guideline for three children, to be increased within the discretion of the court depending upon the circumstances of each case.

B. AGE DIFFERENTIAL

The above orders are to be increased to reflect the cost of raising older children. The following percentages are intended to be applied to the age of the oldest child in the household for whom support is sought under the pending action.

AGE OF OLDEST CHILD	PERCENTAGE INCREASE
0–6	Basic Order Applies
7–12	Basic Order + 10% of Basic Order
13–18	Basic Order + 15% of Basic Order
Over 18	Discretion of the court (and if statute permits)

C. CUSTODIAL PARENT INCOME ADJUSTMENT

Where the custodial parent works and earns income in excess of $15,000 after consideration of day care expenses, the support order is to be reduced by the percentage that the excess represents in relation to the combined incomes of both parents minus the custodial parent's disregard.

Worksheet
Child Support Guidelines

All provisions of the Guidelines should be reviewed prior to the completion of the worksheet. These guidelines will apply (absent a prior agreement acceptable to both parties) in cases where combined gross income of both parties does not exceed $100,000 and where the income of the noncustodial parent does not exceed $75,000.

1. BASIC ORDER

   a) Non-custodial gross weekly income (less prior support orders actually paid, for child/family other than the family seeking this order)   _____

   b) % of gross/number of children (from the chart III A.)   _____%

   c) Basic Order (a) × (b)   (A) _____

2. ADJUSTMENT FOR AGES OF CHILDREN

   a) Age of oldest child   _____

   b) % increase for age (from chart on B.)   _____%

   c) Age add on (2b) × (A)   _____

   d) Adjusted order (A) + (2c)   (B) _____

3. CUSTODIAL PARENT INCOME ADJUSTMENT

   a) Custodial parent gross income   _____

   b) Less $15,000   −$15,000

   c) Less day care cost (annual)   −_____

   d) Custodial adjusted gross   _____

   e) Non-custodial gross (annual)   _____

   f) Total available gross (d) + (e)   _____

   g) Line 3(d) _____   Line 3(f) _____

   h) 3(d) divided by 3(f)   _____ per cent

   i) Adjustment for custodial income (Line 3h %) × (B)   (C) _____

4. CALCULATION OF FINAL ORDER

a) Adjusted order (B) above   (B)_____

b) Less adjustment for
   income (C) above   (C) –_____

c) Less weekly cost of family
   group health insurance [under
   the provisions of section G(1)]   _____

WEEKLY SUPPORT ORDER (B)–(C)–4(c) $_____

Compilation of Margin Definitions

abandonment; constructive abandonment Abandonment occurs when one spouse permanently leaves the marital home. Constructive abandonment occurs when one spouse permanently leaves the marital home in response to the inappropriate behavior of the other spouse.

adjusted basis See *basis*.

adjusted gross income See *gross income*.

admissible evidence Evidence deemed sufficiently reliable to be considered by a court.

adoption The creation of a parent-child relationship. But if either of the parents of the child who is adopted are alive, that legal relationship must first be terminated.

Affinity; consanguinity Two variations of incest. Affinity is a relationship between persons related by marriage. Consanguinity is a relationship between persons related by blood.

agency A legal relationship in which the agent acts on behalf of the principal, and the principal is responsible for the actions of the agent.

alimony; maintenance Support payments made for the benefit of a former spouse.

alternative dispute resolution Nonjudicial methods of dispute resolution.

annulment; divorce An annulment is a judicial termination that a "marriage" never existed. A divorce is a judicial determination that a marriage is legally terminated.

answer Filed by a defendant in response to the plaintiff's complaint.

antenuptial agreement; prenuptial agreement A written agreement made by two persons contemplating marriage, setting forth the disposition of their property upon the dissolution of the marriage.

appeal A process by which a higher court reviews the decisions of a lower court.

arbitration A process by which a dispute is taken outside the judicial system and is determined by a neutral third party. May be either binding or nonbinding.

arrearages Unpaid past due balances of alimony and/or child support.

automatic stay The requirement that creditors stop attempting to collect debts from a debtor immediately upon the filing of a petition of bankruptcy.

bankruptcy A federal court procedure by which a debtor may be legally relieved of the requirement to pay certain debts.

basis; adjusted basis Basis is an amount assigned to an asset (often acquisition cost) used to determine gain or loss upon its sale or transfer. Depreciation or improvement of an asset results in an adjusted basis.

battered woman syndrome Psychological theory that a woman who is repeatedly subjected to physical abuse by her mate may believe that she must kill her mate in self-defense to avoid future abuse.

bigamy; polygamy Bigamy occurs when one person is married to two persons at the same time. Polygamy occurs when one person is married to more than two persons at the same time.

book value; par value Book value is the value of a corporation's net assets less the par value of its preferred stock. Par value is an arbitrary and nominal value assigned to a share of common stock (i.e., $1.00).

brief A written, persuasive argument.

burden of proof The burden to prove all elements of a cause of action. Also, the duty of a plaintiff to present a prima facie case and of a defendant to rebut or contradict the plaintiff's prima facie case.

capital assets Generally, property held for a period of at least one year.

ceremonial marriage A marriage involving a ceremony officiated over by a person authorized by the state to perform weddings.

child support Payments made for the benefit of a minor child not in the permanent custody of the payor.

child support guidelines Statutes that set forth required levels of child support.

civil contempt A judicial remedy available when a person intentionally disobeys an existing court order.

clean hands An equitable doctrine requiring that a person seeking an equitable remedy must be innocent of any wrongdoing.

common-law marriage A marriage that occurs when two persons capable of being married, intend to be married to each other, hold themselves out to the public as being married, and cohabit.

community property; equitable distribution The two theories regarding ownership of marital property. Under community property, each spouse has a one-half ownership in all marital property. Under equitable distribution, each spouse is entitled to an equitable distribution of all marital property between the spouses.

complaint A claim for relief filed by a plaintiff to state a claim against the defendant.

consangunity See *affinity.*

consortium The right to receive society, affection, companionship, and assistance from a spouse.

constructive abandonment See *abandonment.*

contingent fees Legal fees based on the ultimate result obtained by law firm. Not available in divorce cases.

costs of litigation Usually includes all costs other than attorney's fees, such as filing fees, deposition costs, etc.

counterclaim A claim for relief filed by a defendant to state a claim against the plaintiff.

court of general jurisdiction A court having jurisdiction over a wide range of claims.

curtesy; dower Laws providing for the passage of property from a deceased spouse to a widower (curtesy) or a widow (dower).

deductible A payment that results in a deduction from the payor's taxable income by a like amount.

defendant The party defending against the plaintiff's claim.

defense A legal justification for some act. As opposed to a denial of the act.

demonstrative evidence Audio or visual aids used during trial to emphasize or simplify specific issues in controversy.

deposition upon oral examination Questions posed to a live witness, answered orally, under oath.

descent and distribution; intestate distribution The laws that determine the distribution of property when a person dies without a valid will.

dischargeability The quality of a debt that permits a bankruptcy court to discharge, or forgive, the debt. Alimony and child support are not dischargeable in bankruptcy.

discovery The formal process by which parties in litigation are entitled to receive factual information known to other parties.

disengagement letter See *engagement letter.*

divisible divorce A court proceeding that terminates the parties' marriage, but does not adjudicate all of the other issues related to a divorce, i.e., child custody, alimony, etc.

divorce See *annulment; divorce.*

divorce a mensa et thoro; judicial separation; divorce a vinculo matrimonii A judicial separation or divorce a mensa et thoro grants all the relief available in a complete divorce (called a divorce a vinculo matrimonii) except for the right to marry other parties.

domestic violence Abusive behavior between family members or between partners in a romantic relationship.

domestication The process of officially recognizing the validity and authority of a foreign judgment.

domicile A person's permanent place of residence.

dower See *curtesy.*

dowry The property that a wife brings to her husband in marriage.

elements See *prima facie.*

emancipation The process by which a person under the age of majority achieves the legal status of an adult.

emancipation Acts by which a person under the age of majority can be granted the legal rights afforded adults.

engagement letter; disengagement letter; nonengagement letter An engagement letter memorializes the creation of a contract between a client and a law firm. A disengagement letter memorializes the termination of a contract between a client and a law firm. A nonengagement letter memorializes the lack of a contract between a client and a law firm.

equitable distribution See *community property*.

estoppel An equitable theory which prevents a party from claiming one fact to be true after asserting the truthfulness of a contrary fact.

ethics Legal ethics relate to the legal and professional duties that lawyers owe to each other, their clients, and the courts.

ex parte Latin for "on one side only." At an *ex parte* hearing, only one side is present.

expert witness, lay witness Expert witnesses review the facts of a case and give their opinion; lay witnesses testify to what they saw, heard, or did.

final judgment A court judgment that is not subject to further modification.

financial affidavit A court-supplied form that, when completed under oath, details the current financial condition of a party in divorce litigation.

flat fee A preset fee for a specified legal task, such as $500, plus costs of litigation, for an uncontested divorce.

foreign judgment A judgment issued by a court in one state, upon which collection is sought in another state.

full faith and credit U.S. Constitutional guarantee that the judgments and judicial decisions of one jurisdiction will be recognized by other jurisdictions.

garnishment A court order to a person holding property that belongs to a debtor, requiring that some or all of that property be transferred to the court for payment to a creditor.

gross income; adjusted gross income; taxable income Generally, gross income is all income from whatever source derived. Adjusted gross income is gross income less necessary business expenses, payments to qualified retirement accounts, and flexible spending accounts for child care or health care. Taxable income is adjusted gross income less personal exemptions and itemized deductions or the standard deduction, whichever is greater.

guardian ad litem A person appointed to represent the interests of another person in litigation.

hearsay A statement made by an out-of-court declarant for the purpose of proving the truth of statement.

heartbalm statutes Laws abolishing the right of action for alienation of affections, seduction, and criminal conversion.

hourly rate Legal fees based on a specified fee for each hour of labor performed.

illegitimacy See *legitimacy*.

immunity As relates to family law, the traditional prohibition against tort actions between spouses.

in loco parentis Latin for "in the place of a parent."

in personam **jurisdiction** A court's jurisdiction over a person.

in rem **jurisdiction** A court's jurisdiction over a thing.

inception of title theory; source of funds theory Theories relating to ownership of property. Inception of title theory holds that whichever spouse first had the right to acquire title to the property owns it. Source of funds theory bases ownership on the parties' respective contribution toward the acquisition of the property.

includable A payment by a person that results in an addition to the taxable income of the recipient.

interlocutory relief Temporary or nonfinal relief.

interrogatory Written request for information which is responded to in writing and under oath.

intestate; testate A person who dies without a valid will dies intestate. A person who dies with a valid will dies testate.

intestate distribution See *descent and distribution*.

Joint custody; split custody Under joint custody, both parents share full legal and custody of the child. Under split custody, each parent has exclusive custody of the child for extended periods of time.

judicial separation See *divorce a mensa et thoro*.

laches An equitable theory that prevents the prosecution of a legal claim if the claimant delays prosecution until the defending party's ability to defend the claim is impaired.

latchkey children Children who stay at home after school without adult supervision.

laws Specific rules of conduct promulgated by government.

legal custody The legal right to make the most significant decisions regarding child rearing, such as religious training, education, medical treatment, and so forth.

legal capacity As relates to family law, the ability to enter into marriage.

legitimacy; illegitimacy Legitimacy is the legal status that results from being born to parents who are legally married to each other. Illegitimacy is the legal status that results from being born to parents who are not legally married to each other.

levy and sale Court-authorized process of seizing a debtor's property, selling it, and paying the proceeds to a creditor.

"live-in-lover" laws Laws that terminate the right to receive alimony upon a finding that the recipient is cohabitating with another person in a marriage-like relationship.

liquidation value The value of a corporation remaining after all assets are sold and all liabilities are paid.

long-arm statute A state law which gives that state personal jurisdiction over a non-resident of that state.

maintenance See *alimony*.

marital rape Forced sexual activity within the confines of a marital relationship.

marital property Property acquired by either spouse while married; opposite of separate property.

marriage A legal union of two persons.

mediation A process by which parties to a dispute are aided in negotiations by a neutral third party.

mental capacity The ability to understand the consequences of specific actions.

modification The process of revising an existing court order.

motion A request to a court for an order.

motion to dismiss A motion seeking that a claim for relief be dismissed due to a technical deficiency.

motion for summary judgment A motion in which a party seeks a final judgment before trial because there are no material disputes about any significant issues.

motion for judgment on the pleadings A motion in which a party seeks a final judgment immediately after the pleadings are filed because of the lack of any significant issue raised by the pleadings.

motion for a more definite statement A motion seeking that additional details be added to a claim for relief.

motion to strike A motion seeking to eliminate a portion of a claim for relief.

necessities Food, shelter, utilities, medical treatment, etc.

nonengagement letter See *engagement letter*.

nonqualified retirement plan See *qualified retirement plan*.

palimony A slang term for support payment that may be owed to a former partner other than a spouse.

par value See *book value*.

partial performance doctrine The ability to prove the existence of a contract by the performance of at least some of the terms of the contract.

paternity action Litigation initiated to establish the legal identity of a person's father.

paternity index A percentage of probability that a particular male is the biological father of a particular child, based on the results of blood matching tests.

pendite lite Latin for "pending the suit."

personal exemption A specific amount that may be deducted from adjusted gross income.

personal jurisdiction A court's authority to enforce its rulings on a particular person.

physical custody The legal right to the actual physical custody of a child.

physical capacity As relates to family law, the ability to engage in a sexual relationship.

PKPA (Parental Kidnapping Prevention Act) Federal laws designed to deter parents from unlawfully removing a minor child from a particular state.

plaintiff The party who initiates the litigation by filing a complaint against the defendant.

polygamy See *bigamy*.

prenuptial agreement See *antenuptial agreement*.

preponderance of evidence A majority of the evidence.

pretrial conference The court hearing in which the controversies raised by the pretrial order are resolved.

pretrial order An order prepared by the parties detailing the issues to be resolved at trial and the methods that will be employed in resolving them.

prima facie; elements A prima facie case is one in which the plaintiff can present some evidence on each element of his cause of action, thus shifting the burden of persuasion to the defendant. Elements are the individual factors that must be established to prevail in a particular cause of action.

primary caretaker doctrine Theory of child custody that granted permanent child custody to the parent who acted as child's primary caretaker.

privilege for marital communications Prohibition against coerced disclosure of certain statements made within the marital relationship.

privileged information Information obtained through a privileged relationship.

production of documents Written request for documents or other tangible things in the possession, custody, or control of an adverse party or nonparty witness.

purge To take actions that relieve a person of a court order for civil contempt.

putative father An alleged father.

putative spouse doctrine Theory which provides a party who mistakenly, although reasonably, believes they are married, with the legal benefits of marriage.

QDRO (Qualified Domestic Relations Order) A court order to an administrator of a qualified retirement plan to pay benefits to a person other than the participant in the plan.

qualified retirement plan; nonqualified retirement plan A qualified retirement plan does not discriminate in favor of highly compensated employees. A nonqualifed retirement plan favors management and other highly compensated personnel.

recapture Recovery by the IRS of a tax benefit previously taken by a taxpayer.

recission A remedy in a breach of contract action in which the plaintiff seeks that the contract be nullified, or rescinded.

relation back doctrine An annulment relates back in time to the date the "marriage" occurred, thus creating the legal theory that an annulled marriage never existed at all.

relevance The degree to which a piece of evidence tends to prove or disprove a fact in controversy.

request for admission Written request to an adverse party for admission or denial of specific facts at issue in litigation.

res judicata A legal holding that a particular set of circumstances has been fully adjudicated and that no further related litigation will be entertained.

residency As relates to family law, the requirement that a plaintiff seeking a divorce live in the state in which the divorce is filed for a defined minimum period of time.

retainer A lump sum of money paid to a law firm from which hourly fees are deducted.

return on investment value The value of a corporation based on the ability of that corporation to generate earnings.

RURESA; URESA Uniform state laws authorizing state action to recover arrearages of alimony and child support owed by an out-of-state debtor.

separate maintenance In an action for separate maintenance, the parties separate but remain married.

separate property Property owned by a spouse before getting married; opposite of marital property.

service of process Delivery of the summons and complaint upon a defendant.

show cause A court order to a person that he "show cause" why the court should or should not take specific action.

source of funds theory See *inception of title theory.*

specific performance A remedy in a breach of contract action in which the plaintiff seeks a court order compelling the defendant to comply by the terms of the parties' contract.

split custody See *joint custody.*

statute of limitations The period of time permitted by law for a claimant to file a lawsuit.

Statute of Frauds Laws requiring that particular contracts be in writing and signed by the party against whom enforcement of the contract is sought.

subject matter jurisdiction A court's authority to hear a particular case or type of claim.

subpoena; subpoena duces tecum Court order to a nonparty requiring attendance at a deposition or court hearing. A subpoena duces tecum requires the nonparty to also provide access to specific documents or tangible things.

summons Official notification from a court to a defendant that a complaint has been filed against him/her.

taxable income See *gross income*.

tender years doctrine Traditional theory of child custody that usually granted permanent child custody to a child's mother.

testate See *intestate*.

testimony Sworn statements of a witness.

tort A noncriminal wrong, such as negligence or libel.

transmutation of funds theory The theory that holds once marital property and separate property are commingled, the entire property becomes marital property.

trial notebook The working notebook used by the trial team, containing all relevant information needed for trial.

UCCJA (Uniform Child Custody Jurisdiction Act) Uniform laws, adopted by the individual states, that set out the rules for determining venue in interstate child custody disputes.

URESA See *RURESA*.

valuation The process of placing a specific monetary value on a piece of property.

venue The particular county or district in which litigation is to be filed.

void marriage; voidable marriage A void marriage is one that was never considered a valid marriage; a voidable marriage is one that is valid until a court declares it to be void.

witness preparation The process of preparing a witness to testify.

work product Documents or tangible things prepared in anticipation of litigation. Work product is not normally subject to discovery requests.

Index